Tax Treatment of
Compensation and Damages

Tax Treatment of Compensation and Damages

Graham Chase
LLB, AIIT, Solicitor

Butterworths
London, Dublin, Edinburgh
1994

United Kingdom	Butterworth & Co (Publishers) Ltd, Halsbury House, 35 Chancery Lane, LONDON WC2A 1EL and 4 Hill Street, EDINBURGH EH2 3JZ
Australia	Butterworths Pty Ltd, SYDNEY, MELBOURNE, BRISBANE, ADELAIDE, PERTH, CANBERRA and HOBART
Canada	Butterworths Canada Ltd, TORONTO and VANCOUVER
Ireland	Butterworth (Ireland) Ltd, DUBLIN
Malaysia	Malayan Law Journal Sdn Bhd, KUALA LUMPUR
New Zealand	Butterworths of New Zealand Ltd, WELLINGTON and AUCKLAND
Puerto Rico	Butterworths of Puerto Rico Inc, SAN JUAN
Singapore	Butterworths Asia, SINGAPORE
South Africa	Butterworth Publishers (Pty) Ltd, DURBAN
USA	Butterworth Legal Publishers, CARLSBAD, California, and SALEM, New Hampshire

All rights reserved. No part of this publication may be reproduced in any material form (including photocopying or storing it in any medium by electronic means and whether or not transiently or incidentally to some other use of this publication) without the written permission of the copyright owner except in accordance with the provisions of the Copyright, Designs and Patents Act 1988 or under the terms of a licence issued by the Copyright Licensing Agency Ltd, 90 Tottenham Court Road, London, England W1P 9HE. Applications for the copyright owner's written permission to reproduce any part of this publication should be addressed to the publisher.

Warning: The doing of an unauthorised act in relation to a copyright work may result in both a civil claim for damages and criminal prosecution.

© Butterworths & Co Publishers Ltd 1994

A CIP Catalogue record for this book is available from the British Library.

ISBN 0 406 02305 0

Photoset by Phoenix Photosetting, Chatham, Kent
Printed and bound in Great Britain by
Clays Ltd, St Ives plc

PREFACE

The idea for this book came to the author when it became clear that there was no reference work which considered the tax treatment of damages and compensation in detail. This book seeks to fill the void by providing a general commentary on the subject.

The tax treatment of compensatory receipts is of fundamental importance in ascertaining the net amount available to the recipient, as well as its true cost to the payer. Planning may enhance the net return available to the recipient, or may reduce the true cost to the payer. Furthermore, tax may increase or decrease the actual amount of the award properly due; accordingly both the recipient and the payer have a powerful incentive to review the position at an early stage.

In writing this book, I have been helped greatly by David Goy QC, who kindly reviewed the chapters in their various drafts, made many useful suggestions for improvement and contributed generally to the analysis contained in the text. I have also been assisted by various members of Grant Thornton, who provided useful comments on parts of the book and, in particular, prepared the structured settlement example. I would also like to thank Romasa Butt of Counsel for her comments and my colleagues at Laytons for their support. My thanks also go to everyone involved in the production of this book, including Lynn Richards who spent many hours processing and reprocessing the drafts.

Notwithstanding the above contributions, I remain responsible for the book in its final form and all views expressed in it.

The law is as stated at 1 September 1994.

Graham Chase
September 1994

CONTENTS

Preface v
Table of statutes xi
List of cases xv

1 Introduction 1

    The nature of 'damages' 2
    The amount of damages 6
    Tax planning and compensation 13

2 Income tax 19

    General principles and trading receipts 19
    Compensation and trading stock 26
    Loss of profits 27
    The concept of use and capital assets 35
    Trading receipts and assessment 40
    Relief for expenditure 42
    Interest 43
    Profits from land 45
    Defamation 47
    Ex gratia payments 48

3 General principles of capital gains tax 53

    Introduction 53
    The nature of assets 58
    Disposals 69
    Chargeable gains 75

Contents

4 Capital gains tax reliefs 85

The decision in *Zim Properties* 85
The restoration of damaged assets 91
The replacement of assets lost or destroyed 98
Compulsory acquisition 100
Personal compensation 104
Appendix: Extra-statutory Concession D33 105

5 Direct taxes and the defendant 109

The general scheme of the Taxes Act 109
Expenditure for the purposes of the trade 112
Expenditure and provisions 117
Revenue and capital expenditure 120
Compensation and the cessation of trading 122
Compensation and share or business sales 124
Legal fees 126
Investment companies 127
Individuals and interest relief 128
Companies and interest relief 129
Deductions from rental income 129
Relief for capital expenditure 131

6 The position of employees 133

General principles of Schedule E 133
The application of general principles 137
The special statutory scheme 146
Exemption and section 188 152
Termination generally, wrongful and unfair dismissal 154
Retirement 157
Death or disability 161
Redundancy 162
Restrictive covenants 165
National insurance 166
The PAYE system 167
Planning 170
Appendix: Statement of Practice SP 1/94 172

7 Structured settlements 173

Introduction 173
The decision in *Kelly v Dawes* 174
Structured settlements in practice 176
Taxation treatment 179

The insurer and the life office   186
Other considerations   188
Appendix 1: Example   190
Appendix 2: Association of British Insurers—model agreement   199

8 Taxation and quantum   205

The rule in *Gourley*   205
The relevant rule   210
Extension of the *Gourley* rule   216
The position of employees   220
Gourley situations: a summary   226

9 Value added tax   227

The charge to tax   228
The application of the general principle   233
The form of settlement   241
The payment of third party costs   242
VAT and employees   244
The recovery of tax   244

Index   249

TABLE OF STATUTES

References in this Table to *Statutes* are to Halsbury's Statutes of England (Fourth Edition) showing the volume and page at which the annotated text of an Act may be found.

	PARA
Acquisition of Land (Assessment of Compensation) Act 1919	8.04
Administration of Justice Act 1982 (13 *Statutes* 586)	
s 1(1)(a)	1.36
Agricultural Holdings Act 1948	
s 34	3.28
Agricultural Holdings Act 1986 (1 *Statutes* 73)	3.26, 3.28; 9.35
Civil Procedure Act 1833	2.04
Defamation Act 1952 (24 *Statutes* 108)	2.64
Employment Protection (Consolidation) Act 1978 (16 *Statutes* 232)	6.50, 6.73
s 81	Ch 6 Appendix
(2)	6.71
96	6.72
Sch 4	6.72
Fatal Accidents Act 1976 (31 *Statutes* 251)	1.32, 1.39; 3.26
Finance Act 1950 (42 *Statutes* 51):	6.74
Finance Act 1960	6.50
Finance Act 1965	
s 22(1)	3.38
Finance Act 1974 Sch 2	
para 1	6.46
Finance Act 1977 Sch 7	
para 1	6.46
Finance Act 1982	3.73
Finance Act 1988 (42 *Statutes* 923)	3.73; 6.50, 6.76

	PARA
Finance Act 1988 – *contd*	
s 73(2)	5.05
(3)	5.38
78	6.02
Finance Act 1993	2.36
Finance Act 1994	2.36
Immigration Act 1971 (31 *Statutes* 47)	9.48
Income and Corporation Taxes Act 1988 (44 *Statutes* 1):	2.04, 2.06; 8.12
s 1	2.02
9	2.01
15	2.61
(1) Schedule A:	2.60, 2.62; 5.34, 5.37, 5.41, 5.43
para 2	2.62
18(1) Schedule D	
Case I	2.01, 2.52, 2.53; 4.30; 5.01, 5.02, 5.04, 5.05, 5.16; 7.32
Case II	2.01, 2.52; 4.30; 5.01, 5.02, 5.04, 5.05, 5.16
Case III	2.55, 2.58; 5.37; 7.33, 7.34, 7.35
Case VI	2.62
19	6.23
(1) Schedule E:	3.12; 6.01, 6.02, 6.05, 6.06, 6.07, 6.11, 6.12, 6.13, 6.19, 6.20, 6.21, 6.28, 6.40, 6.41, 6.54, 6.74, 6.75, 6.82, Ch 6 Appendix

Table of statutes

	PARA
Income and Corporation Taxes Act 1988 – *contd*	
s 19(1) Schedule E – *contd*	
Case I	6.02, 6.46
Case II	6.02
Case III	6.02, 6.75; 8.39
para 5	6.02
25	5.41, 5.42
(1)	5.05
(2)	5.41
(a)	5.43
(3)	5.41
(a), (b)	5.41
(4)–(9)	5.41
28	5.05
34	2.02
41	2.62
(1), (2)	2.62
60	5.02
74	5.04
(1)(a)	5.04, 5.06
(b)–(k)	5.04
(l)	5.04, 5.21
(m)–(q)	5.04
75	5.37
82	5.39
90	5.05
(1)(a)	5.28
(b)	5.38
(2)	5.05
100(2)	2.11
(a)	2.11
101(3)	2.11
125	7.40
130	5.37
131	6.05, 6.79
135(8)	1.44
148	6.01, 6.31, 6.32, 6.33, 6.34, 6.35, 6.36, 6.37, 6.38, 6.39, 6.40, 6.42, 6.44, 6.48, 6.50, 6.52, 6.58, 6.59, 6.65, 6.68, 6.71, 6.72, 6.73, 6.75, 6.77, 6.78, 6.79, 6.80, 6.82, 6.87, 6.88, Ch 6 Appendix; 8.41, 8.45
(2)	6.32, 6.34, 6.70
(3)	6.37
(4)	6.36
(6)	6.39
Pt V Ch II (ss 153–168G)	6.40
s 154	6.01, 6.31, 6.40, 6.41, 6.42, 6.43, 6.50, 6.68, 6.82
Income and Corporation Taxes Act 1988 – *contd*	
s 154(1)	6.40
156(1)	6.43
188	6.01, 6.31, 6.32, 6.37, 6.42, 6.44, 6.50, 6.51, 6.54, 6.58, 6.68, 6.70, 6.71, 6.77, 6.82, 6.90; 8.07, 8.38, 8.45
(1)	6.44
(a)	6.68
(3)	6.45, 6.47; 8.40
(4)	6.48; 8.41
(5)	6.51
(6)	6.58
(7)	6.51
193(1)	6.46
202A, 202B	6.36
203	6.81
209(4)	6.91
313	5.05; 6.31, 6.74, 6.75, 6.77, 6.78, 6.79, 6.82
(4)	6.75
329	2.59
(1)	7.01
(3)	2.59
337(2)	5.40
338	5.40
(5)(b)	5.40
Pt IX (ss 347A–379)	5.39
s 348	7.33
349(2)	5.39
354, 359, 360	5.39
401	5.03
577	5.12
579(1)	6.72, Ch 6 Appendix
(2)	5.05, 5.28
(a), (b)	5.05
(3)	5.05, 5.38
(4)	5.05
580(3)	6.72, Ch 6 Appendix
588(4)	5.38
589	5.05
Pt XIV Ch I (ss 590–612)	6.31, 6.88
s 595	6.59, 6.65
599	6.34
611	6.62
612	6.59, 6.63
(1)	6.62, 6.64
656	7.33
839(8)	6.35
840	6.51

Table of statutes

	PARA
Income and Corporation Taxes Act 1988 – *contd*	
Sch 11	
para 3	6.45, 6.48
9	6.49
10	6.46
Income Tax Act 1842	5.08
Indemnity Act 1920	2.48
Landlord and Tenant Act 1954:	3.30; 9.35
Leasehold Reform, Housing and Urban Development Act 1993	4.35
Race Relations Act 1976 (6 *Statutes* 828)	1.14, 1.38
Restriction of Ribbon Development Act 1935	2.51
Restrictive Trade Practices Act 1956	
s 6(3)	6.66
Social Security Contributions and Benefits Act 1992 (40 *Statutes* 492)	
s 3	6.79
4(4)	6.79
Taxation of Chargeable Gains Act 1992 (43 *Statutes* 1439)	
s 1(1)	3.15
2(1)	3.03
(2)	3.05
3–5	3.04
6(4)	3.04
7	3.04
8	3.02
(1)	3.05
(4)	3.11
10, 12	3.03
16(2)	3.05
17	3.18, 3.58, 3.70; 4.06
(1)(a)	4.06
(2)	3.35, 3.42
18	3.58
(3)	3.05
19(1)	3.52
21(1)	3.16
(c)	3.25
(2)	4.28
(b)	3.44
22	3.17, 3.49, 3.54; 4.15, 4.16
(1)	3.28, 3.43, 3.49; 4.09, 4.17, 4.21
(a)	3.10, 3.19, 3.32, 3.49, 3.50, 3.51, 3.52, 3.54; 4.23

	PARA
Taxation of Chargeable Gains Act 1992 – *contd*	
s 22(1)(b)	3.32, 3.49, 3.50, 3.54; 4.23
(c)	3.18, 3.32, 3.49, 3.55
(d)	3.32, 3.49, 3.56
(2)	3.32; 4.04
(3)	3.49
23	3.49; 4.15, 4.16, 4.17, 4.18, 4.20, 4.21, Ch 4 Appendix
(1)	4.17, 4.18
(a)	4.19
(b)	4.19, 4.22, 4.23
(c)	4.22
(2)	4.20
(3)	4.23
(4)	4.24, 4.27
(5)	4.27
(6)	4.21
24(1)	3.51
26	3.49
Pt II Ch III (ss 35–52)	3.57
s 37	3.11, 3.12, 3.13, 3.49
(1)	3.09
38	3.66, 3.68
(1)(a)	3.64, 3.70; 5.44
(b)	3.71, 3.72; 5.45
(2)	3.69
39	3.13, 3.14
42(2)	3.45
44	3.07
(1)	4.34
45	3.07
46	4.21
48	3.21, 3.58, 3.67
49	3.21, 3.59, 3.60, 3.61, 3.66; Ch 4 Appendix
(1)	3.59
(c)	3.62, 3.64
51	7.30
(1)	7.30
(2)	4.36, Ch 4 Appendix; 7.01
52(2)	3.12
(4)	4.29
Pt II Ch IV (ss 53–57)	3.57, 3.74
s 53(3)	4.18
54(1), (3)	3.74
57	4.18, 4.25
58	3.06, 3.58
62(2)	3.05
115	3.07

xiii

Table of statutes

	PARA
Taxation of Chargeable Gains Act 1992 – *contd*	
s 154	4.34
(7)	4.34
161	2.14
171	3.58
188	3.12
204	3.51
(1), (2)	3.54
210, 222, 237	3.07
242	3.47
(7)	3.47
243	3.47, 3.48
(1)(b)	3.48
(4)	3.48
244	3.47, 3.48
245	4.28, 4.29
(1)	4.29
(2)	4.28
246	4.28
247	4.28, 4.31, 4.35
(1)(b)	4.31
(2)	4.31
(5)(b)	4.32
(6)	4.28
248	4.34
(1)	4.32
(3)	4.34
251, 252, 254	3.07
256	3.06
262, 263, 268	3.07
272(1)	3.18; 4.08
280, 286	3.58
Sch 1	3.04
Taxation of Chargeable Gains Act 1992 – *contd*	
Sch 2, 3	3.57
Sch 4	3.57
para 1, 2	4.18, 4.33
3, 4	4.33
Sch 8	3.57
Taxes Management Act 1970 (42 *Statutes* 124)	
s 33	2.46, 2.47; 8.11
Town and Country Planning Act 1962	8.29
Town and Country Planning Act 1971	
s 164(1)	8.31
Value Added Tax Act 1994	
s 1	9.01
(2)	9.02
3(1)	9.04
4(1)	9.03
5(2)	9.06
(b)	9.10, 9.22
26	9.43, 9.44
Sch 1	
para 1	9.04
Sch 4	
para 5	9.41, 9.42
Sch 5	
para 4	9.14
Sch 6	
para 6	9.41
Sch 8, 9	9.01
Sch 10	
para 2	9.29, 9.31

TABLE OF CASES

	PARA
Aberdeen Construction Group Ltd v IRC [1978] AC 885, [1978] 1 All ER 962, [1978] 2 WLR 648, 122 Sol Jo 249, [1978] STC 127, 52 TC 281, L(TC) 2675, [1978] TR 25, 1978 SC (HL) 72, 1978 SLT 146	3.40, 3.71
Allison v Murray [1975] 3 All ER 561, [1975] 1 WLR 1578, 119 Sol Jo 712, [1975] STC 524, 51 TC 57, [1975] TR 157	3.72
Anglia Television Ltd v Reed [1972] 1 QB 60, [1971] 3 All ER 690, [1971] 3 WLR 528, 115 Sol Jo 723, CA	1.21
Anglo-Persian Oil Co Ltd v Dale (Inspector of Taxes) [1932] 1 KB 124, [1931] All ER Rep 725, 100 LJKB 504, 145 LT 529, 47 TLR 487, 75 Sol Jo 408, 16 TC 253, 10 ATC 149, CA	2.10, 5.24
Apple and Pear Development Council v Customs and Excise Comrs: 102/86 [1988] 2 All ER 922, [1988] ECR 1443, [1988] 2 CMLR 394, [1988] STC 221, ECJ	9.09
Associated Portland Cement Manufacturers Ltd v Kerr (Inspector of Taxes) [1946] 1 All ER 68, 62 TLR 115, 27 TC 103, CA	6.76
Associated Portland Cement Manufacturers Ltd's Application, Re [1966] 1 Ch 308, [1965] 2 All ER 547, [1965] 3 WLR 1271, 109 Sol Jo 996	8.29
BAZ Bausystem AG v Finanzamt München für Körperschaften: 222/81 [1982] ECR 2527, [1982] 3 CMLR 688, ECJ	9.36
Bacon v Cooper (Metals) Ltd [1982] 1 All ER 397	1.24
Barber v Manchester Regional Hospital Board [1958] 1 All ER 322, [1958] 1 WLR 181, 122 JP 124, 102 Sol Jo 140	8.15
Barr, Crombie & Co v IRC 1945 SC 271, 26 TC 406	2.28
Bartlett v Barclays Bank Trust Co Ltd [1980] Ch 515, [1980] 1 All ER 139, [1980] 2 WLR 430, 124 Sol Jo 85	8.08
Beach v Reed Corrugated Cases Ltd [1956] 2 All ER 652, [1956] 1 WLR 807, 100 Sol Jo 472, [1956] TR 215, 35 ATC 126, 49 R & IT 757	8.04, 8.23
Beak (Inspector of Taxes) v Robson [1943] AC 352, [1943] 1 All ER 46, 112 LJKB 141, 169 LT 65, 59 TLR 90, 87 Sol Jo 13, 25 TC 33, HL	6.74
Bell's Indenture, Re, Bell v Hickley [1980] 3 All ER 425, [1980] 1 WLR 1217, 123 Sol Jo 322	1.12, 8.08
Bird v IRC [1989] AC 300, [1988] 2 All ER 670, [1988] 2 WLR 1237, 132 Sol Jo 790, [1988] STC 312, 61 TC 238, HL	3.08
Bolton (Inspector of Taxes) v Halpern and Woolf (a firm) [1979] STC 761, 53 TC 445, [1979] TR 269; revsd [1981] STC 14, 53 TC 445, [1980] TR 367, CA	5.21
Booth (E V) (Holdings) Ltd v Buckwell (Inspector of Taxes) [1980] STC 578, 53 TC 425, [1980] TR 249	1.43

Table of cases

	PARA
Bowden (Inspector of Taxes) v Russell and Russell [1965] 2 All ER 258, [1965] 1 WLR 711, 109 Sol Jo 254, 42 TC 301, [1965] TR 89, 44 ATC 74:	5.15
Bramwell v Bramwell [1942] 1 KB 370, [1942] 1 All ER 137, 111 LJKB 430, 58 TLR 148, CA	9.28
Bray v Ford [1896] AC 44, [1895–9] All ER Rep 1000, 65 LJQB 213, 73 LT 609, 12 TLR 119, HL	2.66
British Basic Slag Ltd's Agreements, Re [1963] 2 All ER 807, LR 4 RP 116, [1963] 1 WLR 727, 107 Sol Jo 457, CA	6.66
British Insulated and Helsby Cables Ltd v Atherton (Inspector of Taxes) [1926] AC 205, [1925] All ER Rep 623, 95 LJKB 336, 134 LT 289, 42 TLR 187, 10 TC 155, 4 ATC 47, HL	2.10, 5.10, 5.23
British Transport Commission v Gourley [1956] AC 185, [1955] 3 All ER 796, [1956] 2 WLR 41, 100 Sol Jo 12, [1955] 2 Lloyd's Rep 475, [1955] TR 303, 34 ATC 305, 49 R & IT 11, HL	8.02, 8.46
Britwood Toys Ltd v Customs and Excise Comrs LON/86/280, unreported	9.47
Burmah SS Co v IRC 1931 SC 156, 1931 SLT 116, 16 TC 67	2.37
Bush, Beach and Gent Ltd v Road (Inspector of Taxes) [1939] 2 KB 524, [1939] 3 All ER 302, 108 LJKB 801, 161 LT 117, 55 TLR 862, 83 Sol Jo 641, 22 TC 519	2.25, 2.33
Calabar Properties Ltd v Stitcher [1983] 3 All ER 759, [1984] 1 WLR 287, 127 Sol Jo 785, 47 P & CR 285, 11 HLR 20, 268 Estates Gazette 697, [1983] LS Gaz R 3163, CA	1.27
Calvert (Inspector of Taxes) v Wainwright [1947] KB 526, [1947] 1 All ER 282, [1947] LJR 1335, 177 LT 159, 63 TLR 199, 27 TC 475, 40 R & IT 114, 26 ATC 13	6.08
Clayton v Lavender (Inspector of Taxes) (1965) 42 TC 607, [1965] TR 461, 44 ATC 477	6.16
Cooke (Inspector of Taxes) v Quick Shoe Repair Service (1949) 30 TC 460, L(TC) 1483, [1949] TR 87, 28 ATC 24, 42 R & IT 85	5.14
Cooper Chasney Ltd v Customs and Excise Comrs [1990] 3 CMLR 509, LON/89/14092	9.14
Copeman (Inspector of Taxes) v William Flood & Sons Ltd [1941] 1 KB 202, 110 LJKB 215, 24 TC 53, 19 ATC 521	5.15
Countess Warwick SS Co v Ogg (Inspector of Taxes) [1924] 2 KB 292, 93 LJKB 736, 131 LT 348, 8 TC 652	5.22
Cowcher (Inspector of Taxes) v Mills & Co Ltd (1927) 13 TC 216	5.25
Crabb (Inspector of Taxes) v Blue Star Line Ltd [1961] 2 All ER 424, [1961] 1 WLR 1322, 105 Sol Jo 300, [1961] 1 Lloyd's Rep 376, 39 TC 482, [1961] TR 69, 40 ATC 81	2.40
Creed (Inspector of Taxes) v H and M Levinson Ltd [1981] STC 486, [1981] TR 77, 54 TC 477	2.31, 2.68
Customs and Excise Comrs v Bass plc [1993] STC 42	9.23
Customs and Excise Comrs v Moonrakers Guest House Ltd [1992] STC 544, LON/89/1387	9.24
Customs and Excise Comrs v Oliver [1980] 1 All ER 353, [1980] STC 73, [1980] TR 423	9.06
Customs and Excise Comrs v Rosner [1994] STC 228	9.48
Dale (Inspector of Taxes) v de Soissons [1950] 2 All ER 460, 66 (pt 2) TLR 223, 94 Sol Jo 455, 32 TC 118, L(TC) 1519, [1950] TR 221, 43 R & IT 886, 29 ATC 125, CA	6.16
Daniels v Jones [1961] 3 All ER 24, [1961] 1 WLR 1103, 105 Sol Jo 568, CA:	8.21
Davenport (Inspector of Taxes) v Chilver [1983] Ch 293, [1983] 3 WLR 481, 127 Sol Jo 462, [1983] STC 426, 57 TC 661	3.31, 3.52
Davis (Inspector of Taxes) v Powell [1977] 1 All ER 471, [1977] 1 WLR 258, 121 Sol Jo 15, [1977] STC 32, 51 TC 492, L(TC) 2624, [1976] TR 307, 242 Estates Gazette 380	3.28

Table of cases

	PARA
De Bernardy v Harding (1853) 8 Exch 822, 22 LJ Ex 340, 21 LTOS 158, 1 WR 415, 1 CLR 884	1.09
Diamond v Campbell-Jones [1961] Ch 22, [1960] 1 All ER 583, [1960] 2 WLR 568, 104 Sol Jo 249, [1960] TR 131, 53 R & IT 502, 39 ATC 103	2.18
Dott v Brown [1936] 1 All ER 543, 154 LT 484, 80 Sol Jo 245, CA	7.17, 7.20
Drummond (Inspector of Taxes) v Austin Brown [1985] Ch 52, [1984] 2 All ER 699, [1984] 3 WLR 381, 128 Sol Jo 532, [1984] STC 321, 58 TC 67, [1984] LS Gaz R 1844, CA	3.30
Dunlop Pneumatic Tyre Co Ltd v New Garage and Motor Co Ltd [1915] AC 79, [1914–15] All ER Rep 739, 83 LJKB 1574, 111 LT 862, 30 TLR 625, HL	1.17, 9.21
ECC Quarries Ltd v Watkis (Inspector of Taxes) [1977] 1 WLR 1386, [1975] STC 578, 51 TC 153	5.34
Emmerson (Inspector of Taxes) v Computer Time International Ltd [1977] 2 All ER 545, [1977] 1 WLR 734, 121 Sol Jo 224, [1977] STC 170, 50 TC 628, 640, L(TC) 2635, [1977] TR 43, CA	3.72
Ensign Shipping Co Ltd v IRC (1928) 139 LT 111, 17 Asp MLC 472, 12 TC 1169, CA	2.48
Essex County Council v Ellam (Inspector of Taxes) [1989] 2 All ER 494, [1989] STC 317, 61 TC 615, [1989] 19 LS Gaz R 45, CA	7.35
FMS Management Services LON/92/722	9.38
Fairholme v Firth and Brown Ltd (1933) 149 LT 332, 49 TLR 470, 77 Sol Jo 485	8.03
Flockton (Ian) Developments Ltd v Customs and Excise Comrs [1987] STC 394	9.46
Furniss (Inspector of Taxes) v Dawson [1984] AC 474, [1984] 1 All ER 530, [1984] 2 WLR 226, 128 Sol Jo 132, [1984] STC 153, 55 TC 324, HL	1.46, 7.28
Galaxy Equipment (Europe) Ltd, Re MAN/91/1457	9.19
Gallagher v Jones (Inspector of Taxes) [1994] 2 WLR 160, [1993] STC 537, [1993] 32 LS Gaz R 40, CA	5.19
Glantre Engineering Ltd v Goodhand (Inspector of Taxes) [1983] 1 All ER 542, 126 Sol Jo 838, [1983] STC 1, 56 TC 165	6.29
Glenboig Union Fireclay Co Ltd v IRC 1922 SC (HL) 112, 59 SLR 162, 12 TC 427, 1 ATC 142	2.41, 2.43
Gleneagles Hotels plc v Customs and Excise Comrs [1986] VATTR 196	9.11
Gliksten (J) & Son Ltd v Green (Inspector of Taxes) [1929] AC 381, [1929] All ER Rep 383, 98 LJKB 363, 140 LT 625, 45 TLR 274, 14 TC 364, 8 ATC 46, HL	2.17
Godden v A Wilson's Stores (Holdings) Ltd (1962) 40 TC 161, L(TC) 2008, [1962] TR 19, 41 ATC 25, CA	5.32
Gray (Inspector of Taxes) v Lord Penrhyn [1937] 3 All ER 468, 157 LT 164, 81 Sol Jo 749, 21 TC 252	2.21
Great Western Rly Co v Bater (Surveyor of Taxes) [1920] 3 KB 266, 36 TLR 689, 8 TC 231; affd [1921] 2 KB 128, 90 LJKB 550, 125 LT 321, 37 TLR 388, 8 TC 236, CA; revsd [1922] 2 AC 1, 91 LJKB 472, 127 LT 170, 38 TLR 448, 66 Sol Jo 365, 8 TC 231, 1 ATC 104, HL	6.03
Hadley v Baxendale (1854) 9 Exch 341, [1843–60] All ER Rep 461, 23 LJ Ex 179, 23 LTOS 69, 18 Jur 358, 2 WR 302, 2 CLR 517	1.18
Haig's (Earl) Trustees v IRC 1939 SC 676, 1939 SLT 496, 22 TC 725, 18 ATC 226	2.08
Hall & Co Ltd v Pearlberg [1956] 1 All ER 297n, [1956] 1 WLR 244, 100 Sol Jo 187	8.06, 8.15
Hamblett v Godfrey (Inspector of Taxes) [1987] 1 All ER 916, [1987] 1 WLR 357, 131 Sol Jo 361, [1987] STC 60, 59 TC 694, [1987] LS Gaz R 658, CA	6.24
Hanbury, Re, Comiskey v Hanbury (1939) 38 TC 588n, sub nom Re Hanbury, Coniskey v Hanbury 20 ATC 333, CA	7.34

Table of cases

	PARA
Hartley v Sandholme Iron Co Ltd [1975] QB 600, [1974] 3 All ER 475, [1974] 3 WLR 445, 118 Sol Jo 702, [1974] STC 434, 17 KIR 205	8.06
Henley v Murray (Inspector of Taxes) [1950] 1 All ER 908, 31 TC 351, L(TC) 1510, [1950] TR 25, 43 R & IT 328, 29 ATC 35, CA	6.13
Higgs (Inspector of Taxes) v Olivier [1952] Ch 311, [1952] 1 TLR 441, 96 Sol Jo 90, 33 TC 136, L(TC) 1583, [1952] TR 57, 31 ATC 8, 45 R & IT 142, CA	2.44
Hochstrasser (Inspector of Taxes) v Mayes [1959] Ch 22, [1958] 3 All ER 285, [1958] 3 WLR 215, 102 Sol Jo 546, 38 TC 673, L(TC) 1880, [1958] TR 237, 37 ATC 205, 51 R & IT 767, CA; affd [1960] AC 376, [1959] 3 All ER 817, [1960] 2 WLR 63, 104 Sol Jo 30, 38 TC 673, L(TC) 1920, [1959] TR 355, 38 ATC 360, 53 R & IT 12, HL	6.06
Holiday Inns (UK) Ltd, Re MAN/91/1475	9.20, 9.38
Holland (Inspector of Taxes) v Geoghegan [1972] 3 All ER 333, [1972] 1 WLR 1473, 116 Sol Jo 546, 70 LGR 627, 48 TC 482, [1972] TR 141, 51 ATC 153	6.26
Houghton Main Colliery Co Ltd, Re [1956] 3 All ER 300, [1956] 1 WLR 1219, 100 Sol Jo 651, [1956] TR 333, 35 ATC 320, 50 R & IT 189	8.06
Howe (Earl) v IRC [1919] 2 KB 336, [1918–19] All ER Rep 1088, 88 LJKB 821, 121 LT 161, 35 TLR 461, 63 Sol Jo 516, 7 TC 289, CA	7.33, 7.34
Hunter (Inspector of Taxes) v Dewhurst (1932) 16 TC 605, sub nom Dewhurst v Hunter (Inspector of Taxes) 146 LT 510, [1932] All ER Rep 753, 9 ATC 574, HL	6.25
IRC v Alexander von Glehn & Co Ltd [1920] 2 KB 553, 89 LJKB 590, 123 LT 338, 36 TLR 463, 12 TC 232, CA	5.11
IRC v Anglo Brewing Co Ltd (1925) 12 TC 803	5.27
IRC v Bowater Property Developments Ltd [1989] AC 398, [1988] 3 All ER 495, [1988] 3 WLR 423, 132 Sol Jo 1120, [1988] STC 476, 62 TC 1, [1988] NLJR 219, [1988] 34 LS Gaz R 49, HL	1.46, 7.28
IRC v Carron Co (1968) 45 TC 18, [1968] TR 173, 47 ATC 192, 1968 SC (HL) 47, 1968 SLT 305	5.35
IRC v Church Comrs for England [1977] AC 329, [1976] 2 All ER 1037, [1976] 3 WLR 214, 120 Sol Jo 505, [1976] STC 339, 50 TC 516, 588, L(TC) 2605, [1976] TR 187, HL	7.22, 7.26
IRC v Duke of Westminster [1936] AC 1, [1935] All ER Rep 259, 104 LJKB 383, 153 LT 223, 51 TLR 467, 79 Sol Jo 362, sub nom Duke of Westminster v IRC 19 TC 490, 14 ATC 77, HL	1.40
IRC v Newcastle Breweries Ltd (1925) 95 LJKB 936, 135 LT 618, 42 TLR 609, 70 Sol Jo 734, 12 TC 927, CA, sub nom Newcastle Breweries Ltd v IRC (1927) 96 LJKB 735, [1927] All ER Rep 287, 137 LT 426, 43 TLR 476, 12 TC 927, HL	2.16, 2.48
IRC v Niddrie and Benhar Coal Co Ltd (1951) 32 TC 244, [1951] TR 69, 30 ATC 56, 44 R & IT 302	5.20
IRC v Patrick Thomson Ltd (1956) 37 TC 145, [1956] TR 471, 35 ATC 487, 50 R & IT 95, 1957 SLT 235	5.33
IRC v Plummer [1980] AC 896, [1979] 3 All ER 775, [1979] 3 WLR 689, 123 Sol Jo 769, [1979] STC 793, 54 TC 1, [1979] TR 339, HL	7.40
IRC v Ramsay (1935) 154 LT 141, [1935] All ER Rep 847, 79 Sol Jo 987, 20 TC 79, CA	7.17
IRC v Richards's Executors (1969) 46 TC 626, [1969] TR 497, 48 ATC 514, 1970 SC 96, 1970 SLT 137; affd sub nom IRC v Executors of Dr Richards [1971] 1 All ER 785, [1971] 1 WLR 571, 115 Sol Jo 225, 45 TC 626, [1971] TR 221, 50 ATC 249, 1971 SC (HL) 60, 1971 SLT 107	3.72
IRC v Scottish Automobile and General Insurance Co 1932 SC 87, 16 TC 381:	2.12
IRC v Titaghur Jute Factory Ltd [1978] STC 166, 53 TC 675, L(TC) 2679, 1978 SC 96, 1978 SLT 133	5.18

Table of cases

	PARA
IRC v Warnes & Co Ltd [1919] 2 KB 444, 89 LJKB 6, 121 LT 125, 35 TLR 436, 12 TC 227	5.11
IRC v Wesleyan and General Assurance Society [1946] 2 All ER 749, 176 LT 84, CA; affd [1948] 1 All ER 555, [1948] LJR 948, 64 TLR 173, 92 Sol Jo 193, 30 TC 11, [1948] TR 67, 41 R & IT 182, 27 ATC 75, L(TC) 1452, HL	7.25
IRC v Wilkinson [1992] STC 454, CA	3.08
IRC v Wilson's Executors 1934 SC 244, 18 TC 465	5.43
Jarrold (Inspector of Taxes) v Boustead [1964] 3 All ER 76, [1964] 1 WLR 1357, 108 Sol Jo 500, 41 TC 701, L(TC) 2105, sub nom Boustead v Jarrold (Inspector of Taxes) [1964] TR 217, 43 ATC 209, CA	6.27, 6.28
Jarvis v Swans Tours Ltd [1973] QB 233, [1973] 1 All ER 71, [1972] 3 WLR 954, 116 Sol Jo 822, CA	1.29
Jefford v Gee [1970] 2 QB 130, [1970] 1 All ER 1202, [1970] 2 WLR 702, 114 Sol Jo 206, [1970] 1 Lloyd's Rep 107, CA	2.57
John v James [1986] STC 352	1.13, 8.09
Johnston (Inspector of Taxes) v Britannia Airways Ltd [1994] STC 763	5.19
Kelly v Dawes (1990) Times, 27 September	7.02
Kelsall Parsons & Co v IRC 1938 SLT 239, 1938 SC 238, 21 TC 608	2.22
Kirby (Inspector of Taxes) v Thorn EMI plc [1986] 1 WLR 851, 130 Sol Jo 485, [1986] STC 200, 60 TC 519; revsd [1988] 2 All ER 947, [1988] 1 WLR 445, 131 Sol Jo 1456, [1987] STC 621, 60 TC 519, [1987] LS Gaz R 2693, CA	3.20, 3.24
Knight (Inspector of Taxes) v Parry [1973] STC 56, 116 Sol Jo 885, 48 TC 580, L(TC) 2470, [1972] TR 267, 51 ATC 283	5.36
Lang (Inspector of Taxes) v Rice [1984] STC 172, 57 TC 80 (NI CA)	2.34
Leeds Industrial Co-operative Society Ltd v Slack [1924] AC 851, [1924] All ER Rep 259, 93 LJ Ch 436, 131 LT 710, 40 TLR 745, 68 Sol Jo 715, HL:	1.11
Leigh v Customs and Excise Comrs [1990] VATTR 59, LON/89/1387	9.23
Levison v Farin [1978] 2 All ER 1149	8.32
Livingstone v Rawyards Coal Co (1880) 5 App Cas 25	1.15
London and Northern Estates Co Ltd v Harris (Inspector of Taxes) [1939] 1 KB 335, [1937] 3 All ER 252, 106 LJKB 823, 21 TC 197	5.37
London and Thames Haven Oil Wharves Ltd v Attwooll (Inspector of Taxes) [1967] Ch 772, [1967] 2 All ER 124, [1967] 2 WLR 743, 110 Sol Jo 979, L(TC) 2221, [1967] 1 Lloyd's Rep 204, 43 TC 491, [1966] TR 411, 45 ATC 489, CA	2.05, 2.38, 3.10
London Investment and Mortgage Co Ltd v Worthington (Inspector of Taxes) [1959] AC 199, [1958] 2 All ER 230, [1958] 2 WLR 842, 102 Sol Jo 346, 38 TC 86, [1958] TR 149, 37 ATC 125, 51 R & IT 511, HL	2.18
Lothian Chemical Co Ltd v IRC (1926) 11 TC 508, 6 ATC 823	5.02
Lyndale Fashion Manufacturers v Rich [1973] 1 All ER 33, [1973] 1 WLR 73, [1973] STC 32, 117 Sol Jo 54, CA	8.06, 8.22
McGhie & Sons Ltd v British Transport Commission [1963] 1 QB 125, [1962] 2 All ER 646, [1962] 3 WLR 380, 106 Sol Jo 550, [1962] TR 209, 41 ATC 144	8.05
McGowan (Inspector of Taxes) v Brown and Cousins (trading as Stuart Edwards) [1977] 3 All ER 844, [1977] 1 WLR 1403, 121 Sol Jo 645, [1977] STC 342, 52 TC 8, L(TC) 2650, [1977] TR 183, 244 Estates Gazette 133	2.73
McGregor (Inspector of Taxes) v Randall [1984] 1 All ER 1092, [1984] STC 223, 58 TC 110	6.25
MacKinlay (Inspector of Taxes) v Arthur Young McClelland Moores & Co [1990] 2 AC 239, [1990] 1 All ER 45, [1989] 3 WLR 1245, 134 Sol Jo 22, [1989] STC 898, HL	5.07

Table of cases

	PARA
Mairs (Inspector of Taxes) v Haughey [1992] STC 495, (N.I. CA); affd [1994] 1 AC 303, [1993] 3 All ER 801, [1993] 3 WLR 393, [1993] IRLR 551, 137 Sol Jo LB 199, [1993] STC 569, [1993] NLJR 1226, [1993] 37 LS Gaz R 51, HL	6.05, 6.21, 6.40
Mallalieu v Drummond (Inspector of Taxes) [1983] 2 AC 861, [1983] 2 All ER 1095, [1983] 3 WLR 409, 127 Sol Jo 538, [1983] STC 665, 57 TC 330, HL	5.07
Mallett (or Mallet) (Inspector of Taxes) v Staveley Coal and Iron Co Ltd [1928] 2 KB 405, [1928] All ER Rep 644, 97 LJKB 475, 139 LT 241, 13 TC 772, CA	5.25, 5.34
Mansell (Nigel) Sports Co Ltd v Customs and Excise Comrs [1991] VATTR 491, LON/90/6134	9.26
Marren (Inspector of Taxes) v Ingles [1980] 3 All ER 95, [1980] 1 WLR 983, 124 Sol Jo 562, [1980] STC 500, 54 TC 76, [1980] TR 335, HL	3.20, 3.21, 7.30
Marshall v Westminster City Council (8 March 1991, unreported)	7.31
Mercer v Pearson (Inspector of Taxes) [1976] STC 22, 51 TC 213, [1975] TR 295, 54 ATC 335	6.39
Mersey Docks and Harbour Board v Lucas (1883) 8 App Cas 891, 53 LJQB 4, 49 LT 781, 48 JP 212, 32 WR 34, 2 TC 25, HL	5.17
Mitchell (Inspector of Taxes) v B W Noble Ltd [1927] 1 KB 719, [1927] All ER Rep 717, 96 LJKB 484, 137 LT 33, 43 TLR 245, 71 Sol Jo 175, sub nom B W Noble Ltd v Mitchell (Inspector of Taxes) 11 TC 372, 43 TLR 102, CA	5.26
Moore v Griffiths (Inspector of Taxes) [1972] 3 All ER 399, [1972] 1 WLR 1024, 116 Sol Jo 276, 48 TC 338, L(TC) 2450, [1972] TR 61, 51 ATC 61:	6.10
Morley v Lawford & Co (1928) 140 LT 125, 45 TLR 30, 72 Sol Jo 825, 14 TC 229, CA	5.13
Murray (Inspector of Taxes) v Goodhews [1978] 2 All ER 40, [1978] 1 WLR 499, 121 Sol Jo 832, [1978] STC 207, 52 TC 86, L(TC) 2665, [1977] TR 255, CA	2.71
National Bank of Wales Ltd, Re [1899] 2 Ch 629, [1895–9] All ER Rep 715, 68 LJ Ch 634, 81 LT 363, 48 WR 99, 15 TLR 517, 43 Sol Jo 705, 6 Mans 119, CA; affd sub nom Dovey v Cory [1901] AC 477, [1895–9] All ER Rep 724, 70 LJ Ch 753, 85 LT 257, 50 WR 65, 17 TLR 732, 8 Mans 346, HL	2.56
O'Brien (Inspector of Taxes) v Benson's Hosiery (Holdings) Ltd [1979] Ch 152, [1978] 3 All ER 1057, [1978] 3 WLR 609, 122 Sol Jo 439, [1978] STC 549, 53 TC 241, [1978] TR 147, CA; revsd [1980] AC 562, [1979] 3 All ER 652, [1979] 3 WLR 572, 123 Sol Jo 752, [1979] STC 735, 53 TC 241, [1979] TR 335, HL	3.18, 3.38
O'Keeffe (Inspector of Taxes) v Southport Printers Ltd [1984] STC 443, 58 TC 88, [1984] LS Gaz R 1685	5.28
Oram (Inspector of Taxes) v Johnson [1980] 2 All ER 1, [1980] 1 WLR 558, 124 Sol Jo 188, [1980] STC 222, 53 TC 319, [1980] TR 5	3.71, 5.20
O'Sullivan v Management Agency and Music Ltd [1985] QB 428, [1985] 3 All ER 351, [1984] 3 WLR 448, 128 Sol Jo 548, CA	8.11
Ounsworth (Surveyor of Taxes) v Vickers Ltd [1915] 3 KB 267, 84 LJKB 2036, 113 LT 865, 31 TLR 530, 6 TC 671	2.09
Overy v Ashford, Dunn & Co Ltd (1933) 49 TLR 230, 17 TC 497	5.29
P and O European Ferries (Dover) Ltd v Customs and Excise Comrs LON/91/2146, LON/91/2532, unreported	9.49
Parsons v BNM Laboratories Ltd [1964] 1 QB 95, [1963] 2 All ER 658, [1963] 2 WLR 1273, 107 Sol Jo 294, [1963] TR 183, 42 ATC 200, CA	8.35
Pennine Raceway Ltd v Kirklees Metropolitan Council (No 2) [1989] STC 122, 58 P & CR 482, [1989] RVR 12, [1989] 1 EGLR 30, [1989] 23 EG 73, CA	8.31

Table of cases

PARA

Pepper (Inspector of Taxes) v Hart [1993] AC 593, [1993] 1 All ER 42, [1992] 3 WLR 1032, [1993] ICR 291, [1993] IRLR 33, [1993] RVR 127, [1992] STC 898, [1993] NLJR 17, HL 6.38
Peters (George) & Co Ltd v Smith (1963) 41 TC 264, [1963] TR 329, 42 ATC 389 .... 5.28
Phipps v Orthodox Unit Trusts Ltd [1958] 1 QB 314, [1957] 3 All ER 305, [1957] 3 WLR 856, 101 Sol Jo 884, [1957] TR 277, 36 ATC 267, CA 8.16
Practice Direction [1992] 1 All ER 862, sub nom Practice Note [1992] 1 WLR 328 .... 7.15
Praet (Julien) et Cie, SA v H G Poland Ltd [1962] 1 Lloyd's Rep 566 .... 8.35
Pritchard (Inspector of Taxes) v Arundale [1972] Ch 229, [1971] 3 All ER 1011, [1971] 3 WLR 877, 115 Sol Jo 658, 47 TC 680, L(TC) 2422, [1971] TR 277, 50 ATC 318 .... 6.27
Pyrah (Inspector of Taxes) v Annis & Co Ltd [1957] 1 All ER 196, [1957] 1 WLR 190, 101 Sol Jo 128, 37 TC 163, [1956] TR 423, 35 ATC 431, 50 R & IT 174, CA 5.34
RTZ Oil and Gas Ltd v Elliss (Inspector of Taxes) [1987] 1 WLR 1442, 131 Sol Jo 1188, [1987] STC 512, 61 TC 132, [1987] LS Gaz R 2196 .... 5.17
Raja's Commercial College v Gian Singh & Co Ltd [1977] AC 312, [1976] 2 All ER 801, [1976] 3 WLR 58, 120 Sol Jo 404, [1976] STC 282, PC ... 2.61, 8.46
Ramsay (W T) Ltd v IRC [1982] AC 300, [1981] 1 All ER 865, [1981] 2 WLR 449, 125 Sol Jo 220, [1981] STC 174, 54 TC 101, [1982] TR 123, HL 1.41, 1.45, 7.28
Randall v Plumb [1975] 1 All ER 734, [1975] 1 WLR 633, 119 Sol Jo 188, [1975] STC 191, 50 TC 392, [1974] TR 371 .... 3.60
Ransom (Inspector of Taxes) v Higgs [1974] 3 All ER 949, [1974] 1 WLR 1594, 118 Sol Jo 849, [1974] STC 539, 50 TC 1, [1974] TR 281, HL 5.15
Renfrew Town Council v IRC 1934 SC 468, 19 TC 13 .... 2.06, 5.09
Riches v Westminster Bank Ltd [1947] AC 390, [1947] 1 All ER 469, [1948] LJR 573, 176 LT 405, 63 TLR 211, 91 Sol Jo 191, 28 TC 159, 26 ATC 85, 40 R & IT 559, HL 2.04, 2.55
Riley (Inspector of Taxes) v Coglan [1968] 1 All ER 314, [1967] 1 WLR 1300, 111 Sol Jo 606, 44 TC 481, [1967] TR 155, 46 ATC 162 .... 6.30
Robinson (Inspector of Taxes) v Scott Bader Co Ltd [1981] 2 All ER 1116, [1981] 1 WLR 1135, 125 Sol Jo 429, [1981] STC 436, 54 TC 757, L(TC) 2831, [1981] TR 231, CA 5.12
Robinson (Jesse) & Sons v IRC (1929) 12 TC 1241 .... 2.49
Rolfe (Inspector of Taxes) v Nagel [1982] STC 53, 55 TC 585, [1981] TR 373, CA 2.72
Rolfe (Inspector of Taxes) v Wimpey Waste Management Ltd [1989] STC 454, 62 TC 399, CA 5.20
Rookes v Barnard [1964] AC 1129, [1964] 1 All ER 367, [1964] 2 WLR 269, 108 Sol Jo 93, [1964] 1 Lloyd's Rep 28, HL 1.16
Rownson, Drew and Clydesdale Ltd v IRC (1931) 16 TC 595 .... 2.17
Royal Insurance Co v Watson (Surveyor of Taxes) [1897] AC 1, 66 LJQB 1, 75 LT 334, 61 JP 404, 13 TLR 37, 3 TC 500, HL 5.31
Rubber Improvement Ltd v Daily Telegraph Ltd [1964] AC 234, [1963] 2 WLR 1063, 107 Sol Jo 356, sub nom Lewis v Daily Telegraph Ltd [1963] 2 All ER 151, HL 2.65, 8.46
Russell (Neville) v Customs and Excise Comrs [1987] VATTR 1949.11
Sabine (Inspector of Taxes) v Lookers Ltd (1958) 38 TC 120, [1958] TR 213, 37 ATC 227, CA 2.29
St John's School (Mountford and Knibbs) v Ward (Inspector of Taxes) [1975] STC 7n, 49 TC 524, CA 5.20
Saunders v Edwards [1987] 2 All ER 651, [1987] 1 WLR 1116, 131 Sol Jo 1039, [1987] NLJ Rep 389, [1987] LS Gaz R 2193, 2535, CA 1.42

Table of cases

	PARA
Scottish Investment Trust Co v Forbes (1893) 3 TC 231	2.12
Severne (Inspector of Taxes) v Dadswell [1954] 3 All ER 243, [1954] 1 WLR 1204, 98 Sol Jo 591, 35 TC 649, L(TC) 1706, [1954] TR 319, 33 ATC 366, 47 R & IT 584	2.48
Sharkey (Inspector of Taxes) v Wernher [1956] AC 58, [1955] 3 All ER 493, [1955] 3 WLR 671, 99 Sol Jo 793, 36 TC 275, L(TC) 1748, [1955] TR 277, 48 R & IT 739, 34 ATC 263, HL	2.14
Shilton v Wilmshurst (Inspector of Taxes) [1991] 1 AC 684, [1991] 3 All ER 148, [1991] 2 WLR 530, 135 Sol Jo 250, [1991] STC 88, HL	6.06, 6.09, 6.18
Short Bros Ltd v IRC (1927) 136 LT 689, 12 TC 955, CA	2.19, 2.21
Shove v Downs Surgical plc [1984] 1 All ER 7, [1984] ICR 532, [1984] IRLR 17, 128 Sol Jo 221	8.18, 8.38, 8.42, 8.46
Shove (Inspector of Taxes) v Dura Manufacturing Co Ltd (1941) 85 Sol Jo 349, 23 TC 779	2.24
Simmons v IRC [1980] 2 All ER 798, [1980] 1 WLR 1196, 124 Sol Jo 630, [1980] STC 350, 53 TC 461, HL	2.13, 2.14
Simpson (Inspector of Taxes) v John Reynolds & Co (Insurances) Ltd [1975] 2 All ER 88, [1975] 1 WLR 617, 119 Sol Jo 287, [1975] STC 271, 49 TC 693, L(TC) 2549, [1975] TR 33, 54 ATC 10, [1975] 1 Lloyd's Rep 512, CA	2.69
Smith (Surveyor of Taxes) v Incorporated Council of Law Reporting for England and Wales [1914] 3 KB 674, 83 LJKB 1721, 111 LT 848, 30 TLR 588, 6 TC 477	5.14
Smith, Hogg & Co Ltd v Black Sea and Baltic General Insurance Co Ltd [1940] AC 997, [1940] 3 All ER 405, 109 LJKB 848, 163 LT 261, 56 TLR 893, 84 Sol Jo 681, 19 Asp MLC 382, 46 Com Cas 44, HL	6.41
Snook (James) & Co Ltd v Blasdale (Inspector of Taxes) (1952) 33 TC 244, L(TC) 1598, [1952] TR 233, 31 ATC 268, CA	5.30
Sothern-Smith v Clancy (Inspector of Taxes) [1941] 1 KB 276, [1941] 1 All ER 111, 110 LJKB 189, 164 LT 210, 57 TLR 247, 85 Sol Jo 69, 24 TC 1, CA	7.26
Southern (Inspector of Taxes) v Aldwych Property Trust Ltd [1940] 2 KB 266, 109 LJKB 719, 163 LT 364, 56 TLR 808, 84 Sol Jo 584, 23 TC 707	5.37
Southern (Inspector of Taxes) v Borax Consolidated Ltd [1941] 1 KB 111, [1940] 4 All ER 412, 110 LJKB 705, 85 Sol Jo 94, 23 TC 597, 19 ATC 435	5.34
Southern Rly of Peru Ltd v Owen (Inspector of Taxes) [1957] AC 334, [1956] 2 All ER 728, [1956] 3 WLR 389, 100 Sol Jo 527, 36 TC 602, L(TC) 1778, [1956] TR 197, 32 ATC 147, 49 R & IT 468, HL	5.18
Spofforth and Prince v Golder (Inspector of Taxes) [1945] 1 All ER 363, 173 LT 77, 26 TC 310	5.36
Stanton (Inspector of Taxes) v Drayton Commercial Investment Co Ltd [1983] 1 AC 501, [1982] 2 All ER 942, [1982] 3 WLR 214, 126 Sol Jo 497, [1982] STC 585, 55 TC 286, HL	3.70
Stewart v Glentaggart [1963] TR 345, 42 ATC 318, 1963 SC 300, 1963 SLT 119	8.42
Stoke-on-Trent City Council v Wood Mitchell & Co Ltd [1979] 2 All ER 65, [1980] 1 WLR 254, 124 Sol Jo 168, [1979] STC 197, [1978] TR 471, 38 P & CR 126, 248 Estates Gazette 871, CA	2.45, 4.29
Stow Bardolph Gravel Co Ltd v Poole (Inspector of Taxes) [1954] 3 All ER 637, [1954] 1 WLR 1503, 98 Sol Jo 870, 35 TC 459, L(TC) 1717, [1954] TR 365, 33 ATC 378, 48 R & IT 46, CA	2.12
Strong & Co of Romsey Ltd v Woodifield (Surveyor of Taxes) [1906] AC 448, [1904–7] All ER Rep 953, 75 LJKB 864, 95 LT 241, 22 TLR 754, 50 Sol Jo 666, 5 TC 215, HL	5.08

Table of cases

	PARA
Sun Insurance Office v Clark [1912] AC 443, [1911–13] All ER Rep 495, 81 LJKB 488, 106 LT 438, 28 TLR 303, 56 Sol Jo 378, 49 SLR 1038, 6 TC 59, HL	5.18
Tate and Lyle Industries Ltd v Greater London Council [1981] 3 All ER 716, [1982] 1 WLR 149, 125 Sol Jo 865; on appeal [1982] 2 All ER 854, [1982] 1 WLR 971, 80 LGR 753, [1983] 2 Lloyd's Rep 117, CA; affd [1983] 2 AC 509, [1983] 1 All ER 1159, [1983] 2 WLR 649, 127 Sol Jo 257, 81 LGR 433, 46 P & CR 243, [1983] 2 Lloyd's Rep 117, HL	8.28
Taylor v O'Connor [1971] AC 115, [1970] 1 All ER 365, [1970] 2 WLR 472, 114 Sol Jo 132, [1970] TR 37, 49 ATC 37, HL	8.25, 8.26
Tilley v Wales (Inspector of Taxes) [1943] AC 386, [1943] 1 All ER 280, 112 LJKB 186, 169 LT 49, 59 TLR 178, 87 Sol Jo 76, 25 TC 136, 22 ATC 74, HL	6.05, 6.12
Tolsma v Inspecteur der Omzetbelasting Leeuwarden: C–16/93 [1994] ECR I–743, [1994] STC 509, ECJ	9.32
Trafalgar Tours Ltd v Customs and Excise Comrs [1990] 3 CMLR 68, [1990] STC 127, CA	9.07
Try Ltd v Johnson (Inspector of Taxes) [1946] 1 All ER 532, sub nom Johnson (Inspector of Taxes) v Try Ltd 174 LT 399, 62 TLR 355, 27 TC 167, 25 ATC 33, CA	2.51
Tucker (Inspector of Taxes) v Granada Motorway Services Ltd [1979] 2 All ER 801, [1979] 1 WLR 683, 123 Sol Jo 390, [1979] STC 393, 53 TC 92, [1979] TR 179, HL	2.07, 5.22, 5.23
Turner (t/a Turner Agricultural) v Customs and Excise Comrs [1992] STC 621:	9.43
Vallambrosa Rubber Co Ltd v Farmer (Surveyor of Taxes) 1910 SC 519, 5 TC 529	2.09
Van den Berghs Ltd v Clark (Inspector of Taxes) [1935] AC 431, [1935] All ER Rep 874, 104 LJKB 345, 153 LT 171, 51 TLR 393, 19 TC 390, 14 ATC 62, HL	2.27
Vaughan (Inspector of Taxes) v Archie Parnell and Alfred Zeitlin Ltd (1940) 23 TC 505	2.19
Vaughan-Neil v IRC [1979] 3 All ER 481, [1979] 1 WLR 1283, 123 Sol Jo 506, [1979] STC 644, 54 TC 223, [1979] TR 257	6.75
Vestey v IRC [1962] Ch 861, [1961] 3 All ER 978, [1962] 2 WLR 221, 40 TC 112, L(TC) 1996, [1961] TR 289, 40 ATC 325	7.25
Victoria Laundry (Windsor) Ltd v Newman Industries Ltd [1949] 2 KB 528, [1949] 1 All ER 997, 65 TLR 274, 93 Sol Jo 371, CA	1.18
Walker (Inspector of Taxes) v Joint Credit Card Co Ltd [1982] STC 427, 55 TC 617	5.26
Wallman Foods Ltd v Customs and Excise Comrs MAN/83/41, unreported:	9.44
Warnett (Inspector of Taxes) v Jones [1980] 1 WLR 413, [1980] ICR 359, 124 Sol Jo 48, [1980] STC 131, 53 TC 283, [1979] TR 447	6.52
Watney Combe Reid & Co Ltd v Pike (Inspector of Taxes) (1982) 126 Sol Jo 626, [1982] STC 733, 57 TC 372	5.12
West African Drug Co Ltd v Lilley (Inspector of Taxes) (1947) 28 TC 140, 26 ATC 256, 41 R & IT 30	5.25
West Suffolk County Council v W Rought Ltd [1957] AC 403, [1956] 3 All ER 216, [1956] 3 WLR 589, 120 JP 522, 100 Sol Jo 619, 54 LGR 473, 6 P & CR 362, [1956] TR 327, 35 ATC 315, 49 R & IT 561, HL	2.45, 8.04, 8.15
White's Metal Co, Re LON/86/6862	9.12
Wicks v Firth (Inspector of Taxes) [1981] 1 All ER 506, [1981] 1 WLR 475, 124 Sol Jo 829, [1981] STC 28, 56 TC 318, [1980] TR 377; revsd [1982] Ch 355, [1982] 2 All ER 9, [1982] 2 WLR 208, [1982] IRLR 25, 126 Sol Jo 82, [1982] STC 76, 56 TC 318, [1981] TR 517, CA; on appeal [1983] 2 AC 214, [1983] 1 All ER 151, [1983] 2 WLR 34, [1983] IRLR 80, 127 Sol Jo 37, [1983] STC 25, 56 TC 318, 133 NLJ 61, HL	6.40, 6.41

Table of cases

	PARA
Youssoupoff v Metro-Goldwyn-Mayer Pictures Ltd (1934) 50 TLR 581, 78 Sol Jo 617, CA	2.64
Zim Properties Ltd v Procter (Inspector of Taxes) (1984) 129 Sol Jo 68, [1985] STC 90, 58 TC 371, [1985] LS Gaz R 124	3.36, 4.01, 4.02, 7.30

Chapter 1

INTRODUCTION

1.01 In any dispute where compensation is paid, tax can be the single most important factor determining the net amount actually available to the recipient and its true cost to the payer. For example, an employee who is dismissed with immediate effect may claim damages calculated by reference to the salary which he has lost as a result of not being given proper notice. For reasons set out in Chapter 6, those damages may be received free of tax, whereas if the employee had actually worked out his notice period his salary would have been subject to income tax and national insurance in the normal way. Because damages may not be claimed for more than the employee's net loss, they are liable to reduction on account of their favourable taxation status—which reduces the cost of the claim to the employer. The taxation treatment of damages can therefore be different from the loss for which they compensate, and that difference may be taken into account in computing the damages actually due.

1.02 Given the many diverse reasons for which compensation may be paid, no coherent taxation regime may be identified solely by reference to the nature of payments in what may be termed the 'litigation sense'. For example, it is not possible to say that all damages for loss of profits following from a contractual breach are taxable as trading profits. Some may be so treated, but not all.

The status of the payment in the litigation sense is of importance however, and in this respect it is necessary to take some care over terminology. The term 'compensation' is used in this book in a general sense, where a reference to a more precise term such as damages is too restrictive. The terms 'plaintiff' and 'defendant' are also used to refer respectively to the person with a right of action and therefore the recipient of compensation, and to the person against whom an action lies and who is therefore the payer of compensation.

1.03 The taxation treatment of compensation is essentially concerned with the following:

(a) Is the compensation subject to income tax or corporation tax on income profits upon its receipt?

- (b) If not chargeable by reference to income, is the amount subject to capital gains tax or corporation tax on capital gains upon its receipt?
- (c) Is tax relief available for the payment of compensation, or in respect of the costs of pursuing or defending a claim?
- (d) Does the incidence of tax affect the amount actually paid?
- (e) Should VAT be paid in respect of compensation?

The structure of this book reflects the general issues set out above. Chapter 2 deals with the incidence of income tax and corporation tax on income profits. Chapters 3 and 4 are concerned with capital gains. The availability of relief for the payer of compensation, as well as the status of legal and other professional fees, is dealt with in Chapter 5. Distinct rules apply in relation to employees and accordingly a whole chapter, Chapter 6, is devoted to the relevant issues. Chapter 7 deals with structured settlements, a tax driven structure for paying damages in the context of personal injury. As mentioned above, the incidence of tax may affect the amount of damages actually due. The circumstances in which adjustments should be made are dealt with in Chapter 8. Finally, the scope of the charge to VAT is considered in Chapter 9.

1 THE NATURE OF 'DAMAGES'

1.04 The term 'damages' bears a specific and precise meaning in English law. Essentially, damages are the monetary (or pecuniary) compensation which is obtained by success in an action for a wrong which is either a tort (such as negligence or trespass) or a breach of contract. Damages are awarded in the form of a lump sum, subject to the use of structured settlements in personal injury cases, and are generally expressed in English currency. To constitute damages, the compensation must be awarded unconditionally by the court, as distinct from an amount which a party to a dispute agrees to pay so as to settle the action or threatened action against him. This distinction is not of great significance in itself in the context of direct tax, ie income tax, corporation tax and capital gains tax. Accordingly, the chapters which follow use the term 'damages' to include compensation payable under a settlement, provided the compensation would have constituted damages if awarded by the court.

1.05 The definition is therefore a narrow one, as it excludes compensation other than for a tort or breach of contract. The nature of damages and their measure is dealt with in this chapter by reference to the structure of analysis adopted by Harvey McGregor,[1] who identified four categories where an amount may be received by reason of a legal action which falls outside the scope of the term damages. These are actions:

- (a) for monies due under the terms of a contract;
- (b) in quasi-contract;
- (c) in equity; and
- (d) under statute, where the equitable or statutory right to recover is independent of any tort or breach of contract.

The commentary which follows is written in very general terms, with a view to giving a broad outline of the possible taxation treatment rather than a definitive analysis.

1 *McGregor on Damages* (15th edn, 1988) Sweet & Maxwell.

ACTIONS FOR MONEY PAYABLE

1.06 The first category identified as falling outside the term 'damages' consists of actions for money payable; essentially amounts due under the terms of a contract. For example, an action for rent due under a lease, for wages under a contract of employment or the price of goods delivered to a purchaser. In each case the action is for the amount due pursuant to the terms of the contract itself, as distinct from an amount due for a breach of that contract.

It is considered that the existence of such an action does not have a taxation effect in itself. To take one of the above examples, money received for the price of goods will enjoy the same status for tax purposes whether the recipient pays for those goods on time and without dispute, or has to be sued for the same.

ACTIONS IN QUASI-CONTRACT

1.07 The second category identified consists of actions in quasi-contract. The nature of quasi-contract may be described as a liability to pay based on the ground of unjust benefit, and includes actions for money:

(a) paid under a mistake of fact;
(b) paid under a contract, the legal effect of which is in some way destroyed. These may include instances where there has been a total failure of consideration or where the contract is void or illegal; and
(c) paid to a third party but which are recoverable from the defendant because he is primarily liable.

In each of the above, a successful action should not be regarded as having any tax effect other than to cancel the original loss for which the action compensates.

EXAMPLE

Maria owns a shop and agrees to purchase some goods for resale from Philip. £10,000 is paid to Philip upon delivery of the goods to Maria, but before she can resell them they are found to be stolen and Maria is obliged to return them to their rightful owner. A total failure of consideration has occurred under the contract, in consequence of which Maria is entitled to recover the £10,000 paid to Philip. If successful, her trading profits should be computed without reference to the £10,000 expense or subsequent recovery.

1.08 Of course, not all actions are wholly successful or result in the plaintiff being fully reimbursed. If Maria had made a partial recovery only from

1.08 *Introduction*

Philip in the above example, the irrecoverable element should have been deductible for the purposes of computing Maria's profits subject to income tax. While Maria derived no benefit from the expenditure, it had no element of non-trade purpose and therefore could have been deducted. These issues are dealt with in Chapter 5.

Quantum meruit

1.09 A claim on a quantum meruit is a remedy in quasi-contract which operates where the plaintiff seeks a reasonable remuneration for services rendered, there being no precise sum otherwise due to him. This claim is an alternative to an action for damages for breach of contract.

The case of *De Bernardy v Harding*[1] may be used to illustrate the nature of the remedy. In that case the plaintiff agreed with the defendant to advertise and sell tickets to view the funeral of the Duke of Wellington in return for a commission. The defendant wrongfully revoked the plaintiff's authority before he had sold any tickets, but not before he had incurred expense on the preparation of advertisements and printing costs. It was decided that the plaintiff could sue on a quantum meruit for the work which he had performed:

> 'Where one party has absolutely refused to perform, or had rendered himself incapable of performing his part of the contract, he puts it in the power of the other party either to sue for a breach of it or to rescind the contract and sue on a quantum meruit for the work actually done.'[2]

---

1 (1853) 8 Exch 822.
2 Per Alderson J, ibid at 824.

1.10 It is considered that a sum received pursuant to a quantum meruit claim should have the same taxation status as the sums which were anticipated under the contract forming the basis of that claim. In *De Bernardy* the plaintiff was due to receive a commission. If the commission had been received following a successful conclusion of the contract it would have been regarded as a trading receipt for income tax purposes. The compensation he actually received pursuant to his claim should be regarded in the same light. Furthermore, his advertising expenses should have given rise to a deductible revenue expense with a fiscally neutral result. These issues were not considered in *De Bernardy*, but the position would not appear to be in doubt having regard to the general principles set out in Chapter 2.

ACTIONS IN EQUITY

1.11 The third category consists of actions claiming money in equity. Actions in tort and contract are both actions in law, as distinct from actions in equity which, broadly speaking, may be regarded as a gloss on the common law developed for reasons of natural justice; the concept of the trust is a creature of the equitable jurisdiction. From a taxation point of view the distinction between actions in law and equity would not of itself appear to be important. However, awards under the equitable jurisdiction may not, strictly speaking, be damages and they therefore require some explanation.

Equitable awards not included within the definition of damages essentially consist of two types. First, an award may be given for breach of a purely equitable right, or for a tort or breach of contract merely apprehended. For example, in *Leeds Industrial Co-Operative Society, Ltd v Slack*[1] an award was made in lieu of an injunction in the case of a threatened injury. Second, an award may be made following an action for an account. This remedy may in turn be divided into two sub-categories: namely those which do and those which do not involve the defendant handing over or accounting for profits.

1 [1924] AC 851.

Actions for account
1.12 The most commonly encountered example of an action which does not involve the handing over of profits by the defendant is that of an action for breach of trust where the breach in question is the loss of trust property. An amount received in compensation for such a loss should not be regarded as having a taxation effect in itself, because the defendant is merely making good the loss caused in consequence of his breach. However, the loss in question may relate to an asset with an inherent gain, the disposal of which in breach of trust gives rise to a capital gains tax charge.

As a general principle, a trustee is liable to make good all loss which arises by reason of a breach of trust. If that loss were to include an element in respect of tax the trustee would be liable for it, if the Revenue were not willing to grant some form of concessionary relief. On the other hand, a profit realised by a beneficiary may be retained, so a higher base cost in respect of an asset restored to the trust, for example, should not be regarded as reducing the trustee's liability.[1]

1 See *Re Bell's Indenture* [1980] 1 WLR 1217, Ch D at 1236.

Actions for an account of profits
1.13 The second type of action for account involves the handing over of profits by the defendant. The most commonly encountered example is the handing over of profits made in breach of a fiduciary duty. Such a duty exists between trustee and beneficiary, solicitor and client, partner and co-partner amongst others. For taxation purposes it would appear that the profits in question should be imputed to the plaintiff, with the result that the plaintiff is charged to tax in like manner as if he had realised that profit himself.

This view is based upon the nature of the obligation upon the defendant to hold profits accruing by reason of the abuse of his position for the benefit of the plaintiff. The defendant is a constructive trustee, and a person who receives trust property (not being a bona fide purchaser for value without notice of the trust) becomes a trustee of that property. The profit should therefore be imputed to the plaintiff, and any charge to tax determined by the circumstances of the plaintiff.

The restitution of property or payment of profits should be fiscally neutral from the defendant's point of view. The defendant was never entitled to the property or profits in question, and accordingly they should not enter his profit and loss account. The lapse in time between realising profits and accounting for them pursuant to an action may, however, be such that the

1.13 *Introduction*

defendant will have incurred tax liabilities in respect of them. If such profits are more than six years ago the defendant is out of time so far as concerns obtaining a repayment of tax, although Nicholls LJ in *John v James*[1] was of the view that the defendant in that case would obtain relief notwithstanding this restriction.

---

1 [1986] STC 352 at 360.

ACTIONS CLAIMING MONEY UNDER STATUTE

1.14 The fourth and final category identified as falling outside the term 'damages' refers to claims which are independent of any wrong in tort or breach of contract. These include, by way of example, claims under the Race Relations Act 1976 in respect of discriminatory acts. The diverse nature of such receipts does not lend itself to a separate and self-contained commentary. Such receipts may therefore be considered by reference to a general scheme of analysis, which should first consider whether the amount is subject to income tax or corporation tax on income. If not, it should be considered whether it may be taxed as a capital gain. Finally, the status of the payment for the purposes of value added tax should be considered.

2 THE AMOUNT OF DAMAGES

1.15 As a general rule, the damage for which a plaintiff may be compensated is all damage caused by the defendant's breach of contract or tortious act, save for that which is too remote. The concept of remoteness of damage prevents a plaintiff from recovering for damage which results from the defendant's actions, but which is too unusual or unexpected to qualify for recompense.

The amount of damages may be divided between those ascertained in accordance with their normal measure and those not based strictly on compensation. The normal measure of damages needs to be considered separately in relation to contract and tort, although the basic principle for that measure remains the same: namely that of 'restitutio in integrum'. In *Livingston v Rawyards Coal Co*[1] which was concerned with a tortious action, Lord Blackburn stated the principle in the following terms:

> '... where any injury is to be compensated by damages, in settling the sum of money to be given for reparation ... you should as nearly as possible get at that sum of money which will put the party who has been injured, or who has suffered, in the same position as he would have been in if he had not sustained the wrong for which he is now getting his ... reparation.'[2]

Damages not based strictly on compensation consist of nominal, exemplary and liquidated damages. Nominal damages refer to the award of a token sum and must be distinguished from compensation for a small loss; modern awards of nominal damages range from £1 to £5.

1 (1880) 5 App Cas 25.
2 Ibid at 39.

Exemplary damages

1.16 Exemplary damages are not compensatory but are awarded to punish the defendant and to deter him from engaging in such behaviour in the future. The circumstances in which exemplary damages may be awarded are very limited, as a result of the decision of the House of Lords in *Rookes v Barnard*[1] the facts of which are not relevant here. It is now clear that such damages may be awarded only in cases:

(a) of oppressive, arbitrary or unconstitutional acts by government servants;
(b) where the defendant's conduct had been calculated by him to make a profit for himself which might exceed the compensation payable to the plaintiff; and
(c) where the award is expressly authorised by statute.

The nature of exemplary damages would appear to be such that no tax should be charged in respect of their receipt. Specifically, they are not calculated by reference to any loss of income profits by the plaintiff, and accordingly should not be regarded as subject to income tax by virtue of the general rule formulated by Lord Diplock in the *Attwooll* case.[2] So far as capital gains are concerned, such damages are unlikely to be derived from any asset other than, possibly, the 'right to sue' itself, which is considered in Chapters 3 and 4. Having regard to Inland Revenue Concession D33, considered in Chapter 4, such damages would appear to be free of capital gains tax.

1 [1964] AC 1129.
2 See **2.05** below.

Liquidated damages

1.17 Rather than leave the amount of damages to be computed by the court, the parties to a contract may agree in advance what sum should become payable in the event of a contractual breach. To the extent that the sum is a genuine pre-estimate of the loss caused by the breach, it falls to be treated as liquidated damages which the plaintiff may recover without having to prove his actual loss. The ability to fix damages in advance of a breach may of course be abused—the amount of the damages may be fixed at a high level to ensure that the other party performs his part of the contract. A sum so fixed is known as a penalty, and is subject to the equitable jurisdiction of the court. In the case of a penalty the amount due may be reduced by the court to the actual loss suffered.

The nature of liquidated damages and penalties were considered in the case of *Dunlop Pneumatic Tyre Co Ltd v New Garage and Motor Co Ltd*.[1] In that case a sum of £5 was reserved in the contract as being payable by way of liquidated damages in respect of every tyre sold or offered for sale in breach

1.17 *Introduction*

of a so-called 'Price Maintenance Agreement'. It was held that although the resulting damage to Dunlop of a single tyre being sold in breach of the agreement was likely to be trifling, news of price reductions could spread and Dunlop's profits might be threatened. The damages were therefore reasonably fixed, and could be recovered.

1 [1915] AC 79.

Contract: the amount of damages

1.18 Damages for a breach of contract represent recompense for the loss suffered by the plaintiff by reason of that breach. The plaintiff is, so far as money allows, to be placed in the same position as if the contract had been performed. It is therefore implicit that a net loss approach should apply: gains realised by the defendant by reason of the breach must be taken into account. For example, the defendant may be relieved from an obligation to pay for goods or services under the contract in question.

The losses for which damages may be obtained for a breach of contract may be divided into three heads:

(a) basic pecuniary, or monetary, losses;
(b) consequential pecuniary losses; and
(c) non-pecuniary losses.

The distinction between basic and consequential pecuniary losses reflects the distinction between losses that occur in the usual course of things and those which arise because of special or exceptional circumstances, for which the defendant is liable only if they were contemplated or may reasonably be supposed to have been in the contemplation of the parties at the time the contract was made.[1]

1 *Hadley v Baxendale* (1854) 9 Exch 341; and *Victoria Laundry (Windsor) Ltd v Newman Industries Ltd* [1949] 2 KB 528, [1949] 1 All ER 997, among others.

BASIC PECUNIARY LOSSES

1.19 For the purposes of computing the basic pecuniary loss, breaches of contract may be classified into three basic forms: non-performance, delayed performance and defective performance. In each case, the normal basic measure of damages is arrived at by reference to the market value of the supply which should have been made under the contract in question, compared with its cost.

EXAMPLE

Victoria agrees to buy an antique chair from John for £800, but he subsequently refuses to deliver. Victoria buys an equivalent chair elsewhere at a cost of £1,000, the best price obtainable. Victoria's basic pecuniary loss is £200.

1.20 In the case of delayed performance, the basic measure of damages is ascertained by reference to the change in the market value of the goods or services at their contractual date of delivery, compared with their actual date of delivery. In the case of defective performance, the comparison is with the market value of the goods or services as represented, compared with their value as actually delivered.

Similar principles apply to a case involving a breach of contract by the transferee, of which non-performance is the most important, ie a failure to pay for the goods or services in question. In such cases, the basic measure of damages is ascertained by reference to the contract price which should have been received, compared with the market value which can be realised by the plaintiff.

EXAMPLE

To follow the example above, Victoria refuses to perform her part of the contract by accepting delivery of the chair from John at the agreed price of £800. John therefore sells the chair elsewhere, but can only realise £650; his basic pecuniary loss is £150.

The alternative measure

1.21 An alternative measure of damages for basic pecuniary loss is to sue in respect of expenses rendered futile by reason of the contractual breach. This measure may be illustrated by reference to the case of *Anglia Television v Reed*.[1] In that case, Mr Reed contracted to play a leading part in a play to be produced by Anglia Television Ltd. A few days later he repudiated the contract and Anglia Television sued for, and obtained, damages for their total wasted expenditure. In the words of Lord Denning MR:

> '*If the plaintiff claims the wasted expenditure, he is not limited to the expenditure incurred after the contract was concluded. He can claim also the expenditure incurred before the contract, provided that it was such as would reasonably be in the contemplation of the parties as likely to be wasted if the contract was broken. Applying that principle here, it is plain that, when Mr Reed entered into this contract, he must have known perfectly well that much expenditure had already been incurred on director's fees and the like. He must have contemplated—or, at any rate, it is reasonably to be imputed to him—that if he broke his contract, all that expenditure would be wasted, whether or not it was incurred before or after the contract. He must pay damages for all the expenditure so wasted and thrown away.*'[2]

The alternative measure was advanced by Anglia Television in the case as it was unclear what, if any, profit would have been realised from the production of the play.

---

1 [1972] 1 QB 60.
2 Ibid at 64.

Consequential pecuniary losses

1.22 Damages for consequential pecuniary losses may be classified into three heads, which comprise those in respect of:

(a) gains prevented by the breach;
(b) expenses caused by the breach; and
(c) expenses rendered futile by the breach.

1.23 The most encountered head of damage in respect of gains prevented by the breach is for the loss of profits caused by being deprived of the use of the property which should have been provided under the contract in question. The loss of profits may arise by reason of the loss of a specific sale or general custom.

EXAMPLE

A Ltd contracts to purchase a machine for the manufacture of computer disc drives. The machine is delivered one month late, during which time it would have produced 10,000 disc drives with a profit element of £10 each. A Ltd may claim damages for consequential pecuniary loss in the sum of £100,000.

1.24 A wide variety of expenditure may be recovered under the second head of expenses caused by the breach. The case of *Bacon v Cooper (Metals) Ltd*[1] may be used to illustrate the general principle. The plaintiff was a dealer in scrap metal. When he fed a consignment of steel purchased from the defendant into a machine used to produce fragmented scrap steel, the rotor broke. In order to continue his business the plaintiff obtained a new rotor, the direct and financing cost of which was included in the award of damages.

---

1 [1982] 1 All ER 397.

1.25 Damages for expenses rendered futile by the breach may be claimed as an alternative to recovery in respect of gains prevented by the breach. The alternative is usually encountered where the plaintiff is unable to prove a loss of profits, as in the *Anglia Television* case.[1]

---

1 See **1.21** above.

Non-pecuniary losses

1.26 Damages for contractual breach are usually concerned with commercial losses, but it is possible to receive compensation for a number of heads of non-pecuniary loss. Such heads include:

(a) physical inconvenience and discomfort;
(b) pain and suffering, loss of amenities and of expectation of life; and
(c) mental distress.

1.27 Damages may be recovered for physical inconvenience and discomfort in a wide variety of circumstances. The case of *Calabar Properties Ltd v Stitcher*[1] was concerned with a flat which suffered from dampness and water damage in consequence of external defects. In awarding damages to the owners of the flat, a sum was included in order to compensate them for their discomfort, loss of enjoyment and health as a consequence of living in the damp and deteriorating flat.

1 [1984] 1 WLR 287.

1.28 Damages for pain and suffering (etc) are more often encountered in the context of an action in tort, and are therefore dealt with below.

1.29 Damages for mental distress may be recovered in a contractual action in certain limited circumstances. In *Jarvis v Swans Tours*[1] damages were awarded following a spoiled holiday in which the promised facilities did not exist. The basis for that award was simply put by Lord Denning MR:

> '[Mr Jarvis] went to enjoy himself with all the facilities which the defendants said he would have. He is entitled to damages for the lack of those facilities, and for his loss of enjoyment.'[2]

1 [1973] QB 233.
2 Ibid at 238.

Tort: the amount of damages

1.30 The importance of the respective heads of damages in tort and contract are reversed. Because tort primarily protects interests such as a person's personal well being and safety, rather than a person's commercial interests, damages for pecuniary losses do not figure so highly. Conversely, damages for non-pecuniary losses are more important. Again, the losses for which damages may be obtained may be divided into three heads, comprising basic pecuniary losses, consequential pecuniary losses and non-pecuniary losses.

Pecuniary losses

1.31 Damages for basic pecuniary losses arise in connection with tortious damage to property. As in contract, the basic measure of damages is calculated by reference to the diminution in the value of the plaintiff's goods, measured by the cost of repair, or replacement if the goods are destroyed. In the context of land, adverse occupation may be compensated by an award of damages calculated by reference to the land's rental value, known as mesne profits.

A similar classification of damages in respect of pecuniary losses may be adopted for tort as in contract, by reference to three heads:

(a) gains prevented by the tort;
(b) expenses caused by the tort; and
(c) expenses rendered futile by the tort.

1.32 As with contract, damages for gains prevented by the tort may be awarded for loss of business profits. Such an award may arise not only in the context of the plaintiff's goods being damaged, destroyed or misappropriated, but also where the tort in question relates to the plaintiff's person. Examples include damages for false imprisonment, malicious prosecution, libel and slander. Damages for loss of profits may also arise in the context of inducements of breach of contract, and the use of confidential information. A further ground for damages which may be put under this head is that of damages for the loss of the services of a relative killed by a tortious action (for which see the Fatal Accidents Act 1976).

1.33 As with the contractual position, expenses incurred as a result of the tort may be recovered by an award of damages. Such expenses may include the hiring of substitute property while the plaintiff's assets undergo repair, and medical expenses in the case of physical injury amongst others.

1.34 A claim may be made for expenses rendered futile by the tort, as an alternative measure to that afforded by recovery for gains prevented by the tort. The claim does not, however, have the same importance in tort as in contract. This is because the plaintiff is not acting in reliance on the defendant's promise to perform his part of the contract.

NON-PECUNIARY LOSSES

1.35 Protection afforded under the law of tort is primarily concerned with interests such as personal health, safety and reputation. Accordingly, tort recognises a wide array of non-pecuniary loss:

(a) pain and suffering, loss of amenities and expectation of life;
(b) physical inconvenience and discomfort;
(c) social discredit: injury to reputation;
(d) mental distress; and
(e) for bereavement.

1.36 Where a plaintiff seeks damages in respect of a physical injury tortiously inflicted, the head afforded in respect of 'pain and suffering' is one of the most basic. This head may be summarised as follows:

> '... "pain" needs no further elucidation; suffering would include fright at the time of the injury, fear of future incapacity, either as to health or possible death, to sanity or to the ability to make a living, and humiliation, sadness and embarrassment caused by disfigurement.'[1]

Damages for pain and suffering caused or likely to be caused by an awareness that expectation of life has been reduced, is a head which is confined to torts not resulting in physical injury to the plaintiff, for example injury to health by reason of shock.[2] The reference to 'loss of amenities' is to physical injury suffered by the plaintiff which results in disablement, so reducing or preventing the enjoyment of activities formerly pursued. For example, the loss of a limb will have such a result.

---

1 *McGregor on Damages* (15th edn, 1988) Sweet & Maxwell, para 81.
2 Which confinement was effected by the Administration of Justice Act 1982 s 1(1)(a).

1.37 Damages for physical inconvenience and discomfort may be recovered for torts which interfere with the plaintiff short of physical injury. Such damages have been awarded in cases of deceit, false imprisonment, nuisance and negligence.

1.38 Damages for social discredit (and injury to reputation) may be recovered for defamation, malicious prosecution and false imprisonment. Damages for mental distress are primarily confined to those torts which protect reputation, such as libel, slander and malicious prosecution. Such damages also exist as a head in cases of assault, deceit, trespass to property and nuisance. Damages for mental distress may also be recovered under the statutory torts established by the Race Relations Act 1976 for discriminatory acts.

1.39 Damages for bereavement may be recovered by the spouse or parent of the person killed by the tortious act in question, by reason of the Fatal Accidents Act 1976.

3 TAX PLANNING AND COMPENSATION

1.40 It is a well-established principle of UK tax law that a taxpayer may arrange his affairs so as to reduce his liability to tax. Motive does not invalidate a transaction, which must be considered according to its legal effect. Authority for the principle may be found in the case of *IRC v Duke of Westminster*,[1] the facts of which are not relevant here. In the House of Lords, Lord Tomlin was of the view that:

> '*Every man is entitled, if he can, to order his affairs so that the tax attaching . . . is less than it otherwise would be. If he succeeds in ordering them so as to secure this result, then however unappreciative the Commissioners of Inland Revenue or his fellow taxpayers may be of his ingenuity, he cannot be compelled to pay an increased tax.*'[2]

The principle is subject to caveats, especially following the decisions of the House of Lords in the cases of *Ramsay* and *Furniss v Dawson*. It remains important however, not only as a starting point, but for defining the limits of acceptable tax avoidance. If two or more parties to a transaction agree to structure a transaction in a particular manner, which secures certain tax advantages, the Revenue cannot attribute a different character to that transaction so as to counter the advantages which would otherwise have been obtained.

A different character may only be attributed if:

(i) the transaction is not genuine, or
(ii) it falls to be reassessed in accordance with the so-called '*Ramsay* doctrine', or
(iii) a specific statutory provision applies to it.

---

1 [1936] AC 1, [1935] All ER Rep 259, 19 TC 490.
2 [1935] All ER Rep 259 at 267.

1.41 *Introduction*

IS THE TRANSACTION GENUINE?

1.41 It is a question of fact whether a document or transaction is genuine or a sham. In the words of Lord Wilberforce:

> '. . . to say that a document or transaction is a "sham" means that, while professing to be one thing, it is in fact something different. To say that a document or transaction is genuine, means that, in law, it is what it professes to be, and it does not mean anything more than that.'[1]

It therefore follows that where a particular structure has been genuinely adopted in respect of any transaction, the Revenue are not entitled to go behind it to some supposed underlying substance. But, in construing effect, Lord Wilberforce was clear as to the nature of the court's task:

> 'While obliging the court to accept documents or transactions, found to be genuine, as such, it does not compel the court to look at a document or a transaction in blinkers, isolated from any context to which it properly belongs.'[2]

---

1 *WT Ramsay Ltd v IRC* [1981] 1 All ER 865, HL at 871.
2 Ibid.

1.42 Whether any particular transaction can be said to be genuine should be considered not only by reference to its subject matter, but also by reference to any apportionment of consideration as between two or more different items. Any apportionment should be effected on a fair and reasonable basis; for the consequences of not doing so reference may be made to the decision in *Saunders v Edwards*.[1] In that case the price paid for a flat was apportioned so as to allocate a far greater sum in respect of chattels than their actual worth, with the intent to reduce the stamp duty payable. On the facts, the court disregarded the plaintiffs' illegality and allowed them to sue the defendant for fraudulent misrepresentation, but Nicholls LJ added the following note of caution:

> 'Although the deliberate overstatement of the price being paid for the chattels, and hence the deliberate understatement of the consideration being paid for the flat, have not affected the outcome of the plaintiffs' claim in this action, it should not be assumed that this will always be so in other cases where such deliberate misstatements are present.'[2]

The learned judge continued so as to spell out the possible consequences:

> 'In particular, it may not be sufficiently appreciated that, where a party to a contract containing deliberate misstatements in the apportionment of the overall purchase price, made to facilitate the fraudulent evasion of stamp duty . . . seeks to enforce that contract, he may . . . find that the court will decline to assist him because of the unlawful purpose . . . Furthermore, there may be a criminal liability on persons who are involved in such activities with the intent of defrauding the Crown.'

---

1 [1987] 2 All ER 651.
2 Ibid at 665.

1.43 Reference may also be made to the case of *E V Booth (Holdings) Ltd v Buckwell*[1] in which it was held that where parties to a composite transaction had, as a result of negotiation, agreed to apportion the consideration as between different parts, they could not subsequently seek to reallocate the consideration for tax purposes. Conversely, the Inland Revenue's position might well have been different, but then the Revenue was not a party to the transaction.[2]

1 [1980] STC 578.
2 Per Browne-Wilkinson J, ibid at 584.

1.44 Where the parties to a dispute agree to settle, with compensation being paid in respect of two or more items which attract a different taxation treatment, care should be taken to ensure that any apportionment agreed between the parties is fair. For example, the termination of an employee's contract of service may give rise to an action for damages in respect of that employee's loss of salary. For reasons discussed in Chapter 6, that compensation may be free of income tax. The termination may also enable the employee to exercise share option rights. If it is agreed that the employee will surrender or refrain from exercising those rights, the compensation for that agreement will be subject to income tax[1] and this element of the compensation package should be identified in the settlement by reference to a fair apportionment.

In circumstances where the claim for compensation is not admitted, but a sum is being paid in settlement less than that claimed, there may be scope for agreeing a tax-effective apportionment. For example, in the case of a disputed loan, the plaintiff's claim may comprise two elements, the principal of the loan and the interest due thereon. If the dispute is settled by the defendant agreeing to pay a sum less than the disputed principal, it may be open to the plaintiff to regard the entire receipt as a capital payment, with no charge to tax. Any amount expressed to be interest would give rise to a charge to income tax or corporation tax on income, and is therefore to be avoided in this example.

1 By virtue of TA 1988 s 135(8).

THE '*RAMSAY* DOCTRINE'

1.45 Whilst the courts are obliged to accept documents or transactions found to be genuine, tax avoidance may be countered by reference to a transaction taken as a whole without being tied to the status of each transaction in a series—the so-called '*Ramsay* doctrine'.

Until the decision in *Ramsay*,[1] the widely-held view was that the taxation status of a series of transactions fell to be considered by the tax effect of each transaction in the series, not the series as a whole. This approach was relied upon in order to produce tax advantages, notwithstanding that the overall position of the taxpayer might be unchanged at the end of the series in question, save for the attendant professional fees. In *Ramsay* the court was concerned with a scheme for the manufacture of a capital loss, which involved the injection of funds into a chargeable asset for capital gains tax

1.45 *Introduction*

purposes, but their extraction from a non-chargeable asset. In the words of Lord Wilberforce:

> 'The general nature of [the adopted scheme] was to create out of a neutral situation two assets one of which would decrease in value for the benefit of the other. The decreasing asset would be sold, so as to create the desired [capital] loss; the increasing asset would be sold, yielding a gain which it was hoped would be exempt from tax.'[2]

It was accepted in the House of Lords that the courts have no general power to counter tax avoidance, this being a matter for Parliament. However, this did not prevent the courts from considering a series of transactions, effected as a scheme, by reference to their effect as a whole. The courts would not be forced to adopt a step by step, dissecting, approach. In finding in favour of the Crown, Lord Wilberforce said:

> '... it would be quite wrong, and a faulty analysis, to pick out, and stop at, the one step in the combination which produced the loss, that being entirely dependent on, and merely a reflection of, the gain. The true view, regarding the scheme as a whole, is to find that there was neither gain nor loss, and I so conclude.'[3]

---

1 *WT Ramsay Ltd v IRC* [1981] All ER 865, HL.
2 Ibid at 869.
3 Ibid at 874.

1.46 The subsequent decision of the House of Lords in *Furniss v Dawson*[1] rejected the view that the decision of *Ramsay* was confined to schemes of a self-cancelling transaction with no commercial end result. *Furniss v Dawson* was concerned with a share sale by the taxpayer to an unconnected third party, which was effected via an Isle of Man company pursuant to an intermediate share exchange. The share exchange was effected so that the sale proceeds from the ultimate purchaser would be received and retained tax free in the Isle of Man. The House of Lords held that the scheme was one to which the principle in *Ramsay* applied, with the result that the taxpayer was chargeable as though he had sold his shares direct to the third party in consideration of a cash payment to the Isle of Man company, which had issued shares to the taxpayer in respect of the same. For the principle to apply, Lord Brightman noted that two findings of fact were necessary preconditions:

> 'First, there must be a pre-ordained series of transactions, or, if one likes, one single composite transaction. This composite transaction may or may not include the achievement of a legitimate commercial (ie business) end . . . Second, there must be steps inserted which have no commercial (business) purpose apart from the avoidance of a liability to tax, not "no business effect". If those two ingredients exist, the inserted steps are to be disregarded for fiscal purposes. The court must then look at the end result. Precisely how the end result will be taxed will depend on the terms of the taxing statute sought to be applied.'[2]

What constitutes a 'pre-ordained series of transactions' for the purposes of the first finding has been the subject of argument in a number of cases. The essential features were identified by Lord Oliver:

'(1) that the series of transactions was, at the time when the intermediate transaction was entered into, pre-ordained in order to produce a given result;
(2) that transaction had no other purpose than tax mitigation;
(3) that there was at that time no practical likelihood that the pre-planned events would not take place in the order ordained, so that the intermediate transaction was not even contemplated practically as having an independent life; and
(4) that the pre-ordained events did in fact take place.'[3]

1 [1984] AC 474, [1984] 1 All ER 530, 55 TC 324.
2 [1984] 1 All ER 530 at 543.
3 In *IRC v Bowater Property Developments Ltd* [1988] STC 476 at 507.

1.47 The circumstances in which damages and other compensatory amounts are paid rarely require consideration of the *Ramsay* doctrine, with the possible exception of structured settlements which are dealt with in Chapter 7. Accordingly, the commentary in this chapter has been limited to an overview of the general principle.

Chapter 2

INCOME TAX

2.01 This chapter is primarily concerned with the treatment of compensation chargeable under Cases I or II of TA 1988 Schedule D as receipts to be included in the profits of a trade, profession or vocation of the recipient. The nature of the distinction between income and capital is first reviewed before the general principles applicable to compensation as trading (etc) receipts. The remainder of the chapter is concerned with the taxation treatment of compensation as interest, in respect of land and, finally, ex gratia payments.

References in this chapter to income tax are intended to include the charge to corporation tax on income profits, which is computed in accordance with the same principles.[1]

---

1 TA 1988 s 9.

---

1 GENERAL PRINCIPLES AND TRADING RECEIPTS

2.02 In examining the charge to income tax, a distinction must be drawn between those receipts of a revenue or income nature and those of a capital nature. This distinction is fundamental to the UK system of direct taxation; however, there is no statutory definition of 'income' beyond the statement in TA 1988 s 1 to the effect that income tax is to be charged in respect of 'all property, profits or gains respectively described or comprised in the Schedules'.

The general scheme of TA 1988 is to impose a charge to tax if a receipt falls under one or other of the prescribed heads of charge. Certain heads use express words to charge particular receipts as income, even though such receipts would not be regarded as income under general principles. For example, premiums for leases (which are capital in nature) may be treated as rent pursuant to s 34 of the Act. The more general heads of charge, however, may only impose a charge to tax in respect of income falling under it, which presupposes the distinction between income and capital.

2.02 *Income tax*

Income must be money or something which is capable of being converted into money. Unless expressly charged, the possession of a right or the receipt of a benefit is not the receipt of income; this position may be contrasted with the charge to capital gains tax where the possession of rights can be more significant.

2.03 Payments may of course comprise both an income and a capital element, but no general method of apportionment is provided. The requirement to detail each element of loss in an action for damages will sometimes provide the necessary framework within which any apportionment should be made. For example, an action in respect of damage caused to a capital asset may comprise two elements, being:

(a) the cost of repair, and
(b) compensation for loss of profits for the period of that repair.

For reasons explored at **2.38** the former should represent a capital receipt; the latter should be an income receipt.

LIABILITY AND THE EFFECT OF COMPULSION

2.04 The fact that compensation is paid under compulsion would appear to be immaterial so far as concerns its taxation status. The charging provisions of TA 1988 should be considered to ascertain whether the receipt would fall within them if made without an order, with the consequence that the income tax charge is the same whether compensation is awarded by the court or a settlement is negotiated voluntarily.

In the words of Lord Simonds in the context of an additional award by way of interest:

> '*I come then to* . . . *ask what is the character of interest allowed [to be awarded by the court under the Civil Procedure Act of 1833]. Here the argument is that, call it interest or what you will, it is damages, and, if it is damages, then it is not "interest in the proper sense" or "interest proper"* . . . *This argument appears to me fallacious. It assumes an incompatibility between the ideas of interest and damages for which I see no justification. It confuses the character of the sum paid with the authority under which it is paid.*'[1]

His Lordship concluded that the essential character of the payment is the same, whether it is paid under the compulsion of a contract, a statute or a judgment of the court.

---

1 *Riches v Westminster Bank Ltd* [1947] AC 390 at 406.

Principles

2.05 The main principles to apply in determining whether or not a compensatory receipt should be taken into account for the purposes of computing trading profits may be stated as follows. Compensation:

(a) in respect of trading stock is income, so that damages arising under a breach of contract or tort or upon compulsory acquisition are equated with sale proceeds;
(b) to make good a loss of profit which would otherwise have accrued is income, unless the compensation is for a breach of contract which relates to the whole structure of the recipient's trade;
(c) arising under a breach of contract or tort and relating to the use of a capital asset is income (that relating to physical repair of the asset may be capital);
(d) relating to the realisation or sterilisation of a capital asset is capital; and
(e) for the loss of opportunity to create goodwill is income.

The authorities for the income tax treatment in items (a), (b) and (c) above may be considered examples of a more general underlying principle. In this respect Diplock LJ laid down some guidelines in the case of *London & Thames Haven Oil Wharves Ltd v Attwooll*[1]:

> 'Where, pursuant to a legal right, a trader receives from another person compensation for the trader's failure to receive a sum of money which, if it had been received, would have been credited to the amount of profits . . . arising in any year from the trade carried on by him at the time when the compensation is so received, the compensation is to be treated for income tax purposes in the same way as that sum of money would have been treated if it had been received instead of the compensation.
>
> The rule is applicable whatever the source of the legal right of the trader to recover the compensation. It may arise from a primary obligation under a contract, such as a contract of insurance; from a secondary obligation arising out of non-performance of a contract, such as a right to damages, either liquidated, as under the demurrage clause in a charterparty, or unliquidated; from an obligation to pay damages for tort, as in the present case; from a statutory obligation; or in any other way in which legal obligations arise.'[2]

---

1 [1967] 2 All ER 124, 43 TC 491, CA.
2 2 All ER 124 at 134.

2.06 Income tax is usually in question only in respect of damages obtained for a breach of contract or tort and which comprise basic pecuniary losses or consequential pecuniary losses. Non-pecuniary losses should not, as a general rule, be regarded as subject to income tax. It is clear from the examples given in Chapter 1, by reference to the decisions in *Calabar Properties* (**1.27** above) and *Jarvis* (**1.29** above), that the damages there in question should not be regarded as falling within any head of charge imposed by TA 1988.

There may be circumstances, however, where damages for personal injuries received by a trader or professional person, and computed by reference to a loss of profits, might be subject to income tax. In *Renfrew Town Council v IRC*[1] Lord Clyde commented in the following terms:

> 'If he is permanently disabled, the damages would appear to be a capital increment in so far as he is concerned, but if he is only knocked out for, say, six months, during which time he loses, say, professional income, the damages look like a revenue receipt just as the professional income (if earned) would have been.'[2]

Lord Clyde based this dictum on *Burmah Steam Ships Co v IRC*,[3] which is considered at **2.37** below.

2.06 *Income tax*

---

1 (1934) 19 TC 13.
2 Ibid at 19.
3 1931 SC 156, 16 TC 67.

LIMITATIONS OF CASE LAW

2.07 The authorities which form the basis of the general statements above are considered in more detail in this chapter, but the inherent limitations of the case law should always be kept in mind. Lord Wilberforce noted that:

> '. . . we have been warned more than once not to seek automatically to apply to one case words or formula which have been found useful in another . . .'[1]

---

1 *Tucker v Granada Motorway Services Ltd* (1979) 53 TC 92 at 107.

The identification of capital assets

2.08 It can be very difficult to decide whether a particular receipt has an income or a capital nature, which is reflected in the wealth of case law on the subject. A metaphor encountered in a number of cases concerning income and capital is that of 'the tree and the fruit'. The tree represents the capital assets of the business and the fruit represents the income produced from it. Capital assets are equated with the 'tree'. In the case of *Haig's (Earl) Trustees v IRC*[1] the metaphor was referred to in the following terms:

> '. . . the differentiation in any particular case of profits as resulting in capital appreciation on the one hand or on the other in accruer of income may be expected to introduce questions of difficulty. In determining any such question, however, it may perhaps be helpful to distinguish between a fruit-bearing subject and its fruits . . . When fruits are . . . realised, this in general results in an addition to income . . . When the subject which provides the fruits is realised on the other hand, this generally results in a transaction on capital account.'[2]

Two other general tests may also be applied: those of recurrence and enduring benefits.

---

1 (1939) 22 TC 725.
2 Per Lord Moncrieff, ibid at 737.

RECURRENCE

2.09 Where expenditure is repeated or has a periodical or recurrent quality, it points towards an income nature. On the other hand, capital expenditure may be said to be spent once and for all (see *Vallambrosa Rubber Co Ltd v Farmer*[1]). Expenditure on trading stock is recurrent, as the trading stock is sold it must be replaced.

In the case of *Ounsworth v Vickers Ltd*[2] the cost of dredging a channel and forming a deep water berth in connection with the construction of a ship was held to be capital expenditure:

'*[The taxpayer company] did not dredge only to enable their ships to get out merely by virtue of the dredging; they adopted a different plan, namely, by constructing a deep water berth in which their ships could lie between the two tides. . . . The position is just the same as if they had found that there was some new way by which they could get to the sea by digging a new channel at an insignificant expense. I think the true view of the facts in this case is that the whole of this expenditure by the respondents was incurred in making what was in fact a new means of access from their works to the sea, and that it was therefore not income expenditure but capital expenditure, and cannot therefore be deducted.*'[3]

1 (1910) 5 TC 529.
2 [1915] 3 KB 267, 6 TC 671.
3 [1915] 3 KB 267 at 276 per Rowlatt J.

ENDURING BENEFITS

2.10 Expenditure made for the purposes of securing a continuing advantage, or to dispose of an item of fixed capital which is onerous, will usually be regarded as capital. The classic formulation of the principle was made by Lord Cave in *British Insulated and Helsby Cables Ltd v Atherton*:[1]

'*When an expenditure is made, not only once and for all, but with a view to bringing into existence an asset or an advantage for the enduring benefit of a trade, I think that there is very good reason (in the absence of special circumstances leading to an opposite conclusion) for treating such an expenditure as properly attributable not to revenue but to capital.*'[2]

Subsequent decisions have focused on the meaning of the words 'enduring benefit'. A payment which results in an advantage being secured for a number of years will not automatically be regarded as capital, if the advantage in question cannot be said to endure as fixed capital does.[3]

1 [1926] AC 205, 10 TC 155.
2 [1926] AC 205 at 213–214.
3 *Anglo-Persian Oil Co Ltd v Dale* [1931] All ER 725, 16 TC 253.

The statutory definition of trading stock

2.11 In general, trading stock (or stock in trade) comprises all those assets which are purchased for resale, or purchased and manufactured for resale. In the case of manufacturing, the term will include unfinished goods. What comprises trading stock will vary from business to business. For example, a car is stock so far as concerns the car manufacturer or dealer, but a capital asset so far as concerns most other businesses.

The term 'trading stock' is defined by TA 1988 s 100(2). There are two limbs to the definition; the first is given in relation to any trade, and refers to property of any description, being either:

'(i) property such as is sold in the ordinary course of the trade, or would be so sold if it were mature or if its manufacture, preparation or construction were complete; or

2.11 *Income tax*

> *(ii) materials such as are used in the manufacture, preparation or construction of any such property as is referred to in sub-paragraph (i) above . . .'*[1]

The second limb of the definition is concerned with work in progress in relation to any profession or vocation. Any services, articles or materials which may be taken into account as work in progress for the purposes of TA 1988 s 101 are included, which comprise:

> '*(a) any services performed in the ordinary course of the profession or vocation, the performance of which was wholly or partly completed at the time of the discontinuance and for which it would be reasonable to expect that a charge would have been made on their completion if the profession or vocation had not been discontinued; and*
> *(b) any article produced, and any such material as is used, in the performance of any such services.*'[2]

---

1 TA 1988 s 100(2)(a).
2 Ibid s 101(3).

2.12 The statutory definition is therefore wide ranging; it encompasses property held for resale as well as unfinished goods and manufacturing materials. It also includes services completed and unbilled, or still being performed. In most cases the identification of trading stock is not difficult, save in respect of borderline cases. A full review of trading stock[1] is outside the scope of this book, but some general points may be made.

First, the right to do something leading to the acquisition of trading stock may not in itself be stock in trade. This is particularly applicable in relation to extraction activities—so that rights over a gravel bed, for example, are not stock in trade, notwithstanding that the gravel extracted therefrom would be.[2]

Second, the status of assets must be determined by reference to the class of business undertaken. The sale of assets commonly viewed as 'investments', such as shares and land, will give rise to an income treatment if such sales may be regarded as essential parts of the business carried on. The buying and selling of investments as a means of managing surplus funds or reserves, distinct from the other trading activities of the person in question, will be on capital account.[3]

Third, the absence of any trading intention in relation to an asset militates against a finding that the asset is an item of stock in trade. The question of whether an intention to trade exists or not has often arisen in the context of property sales.

---

1 For which see *Simon's Taxes* B3.1001 to B3.1009.
2 *Stow Bardolph Gravel Co Ltd v Poole* [1954] 3 All ER 637.
3 See the decisions in *Scottish Investment Trust Co Ltd v Forbes* (1893) 3 TC 231 and *IRC v Scottish Automobile and General Insurance Co Ltd* (1932) 16 TC 381.

INTENTION

2.13 The leading case of *Simmons (as liquidator of Lionel Simmons Properties Ltd) v IRC*[1] is indicative of the approach taken by the courts in relation to intention. The case involved the status of certain property sales made by the taxpayer company and two of its subsidiaries. The properties in question had been acquired with a view to their retention as investments yielding rental income, the ultimate intention being to secure a public quotation for the group based on an attractive property portfolio. As circumstances changed, it was decided not to proceed with the plan and instead the properties were sold. The Revenue sought to assess the profits on the basis that they were derived from sales of trading stock. The Revenue's contentions were rejected by the House of Lords, where Lord Wilberforce focused upon the intention of the taxpayer:

> 'Trading requires an intention to trade; normally the question to be asked is whether this intention existed at the time of the acquisition of the asset. Was it acquired with the intention of disposing of it at a profit, or was it acquired as a permanent investment? Often it is necessary to ask further questions: a permanent investment may be sold in order to acquire another investment thought more satisfactory; that does not involve an operation of trade, whether the first investment is sold at a profit or at a loss.'[2]

Lord Wilberforce then applied the statement of principle to the facts in question:

> 'Mr Simmons wanted to build up an investment portfolio: he formed investment companies, allied himself with an investment trust, caused each (relevant) company to acquire one property, or at most two properties, to develop and let it, and was forced into a realisation of these completed investments. This was simply a realisation of capital.'[3]

1 [1980] 2 All ER 798.
2 Ibid at 800.
3 Ibid at 803.

SPECIFIC STATUS

2.14 The Inland Revenue do not accept the concept of an asset without specific status.[1] At any point in time it must be held either on capital account as an investment, or on revenue account as trading stock. Stress is laid on the reference to 'any point in time'; as the status of an asset may change, a mixture of case law and statutory provision provides for the direct tax consequences which follow.[2] Essentially, a change in status from trading asset to investment will lead to a charge to income tax based on the market value of the asset at the time of the change, less attributable costs. An asset may, however, change in status from being held as an investment to an item of trading stock without a direct tax cost, provided the appropriate election is made.

1 With justification given Lord Wilberforce's comments in *Simmons v IRC* [1980] 2 All ER 798 at 800.
2 See *Sharkey v Wernher* [1956] AC 58 and TCGA 1992 s 161.

2.15 Income tax

2 COMPENSATION AND TRADING STOCK

2.15 Compensation in respect of trading stock is income. The nature of the event giving rise to the compensation is immaterial. The rationale for such a treatment is that the compensation is analogous to sale proceeds upon the disposal of goods held for resale, albeit that disposal has not occurred in the normal course of trading. In drawing up the profit and loss account for the trade, all amounts received in respect of trading stock should be taken into account as sale proceeds. The cost of making the disposal, represented by the cost of acquiring the trading stock or its diminution in value after partial loss, is entered as cost of sales.

EXAMPLE

John, who is a car dealer, hires Andrew to transport two cars from one garage to another. Unfortunately, Andrew is involved in an accident; one car with a market value of £7,600 is a complete loss, save for a residual scrap value of £400. The second car suffers £2,600 worth of damage; its residual value is put at £4,000.

Assuming John is compensated in full for his loss of £9,800 (ie £7,600−£400, plus £2,600) and further assuming that each car cost £4,900, John's profit and loss account should reflect the following:

	£	£
Sales		9,800
Cost of sales:		
car 1 (£4,900−400)	4,500	
car 2 (£4,900−4,000)	900	
		(5,400)
Profit		4,400

John will carry forward stock to the value of £4,400, representing the scrap value of car 1 and the market value of car 2.

2.16 In the case of *IRC v Newcastle Breweries Ltd*[1] compensation was received by the taxpayer pursuant to a War Compensation Court ruling following the requisition of rum by the Admiralty. The fact that the brewery was not in a position to prevent the acquisition did not affect the taxation treatment:

> 'The rum in question was a commercial asset capable of being put to a use by which gain might be acquired. It has been put to such a use and gain has been so acquired, and it seems to me . . . the fact that the [Brewery] were not free agents in the matter is irrelevant. It was no doubt an unusual mode of deriving gain from the particular asset, but . . . this fact is not enough to prevent that gain from entering into the account of profits arising from the business of which it was an asset.'[2]

---

1 (1927) 12 TC 927.
2 Per Warrington LJ, ibid at 947.

2.17 Insurance recoveries upon stock destruction are also examples of income receipts. In *Rownson Drew & Clydesdale Ltd v IRC*[1] the taxpayer company suffered loss as a result of fire and marine casualties in 1918, which happened by an oversight not to be insured. Whilst having no legal claim upon the underwriters, the claims were met in full in 1919. It was held that the receipts should be regarded as trading receipts and credited to the 1918 year of account.

Reference may also be made to the decision of the House of Lords in *J Gliksten & Son Ltd v Green*[2] which was concerned with an insurance recovery in respect of timber owned by the taxpayer company, who carried on business as timber merchants. It was decided that the whole payment was a trading receipt:

> 'Ought the total amount of these insurance moneys to be regarded as part of the profits and gains of the trade? My Lords, in my opinion they ought, and for this reason: What has happened has been this, that the [stock] which the appellants held has been converted into cash. It is quite true it has been converted into cash through the operation of the fire, which is no part of their trade, but loss due to it is protected through the usual trade insurances, and the [stock] has thus been realised. It is now represented by money, . . . If this results in a gain, as it has done, it appears to me to be an ordinary gain. . . .'[3]

1 (1931) 16 TC 595.
2 [1929] AC 381.
3 Per Lord Buckmaster, ibid at 384.

2.18 Compensation for breach of contract in relation to the acquisition of trading stock may also attract an income charge. In *Diamond v Campbell-Jones*[1] the plaintiff agreed to purchase a leasehold house from the defendants for development purposes. The defendants wrongfully repudiated the contract and the plaintiff sued for his loss.

The case was primarily concerned with the measure of loss to be applied in respect of those damages, but it was also decided that such damages would be liable to income tax in the hands of the plaintiff, in respect of which the decision in *London Investment and Mortgage Co Ltd v Worthington*[2] was cited in support. The *Worthington* case is an example of damages for the loss of stock in trade being subject to an income tax treatment. In the *Campbell-Jones* case the taxpayer was receiving damages in respect of property which would have formed part of his stock in trade had it been received, and therefore the same principles were applied.

1 [1961] Ch 22.
2 [1959] AC 199, [1958] 2 All ER 230.

3 LOSS OF PROFITS

2.19 Compensation to make good a loss of profit will in general be income, ie compensation for amounts which should have been earned are taxed in

2.19 *Income tax*

the same manner as if they had been so earned. An exception to the rule applies in circumstances where the compensation is for a breach of contract which relates to the whole structure of the recipient's trade.

The principle that compensation for loss of profit is an income receipt has been consistently applied, not only to that arising from contractual breach, but also in respect of tortious acts and insurance receipts. The nature of the general principle may be considered by reference to two decisions, *Vaughan v Archie Parnell and Alfred Zeitlin Ltd*[1] and *Short Bros Ltd v IRC*.[2]

---

1 (1940) 23 TC 505.
2 (1927) 12 TC 955.

2.20 In the *Archie Parnell* case the taxpayer had acquired a licence to tour the UK showing Noel Coward's *Cavalcade*. The licence provided that no film of the play would be made during its five-year term, but in fact such rights had already been sold and a film was extensively shown during the currency of the licence.

The taxpayer company commenced an action against the licensors, and was awarded substantial damages for breach of contract. The High Court decided that the measure of damages was the taxpayer's loss of profit, and that the damages were properly included in the computation of its trading profits. Although the licence was for an initial period of five years, the acquisition of such a licence was an ordinary incident of the taxpayer's business and it did not constitute a capital asset.

2.21 In the *Short Brothers* case the taxpayer received compensation of £100,000 following the termination of an agreement to buy ships from the taxpayer, such ships having become surplus to the requirements of the purchaser owing to a slump in the shipping trade. In the Court of Appeal it was unanimously decided that the damages should be included as a trading receipt for the purposes of computing the taxpayer's profits subject to tax. In the words of Lord Hanworth MR:

> '*The £100,000 is paid down as a business proposition to [the taxpayer], and their business is no longer hampered with the contracts which they had entered into with regard to [the] ships. Their business was free to undertake new contracts. Thus there is, in the ordinary course of carrying on their trade, an adjustment made between them and their clients or contractors under which a payment is made to them; they are free from all responsibility in the matter of building ships; they are free to place their yard or ships under contract to fresh customers.*'[1]

A further example of compensation making good a loss of profits being subject to an income treatment is the case of *Gray v Lord Penryhn*.[2] Two employees of the taxpayer trader had misappropriated monies, for which the taxpayer obtained reimbursement from the auditors who admitted negligence on their part. It was held that the sum was a trading receipt. If the fraudulent employees had restored the monies there was no question that they would have been so taken into account, and the court regarded the payment from the auditors in the same light.

1 (1927) 12 TC 955 at 973.
2 (1937) 21 TC 252.

Agency agreements and contracts to supply

2.22 The loss of an income-producing asset, such as an agency contract or contract to supply trading stock, giving rise to compensation is usually regarded as a normal incidence of trading, with the result that the sum received is income in nature.

Compensation received upon the termination of an agency agreement, with one year out of the initial three to run, was unanimously held by the Court of Session to be income in the case of *Kelsall Parsons & Co v IRC*[1]. The agency agreement was at one time one of only two such agreements. However, in the years 1930 to 1934, the year of cancellation, the taxpayer company held between nine and eleven agencies. The agency remained important, notwithstanding the other agencies, by contributing as much as one-half of total commission income prior to termination, but this fact was insufficient to prevent the application of an income treatment.

Lord Normand, in giving judgment in favour of the Inland Revenue, noted that the status of the agency agreement was that of a contract incidental to the normal course of the taxpayer's business; the taxpayer did not act exclusively for one principal. Moreover the taxpayer could not be said to be parting with an enduring asset of the business, in view of its expected termination in the following year with no reasonable expectation of continuance. The effect of the cancellation was considered by Lord Normand in the following light:

> '[The] structure of the business carried on by the [taxpayer] was . . . so designed as to absorb such shocks as the cancellation of a single, albeit an important, agency contract. And it must be remembered that the loss of this agency agreement might be expected to take place in . . . 1935, and the consequential effects on their business had to be faced by the [taxpayer] as at that date. The shock, therefore, such as it was, consisted merely in this, that the end of the agency came by agreement 12 months earlier than its contemplated term.'[2]

1 (1938) 21 TC 608.
2 Ibid at 621.

2.23 In the above case cancellation was regarded as an ordinary incident of the taxpayer's business and, as such, the receipt of compensation had to be income. This is reflected in the views of Lord Fleming:

> 'There is no finding that in consequence of the termination of [the agency] agreement any capital asset was depreciated in value, or became of less use for the purpose of the [taxpayer's] business, or that what has been called the structure of the business received any disturbance other than it might be expected to receive in ordinary course.'[1]

The fact that only one year was left to run of the agency agreement is an important factor in the decision. Lord Fleming accepted that a different

2.23 *Income tax*

decision might have been forthcoming if the agreement was terminated whilst having a period of ten years to run. In these circumstances the compensation for contractual breach might have been regarded as capital in nature, on the basis that the whole structure of the recipient's business was affected; this is considered in further detail below.

1 (1938) 21 TC 608 at 622.

2.24 The case of *Shove v Dura Manufacturing Co Ltd*[1] may also be cited. In that case the court gave the following reasons for treating a sum received upon the cancellation of an agency contract as an income receipt:

> '*No money was spent to secure [the contract]; no capital asset was acquired to carry it out; its cancellation was only an ordinary method of modifying and realising the profit to be derived from it.*'[2]

1 (1941) 23 TC 779.
2 Per Lawrence J, ibid at 783.

CONTRACTS TO SUPPLY

2.25 Similar reasoning to that applied in *Dura Manufacturing* may be found in the decision of the High Court in *Bush, Beach & Gent Ltd v Road*.[1] That case was concerned with compensation received following the termination of a contract to supply the taxpayer with certain agricultural chemicals for resale. The sale of agricultural chemicals represented a new branch of the taxpayer's business, and the taxpayer argued that the compensation should be regarded as a capital receipt because the termination of the contract destroyed that business by removing the source of supply. It was also contended that the compensation should be regarded as compensation for the sterilisation of a capital asset. Both arguments failed in the High Court.

The agreement of the supplier not to provide chemicals to competitors of the taxpayer during the life of the contract was not considered to affect the taxation treatment, such a provision being regarded as a standard contractual provision. The payment was held to be an income receipt, representing profits which the taxpayer would or might have made under the contract.

1 [1939] 2 KB 524, 22 TC 519.

The business structure

2.26 It is to be expected that not every contract will be successfully performed. Decided cases reflect this by regarding compensation in the same light as the profit which would otherwise have been earned and by which the compensation is calculated. However, this treatment becomes untenable the more fundamental the contract in question is to the business, given the effect on the business that such a breach may have. To reflect that different

Loss of profits **2.28**

effect, an exception to the income treatment exists where the breach of contract relates to the whole structure of the profit-making business. The fact that damage may be measured by reference to annual receipts (ie which would otherwise have been earned under the contract) does not render the resulting compensation income in nature.

2.27 The leading case of *Van Den Berghs Ltd v Clark*[1] was concerned with the receipt of compensation following the cancellation of a profit pooling arrangement, which had 13 years to run. The agreement was entered into in 1912 and was to last until 1926, although subsequent variations extended the period to 1940. It provided a framework within which the taxpayer and a competing Dutch company would operate their respective businesses, including prices, supply and the sharing of profits between them. The First World War interrupted the activities of the Dutch company, which agreed to pay the taxpayer damages for cancellation in 1927.

The nature of the cancelled contract was considered in the House of Lords by Lord Macmillan, who began his analysis by querying what the taxpayer had given up:

> '*They gave up their whole rights under the agreements for thirteen years ahead. These agreements are called . . . "pooling agreements," but that is a very inadequate description of them, for they did much more than merely embody a system of pooling and sharing profits . . .*
>
> *On the contrary the cancelled agreements related to the whole structure of the [taxpayer's] profit-making apparatus. They regulated the [taxpayer's] activities, defined what they might and what they might not do, and affected the whole conduct of their business.*'[2]

The money received for the cancellation was in respect of a matter fundamental to the organisation of the taxpayer's trading activities. Such compensation could not be regarded as an ordinary incidence of trading activity and could not therefore be regarded as income. Accordingly, the case was decided in favour of the taxpayer, to the effect that the cancellation monies were capital in nature and therefore free of tax. If the facts of the case were to be repeated today, the cancellation monies would appear to be subject to tax on capital gains, having regard to the principles in Chapters 3 and 4.

---

1 [1935] AC 431.
2 Ibid at 442.

2.28 The above approach was also applied in the case of *Barr, Crombie & Co Ltd v IRC*.[1] In that case the taxpayer company's business almost exclusively comprised the management of ships on behalf of another company under an agreement with some eight years to run. That customer went into liquidation so that the appellant's business was effectively lost. For the 16 years in which the contract ran, 88.23% of the taxpayer company's income was derived from it. The importance of the profits generated from the contract was referred to by Lord Normand:

> '. . . *virtually the whole assets of the [Taxpayer] Company consisted in this agreement. When the agreement was surrendered or abandoned practically nothing*

remained of the Company's business. It was forced to reduce its staff and to transfer into other premises, and it really started a new trading life. Its trading existence as practised up to that time had ceased with the liquidation of the [contractor]. The proportions of its profits . . . demonstrate that.'²

His Lordship concluded:

'And where you have a payment for the loss of the contract upon which the whole trade of the Company has been built, where the expected profits of the contract are used to measure the loss of them for a period of future years, and where in consequence of the loss the Company's structure and character are greatly affected, the payment seems to me to be beyond doubt a capital payment.'

The receipt was therefore free of tax in the hands of the taxpayer company.

1 1945 SC 271, 26 TC 406.
2 26 TC 406 at 411.

VARIATION OF AGREEMENTS

2.29 Compensation which becomes payable as a result of the variation, as distinct from the cancellation, of an agreement which affects the whole conduct of the recipients business may also attract a capital treatment.

In the case of *Sabine v Lookers Ltd*[1] the respondent's business was principally based on its distributor agreement with Austin Motor Car Ltd. Whilst that agreement was yearly only, it contained a clause whereby the respondent could renew it. Austin made certain alterations to the agreement, weakening the clause on continuity, and as a result paid a sum in compensation. It was held that that sum was a capital receipt, notwithstanding the fact that the agreement remained in existence. In finding in favour of Lookers Ltd, the court reviewed the effect of the distributor agreement and its variation:

'The agreement did not merely lay down terms in regard to the purchase and sale of vehicles but in effect laid down the conditions under which Lookers had to trade and earn their profits. Thus it in effect limited their trade to Austin vehicles; it provided that Lookers had to set up a particular sales organisation; it limited the prices at which sales could be made; and it required them to service and repair Austin vehicles. The distributorship . . . governed Lookers' whole trade . . . Accordingly, if Austins had told Lookers that no renewal would be granted . . . and had paid Lookers compensation . . . [it] would in my view have been a capital receipt in Lookers' hands; and I think the same result would follow as regards any material variation in the continuity clause.'²

1 (1958), 38 TC 120, CA.
2 Per Jenkins LJ, ibid at 133.

2.30 It is clear that not all compensation payments for the variation of a contract fundamental to the trade will be treated as a capital receipt. In the *Lookers* case the variation went to the very heart of the contract, in that the taxpayer could not be certain from year to year that the contract would

Loss of profits **2.32**

continue. This was a fundamental change, as the taxpayer would be forced to make contingency plans, or enter into alternative arrangements, with a view to safeguarding the business in the event that the contract was not renewed.

THE DIVIDING LINE

2.31 The dividing line between revenue receipts for contractual breach on the one hand, and capital receipts relating to the whole structure of the trade on the other, can be difficult to draw.

The decision of the High Court in the case of *Creed v H & M Levinson Ltd*[1] illustrates the grey areas which exist. The taxpayer company made hats, a substantial part of its production being sold to Marks & Spencer Ltd, who decided against selling hats. To keep that decision from the millinery trade in general, it agreed to continue accepting hats from the taxpayer and to assist it with converting to new forms of light clothing production. After a year or so the store declined to purchase any further light clothing; a writ followed and the action was settled in return for a payment to the taxpayer company.

In allowing the Revenue's appeal to treat the compensation as income, Slade J noted that the payment was not made by way of compensation for the cancellation of the existing millinery business, but for the loss of an opportunity to extend its business, ie by the production of light clothing.

The following points were made in the context of denying that the compensation related to the whole structure of the taxpayer company's business:

(a) that its business with the department store had never constituted nearly the whole of the source of its profits; and
(b) there was no evidence to suggest that the whole structure of its trade was altered after its arrangements with the department store ceased, notwithstanding the foray into light clothing production.

---

1 [1981] STC 486, 54 TC 477.

2.32 The requirement that the contract in question must relate to the whole structure of the trade is a difficult one to meet. In the *Levinson* case Marks & Spencer took proportions of the taxpayer's total production ranging from 47.4 to 90.5% in any one year. The light clothing production was a new form of production for the company, only entered into in view of the department store's decision to cease to sell hats. Viewed in this context, the Learned Judge's distinction that the damages related to the loss of opportunity to build up goodwill elsewhere, and were therefore income in nature, appears somewhat fine.

The decision may be contrasted with that in the earlier case of *Barr, Crombie & Co*,[1] the facts of which bear certain similarities. The distinction drawn as to the nature of the damages in the *Levinson* case however, was fundamental to the different taxation treatment applied:

> 'So far as one can determine the Commissioners' reasons from their decision, it would appear that they directed their attention primarily to the fact that the business with Marks & Spencer had at one time represented a substantial part of the

2.32 *Income tax*

company's business, overlooking the fact that the payment did not represent a payment for the cancellation of this business, but was for something quite different, consisting of the loss of an opportunity to build up goodwill with other persons.'[2]

1 **2.28** above.
2 Per Slade J, 54 TC 477 at 487.

2.33 The case of *Bush, Beach & Gent Ltd v Road*[1] is a further example of the reluctance of the courts to assist in meeting the 'whole structure' requirement. As mentioned above, the case concerned the termination of a contract to supply the appellant with agricultural chemicals upon payment of £4,500 compensation.

The taxpayer contended that:

(a) the selling of industrial (its main business) and agricultural chemicals were two separate and distinct businesses;
(b) that the cancellation of the contract destroyed the whole of the agricultural chemical business, the £4,500 was agreed compensation for that loss; and
(c) the £4,500 was paid by way of compensation for the sterilisation of a capital asset, as the contract established not only a source of supply but also a market in view of non-competition clauses in favour of the appellant.

The arguments were rejected by Lawrence J:

'The sum paid, in my view, represented profits which the appellant company would or might have made under the contract, not the purchase price of the contract itself . . . Nor do I accept the argument that the structure of the appellant company was affected by the contract or its cancellation . . . The appellant company could always have sold agricultural chemicals and it can still do so. The contract was made in the ordinary course of the company's business, although in a new field, and the exclusion of competition is an ordinary incident of such contracts . . .'[2]

1 **2.25** above.
2 [1939] 2 KB 524 at 533.

2.34 A further point which may be made is that the fact that the taxpayer actually ceases to trade by reason of damage for which he is compensated is not sufficient in itself to convert what would otherwise be a revenue payment for loss of profits into a capital sum. This conclusion was reached by the Court of Appeal (Northern Ireland) in the case of *Lang v Rice*[1] which was concerned with compensation for loss of profits pending reinstatement of the taxpayer's business, whose premises were destroyed by bombings in 1971 and 1973. Whilst that case was not concerned with contractual breach, the decision in *Barr, Crombie & Co* was considered to be in point.

1 [1984] STC 172.

Lloyd's losses

2.35 Many members of Lloyd's have been engaged in actions for damages for losses suffered by virtue of their membership of unsuccessful syndicates. The actions are brought in a variety of ways: against the lead underwriters of their syndicates, the agents managing the syndicate and member's agents, as well as against the Corporation of Lloyd's for allegedly failing to properly exercise its regulatory functions.

The Revenue's view is that where a member receives a compensatory payment in settlement of a claim, or pursuant to an order of the court, the compensation should be treated as a trading receipt.[1] This view is taken because the compensation makes good the original deficiency. Because the compensation is taken into account for income tax purposes, the Revenue do not accept that it is a sum chargeable to capital gains tax, and in particular do not accept that any exemption from tax may be afforded pursuant to Extra-statutory Concession D33 (for which see Chapter 4).

The Revenue's view would appear to be well supported by case law; in particular, the receipt of such compensation would appear to fall firmly within the ambit of the rule formulated by Diplock LJ in the *Attwooll* case, at **2.05** above.

---

1 *Tax Bulletin* May 1992.

2.36 The basis of assessment applicable to compensation depends upon the circumstances of the recipient, and in particular whether he is a current member, or a former or deceased member. Significant amendments to the basis of assessment for individual members of Lloyd's were effected by the Finance Act 1993, and again by the Finance Act 1994, adding to what was already a complex area. It is understood that in all cases where compensation has been paid the basis of assessment has been agreed with the Inland Revenue, but a review of the relevant principles to apply is outside the scope of this book.

4 THE CONCEPT OF USE AND CAPITAL ASSETS

2.37 In keeping with the 'fruit and tree' metaphor, compensation relating to the use of a capital asset is income, but that relating to its realisation or sterilisation is capital. Sums arising from use represent 'fruit', those from realisation the 'tree' itself.

In *Burmah Steam Ship Co Ltd v IRC*[1] a ship was placed with ship repairers in order to effect an overhaul. The overhaul was not completed by the specified date and the repairers therefore agreed to pay a sum in settlement of the claim brought against them. That sum was held to be a trading receipt, being damages for the loss of profit arising from the ship repairers' breach of contract. In deciding in favour of the Inland Revenue, the nature of the damages received by the appellant taxpayer was considered by reference to the following analogy:

2.37 *Income tax*

> 'Suppose someone who chartered one of the Appellant's vessels breached the charter and exposed himself to a claim of damages . . . there could, I imagine, be no doubt that the damages recovered would properly enter the Appellant's profit and loss account for the year. The reason would be that the breach of the charter was an injury inflicted on the Appellant's trading, making . . . a hole in the Appellant's profits, and damages recovered could not therefore be reasonably or appropriately put . . . to any other purpose than to fill that hole.'[2]

The damages received from the ship repairers were an estimate of the taxpayer's loss of profit caused by the delay, which was an injury inflicted on the taxpayer's trading activities in the same way as the example given above.

1 1931 SC 156, 16 TC 67.
2 Per Lord Clyde 16 TC 67 at 71.

TOTAL AND PARTIAL LOSS

2.38 In the *Attwooll* case[1] the appellant's jetty, which was used in conjunction with its oil storage facility, was damaged by an oil tanker. The tanker owner agreed to pay damages to compensate the appellant for the loss of profit while the jetty was being repaired. That sum was held to be a trading receipt.

The case is important because of the distinction drawn between the total and partial loss of an asset. The different nature of the compensation receivable in each instance was commented upon:

> 'In the case of a total loss, what can be recovered from the assumed wrongdoer is the value of that which has been lost. If the thing lost is a ship or a jetty which is ordinarily used for the purpose of earning profits, the fact of its profitability is an element to be considered in assessing its capital value. In such a case the owner's right is a right to recover the value of the thing which has been lost, and this can no doubt be properly described as "whole and indivisible", even though it includes some element of profitability of the thing lost; in such circumstances what is recovered is . . . a capital receipt.'[2]

On the other hand, where there is only a partial injury, which was the case in *Attwooll*, the compensation will necessarily comprise two elements. First, the plaintiff can recover the whole cost of repair, which is without doubt a capital receipt. Second, he can also recover something in respect of use during the period of repair. Damages recovered under this head are regarded as trading receipts, in that they represent the trading profit which the plaintiff would have earned if he had had use of his asset. In the *Attwooll* case that asset was a jetty.

1 **2.05** above.
2 Per Willmer LJ [1967] 2 All ER 124 at 129.

PRICE REDUCTIONS

2.39 The decision in the *Burmah Steam Ship* case does not mean that compensation for a delay in performing a contractual obligation will invariably be regarded as an income receipt. If the facts in the case had involved the purchase of a capital asset, the delivery of which was delayed, the negotiation of a reduction in the price of that asset should not be regarded as an income receipt. It would merely give rise to a lower capital cost in respect of the acquisition.

2.40 The case of *Crabb v Blue Star Line*,[1] which was concerned with a receipt under an insurance policy against late delivery, may be cited in support of the distinction. The taxpayer company had ordered seven new ships from ship-builders to replace losses caused by enemy action during the Second World War. The taxpayer also effected an insurance policy at Lloyd's under which it was entitled to receive £500 per day for each day's delay in delivery of a ship. Two of the ships were delivered late and payments were made under the policy; the Inland Revenue contended that the payments should be taken into account in computing the taxpayer's profits.

A finding of fact was made to the effect that the taxpayer frequently entered into ship-building contracts under which the purchase price was reduced in the event of delayed delivery and increased in the event of early delivery. In the High Court, Buckley J found in favour of the taxpayer, to the effect that the insurance recoveries should also be regarded as reducing the cost to the taxpayer of acquiring the ships.

The decision in *Burmah Steam Ship* was distinguished on two grounds. First, the method of quantifying a payment by reference to profits is not a conclusive test as to whether that payment has an income nature. Second, the decision in *Burmah Steam Ship* was concerned with assets already owned by the taxpayer, whereas the policies of insurance were entered into as an incident to the acquisition of the ships which did not then exist:

> '... in the particular cases with which I am concerned the contracts with the ship-builders did not contain a clause operating on the price to be paid to the ship-builders in that kind of way; instead of that, the taxpayers covered the position by insurance. There seems to be very great force in the argument that, if the contracts in respect of the two ships with which I am concerned had stipulated that, if the ship-builders did not deliver within fourteen days after the due date of delivery, the purchase price would be reduced by £500 a day over a period of time, then it would be exceedingly difficult, if not impossible, for the Revenue to suggest that that reduction in the price to be paid by the taxpayers could be regarded as a revenue receipt by the taxpayers.'[2]

Because the insurance policy placed the taxpayer in the same position as a price reduction, the case was concluded in favour of the taxpayer:

> '... the sums secured by these policies are not in essence compensation for loss of profits, although in a sense they are associated with the fact that, if due delivery were not made, the taxpayers would be deprived of profits if they then wished to take the ships into service in their business. I think that these policies are really associated with the price which the taxpayers felt justified in paying for the services which the ship-builders were contracting to give, and were insurances against the possibility of the ship-builders not providing as valuable services as by the contract they were promising to provide.'[3]

---

1 [1961] 2 All ER 424.
2 Per Buckley J, ibid at 428.
3 Per Buckley J, ibid at 429.

2.41 *Income tax*

Capital assets and their realisation

2.41 Realisation of a capital asset indicates a capital treatment. Realisation may take various forms other than the complete loss of the asset—these include the acceptance of substantial restrictions, otherwise referred to as 'sterilisation'. This form of realisation may be illustrated by the leading case of *Glenboig Union Fireclay Co Ltd v IRC*[1] in which the taxpayer was concerned with the manufacturing of fireclay goods and owned a bed of fireclay which ran beneath a railway.

A dispute arose between the taxpayer and the railway company over the working of the fireclay bed. Pending an action which was ultimately unsuccessful, the taxpayer was prevented from working the bed but continued to incur expenses in keeping its workings open. On losing that action, the railway company used its statutory powers to require the taxpayer not to work the bed underlying the railway line, and paid it compensation for the loss thereby caused. In addition, the railway company paid damages for the loss to the taxpayer during the period in respect of which it was prevented from working the bed pending the hearing of the railway company's unsuccessful action.

---

1 (1922) 12 TC 427, HL.

2.42 As regards the latter amount, the Court of Session decided that the damages represented the reimbursement of sums incurred by the taxpayer in protecting its capital asset; the sums were not incurred in earning profits. It was therefore considered that the damages were a capital receipt.

The treatment of the latter amount was not disputed further, but that of the statutory compensation was appealed to the House of Lords, following a decision of the Court of Session to the effect that the compensation was also a capital receipt. The House of Lords unanimously held that it was a capital receipt. Although the amount of compensation received was calculated by reference to the quantity of fireclay which would be worked before the bed became exhausted, and when worked the fireclay was trading stock so far as the taxpayer was concerned, the measure of compensation did not affect the quality of the receipt as capital. Until the fireclay was worked, it remained a capital asset in the form of the fireclay bed. So for example, if all the fireclay had been obtained but had then been destroyed, compensation for the destruction would have been regarded as a trading receipt, because it would have been a realisation of trading stock. Such a treatment illustrates the potential for translating certain forms of capital into trading stock, which is particularly acute in the context of extraction industries.

2.43 The taxpayer had sought to argue that the compensation was revenue in nature (this would have been a more favourable result for the purposes of excess profits duty), because the bed would have been fully worked in some two and a half years. The compensation, it was argued, was merely a payment for loss of profits. Having regard to the status of the fireclay bed as a capital asset, the taxpayer's arguments were rejected:

> '*In truth the sum of money is the sum paid to prevent the Fireclay Company obtaining the full benefit of the capital value of that part of the mines which they are*

prevented from working by the Railway Company. It appears to me to make no difference whether it be regarded as the sale of the asset out and out, or whether it be treated merely as a means of preventing the acquisition of profit which would otherwise be gained. In either case the capital asset of the Company to that extent has been sterilised and destroyed, and it is in respect of that action that the sum . . . was paid . . . [It] is now well settled that the compensation payable in such circumstances is the full value of the minerals that are to be left unworked, less the cost of working, and that is of course, the profit that would have been obtained were they in fact worked. But there is no relation between the measure that is used for the purpose of calculating a particular result and the quality of the figure that is arrived at by means of the application of that test.'[1]

1 Per Lord Buckmaster (1922) 12 TC 427 at 463.

2.44 A point which may be made is that the *Glenboig* case involved the complete, as distinct from partial, sterilisation of a capital asset. It is thought that a payment in respect of a restriction for a limited period over a capital asset may also be capital in nature, depending upon the length of the restriction. The shorter the period of time for which the restriction applies, the greater the likelihood that any resulting compensation would be treated as an income receipt. The circumstances of the recipient will also be a material factor. If the recipient's activities are carried on in such a way that the acceptance of restrictions could be regarded as an ordinary incident of those activities, then payments in respect of those restrictions may well constitute income.[1]

Reference may also be made to the decision in *Thomas McGhie & Sons Ltd v British Transport Commission*, which is considered at **8.05** below.

1 *Higgs v Olivier* (1952) 33 TC 136.

COMPENSATION FOR DISTURBANCE

2.45 In *West Suffolk County Council v W Rought Ltd*[1] a local authority compulsorily acquired leasehold factory premises which the taxpayer company occupied for its manufacturing activities. A period of nine months elapsed from the date when the company was able to recommence its manufacturing operations in alternative accommodation. In making its claim for compensation, the company included a head for loss of profits caused by the disturbance.

In an appeal against the award made by the Lands Tribunal, the House of Lords held that this head of damages was liable to income tax, even though the head of loss went to make up the total compensation or purchase price fixed for the acquisition of a capital asset. Reference may also be made to the decision in *Stoke-on-Trent City Council v Wood Mitchell & Co Ltd*[2] which is considered at **4.29** below.

1 [1957] AC 403.
2 [1979] STC 197.

5 TRADING RECEIPTS AND ASSESSMENT

2.46 Compensation chargeable to income tax is not necessarily attributable to the accounting period in which it is received. Accounts for a previous year may be reopened so as to include a subsequent receipt, and the Revenue may raise an additional assessment for the further tax due.

Conversely, if the accounts for a previous year included an anticipated receipt, which turns out to be less than that shown to be due in the accounts, the profits may be reduced and a repayment of tax obtained. The latter adjustment is not automatic where the accounts have been accepted as the basis of assessment and tax has been paid on an assessment which has become final and conclusive; it is necessary for the taxpayer to show an error or mistake in the computation of the accounts for the previous period. Such a claim for relief may be made under TMA 1970 s 33, no later than six years after the end of the year of assessment (or, if the assessment is to corporation tax, the end of the accounting period) in which the assessment is made. For the circumstances in which relief is available, reference may be made to *Simon's Taxes* A3.1001.

RELATING BACK

2.47 As a general rule, compensation received in respect of an action arising in a past accounting period, where the final liability remained open to calculation or agreement, will be related back to the period in which that action arose and tax assessed accordingly. TMA 1970 s 33 is not in question where the effect is to increase, rather than diminish, the profits for the previous period.

EXAMPLE

John employs Jane to refurbish his restaurant in August 1994 and the contract specifies that the refurbishment is to be completed within five weeks. In breach of contract the refurbishment is completed three weeks late and John sues for damages on account of his loss of profit for the three-week period.

In drawing up his accounts for the year to 31 December 1994, John includes the sum of £2,000 on account of his claim, having been advised that this is the minimum amount which he should receive and that Jane has no valid defence to the action. Some eight months later the claim is compromised and Jane pays £2,700 in settlement. The £700 should be related back to 1994 and assessed accordingly.

2.48 The application of the principle may be illustrated by reference to the decision in the *Newcastle Breweries* case[1] where the brewery received compensation for rum requisitioned by the Admiralty. An initial amount on account was received in 1918 and the balance, pursuant to the Indemnity Act 1920, in 1922. The issue of allocation was particularly important, given the incidence of Excess Profits Duty in 1918 at a rate of 80%. In deciding in favour of the Inland Revenue, so as to allocate the compensation to 1918, it was noted that the requisition was to be treated as a commercial transaction and being so treated:

*'the property in the goods passed by delivery during the accounting period [ie 1918] and the money then became payable, although, owing to a dispute as to the amount, it was not ascertained or paid in full until some years later, and if this be so then the whole amount would . . . be properly dealt with in ascertaining the profits for the accounting period.'*²

A large number of cases may be cited in support of this principle, many of which were also concerned with the imposition of Excess Profits Duty which ceased to apply to accounting periods post 31 March 1921. Reference may be made to *Ensign Shipping Co Ltd v IRC*³ and *Severne v Dadswell*⁴ amongst others.

1 **2.16** above.
2 Per Warrington LJ (1927) 12 TC 927 at 948.
3 (1928) 12 TC 1169.
4 [1954] 3 All ER 243, 35 TC 649.

2.49 So far as concerns the cancellation of contracts, reference may be made to the decision in *Jesse Robinson & Sons v IRC*.¹ In that case a contract to supply was cancelled in consideration of an agreement to supply goods at a lower price, and the payment of the price difference in four instalments. It was held that the taxpayer company had earned the instalment payments at the date of the agreement, and that they were therefore liable to tax at that time and not, as the taxpayer argued, when the instalments were actually paid.

1 (1929) 12 TC 1241.

2.50 In *Rownson, Drew and Clydesdale Ltd*¹ the taxpayer company was a party to three successive agreements with the government for the disposal of surplus stores. The initial result in 1918 was a loss, but subsequent agreements varied the system of payment more favourably to the taxpayer and in 1922, after some arbitration proceedings, a new agreement was made under which the government paid or allowed the taxpayer's expenses, with the result that the loss was made good. The question was whether the cost revisions should be treated as having corrected the original loss, or whether it was to be treated as an independent piece of good fortune to be taken into account in 1922. The court held in favour of the Revenue, to the effect that the loss in 1918 should be revised in accordance with the subsequent agreements.

A further point which arose for consideration was the status of additional sums received by the taxpayer in 1923 at the conclusion of the whole agreement, whereby the taxpayer was paid a certain percentage on a shortfall of turnover during the period. The Revenue argued that the additional sums should be treated as earned rateably over the time, but this argument was rejected. The additional sums arose at the end of the transactions in question, and accordingly were to be included only when they became ascertainable and due, even though the sums were calculated by reference to events during the life of the contract.

1 **2.17** above.

LIMITATIONS

2.51 Limits to the principle of relating back can be identified. For example, in *Rownson* the additional sums were regarded as taxable only at the conclusion of the contract.

The principle is also limited where the right to receive the compensation can be said to be so contingent or uncertain that it may only be taken into account upon actual receipt. This issue was fully considered by the Court of Appeal in *WS Try Ltd v Johnson*.[1] The taxpayer applied for permission to build houses on land which it owned, but the applications were refused in 1936 and again in 1938. The taxpayer sought compensation from the local county council, under the provisions of the Restriction of Ribbon Development Act 1935. By an agreement in 1940, the taxpayer sold the land to the council, part of the puchase price being expressed to be in full and final settlement of the claim for compensation.

Having regard to the uncertainties of the taxpayer's claim to compensation, the Court of Appeal held that it could not be brought into account earlier than the date of the agreement, with the consequence that it was taxable in the year 1941–42. The practical effect of those uncertainties were referred to in the following terms:

> 'Looking at the effect of the Act quite broadly it seems to me that the [taxpayer] . . . has his claim hedged round with uncertainty and speculation. It is quite impossible for him, as a matter of business, or for his accountants as accountants, to put any sort of value or estimate on what he is likely to get if in the end he presses his claim to compensation.'[2]

---

1 [1946] 1 All ER 532.
2 Per Lord Green MR, ibid at 538.

---

6 RELIEF FOR EXPENDITURE

2.52 Expenditure may be incurred in a number of ways which may be the subject of a claim for compensation. These include expenditure incurred:

(a) which is wasted by reason of the defendant's conduct;
(b) by the plaintiff to mitigate his loss; and
(c) by the plaintiff in pursuing his claim for compensation, and specifically legal fees.

In each case the question is raised: is relief from tax to be given on account of such expenditure? The principles to apply are considered in Chapter 5 in the context of the payer or defendant to an action. Such principles would appear to be equally applicable to the plaintiff and are not therefore repeated, but a number of specific points may be made. Expenditure which is wasted may be deducted for the purposes of computing profits subject to Schedule D, Case I or II if it was in the nature of revenue expenditure incurred for trading purposes. The fact that no benefit was ultimately derived is not a material factor.

EXAMPLE

Maria agrees to appear in a film being produced by Andrew, who incurs expenditure in hiring film crews and equipment. Maria subsequently repudiates the contract, as a result of which Andrew's expenditure is wasted. Had the film been produced, the expenses may have been deducted in the normal way, and should continue to be so available.

2.53 If the expenditure has a capital nature (as discussed in Chapter 5) then relief is unlikely to be available; there is rarely an 'asset' against which the expenditure may be offset.

EXAMPLE

Jane and Philip agree to develop a property together, to be held as a rental investment once completed. A joint venture agreement is executed, but Philip repudiates the contract shortly afterwards. Jane's wasted expenditure, comprising legal fees on the proposed purchase which she has had to abandon, will not attract relief for the purposes of capital gains tax or Schedule D, Case I because the fees relate to the acquisition of a capital asset.

2.54 It is considered that expenditure to mitigate loss should give rise to a deduction in circumstances where the loss would be eligible for relief on revenue account, for example, in respect of damage to trading stock. Such expenditure may also be available for relief where it can be said to have been incurred on the grounds of commercial expediency within the principle set out by Viscount Cave LC in *British Insulated and Helsby Cables*.[1]

---

1 See **5.10** below.

---

7 INTEREST

2.55 Compensation may be regarded as interest under Case III of Schedule D TA 1988 and taxed accordingly. In the leading case of *Riches v Westminster Bank Ltd*[1] the House of Lords decided that an additional award made in favour of the taxpayer, in order to compensate him for the length of time for which he was deprived of certain profits fraudulently concealed from him, was interest.

The reasons for this decision are worth considering in detail:

> 'The contention of the appellant may be summarily stated to be that the award . . . cannot be held to be interest in the true sense of that word because it is not interest but damages, that is, damages for the detention of a sum of money due by the respondents to the appellant . . .
>
> The appellant's contention is . . . artificial and is in my opinion erroneous because the essence of interest is that it is a payment which becomes due because the creditor has not had his money at the due date. It may be regarded either as representing the profit he might have made if he had had the use of the money, or

2.55 *Income tax*

> conversely the loss he suffered because he had not that use. The general idea is that he is entitled to compensation for the deprivation.
>
> From that point of view it would seem immaterial whether the money was due to him under a contract express or implied or a statute or whether the money was due for any other reason in law. In either case the money was due to him and was not paid, or in other words was withheld from him by the debtor after the time when payment should have been made, in breach of his legal rights, and interest was a compensation, whether the compensation was liquidated under an agreement or statute . . . or was unliquidated and claimable under the Act as in the present case.
>
> The essential quality of the claim for compensation is the same and the compensation is properly described as interest.'[2]

1 [1947] AC 390.
2 Per Lord Wright, ibid at 399.

2.56 The taxpayer's argument to the effect that an increase in damages to take into account the yearly loss arising is merely part and parcel of the calculation of the award was specifically rejected by Viscount Simon. The earlier decision in *National Bank of Wales Ltd*[1] in which it was decided that damages did not include an element of interest notwithstanding their increase by reference to a percentage rate per annum, was quoted with disapproval.

1 [1899] 2 Ch 629.

2.57 The decision in the *Riches* case should be considered in the light of two possible limitations. First, compensation may in some circumstances be regarded purely as damages for the loss of an asset, notwithstanding that the compensation may have been calculated in part by reference to an interest rate factor. The decision in the *Glenboig* case may be cited as an example.

Second, where compensation is payable pursuant to an agreement between the parties to the dispute, it would appear to be possible to agree to make an undifferentiated payment, ie one which does not expressly identify the interest element:

> 'It is only compulsory to award interest on judgments. When interest is awarded on a judgment, tax is payable on it. It is very different with settlements. If the parties agree expressly that no interest is included, the revenue will not be able to go behind it. It is to the advantage of both parties to settle on these terms, rather than benefit the revenue. There is nothing illegal in it. It is everyday practice to make arrangements with a view to avoiding tax.'[1]

In some circumstances it might be necessary to consider the above view in the light of those cases where the courts have dissected payments into their constituent parts, which are dealt with in the context of structured settlements at Chapter 7. As a general proposition, it would appear permissible for the parties to a dispute to agree an overall settlement which has been arrived at by reference to an interest element, but which is essentially an agreement concluded on a lump sum basis.

1 Per Lord Denning MR in *Jefford v Gee* [1970] 2 QB 130 at 150.

Assessment

2.58 Compensation which falls to be treated as interest chargeable under Case III of Schedule D is taxable when it is actually received by the taxpayer. Interest accrued but not paid is not as a general rule taxable, and accordingly there is no question of an interest element in any compensatory receipt being related back.[1]

1 *Simon's Taxes* B5.102.

Damages for personal injury

2.59 Interest on damages in respect of personal injuries or death are excluded from the charge to income tax by virtue of TA 1988 s 329. The exclusion is extended by s 329(3) so as to apply to payments in satisfaction of a cause of action, which include payments into court. For the purposes of the section 'personal injuries' includes any disease as well as any impairment of a person's physical or mental condition. By Revenue Concession the exclusion is extended to interest on damages awarded in corresponding circumstances by a foreign court, provided the foreign country in question also exempts such interest from tax.[1]

1 Extra-statutory Concession A30.

8 PROFITS FROM LAND

2.60 Profits from land are charged to income tax under TA 1988 Schedule A. Section 15 of that Act provides for tax to be charged, inter alia, on:

> '... receipts arising to a person from or by virtue of his ownership of ... land ... in the UK.'

2.61 In the light of the decision of the Privy Council in *Raja's Commercial College v Gian Singh & Co Ltd*[1] it is clear that damages for trespass (known as mesne profits), which compensate the landlord for the rental loss suffered by reason of a tenant's adverse occupation, are chargeable to income tax. This is in accordance with the general rule that sums paid in place of lost income fall to be treated in the same manner. The fact that the recipient may be an investor in the case of profits from land, rather than a trader, was not considered material:

> 'The damages here were applicable to the purpose of filling the hole in the plaintiffs' income caused by the fact that they were not able to obtain as much rent for the premises as they would have obtained if the appellants had not been in occupation as trespassers.'[2]

The decision of the Privy Council was concerned with the imposition of income tax in Singapore. However, the charging provision under the

2.61 *Income tax*

Singaporean legislation was no different in its ambit than s 15, a point which was expressly made by the court.[3]

---

1 [1976] 2 All ER 801.
2 Per Lord Fraser, ibid at 805.
3 Ibid.

ASSESSMENT

2.62 Unlike interest, the charge to tax under Schedule A is on an arising basis (ie by reference to amounts due and payable in the relevant period). Paragraph 2 of Schedule A refers to the charge to tax by reference to 'the rents or receipts to which a person becomes entitled in the chargeable period'. An arising basis also applies to amounts chargeable under TA 1988 Schedule D Case VI in respect of furnished accommodation.

The arising basis is disapplied, however, if the taxpayer can bring himself within the relieving provisions of TA 1988 s 41. If a claim under this section is accepted, the taxpayer is not regarded as being entitled to the rent in question, and such adjustments are made as are necessary. If the taxpayer subsequently receives an amount which is the subject of relief, then his liability to tax is adjusted. An obligation is placed upon the taxpayer to give the inspector notice of the receipt no later than six months thereafter.[1]

Relief is available only if both the condition in (a) below and one of the conditions in either (b) or (c) below is satisfied. The taxpayer must prove:

> '(a) that he has not received an amount which he was entitled to receive in respect of any rents or receipts on the profits or gains arising from which he would be chargeable under Schedule A; and
> (b) if the non-receipt of that amount was attributable to the default of another person by whom it was payable, that the claimant has taken any reasonable steps available to him to enforce payment; or
> (c) if the claimant waived payment of that amount, that the waiver was made without consideration, and was reasonably made in order to avoid hardship.'[2]

---

1 TA 1988 s 41(2).
2 Ibid s 41(1).

2.63 The conditions are such that no relief may be afforded in circumstances where the taxpayer is seeking to enforce any remedies available to him. Such adjustments as are provided for will therefore rarely be available in the context of compensation until such time as the taxpayer's action is settled or judgment given.

EXAMPLE

Lorna owns an office block which is let at a rent of £280,000 per annum (exclusive of value added tax). At the end of the tenancy period in August 1994, the tenant remains in occupation for a period of six months, against the wishes of Lorna.

In raising an assessment for the year 1994/95 (on a current year basis, tax being due on 1 January 1995 based on a provisional assessment of income), the Inspector may require tax to be paid as if the rental yield of £280,000 per annum continued. If the action is settled in 1996, on the basis that Lorna receives £100,000, the assessment for 1994/95 may be adjusted and a repayment of tax obtained.

9 DEFAMATION

2.64 Defamation is essentially the publication of a statement which is concerned with, or reflects on, a person's reputation, and is such as to lower his reputation in the minds of right-thinking members of society generally, or to tend to make such members shun or avoid him.[1] Two categories of defamation exist: libel and slander. The former consists of a defamatory statement in permanent form, ie writing, but also radio and television.[2] The latter consists of a defamatory statement by spoken word or gesture.

The distinction is important because libel is actionable per se, that is without proof of 'special damages'. Slander is (subject to certain exceptions) only actionable with proof of special damage, in that the plaintiff must prove loss of money or some advantage which can be expressed in money.

1 For example, *Yousoupoff v Metro-Goldwyn-Mayer Pictures* (1934) 50 TLR 581.
2 By virtue of the Defamation Act 1952.

2.65 In the case of *Lewis v Daily Telegraph Ltd*[1] the House of Lords considered the status of an award of damages having regard to the rule in *Gourley*.[2] For the rule to apply, it is a condition that damages are paid in respect of lost income which would have been chargeable to income tax had they been received, and a further condition is that the damages paid are free of income tax in the plaintiff's hands.

Lord Reid was of the view that the rule in *Gourley* did apply to an award of damages for defamation, which therefore means that the damages must be received free of tax in the hands of the plaintiff. Lord Reid's judgment however contains references to damages for loss of income:

> 'A company cannot be injured in its feelings, it can only be injured in its pocket. Its reputation can be injured by a libel but that injury must sound in money. The injury need not necessarily be confined to loss of income. Its goodwill may be injured. But insofar as the company establishes that the libel has, or has probably, diminished its profits, I think that Gourley's case is relevant.'[3]

1 [1964] AC 234.
2 For which see Chapter 8.
3 [1964] AC 234 at 262.

2.66 Why then was Lord Reid of the view that the damages would be tax free, having regard to the weight of case law authority to the effect that compensation for lost income is subject to income tax? It is considered that the decision follows from the nature of the damages in question.

The decision in *Lewis* was concerned with general damages for injury to reputation, which may be recovered without the plaintiff adducing evidence that he has been harmed. In that case no evidence of financial loss as a result of the publication of the defamatory statement was put before the jury, from which it can be concluded that no element of special damage was contained in the award, as such damage must be proved.

In assessing general damages for defamation there is no legal rule which governs the amount due, this is 'peculiarly the province of the jury'.[1] The factors which the jury are entitled to take into account are many and various; they may include the nature of the defamation, whether any apology has been offered, the conduct of the plaintiff and so on.

The fact that general damages may be calculated by reference to a loss of profits does not alter the nature of the damages as that for injury to reputation; an analogy may be drawn with damages for personal injury in this respect. As such, the damages cannot be equated with any taxable source of income and are therefore considered to be free of income tax in the hands of the plaintiff.

1 Lord Herschell in *Bray v Ford* [1896] AC 44 at 52.

2.67 Somewhat different considerations might apply in relation to special damages. To the extent that they make good a specific loss of profits, which have to be pleaded and proved, there would appear to be no reason why an award may not be charged to income tax, having regard to the rule formulated by Diplock LJ in the *Attwooll* case.[1] The loss may be as specific as that flowing from, say, a contractual breach and so subject to income tax in the hands of the plaintiff.

1 **2.05** above.

10 EX GRATIA PAYMENTS

2.68 The distinction between income and capital receipts should not be relevant in the context of ex gratia payments—by their very nature they should be outside the scope of a direct tax charge, with only inheritance tax to consider. A brief review of the case law reveals that the position of ex gratia payments is not so straightforward. A charge to income tax may apply to purely voluntary payments, not only in relation to employees as considered in Chapter 6, but also by reference to the computation of trading profits.

Two general points may be made about ex gratia payments. First, a payment made by way of compromise of a genuinely disputed claim cannot be an ex gratia payment, for which see *Creed v H & M Levinson Ltd*.[1] Second, no charge to capital gains tax can arise in the context of an ex gratia payment, as no 'disposal' of any 'asset' is involved.

1 [1981] STC 486, 54 TC 477.

2.69 The exemption from tax for ex gratia payments was considered by the Court of Appeal in the case of *Simpson v John Reynolds & Co (Insurers)*

*Ltd.*¹ The facts were as follows. The taxpayer had acted as an adviser to a client company for a number of years on all its insurance matters. When that client was taken over, its new parent company required it to place its insurance business elsewhere and therefore wrote to the taxpayer to inform it that its services were no longer required.

Subsequently, the client company volunteered to pay £1,000 per annum for a period of five years in recognition of the taxpayer's services. The facts relevant to the payment were summarised as follows:

> 'First, this was a wholly unexpected and unsolicited gift. Second, it was made after the business connection had ceased. Third, the gift was in recognition of past services rendered by the client company over a long period, though not because those past services were considered to have been inadequately remunerated. Fourthly, the gift was made as a consolation for the fact that those remunerative services were no longer to be performed by the client company for the donor; and, fifthly, there is no suggestion that at a future date the business connection might be renewed.'²

---

1 [1975] 2 All ER 88.
2 Per Russell LJ, ibid at 90.

2.70 Although the payment in *Simpson* might be said to be compensation for loss of profit, its ex gratia nature placed it outside the charge to tax. The reasons cited by the Crown in support of its case were expressed in the following terms:

> 'The Crown sought support, in the general circumstances of the case, from the facts that the gift was in some sort, as I have indicated, measured against past commission earned in relation to the business connection and that the taxpayer included this sum in its accounts as receipts under the heading of gross commission. There was a convenient summary by counsel for the Crown of the circumstances which he said stamped the receipt as coming within the definition of something arising from the trade: first, the fact that it arose on the termination of the trade relationship; secondly, the calculation of the payment by reference to past premiums; thirdly, a five year spread-over of the £5,000; fourthly, the accounts showing the sum as a trading receipt; and, fifthly, that there was not established a case here of a personal testimonial but a recognition only of the value of past trading activities in the course of that connection and as a consolation for the profits of that trading connection coming to an end.'¹

Despite these arguments, a unanimous court found in favour of the taxpayer company, essentially on the grounds that it was an unsolicited voluntary payment made after the termination of the contractual relationship in question:

> '. . . the payment was a purely voluntary one, wholly unexpected by the company. I fully accept that the mere fact that the payment was made voluntarily does not of itself frank a payment made to a trader from the point of view of tax; but when a payment is made purely voluntarily, on the termination of a trading relationship, that termination being so far as the parties can possibly foresee a permanent termination, and is made for no other reason than that the party making the payment is sorry that the relationship has had to terminate and is grateful for the excellent service which the payee has given to it over a very long period of years,

then it appears to me quite clear that the payment does not arise or accrue to the payee by reason of any trade carried on by it.'[2]

1 Per Russell LJ [1975] 2 All ER 88 at 91.
2 Per Walton LJ, ibid at 92.

2.71 The decision in *Murray v Goodhews*[1] may be cited as a further example of the relevant principle. In that case a brewery company terminated certain tenancies as it was entitled to do, and then made ex gratia payments to the tenants. The case was complicated by the fact that the relationship between the brewery and the tenants had not ended, but it was decided that the payments were not taxable because they were voluntary in nature, wholly unexpected and unsolicited. The motives of the brewery in making the payments was to acknowledge its long and friendly relations with the taxpayer, and to maintain its goodwill.

1 [1978] 2 All ER 40, [1978] STC 207, CA.

Pursuing claims

2.72 The fact that a trader has sought compensation is a relevant factor in the taxation treatment. For compensation to be free of income tax as an unsolicited payment, the taxpayer should refrain from pursuing any claim, whether legal or moral, which he may have. Furthermore, the expectation that compensation will be received is a factor against a tax free treatment. In the case of *Rolfe v Nagel*[1] the fact that the taxpayer had pressed his grievance and sought some recompense for what was the loss of a trading benefit was one of the factors taken into account by the Court of Appeal in finding that the compensation was a trading receipt in the taxpayer's hands.

1 [1982] STC 53, CA.

2.73 The decision in the case of *McGowan v Brown and Cousins*[1] may also be referred to. The taxpayers were estate agents who had been paid a sale fee of £525 for acquiring a development site on behalf of a client. The amount of the fee was very low for the work involved, but the taxpayers were willing to do this in the expectation of obtaining the more profitable work of selling property upon completion of the development.

The land in question was sold by the taxpayers' client to C Ltd and the taxpayers asked C Ltd to appoint them as their selling agents. This they refused to do, but offered an ex gratia payment of £1,250 and after some negotiation a figure of £2,500 was agreed. The Inland Revenue sought to tax the payment, but the taxpayers resisted on the basis that the payment was a voluntary one, made by C Ltd who were under no legal or moral obligation to make any such payment. The taxpayers' arguments were rejected by the High Court because the taxpayers had effectively earned the £2,500 in question, although they had no legal obligation to it:

'. . . the gift was plainly earned and not merely deserved. It was earned because the gift was compensation for the loss of an opportunity to earn selling profits and the taxpayers were morally entitled to that opportunity because their past services as purchasing agents had been inadequately remunerated. The gift was not unexpected and was not unsolicited. The gift was in fact . . . ultimately referable to the work which the taxpayers had carried out in the acquisition of the site.'[2]

1 [1977] 3 All ER 844.
2 Per Templeman J, ibid at 852.

Chapter 3

GENERAL PRINCIPLES OF CAPITAL GAINS TAX

3.01 For ease of use, the commentary on capital gains is divided into two chapters. This chapter deals with the general principles, essentially the nature of the requirements for a charge to tax and its calculation. Chapter 4 deals with the specific reliefs available in the context of compensation receipts.

1 INTRODUCTION

3.02 Capital gains tax is charged in respect of chargeable gains realised by persons other than companies. Companies are chargeable to corporation tax in respect of chargeable gains, which are computed in accordance with the principles applicable to capital gains tax.[1] Unless otherwise indicated, any reference in this chapter, or in Chapter 4 to the nature of the charge to capital gains tax, should be taken to include a reference to corporation tax on chargeable gains.

1 TCGA 1992 s 8.

3.03 The general ambit of the charge is first determined by reference to the residence status of the taxpayer. Any person who is resident or ordinarily resident in the UK during a year of assessment is within the scheme of the 1992 Act,[1] which extends to gains realised from both UK and non-UK situate assets. However, persons resident or ordinarily resident but not domiciled in the UK are exempted in relation to gains realised from non-UK situate assets, to the extent that amounts in respect of such gains are not remitted to the UK.[2] Non-UK resident persons are subject to tax in respect of assets used in or for the purposes of a trade, carried on in the UK through a branch or agency.[3]

A full discussion of the nature of the capital gains tax charge is outside the scope of this book. However, some general guidance is included in respect of the following:

3.03 *General principles of capital gains tax*

(a) rates and payment of tax;
(b) losses; and
(c) exemptions and reliefs.

The nature of the interaction between capital gains tax and income tax is then dealt with before turning to the charging requirements.

---

1 TCGA 1992 s 2(1).
2 Ibid s 12.
3 Ibid s 10.

RATES AND PAYMENT OF TAX

3.04 With effect from the tax year 1988–89 onwards, capital gains tax has been levied at income tax rates, and chargeable gains are treated as if they constituted a person's top slice of income.[1] An individual subject to a marginal income tax rate of, say, 40% would also pay capital gains tax at this rate. For years prior to 1988–89 a flat rate of 30% applied. Gains accruing to trustees of an accumulation or discretionary settlement are subject to tax at the sum of the basic rate (25%) and the additional rate (10%).[2] The charge to tax is subject to an annual exemption.[3]

Capital gains tax is payable no later than 1 December following the end of a year of assessment, or 30 days after the issue of a notice of assessment, whichever is later.[4]

Corporation tax imposes a charge to tax on profits, which include both income and chargeable gains.[5] For gains realised on or after 17 March 1987, the same rate of corporation tax applies to both capital gains and income receipts. From 1973 to 1987 however, capital gains were effectively charged at a lower rate by the device of reducing the gain by a fraction (6/7ths for the 1986 financial year), giving an effective rate of 30%.

---

1 TCGA 1992 s 4.
2 Ibid s 5.
3 Ibid s 3. This is £5,800 in the case of individuals for 1994–95. For trustees the amount is halved, TCGA 1992 Sch 1.
4 TCGA 1992 s 7.
5 Ibid s 6(4).

LOSSES

3.05 As a general rule, losses are computed in the same way as chargeable gains. Furthermore, a disposal which can result in a chargeable gain may also result in an allowable loss, but no allowable loss may be realised in relation to a disposal which is exempted from charge.[1] This mirror treatment is disapplied in certain circumstances; for example, losses resulting from transactions between connected persons are subject to restrictions under TCGA 1992 s 18(3).

Losses realised in any year must be set against chargeable gains of the same year. To the extent that losses remain unrelieved against gains, they may be carried forward and set against gains realised in subsequent years.[2] As a general principle, it is not possible to carry losses back.[3] Losses are not available for set-off against anything other than chargeable gains; for example they are not available for set-off against trading profits.

Similar restrictive rules apply in relation to losses realised by companies, which may be set against gains of the same or a later accounting period.[4]

---

1 TCGA 1992 s 16(2).
2 Ibid s 2(2).
3 Subject to the provisions of TCGA 1992 s 62(2) which apply upon death.
4 TCGA 1992 s 8(1).

EXEMPTIONS AND RELIEFS

3.06 A wide array of exemptions and reliefs are provided. These can take the form of a deferment in relation to certain types of transfer. For example, a transfer between husband and wife is treated as being on a no gain / no loss basis, so that any charge is deferred until such time as the asset is realised by the transferee.[1] Other gains may be exempted entirely if realised by a tax favoured person, such as a charity.[2]

The exemptions and reliefs which are particularly important in relation to compensation receipts are those exempting particular classes of asset, which are dealt with below. For the specific reliefs available in relation to compensation, see Chapter 4.

---

1 TCGA 1992 s 58.
2 Ibid s 256.

3.07 Non-chargeable assets, in respect of which neither a chargeable gain nor an allowable loss may be realised, include the following:

(a) motor cars and certain other forms of transportation (TCGA 1992, s 263);
(b) foreign currency bank accounts established for meeting personal expenditure outside the UK (TCGA 1992 s 252);
(c) decorations for valour or gallant conduct acquired otherwise than for value (TCGA 1992 s 268);
(d) rights under a life assurance policy, unless acquired for value by a person other than the original beneficial owner (TCGA 1992 s 210);
(e) debts[1] owed to the original creditor, and qualifying corporate bonds[2] (TCGA 1992 ss 251 and 117);
(f) certain annuity rights (TCGA 1992 s 237);
(g) tangible moveable property which comprises a wasting asset[3] unless capital allowances have been or could have been claimed (TCGA 1992 ss 44 and 45);
(h) tangible moveable property if disposal proceeds amount to £6,000 or less, but subject to a marginal relief if proceeds exceed this figure (TCGA 1992 s 262);
(i) an individual's only or main private residence (TCGA 1992 s 222); and
(j) government gilt-edged securities (TCGA 1992 s 115).

The above list is intended as an outline only of those assets which are exempt and in respect of which compensatory receipts might be

3.07 *General principles of capital gains tax*

encountered. The importance of the exemptions are twofold. First, any amount which might otherwise be subject to tax as discussed in this chapter will be exempted if it derives from an asset within the above. Second, the nature of what is known as the 'underlying asset' in any claim for compensation may determine the taxation status of any monies received in settlement of that claim. This is discussed in Chapter 5 by reference to Extra-statutory Concession D33.

---

1 Other than a debt on a security, essentially a debt which is marketable and capable of realising a gain : *Simon's Taxes* C1.408.
2 Relief may be given in certain circumstances under TCGA 1992 s 254.
3 Essentially, an asset with a predictable life not exceeding 50 years.

Capital gains tax and income

3.08 Capital gains tax was introduced in 1965 by the then Chancellor, James Callaghan, in order to tax profits which were outside the scope of income tax. It would therefore be logical to assume that a charge to capital gains tax may only apply in respect of a capital receipt, in the same way that a charge to income tax may only apply to an income receipt. This is not the case; capital gains tax applies to all gains, save that receipts charged to income tax are excluded. Exclusions also apply in respect of expenditure taken into account for income tax.

In practice the charges to income tax and capital gains tax may be considered as mutually exclusive, but the interaction between the two is such that it sometimes affords the Inland Revenue a choice between an assessment to income tax on the one hand, and to capital gains tax on the other. A double charge to tax may not of course arise:

'. . . *it is not open to the revenue to subject a taxpayer to two different charges to tax in respect of the same receipts.*'[1]

Whilst a double charge to tax may not be imposed, the Inland Revenue may issue alternative assessments in relation to the same receipt; this was considered in *IRC v Wilkinson*.[2]

---

1 Per Lord Keith, *Bird v IRC* [1989] AC 300 at 325.
2 [1992] STC 454.

CONSIDERATION CHARGEABLE TO INCOME TAX

3.09 Amounts chargeable to income tax are excluded from the consideration taken into account for capital gains tax purposes by reason of TCGA 1992 s 37. The exclusion is in the following terms:

'*(1) There shall be excluded from the consideration for a disposal of assets taken into account in the computation of the gain any money or money's worth charged to income tax as income of, or taken into account as a receipt in computing income or profits or gains or losses of, the person making the disposal for the purposes of the Income Tax Acts.*'

3.10 The operation of the exclusion may be illustrated by reference to the facts in the case of *London & Thames Haven Oil Wharves Ltd v Attwooll*.[1] In that case the taxpayer suffered damage to a jetty (a capital asset) as a result of an accident involving an oil tanker, which accident was caused by the negligent handling of the oil tanker. After litigation, damages were paid to the taxpayer in respect of its loss, which included an element representing the loss of income profits for the period required to repair the jetty.

Applying the capital gains tax legislation to the facts of the case, there can be little doubt that the element paid for loss of profits is chargeable, being a sum derived from an asset, namely the jetty, pursuant to TCGA 1992 s 22(1)(a). However, for reasons explored in Chapter 2, that element of the damages was held to be a trading receipt chargeable to income tax. Accordingly, any charge to capital gains tax in relation to that element of the damages is excluded.

1 [1967] 2 All ER 124. The capital gains tax legislation was not actually in question in the case.

3.11 References to income in TCGA 1992 s 37 are construed so as to include references to income chargeable to corporation tax in the context of persons so liable.[1]

1 TCGA 1992, s 8(4).

Profits or gains
3.12 TCGA 1992 s 37 not only excludes amounts actually charged to income tax, as illustrated by reference to the *Attwooll* case above, but also excludes consideration which is taken into account for income tax purposes whether or not any tax becomes payable as a result. Furthermore, the reference to 'profits or gains' includes employment income chargeable under Schedule E.[1]

It would therefore appear to be the case that a termination payment, exempted from income tax under TA 1988 s 188 as considered in Chapter 6, will not be chargeable to capital gains tax by being consideration for the surrender of a right derived from the employment contract. The position would appear to be the same whether the exemption given under s 188 is by reference to the £30,000 'golden handshake' limit, or is without limit, for example in relation to foreign service.

1 TCGA 1992 s 52(2).

THE EXCLUSION FOR INCOME EXPENDITURE

3.13 The exclusion for consideration chargeable to income tax under TCGA 1992 s 37 is coupled with a similar exclusion for expenditure which is taken into account for income tax purposes. In this respect, TCGA 1992 s 39 excludes expenditure:

> '... allowable as a deduction in computing the profits or gains or losses of a trade, profession or vocation for the purposes of income tax or allowable as a deduction in

3.13 *General principles of capital gains tax*

computing any other income or profits or gains or losses for the purposes of the Income Tax Acts . . .'

As for TCGA 1992 s 37, references to income tax include references to corporation tax, and the extension to employment income also applies.

3.14 As a general principle, the nature of compensatory payments is to restore the recipient to the position in which he should have been but for the action resulting in his loss (the subject of compensation). This usually involves a 'net loss' approach, so that s 39 is unlikely to be directly in question. Any compensation paid will take into account expenditure which would otherwise have been incurred by the recipient.

However, the effect of TCGA 1992 s 39 should be borne in mind in circumstances where past revenue expenditure is reflected in the quantum of a claim for compensation for injury to a capital asset. This is best explained by way of example.

EXAMPLE

Robert owns an office building which was originally purchased for £100,000 and refurbished at a cost of £50,000. Of the refurbishment costs, £20,000 related to improvements to the building and was therefore capital expenditure, but £30,000 was eligible to be treated as income expenditure deductible in computing Robert's trading profits.

The office building is destroyed by fire, and Robert receives £150,000 from his insurers representing its value. That insurance receipt is liable to capital gains tax, subject to deductions on account of the original cost of £100,000 and the improvement expenditure of £20,000. The income refurbishment costs of £30,000 are excluded by TCGA 1992 s 39.

The charging requirements of the 1992 Act

3.15 The general nature of the capital gains tax charge having been considered, it is appropriate to turn to the detailed charging requirements with which the remainder of this chapter is concerned. Section 1(1) of the TCGA 1992 provides as follows:

> 'Tax shall be charged in accordance with this Act in respect of capital gains, that is to say chargeable gains computed in accordance with this Act and accruing to a person on the disposal of assets.'

The section can be seen to impose three requirements for a charge to tax. First, there must be an 'asset'. Second, a 'disposal' of that asset, and third a 'chargeable gain' accruing on that disposal. Each of the three requirements is dealt with in turn.

2 THE NATURE OF ASSETS

3.16 The type of 'asset' recognised by the 1992 Act is widely defined. TCGA 1992 s 21(1) provides as follows:

The nature of assets **3.18**

'*All forms of property shall be assets for the purposes of this Act, whether situated in the United Kingdom or not, including—*

(a) options, debts and incorporeal property generally, and
(b) any currency other than sterling, and
(c) any form of property created by the person disposing of it, or otherwise coming to be owned without being acquired.'

The word 'property' is not itself defined but would appear to mean anything capable of being owned, including property which comes into existence only upon its disposal. Interests in land, whether freehold or leasehold, goodwill, stocks and shares, the benefit of a loan or an insurance policy, an interest under a settlement or an intellectual property right are all examples of assets.

3.17 Receipts for injury to or the destruction of an asset are within the charge to tax.[1] The involuntary nature of the realisation does not prevent the compensation from being chargeable to tax, although various reliefs may be applicable. This gives rise to few conceptual difficulties, as the underlying asset which is injured or destroyed should be readily identifiable. However, complications do arise because the examples of assets can be extended to include two further entries. First, the benefit of a claim to statutory compensation, and second, the benefit of an action for damages.

These two entries are specifically dealt with below, but they should be considered in the context of the general principles which apply to the identification of assets. Those principles were considered in the important case of *O'Brien v Benson's Hosiery*.

1 TCGA 1992 s 22.

The decision in *O'Brien v Benson's Hosiery*

3.18 The facts in the case of *O'Brien v Benson's Hosiery*[1] are relatively simple. The issue was whether the sum of £50,000, paid by an employee in consideration for a release from his seven-year service contract with the taxpayer company, was chargeable in the hands of the taxpayer company.

The Inland Revenue contended that the £50,000 was a capital sum from the disposal of assets, consisting of the taxpayer's rights under the service contract. The disposal was effected by the taxpayer agreeing to refrain from exercising his rights under the contract, within what is now TCGA 1992 s 22(1)(c).

While the views of the Inland Revenue found favour with the High Court, the Court of Appeal accepted the taxpayer company's argument that a right to personal services could not constitute an asset. The rights in question were neither assignable nor had a market value. The court considered that such attributes were an implicit requirement for an asset to exist, by virtue of what is now TCGA 1992 s 17 which refers to disposals and the imputation of market value in computing gains.

The Court of Appeal was of the view that to make such provisions workable:

3.18 *General principles of capital gains tax*

> '... any asset to which they are capable of applying must be one for which a market value can be ascertained in accordance with [s 272(1) of the 1992 Act]. A right to personal services under a contract of service is, of course, unassignable. It cannot be bought or sold. Moreover it cannot survive the demise of either of the parties. It can have no actual marketable value, for there can be no market for what is unsaleable.'[2]

1 [1980] AC 562, [1979] 3 All ER 652, [1979] STC 735.
2 Per Buckley LJ [1978] 3 All ER 1057 at 1063.

3.19 The views of the Court of Appeal were rejected by the House of Lords, who restored the decision in favour of the Inland Revenue. In a short judgment, Lord Russell of Killowen rejected the requirement that an asset must be capable of assignment, it was sufficient that it be capable of being turned to account:

> '*It was contended for the taypayer that the rights of an employer under a contract of service were not "property" nor an "asset" of the employer, because they cannot be turned to account by transfer or assignment to another. But in my opinion this contention supposes a restricted view of the scheme of the imposition of the capital gains tax which the statutory language does not permit.*'[1]

His Lordship continued to the effect that rights which could be turned to account were capable of being assets, notwithstanding that the rights in question related to personal services:

> '*If, as here, the employer is able to exact from the employee a substantial sum as a term of releasing him from his obligations to serve, the rights of the employer appear to me to bear quite sufficiently the mark of an asset of the employer, something which he can turn to account, notwithstanding that his ability to turn it to account is by a type of disposal limited by the nature of the asset. In this connection I would also refer to the provisions of [s 22(1)(a)] which appear to me apt to cover a case where damages are recovered by an employer from a third party for wrongful procurement of breach by the employee of his contract of service.*'

The reference to what is now s 22(1)(a) of the 1992 Act is to the charge upon amounts received by way of compensation for any kind of damage or injury to assets, or for their loss, destruction or dissipation.

1 [1979] 3 All ER 652 at 655.

'ASSETS' AND 'PROPERTY'

3.20 The decision in *O'Brien* suggests that something is an asset because a sum of money has been obtained in respect of it. The mere fact of receiving that sum would appear sufficient, in itself, for a capital gains tax charge to apply. Fortunately, subsequent case law has clarified the meaning of the term 'asset' and the use of the word 'property' in defining that term.

It would now appear to be settled, following the decisions of the House of Lords in *Marren v Ingles*[1] and the Court of Appeal in *Kirby v Thorn EMI*,[2] that 'assets' are defined in terms of property. Unless a form of property can be identified no charge to tax may arise. The decision in *O'Brien* is not therefore authority for the proposition that the term assets is wider than the term property, so as to include any right which could be turned to account, whether or not that right constituted a form of property.[3]

The decision in *Marren v Ingles* illustrates the wide ambit of the term 'assets', by applying it to an element of the price paid upon a share sale; that limitations exist is demonstrated by the decision in *Kirby v Thorn EMI*.

---

1 (1980) 54 TC 76.
2 [1987] STC 621.
3 Identified by Warner J in *Zim Properties Ltd v Procter* [1985] STC 90.

MARREN V INGLES

3.21 The case of *Marren v Ingles*[1] was concerned with a sale of shares in a private company by the taxpayer, in consideration of an immediate cash sum of £750 per share and a further cash sum which only became payable if the company were subsequently floated on a stock exchange. The amount of the further cash sum was dependent upon share values on the first day of trading following flotation. It was therefore both contingent and unascertainable at the time of the share sale, in 1970.

Whilst the 1992 Act makes provision for postponed payments and contingent liabilities,[2] no provision is made for a contingent and unascertainable future payment. The 'solution' adopted by the House of Lords was to regard the right to future payment as an asset in itself, so that the consideration for the share sale consisted of two elements:

(a) the cash sum of £750 per share, and
(b) the market value of the right to the further cash sum, valued as at the time of the share disposal.

---

1 (1980) 54 TC 76.
2 TCGA 1992 ss 48 and 49.

3.22 The House of Lords decided that the new asset, consisting of the right to a further cash sum, was disposed of when the further cash sum became due, which analysis requires a further computation. A chargeable gain accrues if the market value at the time of the share disposal proved less than the amount ultimately paid.

Conversely, an allowable loss is realised if the market value proved to be greater than the amount finally paid:

> 'The first question is whether the right to half of the profit is properly to be regarded as a separate asset, or simply as a deferred part of the price of the shareholdings. In my opinion, the former view is correct. "Asset" is defined . . . in the widest terms, to mean *all forms of property* . . .
>
> It is therefore apt to include the incorporeal rights to money's worth which was part of the consideration given for the shareholdings in 1970. The vendors could have disposed of the right at any time . . . by selling it or giving it away and assigning it. If they had done so, there would have been an actual disposal of an asset and the vendors would have been liable for capital gains tax on the amount, if any, by which the price or value of the asset at the date of disposal exceeded its value [in] . . . 1970.'[1]

3.22 *General principles of capital gains tax*

1 Per Lord Fraser, (1980) 54 TC 76 at 98–99.

3.23 The above analysis would, it is thought, have remained the same if the right to the further sum was expressed as personal to the vendor and incapable of assignment, in view of the decision in *O'Brien* as to marketability. The distinction made by Lord Fraser between 'a separate asset' and 'a deferred part of the price' would therefore appear to be a fine one. A deferred part of the price remains just that, provided its method of valuation and payment enables it to be brought within a specific charging provision of the 1992 Act. If it cannot be so brought in, it is a separate asset.

Accordingly, immediate cash payments, delayed cash payments, instalment payments, or any combination of them, whether subject to contingencies or not, may be regarded as part of the consideration for the disposal of an asset within the scheme of the Act. They are to be distinguished, however, from a right to receive a contingent and unascertainable future payment which falls to be treated as an asset.

KIRBY V THORN EMI

3.24 Further problems in identifying an 'asset' were considered by the Court of Appeal in *Kirby v Thorn EMI*.[1] In that case the taxpayer company agreed to procure the sale of shares in certain trading subsidiary companies. As part of the terms, the taxpayer company agreed not to compete with the subsidiary companies in question for a period of five years. The covenant was given in consideration of the sum of $575,000.

The taxpayer company was successful both before the Special Commissioners and in the High Court to the effect that the $575,000 was not consideration for the disposal of an asset, whether that asset consisted of the shares sold or the taxpayer company's freedom to trade. So far as the former was concerned, it was agreed that the amount was derived from the covenant, a reflection of the taxpayer's ability to control its and its subsidiaries' business activities. The price allocated to the shares fully reflected their market value. As to the latter, the freedom to trade was not a form of property capable of being owned and so its restriction could not be a disposal. The scheme of the 1992 Act was such as to require:

'... there to be a disposal of assets, and assets are defined in terms of "forms of property". The freedom of commercial activity of a person or a company is not in my judgment such an asset ... There is no discernible chose in action in such a freedom; nor is there any other right capable of being directly enforced against any other legal person.'[2]

1 [1986] STC 200.
2 Per Knox J, ibid at 212.

3.25 The decision of the court in *Kirby v Thorn EMI* is also authority to the effect that the reference in what is now TCGA 1992 s 21(1)(c) to 'any form of property created by the person disposing of it' does not include property created by the act of disposal. The property in question must be created before its disposal in order to be an asset for the purposes of the 1992 Act.

The Court of Appeal agreed with the above analysis, however judgment was given for the Crown on the basis that consideration was derived from the taxpayer company's goodwill in the business carried on by its subsidiary companies. The giving of a restrictive covenant amounted to a disposal of goodwill and was therefore chargeable in full.

Claims to statutory compensation

3.26 The term 'assets' can include the benefit of a claim to statutory compensation, depending upon the nature of the claimant's rights conferred by the statutory provision in question. In this respect, statutory compensation is used in the sense of an amount which is directed as being due to the plaintiff upon the occurrence of a relevant event, independent of any common law action, rather than an amount which is computed in accordance with, or laid down as being due by statute dependent upon a successful action in tort, contract or otherwise.

An example of the former is compensation under the Agricultural Holdings Act 1986 following the termination of a lease. An example of the latter is damages for bereavement conferred by reason of the Fatal Accidents Act 1976.

3.27 As a general rule, statutory compensation is outside the scope of the capital gains tax charge unless it can be said to create an independent proprietary right in favour of the plaintiff which affords compensation for the loss of, or injury to, an asset. Three cases may usefully be referred to: *Davis v Powell* and *Drummond v Austin Brown*, which were both concerned with compensation payable to tenants, and *Davenport v Chilver*, which was concerned with compensation for the confiscation of property.

THE FREEDOM FROM CHARGE

3.28 The case of *Davis v Powell*[1] was concerned with compensation payable to an agricultural tenant on the surrender of his tenancy upon notice to quit. The compensation was paid pursuant to s 34 of the Agricultural Holdings Act 1948 (which was replaced by the 1986 Act). That section applies where the tenancy of an agricultural holding terminates by reason of a notice to quit with which the tenant complies. Compensation is set at no less than one year's rent, nor more than two years' rent. The tenant must prove his loss in order to obtain more than the lower limit.

The Inland Revenue argued that the compensation derived from the lease, which was the subject of a disposal upon the tenant complying with the notice to quit and therefore was subject to capital gains tax. The Revenue's argument was rejected by the High Court. The object of s 34 is to provide, by statute, that a landlord shall make good to a tenant the loss or expense which he unavoidably incurs in connection with the matters mentioned in the section. To avoid argument, the tenant gets no less than one year's rent or more than two, and if he wants more than one year he must prove his loss.

So far as the question of causation was concerned, and in particular whether what is now TCGA 1992 s 22(1) could bring the receipt into charge, it was decided that the section did not apply:

3.28 *General principles of capital gains tax*

'It does not seem to me that the compensation paid under s 34 is derived from the asset, namely the lease. It is not derived from an asset at all: it is simply a sum which Parliament says shall be paid for expense and loss which are unavoidably incurred after the lease has gone.'[2]

1 [1977] 1 All ER 471.
2 Per Templeman J, ibid at 474.

3.29 Some importance can be placed upon the fact that there was no agreement to pay the compensation to which the tenant was a party. In particular, it could not be said to have been paid:

'... as a result of a bargain in which the tenant says, "If I get out, will you pay me £591?". It is a sum paid where a tenant is faced with a notice to quit and must get out. Parliament says that in these circumstances, which have nothing to do with a surrender, the tenant is to have a sum by way of compensation for irretrievable loss.'[1]

1 Per Templeman J [1977] 1 All ER 471 at 474.

3.30 The decision of the Court of Appeal in the case of *Drummond v Austin Brown*[1] was concerned with similar facts to those in *Davis v Powell*, albeit the compensation there was payable upon the termination of the taxpayer's lease under the Landlord and Tenant Act 1954. Again the decision was in favour of the taxpayer, to the effect that the compensation was neither derived from the lease nor for the loss of an asset, either of which would render the amount taxable. In the words of Fox LJ:

'... the right to compensation is still only a right given by Parliament. If Parliament chose to take it away, the lease by itself would not have conferred it. We do not think that it is accurately described as an "incident" of the lease. It does not attach to the estate as such.'[2]

The scope of the exemption from tax for statutory compensation, illustrated by the decisions in *Davis v Powell* and *Drummond v Austin Brown*, is, however, subject to the decision in *Davenport v Chilver*.

1 [1984] STC 321.
2 Per Fox LJ, ibid at 324.

THE DECISION IN *DAVENPORT V CHILVER*

3.31 There is no general proposition that a statutory right to compensation for irretrievable loss cannot be an asset. This was established by the High Court in *Davenport v Chilver*.[1] That case was concerned with compensation received in respect of property in Latvia, expropriated by the USSR in 1940. The taxpayer received compensation by virtue of two types of claim:

(a) one claim related to property either owned by the taxpayer, or to which she was beneficially entitled following the death of her father before expropriation; and

The nature of assets **3.34**

(b) the remainder related to property owned by the taxpayer's mother who, upon her death after expropriation, had left a share in any compensation which might become payable to the taxpayer.

---

1 [1983] STC 426, 57 TC 661.

3.32 So far as the first element of the compensation was concerned, a charge to capital gains tax applied, subject to computation in accordance with the normal rules of time apportionment and base cost. The fact that the expropriation occurred in 1940, well before the introduction of capital gains tax, did not assist the taxpayer. The disposal was regarded as having occurred at the time the compensation was received in the year 1972–73, by virtue of what are now TCGA 1992, ss 22(1)(a) and (2).

The Latvian property was, of course, physically disposed of in 1940, but no sum was 'derived' from that disposal. The expropriation was on the basis that no compensation would be paid. It was therefore the case that the compensation subsequently received under the statutory scheme by the taxpayer was for the 'loss . . . of an asset' within TCGA s 22(1)(a). Furthermore, the disposal was regarded as having taken place upon receipt of the compensation; in this respect TCGA 1992 s 22(2) provides as follows:

'In the case of a disposal within paragraph (a), (b), (c) or (d) of [s 22(1)], the time of the disposal shall be the time when the capital sum is received as described in that sub-section.'

The compensation was therefore within the charge to tax, notwithstanding that the expropriation occurred some 25 years before the introduction of capital gains tax.

3.33 The second element of the compensation raised somewhat more difficult questions of statutory construction. At the time of death of the taxpayer's mother, the taxpayer neither owned any property in Latvia nor had any right to compensation; she merely had a hope of receiving future compensation. Either way there was no 'asset' from which the compensation could be said to derive. Nourse J agreed with the decision of the Special Commissioners in this respect; after quoting an extract from their decision he noted that it was based on the reasoning of Walton J in the case of *IRC v Montgomery*:[1]

'. . . where the learned judge had adopted the dictionary meaning of "derivation" as being to trace or show the origin . . . To express it in my own words, I do not think that one thing can be said to derive from another unless it is in some sense the fruit of the tree. In Latvia the tree is dead. The fruit has dropped from one rooted in a loftier soil to which the blight cannot attain.'[2]

---

1 [1975] 1 All ER 664, 49 TC 679.
2 [1983] STC 426 at 439.

3.34 The Inland Revenue did, however, succeed on an alternative argument to the effect that the taxpayer's statutory right to compensation was, in itself, an asset. This argument was accepted by Nourse J, in the following terms:

> '... the effect of the [Statutory] Order was to confer on [the taxpayer] a right to share in a designated fund, subject to proof of title and value. That is a right which can, I think, fairly be described as an independent proprietary right, whereas the right to compensation [in Davis v Powell was] a claim against the pocket of the landlord for expense which the tenant's pocket is deemed already to have met.'[1]

Acceptance of the Inland Revenue's argument, however, did not rob the taxpayer of victory, because it was also decided that she acquired her right to compensation upon the Statutory Order coming into operation in 1969, at its then market value. This result was reached because the asset was acquired other than by way of a bargain at arms length so that its deemed acquisition cost, which should have remained equal to that finally paid in 1972–73, completely sheltered the gain.

---

1 [1983] STC 426 at 441.

3.35 If the facts in *Davenport v Chilver* were to be repeated, save that the Statutory Order was to come into operation after 9 March 1981, the compensation would not have been so sheltered. This is because the market value rule upon acquisition would be disapplied by TCGA 1992 s 17(2) which applies to the acquisition of an asset if:

> '(a) there is no corresponding disposal of it, and
> (b) there is no consideration in money or money's worth or the consideration is of an amount or value lower than the market value of the asset.'

Obviously, the exactment of a Statutory Order does not involve any form of disposal, and no amount was paid by the taxpayer in order to acquire the rights conferred by it.

The benefit of an action for damages

3.36 The decision of the High Court in the case of *Zim Properties Ltd v Procter*[1] is central to the consideration of the capital gains tax regime as it applies to compensation. This is because the decision is authority for the proposition that the benefit of an action for damages is itself an asset for the purposes of capital gains tax.

The facts of the case were as follows. The taxpayer company contracted to sell some of its investment properties to a third party purchaser, Courtdeals Ltd. The contract was executed on 12 July 1973, with completion agreed 12 months later. Completion failed to take place as the taxpayer was unable to show good title to one of the properties and the purchaser therefore repudiated the contract, as he was entitled to do.

Believing the repudiation to have been caused by the negligence of its solicitors acting in the sale, the taxpayer issued a writ against them claiming damages totalling £104,138. The greater part of the damages alleged by the taxpayer represented the difference between the agreed sale price and the subsequent value of the properties, which had fallen due to prevailing market conditions. The action was compromised by the solicitors agreeing to pay £69,000 to the taxpayer in full and final settlement of the claim.

1 [1985] STC 90.

3.37 The Inland Revenue assessed the taxpayer to corporation tax on chargeable gains on the basis that the agreed compromise was a disposal by the taxpayer of the right of action against the solicitors, which right constituted an 'asset'. In the High Court, Warner J agreed with the Inland Revenue in the following terms:

(a) a right to bring an action to seek to enforce a claim that was neither frivolous nor vexatious, which right could be turned to account by negotiating a compromise yielding a capital sum, constituted an 'asset' for the purposes of the capital gains tax legislation;
(b) the capital sum that accrued to the taxpayer company was derived not from the investment properties but from the right of the taxpayer to sue his solicitors. Accordingly, the receipt did not fall to be treated as a part disposal of the investment properties; and
(c) the taxpayer acquired its right to sue when the contract for sale of the investment properties was entered into. The acquisition was not 'by way of a bargain at arms length' and accordingly the taxpayer was deemed to have acquired that right for a consideration equal to its then market value, if any. Thus in computing the assessable gain, the market value of the right fell to be deducted.

Each of the above conclusions requires consideration in turn, but the problems associated with the decision and the concessionary relief available in respect of it are explored in Chapter 4.

THE NATURE OF THE RIGHT

3.38 The nature of the right had to be regarded as an asset in *Zim Properties*, having regard to the decision of the House of Lords in *O'Brien*. The nature of the right as an asset is an important point, and it is therefore worth quoting from the decision of Warner J at some length.

The learned judge first noted the taxpayer's argument to the effect that because his action could not be guaranteed to succeed it did not have the hallmarks of an asset:

> 'One way in which counsel for the taxpayer company attacked the decision of the commissioners to the effect that the £60,000 was "derived" from the taxpayer company's right of action against the firm was this . . . He pointed out that, on the pleadings in the action between the taxpayer company and the firm, the outcome of the trial might have depended on whether the court preferred the evidence of [the plaintiff] or that of a partner in the firm. Alternatively, it might have depended on whether the court found as a fact that, if Courtdeals Limited had been told that the 1960 conveyance was missing, Courtdeals Limited would nonetheless have entered into the contract or would have declined to do so. In other words, what the Crown referred to as the taxpayer company's "right of action" against the firm was in reality no more than a claim which might or might not succeed. Such a claim, unlike an

3.38 *General principles of capital gains tax*

undoubted right, was not a form of property and therefore, having regard to the terms of s 22(1) of the Finance Act 1965, was not an "asset" for capital gains tax purposes.'[1]

The Crown's argument against this was that the taxpayer's claim for compensation was a form of property. Alternatively, it was submitted that, if it was not a form of property, it was nonetheless an 'asset' for capital gains tax purposes. The taxpayer's argument to the effect that the so called 'right of action' was merely a claim which may or may not succeed was attacked on the basis that in future cases it would be necessary for the commissioners to decide, on a balance of probabilities, whether a civil action that had in fact been compromised would or would not have succeeded if it had actually gone to trial.

The point was decided in favour of the Crown:

'I have ... come to the conclusion that counsel for the Crown is entitled to succeed ... He is entitled to do so, I think, not on the strength of the various authorities to which he referred me on the scope of the concept of a "chose in action" in English law or on the strength of what it is desirable or undesirable that appellate commissioners should have to decide, but on the strength of the decision of the House of Lords in O'Brien (Inspector of Taxes) v Benson's Hosiery (Holdings) Limited *[1980] AC 562, [1979] STC 735. True the contractual rights that were there held to constitute an asset for capital gains tax purposes were undisputed. They were not a mere claim. But that formed no part of the ratio decidendi of the case. The ratio decidendi was that those rights were an asset for capital gains tax purposes because they were something that could be turned to account.'*[2]

---

1 [1985] STC 90 at 103.
2 Ibid at 104.

3.39 The conclusion has echoes of a circular argument. If a sum of money has been received then it is chargeable because 'something' has yielded a sum of money and that something must therefore be an asset. As discussed however, the decision in *O'Brien* is not authority for such a proposition; there must be some form of underlying property. It may therefore be the case that the decision in *Zim Properties* should have focused more on the scope of the concept of a 'chose in action'.

The causal link

3.40 The compensation in *Zim Properties* was considered as deriving from the right to sue—a separate and distinct asset from the investment properties. The counter argument raised by the taxpayer, was essentially to the effect that the compensation derived from the properties which were the subject of the action. Because the properties were not sold, compensation was received for the loss that the taxpayer suffered by reason of there having been no sale. It was therefore argued that the compensation was derived from the properties as much as the sale price would have been if the properties had been sold. It was suggested that any other decision would transgress the basic rule that capital gains tax is a tax on real gains, not on 'arithmetical differences'. The reference to arithmetical differences is to the dictum of Lord Wilberforce in *Aberdeen Construction Group Ltd v IRC*[1] in which his Lordship was anxious to avoid paradoxical results contrary to business sense. Finally, it was argued that a decision in favour of the Inland Revenue would also be inconsistent with previous case law authorities to the effect that a right to compensation for loss is not an 'asset' for capital gains tax purposes.

However, the taxpayer's arguments were rejected:

> 'It does not . . . seem to me "contrary to business sense" to treat the £69,000 received by the taxpayer company in this case as a gain. The fact is that, after its receipt of that sum, the taxpayer company still owned the properties, unaffected and unimpaired by the fate of its contract with Courtdeals Ltd.'[2]

1 [1978] STC 127 at 131.
2 Per Warner J [1985] STC 90 at 107.

3.41 The court was not willing to concede that the statutory compensation cases cited in support of the taxpayer's case (comprising *Davis v Powell* and *Drummond v Austin Brown*, **3.28** to **3.30** above) evinced anything other than a general principle that 'not every right to a payment is an "asset" for capital gains tax purposes'. Accordingly, the £69,000 compensation was subject to tax.

ACQUISITION OF THE RIGHT TO SUE

3.42 The compensation which was brought into charge in *Zim Properties* was of course subject to a deduction being made available on account of the acquisition of the right to sue by the taxpayer in July 1973. That acquisition occurred upon entering into the contract of sale to Courtdeals Ltd. However, this right was thought unlikely to have anything but a nominal value, the result was therefore to charge the £69,000 in full.

If the acquisition of the right to sue occurred after 9 March 1981 no amount would have been available for deduction in any event because of TCGA 1992 s 17(2).

3 DISPOSALS

3.43 The second requirement for a charge to capital gains tax is that the asset in question is the subject of a 'disposal'. No general definition is given to the word 'disposal', but various provisions extend or limit the word. as a general proposition the word refers to a transfer of the beneficial ownership in an asset from one person to another. This may be effected for full consideration, in money or money's worth, at an undervalue or for no consideration.

In most cases a disposal will consist of an asset transfer under which the transferee acquires the asset in question. However, it is not a requirement that the payer actually acquires an asset.[1]

1 In view of the extension to the term 'disposal' imported by TCGA 1992 s 22(1).

3.44 *General principles of capital gains tax*

Part disposals

3.44 Disposals include part disposals. The concept is often encountered in the context of compensatory receipts, and accordingly a brief overview is necessary. TCGA 1992 s 21(2)(b) provides as follows:

> *'there is a part disposal of an asset where an interest or right in or over the asset is created by the disposal, as well as where it subsists before the disposal, and generally, there is a part disposal of an asset where, on a person making a disposal, any description of property derived from the asset remains undisposed of.'*

3.45 If there is a part disposal, the disposal consideration is fully brought into charge, but only that proportion of the acquisition cost of the asset attributable to the part disposed of may be deducted. The incidental costs of making the part disposal are wholly attributable to the part disposed of and are therefore allowed in full. The apportionment is calculated by reference to the fraction $\frac{A}{(A + B)}$, where A is the amount or value of the consideration for the disposal and B is the market value of the property which remains undisposed of.[1] As a practical matter the apportionment requires a market value to be determined for the part which is retained.

---

1 TCGA 1992 s 42(2).

EXAMPLE

Deborah purchased a garage for £210,000 in December 1982, which she let to a car dealer. Following some general improvements made to the property at a cost of £45,000 in March 1985, Deborah sold part of the garage for conversion into offices in January 1986 and received £180,000. Legal costs of £3,000 were incurred. The market value of the remaining part of the garage immediately following the sale was £160,000. The indexation factor for December 1982 to January 1986 is 0.167 and that for March 1985 to January 1986 is 0.037. The part disposal computation is therefore as follows:

	£	£
Disposal consideration		180,000
Allowable cost:		
$210,000 \times \frac{180,000}{180,000 + 160,000} =$	111,176	
$45,000 \times \frac{180,000}{180,000 + 160,000} =$	23,823	
Indexation allowance:		
0.167 × 111,176 =	18,566	
0.037 × 23,823 =	881	
		(154,446)
Legal fees		(3,000)
Chargeable gain		22,554

3.46 Perhaps because of the requirement to value that part of the property which is retained, the Inland Revenue are willing to treat land disposals in respect of part of an estate as though the land sold was a separate asset. Under this alternative basis costs are apportioned subject to the method of apportionment being fair and reasonable.[1]

1 Inland Revenue Statement of Practice D1.

STATUTORY RELIEF FOR PART DISPOSALS

3.47 Certain part disposals may attract relief pursuant to TCGA 1992 ss 242–244 which apply in relation to so-called 'small part disposals' and disposals to an authority with compulsory powers.

Under s 242, any capital gains tax liability in relation to a transfer of land is deferred until the part retained is the subject of a disposal.[1] For the relief to apply, the amount or value of the consideration for the transfer must not exceed one-fifth of the market value of the land holding immediately before the transfer. Furthermore, the consideration for the transfer must not exceed £20,000. The limit takes into account other land transfers whether relieved under s 242 or not, but, excluding a transfer to which TCGA 1992 s 243 (part disposals to authorities with compulsory powers) applies, in the year of assessment in which the part disposal was made.

Relief is afforded by reducing the allowable expenditure attaching to the part retained, and is therefore subject to there being a sufficient amount of expenditure against which to set off the disposal consideration.[2] No relief is available in respect of wasting assets.[3]

EXAMPLE

James owns Whiteacre which is valued at £120,000. He sells part of Whiteacre to a neighbour for £18,000 and claims relief pursuant to s 242. The disposal proceeds are not more than 20% of Whiteacre nor do the disposal proceeds exceed the £20,000 limit. Assuming that there is no restriction by reference to James' allowable expenditure in relation to Whiteacre, the full amount of the disposal proceeds are received free of tax. Upon a subsequent disposal the £18,000 is deducted from the allowable expenditure otherwise available in respect of the land.

1 *Simon's Taxes* C2.1103.
2 TCGA 1992 s 244.
3 Ibid s 242(7).

3.48 A similar form of relief applies in relation to part disposals to authorities with compulsory powers, whether these powers are actually exercised or not, under TCGA 1992 s 243. Relief is not capped by reference to any financial limit, but is only available where the amount or value of the consideration is 'small' compared with the market value of the part retained. For these purposes small is taken to be 5% or less.[1] It is a condition that the transferor had not taken any steps, by advertising or otherwise, to dispose of his holding, or to make his willingness to dispose known to the authority or

3.48 *General principles of capital gains tax*

others.² Again, the limitations of TCGA 1992 s 244 apply. No relief is available in relation to wasting assets.³ For a full commentary reference should be made to *Simon's Taxes* C2.1117.

For roll-over relief on compulsory acquisition under TCGA 1992 s 247 reference should be made to Chapter 4.

---

1 CCAB Press Release, June 1965.
2 TCGA 1992 s 243(4).
3 Ibid s 243(1)(b).

The provisions of s 22

3.49 The concept of disposal is extended so as to include sums derived from assets which might not constitute a disposal in the general sense. TCGA 1992 s 22(1) initially provides as follows:

> '. . . there is . . . a disposal of assets by their owner where any capital sum is derived from assets notwithstanding that no asset is acquired by the person paying the capital sum . . .'

The general ambit of the section is accompanied by four further specific instances of disposal, which apply in circumstances where capital sums are received:

> '(a) . . . by way of compensation for any kind of damage or injury to assets or for the loss, destruction or dissipation of assets or for any depreciation or risk of depreciation of an asset,
> (b) . . . under a policy of insurance of the risk of any kind of damage or injury to, or the loss or depreciation of, assets,
> (c) . . . in return for forfeiture or surrender of rights, or for refraining from exercising rights, and
> (d) . . . as consideration for use or exploitation of assets.'

The ambit of s 22(1) is subject to TCGA 1992 ss 23 and 26, which are respectively concerned with the receipt of compensation and insurance monies applied in repairing the asset,¹ and mortgages and charges with which this book is not concerned. Paragraphs (a) to (d) above are examples of sums derived from assets, not an exhaustive list of circumstances in which capital sums may be derived from assets.²

The reference to 'capital sums' in s 22 is a reference to any money or money's worth not otherwise excluded for capital gains tax purposes.³ The exclusion is a reference to money or money's worth charged to income tax.⁴

---

1 For which see Chapter 4.
2 This is implicit in the commentary contained in Inland Revenue booklet CGT8 (1980) at para 116.
3 TCGA 1992 s 22(3).
4 For which see ibid s 37.

3.50 In practice, compensation or insurance proceeds for the entire loss, destruction, dissipation, or extinction of an asset chargeable under TCGA

1992 s 22(1)(a) or (b) are regarded as consideration for the disposal of that asset.

EXAMPLE

Peter purchased a painting for £22,000 in August 1986. The painting was destroyed by fire in June 1991, as a result of which Peter received in September 1991 the insured value of £36,000.

		£	£
Consideration for disposal			36,000
Deduct:	Allowable cost:	22,000	
	Indexation allowance		
	(August 1987 to September 1991)		
	0.376 × 22,000	8,272	(30,272)
Chargeable gain			5,728

3.51 However, TCGA 1992 s 24(1) provides that the occasion of the entire loss (etc) of an asset constitutes a disposal of the asset, whether or not any capital sum is received by way of compensation. An alternative analysis is that the loss gives rise to a disposal, which results in a capital loss. The subsequent receipt of compensation is received for a separate asset, comprising the right to receive the compensation. This alternative analysis gives rise to different timing of gains and losses; the indexation allowance may also be different. This alternative argument would appear to be limited to receipts chargeable under TCGA 1992 s 22(1)(a) having regard to the provisions of TCGA 1992 s 204 in relation to policies of insurance.

PHYSICAL DAMAGE

3.52 Compensation for physical damage to an asset will fall within TCGA 1992 s 22(1)(a) given the reference to 'any kind of damage or injury to assets'. The section's primary concern is with compensation payable as a result of some physical loss or damage, and clearly includes damages so recoverable in contract or in tort. The ambit of paragraph (a) was considered in the case of *Davenport v Chilver*:[1]

> '*My first impression of the language of para (a) was that its primary concern is with compensation payable as a result of some physical loss or damage. It clearly includes damages so recoverable in contract or in tort, but the word "compensation" demonstrates that it is not so limited. I would expect it to include, for example, compensation payable under legislation such as the War Damage Acts.*'[2]

The section is not considered to apply in circumstances involving a compulsory acquisition of land. This is because such an acquisition occasions a disposal of the asset within TCGA 1992 s 19(1). A distinction should be drawn between compensation payable as a result of a change of title and that paid as a result of some physical loss or damage. Again in the words of Nourse J:

3.52 *General principles of capital gains tax*

> '... *[There] seems to be no reason for excluding compensation for injurious affection in a case where no land is taken from the claimant. That would be compensation received for the depreciation of an asset. That is a case where there is no change of title to the asset, but a statutory undertaking on adjoining or neighbouring land can hardly be said to cause physical loss or damage to the asset. Again, the phrase "dissipation of assets" could well extend beyond the case of physical loss or damage.*'[3]

The term 'loss' would appear to refer to events which involve no physical damage to the asset but deprive the owner of it by actions which fall short of a disposal. The term comprehends any act of confiscation, nationalisation, expropriation, or similar official act of dispossession.[4]

1 [1983] STC 426.
2 Per Nourse J, ibid at 439.
3 Ibid at 440.
4 Ibid.

3.53 The reference to 'destruction' would appear to be a reference to the loss of an asset by physical damage, for example a fire or earthquake. The phrase 'dissipation of assets' is apt to cover the wasting of an asset, for example the application of incorrect mining methods resulting in a fall in value of the mine in question. It would also appear apt to cover activities engaged on neighbouring land which do not cause physical damage to the asset but result in a loss in value.

Finally, the phrase compensation 'for any depreciation or risk of depreciation' of an asset is a reference to any action which impinges on the integrity of the asset or reduces its value, or action which could lead to such a result.

INSURANCE

3.54 Insurance receipts following damage to an insured asset fall to be assessed to capital gains tax under TCGA 1992 s 22(1)(b). The form of loss in question follows the formulation in s 22(1)(a) in that it refers to 'damage or injury to, or the loss or depreciation of, assets'. It should be noted that a policy of insurance is a prerequisite for a charge to tax. It would therefore appear to follow that damage made good, notwithstanding the lack of a valid policy, will not be subject to charge.

The rights of the insured under a policy of insurance constitute an asset, so that a chargeable gain may accrue upon their disposal; for example, by assignment of the rights to a third party. This treatment only applies to the extent that the rights relate to an asset upon which a chargeable gain may accrue.[1]

As referred to at **3.50** and **3.51** above, sums received under a policy of insurance are regarded as derived from the asset damaged or lost (etc) for the purposes of TCGA 1992 s 22.[2]

1 TCGA 1992 s 204(1).
2 Ibid s 204(2).

FORFEITURE OR SURRENDER

3.55 Payment in return for the forfeiture or surrender of rights, or for refraining from exercising rights is chargeable under TCGA 1992 s 22(1)(c). Compensation in return for releasing another person from a contract, or restrictive covenant, may be charged under this head.

USE OR EXPLOITATION

3.56 Sums received in consideration for the use or exploitation of assets are subject to capital gains tax under TCGA 1992 s 22(1)(d). Obvious examples include sums for the right to exploit a copyright, or to use goodwill.

As such, compensation is unlikely to be taxed under this head, but one important point may be made. Compensation for the 'use' of an asset, in the sense that damages are calculated by reference to the loss of an asset for a period of time as considered in Chapter 2, would not be charged under this head. The amount received in such circumstances is calculated by reference to the 'use' of the asset, but is not consideration for that 'use'.

4 CHARGEABLE GAINS

3.57 Chapters III and IV of Pt II TCGA 1992 contain the main rules relating to the computation of gains. Those rules are modified by special provisions relating to assets held on 6 April 1965 and 31 March 1982,[1] and in respect of leases with a term of less than 50 years.[2]

The computation of gains is achieved by bringing into charge the consideration for the disposal in question, subject to deducting therefrom such expenditure as is allowed—essentially the acquisition cost of the asset together with incidental costs on disposal, such as legal fees. In addition, the gain is modified by the indexation allowance which is intended to remove inflationary gains from charge. As a general rule, losses are computed in the same way as gains. Computation is therefore dependent upon:

(a) disposal consideration;
(b) allowable expenditure and deductions; and
(c) indexation.

The commentary which follows on the computational factors is selective, concentrating on those aspects which are likely to be of immediate relevance to compensatory receipts.[3]

---

1 TCGA 1992 Schs 2, 3 and 4.
2 Ibid Sch 8.
3 For a more complete analysis see *Simon's Taxes* C2.101.

Disposal consideration

3.58 The disposal consideration is the actual consideration given, unless the 1992 Act provides otherwise. Market value may be substituted in the context of asset disposals between 'connected' persons, or transactions not at arm's length.[1] Furthermore, certain disposals are deemed to be made for such a consideration as gives rise to neither a gain nor a loss, which includes transfers between husband and wife [2] and companies in the same group.[3]

When it is the actual consideration which applies, its amount must be ascertained at the date of disposal. As a general rule, the date of payment is irrelevant, although some relief from the basic rule may be available in the case of instalment payments.[4] Contingent sums are brought into account without regard to the risk of non-payment, but are subject to subsequent adjustment if the amounts brought into account are not paid.[5]

1 TCGA 1992 ss 17, 18 and 286.
2 Ibid s 58.
3 Ibid s 171.
4 Ibid s 280.
5 Ibid s 48.

CONTINGENT LIABILITIES

3.59 The treatment of contingent liabilities is governed by TCGA 1992 s 49. In the first instance, no allowance is made in the computation of the gain in three circumstances, detailed at s 49(1):

> '(a) in the case of a disposal by way of assigning a lease of land or other property, for any liability remaining with, or assumed by, the person making the disposal by way of assigning the lease which is contingent on a default in respect of liabilities thereby or subsequently assumed by the assignee under the terms and conditions of the lease,
> (b) for any contingent liability of the person making the disposal in respect of any covenant for quiet enjoyment or other obligation assumed as vendor of land, or of any estate or interest in land, or as a lessor,
> (c) for any contingent liability in respect of a warranty or representation made on a disposal by way of sale or lease of any property other than land.'

If it is subsequently shown that any such contingent liability within items (a) to (c) above has become enforceable, and is being or has been enforced, all appropriate adjustments are made to the original assessment.

Item (a) above applies to the liabilities which remain with a tenant notwithstanding the assignment of a lease or other property. For example, the original tenant remains liable under his lease for breaches of covenant for the entire life of the lease. If a purchaser of the lease is in breach of a covenant, such as the covenant to pay rent, the landlord may look to the original tenant to make good the loss. Item (b) above applies to the liabilities which remain with a vendor or lessor of land notwithstanding a sale or leasehold grant.

EXAMPLE

A Ltd takes a lease for 25 years at a full market rent. A Ltd transfers the lease some seven years later to B Ltd. Due to trading difficulties B Ltd becomes insolvent three years after taking the lease. The landlord can now revert to A Ltd, as the original tenant, for payment of rent and all other sums due under the terms of the lease.

3.60 The ambit of TCGA 1992 s 49 was considered in the case of *Randall v Plumb*.[1] It was there concluded that contingencies expressly mentioned by the section were to be disregarded, but if such a contingent liability actually arose, the amount paid would be taken into account by way of adjustment. Conversely, if the contingency was not expressly mentioned, it must be taken into account in valuing the disposal consideration (with the practical difficulties this entails) but no subsequent adjustment is to be made:

> '... *unless the contingency is one which is expressly mentioned in one or other of these sub-paragraphs, in which case the contingency is to be disregarded but justice will be done to the taxpayer if the contingency actually turns out the wrong way by an adjustment of tax, it must (if it can as a matter of valuation) be taken at once into account in establishing the amount of the consideration received by the taxpayer, this being the only possible method of arriving at a figure for the amount of the consideration which truly reflects the contingency to which the matter is subject. Of course, this will not do ideal justice, or even such justice as an adjustment to the tax actually paid will effect, because obviously the valuation of the contingency must lie between the extremes of its happening and its not happening, whereas finally it will either happen or not happen; but this is a chance which may rebound to the advantage or to the disadvantage of either party.*'[2]

---

1 [1975] 1 WLR 633, 50 TC 392.
2 Per Walton J [1975] 1 WLR 633 at 637.

3.61 If the vendor assumes an actual liability upon the disposal of an asset, as distinct from a contingent liability, the amount of that liability should be deducted from the vendor's disposal consideration. Similarly, if the purchaser assumes liabilities, their amount should be taken into account so far as concerns the purchaser's acquisition cost.

In the case of an contingent liability which does not fall to be taken into account under TCGA 1992 s 49 and where a liability arises in excess of the value (if any) placed upon it, there is no mechanism for adjusting the vendor's disposal consideration. On the other hand, a vendor may benefit if the liability never arises, in which case his true gain is greater than that taxed.

EXAMPLE

Harold assigns a lease in respect of an industrial site for £100,000, on terms which provide for the repayment of the purchase consideration if planning permission is not obtained for the unit in the manner proposed by the tenant. It is considered that a 20% risk exists of the local authority restricting the use to which the unit may be put. The value of the contingent liability is therefore 20% of £100,000, namely £20,000. Accordingly, the disposal consideration brought into account is £80,000. If permission is not given the vendor must repay £100,000, but his disposal consideration remains in the sum of £80,000.

THE STATUS OF WARRANTIES

3.62 Contingent liabilities in respect of a warranty or representation are specifically provided for by TCGA 1992 s 49(1)(c). Given that warranties are express representations made to a purchaser of an asset, the reference to 'representation' would appear to include those which are implied. Not all representations are included; those in respect of land are excluded.

In the normal course of events, a payment in settlement of a warranty claim is made by the vendor of an asset to the purchaser in order to compensate the purchaser for the reduction in value of the asset resulting from the warranty breach. Such a payment amounts to an adjustment of the disposal consideration as between purchaser and vendor. This gives a fiscally neutral result.

EXAMPLE

A Ltd agrees to sell the entire share capital in a subsidiary to B Ltd for £1,000,000. As part of the sale agreement, A Ltd warrants that the subsidiary's plant and machinery is in good working order and worth no less than £200,000. After B Ltd's acquisition it is discovered that the plant and machinery is in a poor state of repair and only worth £50,000. As a result of the breach, A Ltd pays £150,000 by way of compensation.

In computing A Ltd's capital gain, the disposal consideration is reduced by £150,000 to £850,000. Similarly, B Ltd's acquisition expenditure is reduced to £850,000.

3.63 It is not clear how the adjustment is made so far as concerns the purchaser's acquisition cost, given that there is no express mechanism provided. However, it is reasonable to expect that an adjustment to the vendor's disposal consideration should be reflected in a corresponding adjustment to the purchaser's allowable expenditure. One analysis is to regard the warranty payment as consideration for a part disposal by the purchaser, but the reference to adjustments 'otherwise' than by discharge or repayment of tax would appear to allow the simple device of a corresponding adjustment to the purchase price. Whatever the technical merits, the second interpretation is to be preferred from the practical point of view, and is understood to reflect the practice of the Inland Revenue.

Warranties may not always be given by all the vendors, for example upon a share sale where minority shareholders with no active involvement in the management of the company are not expected to join with the majority shareholders in giving warranties. In such a case the enforcement of a warranty claim may distort the gains realised as between the various shareholders. However, this should not prevent an adjustment from being made available to those shareholders who actually meet the cost of the warranty claim.

Representations by the purchaser

3.64 In some circumstances, the purchaser will warrant a state of affairs to the vendor upon a disposal. This raises the question: If a claim is made by the vendor which is met by the purchaser, does this give rise to an adjustment for the purposes of computing the purchaser's base cost? The answer is unclear, but it is thought to be 'no' because sub-s (c) refers to a 'disposal' only, not an 'acquisition'.

EXAMPLE

Andrew operates a printing business which he agrees to sell to Richard for £100,000. The agreement is envisaged to constitute a business transfer as a going concern, so that no VAT is chargeable upon the sale. Richard warrants that he will conduct the business after the sale in the same manner as before. The business is transferred and no VAT is paid.

In breach of the warranty Richard merely stores the assets acquired. Customs require VAT of £17,500 to be paid in relation to the sale, in consequence of which Andrew claims that amount from Richard pursuant to the breach of warranty.

So far as Andrew is concerned the £17,500 recovered is paid to Customs and his net position remains the same. So far as Richard is concerned however, he requires his acquisition cost to be increased by £17,500—assuming the VAT to be irrecoverable. However, such an adjustment would not appear to be available under TCGA 1992 s 49(1)(c) if the claim is by way of damages for breach of warranty. Conversely, the amount might be capable of being added to Richard's acquisition cost under TCGA 1992 s 38(1)(a) if the contract contained a mechanism providing for the VAT element to be paid as part of the purchase price.

Indemnities

3.65 Indemnities may be given in a wide variety of circumstances, and are often encountered in the context of share sales as affording protection to the purchaser in addition to the comfort given by warranties.

An indemnity is essentially a promise to pay an amount in the event that certain contingent liabilities fall due. The factors relevant to the indemnity calculation are specifically agreed between the parties. This may be contrasted with the position under a warranty, in which case the amount payable for breach is dependent upon the actual loss suffered by the purchaser, although its quantification may be subject to express terms.

3.66 There would appear to be no good reason for distinguishing between payments made under a warranty as between vendor and purchaser, and those made under an indemnity. However, indemnities are not specifically mentioned in TCGA 1992 s 49 so that the mandatory mechanism for adjustment applicable to warranties does not apply. Three possible treatments would appear to be available.

First, payments under an indemnity could amount to an adjustment of the disposal consideration and acquisition cost of the vendor and purchaser respectively. Such adjustment could be made under TCGA 1992 s 38 so far as the purchaser is concerned, on the basis that the amount or value of the consideration given would be artificially inflated if the subsequent payment under the indemnity was not taken into account. The adjustment so far as the purchaser was concerned should be mirrored by a corresponding adjustment to the vendor's position.

Second, the indemnity could be regarded as a contingent liability of the vendor at the time of the sale, such liability falling outside TCGA 1992 s 49 and so subject to the rule in *Randall v Plumb*, **3.60** above.

Third, payments under the indemnity could be regarded as disposal consideration in respect of the purchaser's 'right to sue', in accordance with *Zim Properties*.[1] The result would be to charge in full the resulting payment in the purchaser's hands, no relief being available so far as the vendor is concerned.

1 **3.37** above.

3.67 It is considered that the first treatment will apply in most instances. The Inland Revenue accept that payments made under an indemnity between vendor and purchaser should be treated in the same way as a payment made under a warranty, with appropriate adjustments to the disposal consideration and acquisition cost:

> 'The principle in Zim Properties Limited *is not regarded as applicable to payments made under a warranty or indemnity included as one of the terms of a contract of purchase and sale. If after the completion of the sale a payment is made under a warranty or indemnity by the vendor to the purchaser, the purchaser's cost of acquisition in the event of a further disposal is reduced by the sum received, and the sale proceeds of the vendor are adjusted under [TCGA 1992 s 49]. Where such a payment is not made in accordance with the terms of the contract, the principle in* Zim Properties *may apply and the sums received by the vendor or purchaser as appropriate may be identified as capital sums derived from the asset, or from the right of action, depending on the facts of the case.*'[1]

It should be noted that for the first treatment to apply, payments must be made between vendor and purchaser, not by the vendor to some other person such as a company whose share capital is the subject of a sale; hence the practice for any tax deed of indemnity in respect of such a sale to be between the purchaser and vendor only.

1 Extra-statutory Concession D33, para 13.

Allowable expenditure and deductions

3.68 The disposor of an asset may offset against the disposal consideration such expenditure as is allowed under TCGA 1992 s 38. Three classes of expenditure are so allowed, which are restricted to:

> '(a) *the amount or value of the consideration, in money or money's worth, given by him or on his behalf wholly and exclusively for the acquisition of the asset, together with the incidental costs to him of the acquisition or, if the asset was not acquired by him, any expenditure wholly and exclusively incurred by him in providing the asset,*
> (b) *the amount of any expenditure wholly and exclusively incurred on the asset by him or on his behalf for the purpose of enhancing the value of the asset, being expenditure reflected in the state or nature of the asset at the time of the disposal, and any expenditure wholly and exclusively incurred by him in establishing, preserving or defending his title to, or to a right over, the asset,*
> (c) *the incidental costs to him of making the disposal.*'

3.69 The section continues to define what is meant by incidental costs, namely expenditure wholly and exclusively incurred for the purposes of the acquisition or disposal, consisting of fees paid to surveyors, valuers, auctioneers, accountants, agents and legal advisers and the costs of transfer or conveyance including stamp duty.[1] Furthermore, advertising expenditure is

Chargeable gains **3.72**

included, whether for finding a seller or buyer, as are costs incurred in making any valuation or apportionment required for the computation of the gain, and expenses in ascertaining market value where required by the Act.

1 TCGA 1992 s 38(2).

AMOUNT OR VALUE OF THE CONSIDERATION

3.70 Section 38(1)(a) of TCGA 1992 allows expenditure consisting of the amount or value of the consideration upon acquisition to be deducted.

The reference to 'amount' obviously applies if the acquisition is made for money. If it is not made for money then the value of the consideration will be equal to the value agreed by the parties, provided they are acting at arm's length with no suggestion of mala fides. Only if the acquisition falls within TCGA 1992 s 17, or mala fides exists, will the reference to value be to the market value of the asset acquired.[1]

1 *Stanton v Drayton Commercial Investment Co* (1982) 55 TC 286.

ENHANCEMENT EXPENDITURE AND PRESERVATION OF TITLE

3.71 Expenditure may be deducted under one of two limbs pursuant to TCGA 1992 s 38(1)(b). First, a deduction is available for enhancement expenditure on the asset. Second, a deduction is available for expenditure incurred in establishing, preserving or defending title to, or a right over, the asset. The reference to 'expenditure' precludes a deduction being available in respect of the taxpayer's own labour.[1]

So far as the first limb is concerned two points may be made. First, the expenditure in question must be incurred 'on' the asset; it is not sufficient that expenditure has the effect of enhancing the value of the asset in question. In *Aberdeen Construction*[2] an argument to the effect that a loan waiver in favour of a company could be regarded as enhancement expenditure so far as its shares were concerned was rejected. Second, the expenditure must be reflected in the state or nature of the asset at the time of its disposal.

1 *Oram v Johnson* (1980) 53 TC 319.
2 *Aberdeen Construction Group Ltd v IRC* [1978] 1 All ER 962, 52 TC 281, HL.

3.72 The application of the second limb in TCGA 1992 s 38(1)(b) raises some interesting problems. The reference to 'establishing' title is to something done once the asset in question has been acquired, not to something done upon its acquisition.[1] In *IRC v Richards Executors*[2] solicitors' fees incurred in investigating title to, and valuation of, stocks and shares were allowed to be deducted in the probate context. The valuation aspect was regarded as incidental to the investigation with the result that the 'wholly and exclusively' test was satisfied.

A case of particular interest is that of *Emmerson v Computer Time International*.[3] This was concerned with a leasehold property in respect of which the liquidator to the tenant paid rent arrears so as to obtain the landlord's consent to assign. The Court of Appeal rejected the liquidator's claim to relief—the second limb to s 38(1)(b) was considered to apply to expenditure incurred in such matters as evicting a squatter or registering a charge over property.

1 *Allison v Murray* (1975) 51 TC 57.
2 (1971) 46 TC 626.
3 (1977) 50 TC 628.

Indexation

3.73 Having established the disposal consideration and the expenditure allowable as a deduction therefrom, one further factor must be taken into account so as to complete the computation. This factor is the indexation allowance. Prior to the introduction of the indexation allowance by the Finance Act 1982, the capital gains tax charge was the subject of frequent criticism on the basis that it taxed inflationary, as distinct from real, gains. The basic rule is that the acquisition cost of the asset, and any enhancement expenditure thereon, is increased by a factor derived from the change in the retail price between the cost or expense being incurred and the asset being disposed of.

As originally introduced, pre-1982 inflationary gains were left unrelieved, but this position was rectified by the Finance Act 1988 which provided for the whole pre-1982 gain to be taken out of charge. This is achieved by substituting the asset's March 1982 value for its original cost, a process called 'rebasing'. Rebasing applies to assets acquired before 1 April 1982 and disposed of after 5 April 1988.

EXAMPLE

Susan acquired a chargeable asset in 1975 for £15,000, which she sold in June 1989 for £140,000. The actual gain on disposal is therefore £125,000. However, the acquisition cost of the asset is rebased to its March 1982 value, say £95,000. The gain is therefore reduced to £45,000 and will be further reduced on account of the indexation allowance.

CALCULATION

3.74 The calculation of the indexation allowance is governed by Ch IV Pt II TCGA 1992, which provides for the allowance to be equal to the allowable expenditure in question multiplied by a figure expressed as a decimal and determined by the formula:

$$\frac{(RD - RI)}{RI}$$

For these purposes 'RD' is the retail prices index for the month in which the disposal occurs, and 'RI' is the retail prices index for March 1982 or the month in which the expenditure was incurred, whichever is the later.[1]

The resulting figure is rounded to the nearest three decimal places.[2] If there are several different items of allowable expenditure which were incurred at different times, it is necessary to calculate the indexation allowances separately for each item.

---

1 TCGA 1992 s 54(1).
2 Ibid s 54(3).

EXAMPLE

CH acquired a chargeable asset in March 1984 for £20,000, in respect of which he incurred enhancement expenditure of £15,000 in January 1986. On October 1992 the asset is sold for £65,000. The Retail Prices Index for March 1984 was 87.48, for January 1986 it was 96.25 and for October 1992 it was 139.90.

		£	£
Sale Proceeds			65,000
Deduct:	acquisition cost	20,000	
	enhancement expenditure	15,000	

Indexation allowance:

$$\frac{139.9 - 87.48}{87.48} = 0.599$$

0.599 × 20,000   11,980

$$\frac{139.9 - 96.25}{96.25} = 0.453$$

0.453 × 15,000   6,795   (53,775)

Chargeable gain   11,225

Chapter 4

CAPITAL GAINS TAX RELIEFS

4.01 This chapter is concerned with the specific reliefs which are available in relation to compensation receipts. This is explored by reference to:

(a) Extra-statutory Concession D33, which is concerned with the decision in '*Zim Properties*';
(b) the restoration of damaged assets;
(c) the replacement of assets lost or destroyed;
(d) compulsory acquisitions; and
(e) personal compensation.

For the treatment of grants for giving up agricultural land reference should be made to *Simon's Taxes* C1.329.

1 THE DECISION IN *ZIM PROPERTIES*

4.02 The decision in *Zim Properties Ltd v Procter*[1] was explored in detail in Chapter 3. Essentially, it is authority for the proposition that a right to bring an action to enforce a claim, which claim may or may not succeed but is neither frivolous nor vexatious, is itself an 'asset' for capital gains tax purposes. Accordingly, any sum paid in settlement of that right by way of a compromise is chargeable as disposal consideration.

The decision in *Zim Properties* is in many respects inconvenient and has been widely criticised. It introduces a new asset in the form of the right to take legal action, in addition to any other assets of the plaintiff which may be regarded as forming the basis of that right. This can result in a mis-match between disposal proceeds and expenditure, and give problems in relation to the availability of reliefs.

---

1 [1985] STC 90.

4.02 *Capital gains tax reliefs*

EXAMPLE

Jane owns an exotic car worth £100,000. Due to the negligence of Philip its value falls by £60,000, under circumstances in which Jane can sue for her loss. The car is an exempt asset for capital gains tax purposes, so any disposal proceeds in respect of it are free of tax. However, Jane's rights against Philip comprise a separate asset which is not exempt. If the action were compromised by Philip agreeing to pay £60,000 that sum could be chargeable in full under the principle in *Zim Properties*.

4.03 To address this and other problems the Inland Revenue introduced Extrastatutory Concession D33. The problems are expressed in para 7 of the Concession:

> '*Some forms of compensation are specifically exempted from liability to capital gains tax . . . and these remain exempt despite the decision in* Zim Properties. *But other statutory reliefs and exemptions are not available where the receipt of the compensation is regarded as giving rise to a disposal of the right of action, not of any underlying asset to which the relief or exemption might apply. These include deferment relief for compensation applied in restoring or replacing an asset, roll-over relief for the replacement of business assets, retirement relief and private residence relief.*'

The Concession is central to the treatment of compensatory receipts and it is therefore reproduced in full in the appendix to this chapter. The Concession is expressed to apply to all open cases as at its date of issue: 19 December 1988. It should be borne in mind that the concession is concerned with capital gains tax only; it has no application to receipts which are revenue in nature.

The strict position

4.04 The Concession first considers the strict position established by the decision in *Zim Properties*. This may be summarised in the following terms:

(a) a capital gain will be realised if the compensation received in respect of the right of action exceeds that which may be deducted on account of its acquisition cost;
(b) such a right will almost invariably be acquired otherwise than by way of bargain made at arm's length, for example a right acquired by reason of a breach of contract;
(c) if the right was acquired before 10 March 1981, it is deemed to have been acquired for a sum equal to its market value on the date of acquisition. However, if it was acquired after that date it will usually be treated as having been acquired without cost;
(d) if the right was held on 31 March 1982 and disposed of after 5 April 1988, any gain will be computed by reference to the market value of the right on 31 March 1982 under the 'rebasing' rules;
(e) in computing the chargeable gain, legal or other professional costs may be deducted in the normal way; and
(f) the right of action is treated as disposed of when compensation in respect of it is actually received, in accordance with the rule in TCGA 1992 s 22(2). If a series of payments are made then each receipt is regarded as the occasion of a separate disposal.

THE APPLICATION OF THE STRICT POSITION

4.05 The strict position will be in question if the Revenue deny the availability of the concessionary treatment. In addition, it is noted that a taxpayer need not claim the concessionary treatment, indeed the application of the strict position may be beneficial in some circumstances. These may include instances where compensation is paid:

(a) in relation to a right of action acquired before 10 March 1981 which had a high market value upon its acquisition;
(b) in relation to a right of action held on 31 March 1982 with a significant open market value at that time;
(c) at a time when the taxpayer is not UK resident, so that any gain is free of tax;
(d) which allows the taxpayer to utilise personal exemptions which would otherwise be lost, or gain accelerated relief for capital losses; and
(e) which is subject to tax but at a lower rate than would otherwise apply in relation to a gain realised in a subsequent tax year.

EXAMPLE

Michael purchases a property for investment purposes for £600,000 in 1989. Due to the negligence of his solicitors a title defect in relation to the property was not identified, and Michael brings a claim for £75,000, being the fall in value of the property as a consequence of the defect. His solicitors acknowledge that they were at fault and damages are agreed in the sum of £60,000. This is paid in 1992.

If the strict position were to apply, the £60,000 would be taxable in full. If Michael were a non-UK resident in 1992 however, no capital gains tax would be payable, and upon an eventual disposal of the property at a time when he is so resident, the chargeable gain which would otherwise have arisen is effectively reduced by reference to the £60,000 damages.

THE DATE OF ACQUISITION

4.06 Where a right of action is acquired as a consequence of some contractual breach, or tortious action, it is regarded as having been acquired otherwise than by way of a bargain made at arm's length under TCGA 1992 s 17(1)(a).

The normal rule applicable to an acquisition which falls within s 17 is to treat it as effected for a consideration equal to the market value of the asset acquired. However, this is disapplied if the right was acquired after 9 March 1981, in which case only the actual consideration given for the right will be taken into account. Invariably, this means that no acquisition cost is available to the taxpayer in computing any gain upon the disposal of the right.

4.07 So far as concerns the time when a cause of action is regarded as occurring, this will follow the general principles of contract law or tort, as appropriate. In general, a right will be acquired when there is a factual situation which, if proved, provides the plaintiff with a remedy against the defendant in question. If the right accrues by reason of a breach of contract, then it accrues when that breach occurs. The fact that no damage is suffered until some time after the breach does not delay the time of acquisition. If the right accrues by reason of the commission of a tort which is not actionable unless actual damage is proved, as is the case with negligence, then it does not accrue until damage is in fact suffered.

In *Zim Properties* the right of action arose by reason of a breach of contract, occasioned by the solicitors' alleged failure to exercise due care in acting in the sale. The contract of sale was entered into on 12 July 1972. Completion was one year later in July 1973 when the purchaser refused to take the conveyance. It was decided by Warner J that the right accrued in July 1972, because that was the date upon which the taxpayer acted to its detriment in entering into a contract in inappropriate terms and so became subject to the risk of financial loss. The fact that the loss did not crystallise until 1973 did not delay the time of acquisition.

Rights and values

4.08 As stated above, the value of a right of action is in question if it was acquired before 10 March 1981 or was held on 31 March 1982. The valuation of that right should be determined according to its 'market value', which TCGA 1992 s 272(1) defines as: 'the price which [the asset in question] might reasonably be expected to fetch on a sale in the open market'.

The uncertainties associated with many legal actions will often result in the market value of the right of action being heavily discounted from the sum which is likely to be received if the action is successful. Furthermore, when the action arises by reason of a breach of contract, at a time when no loss has occurred or is certain to occur, it will be difficult to establish any value at all. In *Zim Properties* the right accrued in July 1972, but there was no loss until the following year. Whichever date was taken, Warner J was doubtful that the taxpayer's right of action could be said to have any market value.

The terms of the Concession

4.09 The strict position having been considered it is appropriate to turn to the terms of Concession D33, which may be summarised as follows:

(a) compensation derived from a right of action following the total or partial loss or destruction of, or damage to, a form of property which is an asset for capital gains tax purposes, or because some loss or disadvantage in connection with such a form of property was suffered, may be treated as if it derived from the property ('the underlying asset') and not from the right of action;
(b) as a result of the analysis in (a), a proportion of the cost of the underlying asset on normal part-disposal rules may be taken into account in computing the chargeable gain;
(c) if a relief would have been available in relation to a disposal of the underlying asset, it will also be available on the disposal of the right of action; and
(d) if a right of action is acquired in connection with some matter which does not involve a form of property which is an asset for capital gains tax purposes, then any gain accruing on its disposal is exempt from tax.

Rather confusingly, the wording in (a) shares elements in common with the provisions of TCGA 1992 s 22(1), but in practice the principle in *Zim*

Underlying assets

4.10 The operation of the Concession relies upon the concept of what is referred to as the 'underlying asset' to the right of action. It will be remembered that in *Zim Properties* the taxpayer argued, unsuccessfully, that the compensation should have been regarded as derived from the properties which would have been sold but for the alleged negligence of its solicitors. This argument was advanced on the basis that the compensation was as much derived from the properties as the sale price, had they been sold.

The adoption of the 'underlying asset' concept in the Concession gives effect to the taxpayers argument. If the Concession were applied to the facts in *Zim Properties*, the compensation received would be regarded as derived from the properties, and a normal part-disposal calculation would have applied.

EXAMPLE

Harry owns an office block which he acquired in May 1984 for £167,000. He entered into negotiations to sell the office block and a contract was entered into in December 1989, completion being delayed until December 1990. Due to the negligence of Harry's solicitors, he was unable to show good title and his purchaser refused to complete the purchase, which he was entitled to do.

The refusal was made in the context of a falling property market. Harry had contracted to sell the office block for £435,000, but in December 1990 it was valued at only £385,000. He sued his solicitors for the loss of the £50,000 in question, and the action was eventually compromised in February 1991 by the payment of £42,000. At that time the value of the office block was estimated at £350,000.

The application of the concessionary treatment gives the following result:

	£	£
Disposal proceeds		42,000
Deduct: Allowable expenditure		
$167{,}000 \times \dfrac{42{,}000}{42{,}000 + 350{,}000} =$	17,893	
Indexation allowance (May 1984–February 1991)		
$0.471 \times £17{,}893 =$	8,428	
		(26,321)
Chargeable gain		£15,679

If the strict position were applied, the £42,000 would be chargeable in full.

4.11 The Concession is silent as to the identification of 'underlying assets', although an example is given in the following terms:

> '... if compensation is paid by an estate agent because his negligence led to the sale of a building falling through, an appropriate part of the cost of the building may be deducted in computing any gain on the disposal of the right of action.'

4.11 *Capital gains tax reliefs*

The example given can be seen to be analogous to the facts in *Zim Properties*. The failure by the estate agent to exercise due care in the example results in the taxpayer being unable to realise a sale in relation to his property, in the same way as the failure in *Zim Properties*. Another example which might be given is where a taxpayer suffers damage to property, but, due to the negligence of his solicitors the action in relation to the taxpayer's loss becomes time-barred.

It would appear that the identification of the underlying asset is intended to be a reflection of the loss to which the right of action relates. If the loss relates, ultimately, to some damage or disadvantage in connection with an asset, then the part-disposal rules will apply in relation to that asset. The Concession does not explain what is to happen in circumstances where the underlying asset is sold prior to the receipt of any compensation. Presumably, a normal calculation to ascertain the gain or loss is carried out in relation to the asset, the receipt of compensation giving rise to a subsequent charge to tax. The disposal of the underlying asset will mean that any loss will be realised prior to any gain in relation to the compensation. Because losses may be carried forward and offset the position should be neutral subject to changes in tax rates, and the availability of personal allowances.

In most cases it is thought that the underlying asset will be readily identifiable, but a right of action may accrue independently of any underlying asset. This distinction, and the different tax treatment which applies, may prove a fertile ground for dispute, but ultimately the nature of the concessionary treatment gives the Inland Revenue something akin to a deciding vote in borderline cases.

No underlying asset
4.12 If a right of action yields a sum upon a disposal, but that right was not acquired in connection with a matter involving a form of property which is an asset for capital gains tax purposes then, as stated above, any gain is exempted from charge. This aspect of the concessionary treatment goes to the heart of the decision in *Zim Properties*, by reversing the rule that a right of action is by itself an asset.

The Concession gives some limited guidance as to those instances where no underlying asset will be regarded as existing; these include rights acquired:

(a) where professional advisers are negligent in connection with a tax or other financial matter. A reference is made to the giving of misleading advice or a failure to claim a tax relief within time; and
(b) in relation to a private or domestic matter.

4.13 Whilst the guidance is welcome, it leaves questions unanswered. So far as concerns the first limb to item (a) above, negligent advice in relation to tax clearly involves no form of underlying asset; the plaintiff's loss relates only to the additional tax burden which arises as a consequence of the advice—no property suffers damage or other disadvantage. However, the guidance to the effect that compensation for negligent advice in relation to some other financial matter is a more difficult area. For example, if a person suffered a loss in connection with shares by reason of his stockbroker's negligent advice, any compensation could be subject to tax on a part disposal basis by reference to the shares in respect of which the losses relate.

So far as concerns item (b) above, the reference to a 'private' matter would appear to be a reference to a matter which is individual or special to the taxpayer in question. The reference to a domestic matter would appear to be to something arising in the context of the home or family of the taxpayer, for example, damages for nuisance caused by a neighbour.

Other reliefs and exemptions
4.14 In addition to the application of the part-disposal rules, the Concession also provides that reliefs which are available in respect of the underlying asset are also available in relation to a compensatory receipt. For example, if the facts were the same as in *Zim Properties*, except the claim related to the private residence of an individual taxpayer, the sale of which would be free of capital gains tax, compensation payable by his solicitors for acting negligently in the sale would also be free of tax.

The Concession makes the full range of exemptions and reliefs available; specifically mentioned are the private residence relief (as in the above example), retirement relief and roll-over relief, as well as the specific exemptions available in relation to particular assets such as motor cars.

2 THE RESTORATION OF DAMAGED ASSETS

4.15 As discussed in Chapter 3, compensation, including insurance receipts, in respect of damage or injury to an asset is chargeable under TCGA 1992 s 22. If the asset is not lost or destroyed, then the receipt of compensation involves a part disposal, so that an appropriate part of the allowable expenditure is available. Under s 22 the time of disposal is the date upon which the compensation is received.

Accordingly, if restoration expenditure is incurred before the compensation is received, it will be taken into account in calculating the chargeable gain. Conversely, if no restoration costs have been incurred the gain will be computed by reference to the value of the asset in its unrestored state, which will normally result in a higher gain being realised.

EXAMPLE

David owns an asset which was acquired in April 1985 for £50,000. In June 1991 the asset suffered damage of some £25,000 caused by Elizabeth. An action brought by David against Elizabeth is settled by payment of the £25,000 in question in September 1991. At that time the asset, which remained in its damaged state, was worth £105,000.

4.15 *Capital gains tax reliefs*

	£	£
Disposal consideration		25,000
Deduct: Allowable expenditure		
$50{,}000 \times \dfrac{25{,}000}{25{,}000 + 105{,}000} =$	9,616	
Indexation allowance (April 1985–September 1991)		
$0.420 \times 9{,}616 \quad =$	4,039	
		(13,655)
Chargeable gain		11,345

However, the restoration of an asset before any compensation is received will normally reduce the chargeable gain which would otherwise accrue. For example, if David were to restore the asset at a cost of £25,000 in June 1991, and as a consequence the restored asset is worth £130,000 in September 1991 when the compensation is received, the calculation (ignoring the effect of TCGA 1992 s 23 at **4.17**) would be as follows:

	£	£
Disposal consideration		25,000
Deduct: Allowable expenditure		
Acquisition cost: $£50{,}000 \times \dfrac{25{,}000}{25{,}000 + 130{,}000} =$	8,065	
Enhancement cost: $£25{,}000 \times \dfrac{25{,}000}{25{,}000 + 130{,}000} =$	4,032	
Indexation allowance		
Acquisition cost (April 1985–September 1991)		
$0.420 \times £8{,}065 \quad =$	3,387	
Enhancement cost (June 1991–September 1991)		
$0.004 \times £4{,}032 \quad =$	16	
		(15,500)
Chargeable gain		9,500

4.16 The tax saving achieved by reason of the restoration expenses is a function of the value of the damaged asset after restoration. In the above example it is assumed that restoration costs of £25,000 increase the value of the asset by an equal amount, but this is not necessarily so. If the value of the asset increases by a greater amount than the expense, then the effect is to proportionally increase the gain. The position is reversed if the value of the asset increases by a lesser amount than that applied in restoration.

Compensatory receipts chargeable under TCGA 1992 s 22 may be sheltered to some extent by reinstating the asset as demonstrated above, but such reinstatement will not wholly shelter an inherent gain which would otherwise be realised. However, a specific form of relief is available where

The restoration of damaged assets **4.17**

the compensation is used to reinstate a damaged asset, in which case a deferment of the charge may be obtained pursuant to TCGA 1992 s 23.

The relieving provisions of s 23

4.17 Relief may be claimed by the taxpayer in respect of compensation for damage to assets where the compensation is applied in restoring the asset. TCGA 1992 s 23(1)) provides that the receipt of a capital sum within any one of paras (a) to (d) of TCGA 1992 s 22(1) is not to be treated as a disposal of the asset if:

(a) the capital sum is wholly applied in restoring the asset; or
(b) the capital sum is applied in restoring the asset except for a part of the capital sum which:
 (i) is not reasonably required for the purpose; and
 (ii) which is 'small' as compared with the whole capital sum; or
(c) the amount of the capital sum is small, as compared with the value of the asset.

Where s 23 applies, the compensation is not treated as a disposal receipt, but is deducted from the allowable expenditure available in relation to the asset, in computing any gain upon its subsequent disposal. For these purposes the allowable expenditure does not include an indexation allowance. The immediate effect is therefore to postpone any charge to capital gains until such time as the restored asset is sold or otherwise disposed of, but the overall effect is not necessarily fiscally neutral.

EXAMPLE

Julie owns a painting which cost £26,500 in May 1984. It was damaged by fire in January 1989 and Julie's insurance company paid £23,000 in March 1989 in respect of the damage suffered. At that time the asset was worth £53,500 in its damaged state. Julie applied the full £23,000 in restoring the asset in June 1989.

If no claim were made under s 23, the position would be as follows:

1988/89

	£	£
Disposal consideration		23,000
Deduct: Allowable expenditure		
Acquisition cost: £26,500 × $\frac{23,000}{23,000 + 53,000}$ =	8,020	
Indexation allowance (May 1984–March 1989) 0.262 × £8,020 =	2,101	
		(10,121)
Chargeable gain		12,879

If the asset were sold for £87,000 in February 1990, the position would be as follows:

4.17 *Capital gains tax reliefs*

1989/90

	£	£	£
Disposal consideration			87,000
Deduct: Allowable expenditure			
Acquisition cost: (26,500 − 8,020)		18,480	
Restoration Expenditure		23,000	
Indexation allowance:			
Acquisition cost (May 1984–February 1990) 0.351 × £18,480	6,486		
Enhancement cost (June 1989–February 1990) 0.042 × £23,000	966		
		7,452	
			(48,932)
Chargeable gain			38,068

Total gains of £50,947 have been realised. Conversely, if a claim is made under s 23, the compensation receipt is deemed not to be a disposal but is deducted from the allowable expenditure. In this example therefore, the acquisition cost of £26,500 which would otherwise be available, is reduced by £23,000 and no gain is realised in 1988/89.

If the asset were sold for £87,000 in February 1990, the position would be as follows:

	£	£	£
Disposal consideration			87,000
Deduct: Acquisition cost (as reduced)		3,500	
Restoration expenditure		23,000	
Indexation allowance:			
Acquisition cost (May 1984–February 1990) 0.351 × £26,500	9,301		
Restoration expenditure (June 1989–February 1990) 0.042 × £23,000	966		
Less: Indexation adjustment (Indexation on insurance receipt from March 1989 to February 1990) 0.070 × £23,000	(1,610)		
		8,657	
			(35,157)
Chargeable gain			51,843

4.18 The making of a claim under s 23 may therefore result in a higher total gain being realised; in the above example £51,843 as compared with £50,947. This arises because of the adjustments made on account of the indexation allowance. TCGA 1992 ss 53(3) and 57 together provide for the indexation allowance to be computed by reference to all expenditure in respect of the asset, which includes amounts relieved pursuant to TCGA 1992 s 23(1). A corresponding indexed adjustment is deducted upon a subsequent disposal.

For compensation received prior to 6 April 1988 in respect of an asset held by the taxpayer on 31 March 1982, a special relief applies in lieu of rebasing.[1]

1 TCGA 1992 Sch 4 paras 1 and 2. See *Simon's Taxes* C1.325.

4.19 The requirement under TCGA 1992 s 23(1)(a) or (b) to apply compensation in restoring the damaged asset would not appear to preclude the possibility of the restored asset being in a better and more valuable condition than before it was damaged.

LIMITATIONS

4.20 If the compensatory receipt falls within para (b) (partial restoration) or (c) ('small' receipts) of TCGA 1992 s 23(1), but there is no allowable expenditure in relation to the asset, then no relief is available and the compensation is taxable in full. If there is allowable expenditure but this is less than the compensation, then the taxpayer may elect to deduct all of that allowable expenditure from the compensation, which is then chargeable as to the excess. The expenditure so deducted is not available on a subsequent disposal of the asset.

Again, the immediate effect of making a claim is to postpone a charge to tax, in relation to so much of the compensation as equals the allowable expenditure to date.

EXAMPLE

Hilary owns an asset which was originally acquired for £11,500 in February 1986. In June 1989 it is damaged, and its value is reduced to £11,800, Hilary receives £13,000 compensation in October 1989, of which £12,500 is applied, in December 1989, in restoring the asset. It is the subject of a sale for £28,500 in May 1990.

If an election were made under TCGA 1992 s 23(2), a chargeable gain of £1,500 (ie £13,000 − £11,500) would be realised for the year 1989/90. Upon the subsequent disposal the position would be as follows:

1988/89

	£	£	£
Disposal consideration			28,500
Deduct: Acquisition cost (as reduced)		nil	
Restoration expenditure		12,500	
Indexation allowance:			
Acquisition cost (Feb 1986–May 1990) 0.306 × £11,500	3,519		
Restoration expenditure (Dec 1989–May 1990) 0.062 × £12,500	775		

4.20 *Capital gains tax reliefs*

	£	£	£
Indexation adjustment (Oct 1989–May 1990) 0.074 × £13,000	(962)		
		3,332	
			(15,832)
Chargeable gain			12,668

If no election were made, a gain would be realised in 1988/89, calculated on the normal part disposal basis, of £5,670. A further gain is realised by reason of the sale, as follows:

1989/90

	£	£	£
Disposal consideration			28,500
Deduct: Acquisition cost (11,500 − 6,028)		5,472	
Restoration expenditure		12,500	
Indexation allowance:			
Acquisition cost (Feb 1986–May 1990) 0.306 × £5,472	1,674		
Restoration expenditure (Dec 1989–May 1990) 0.062 × £12,500	775		
		2,449	
			(20,421)
Chargeable gain			8,079

WASTING ASSETS

4.21 In no case is relief available under TCGA 1992 s 23 in respect of a wasting asset.[1] However, the Inland Revenue are willing to grant relief by concession; in the case of leases, Extra-statutory Concession D1 provides as follows:

> 'Where property is held on a lease which has 50 years or less to run insurance payments received by the lessee in respect of the property will not be treated as a capital sum derived from the lease within the meaning of [TCGA 1992 s 22(1)], to the extent that they are applied by the lessee in discharging an obligation to restore any damage to the property.'

Where the Concession applies, an immediate charge to tax on the receipt is waived to the extent that it is applied in making good the damage. The Concession is silent as to the capital gains tax effect of the restoration expenditure; it would appear that such expenditure will be subject to the straightline restriction over the life of the lease provided for by TCGA 1992 s 46.

1 TCGA 1992 s 23(6).

THE USE OF THE TERM 'SMALL'

4.22 The Inland Revenue interpret the term 'small' as meaning no more than 5% in value of the sum received, in a case falling within TCGA 1992 s 23(1)(b). In a case within s 23(1)(c), the comparison would appear to be by reference to the value of the asset before any damage.

EXAMPLE

Alison owns a rare painting worth £31,000, which is damaged by reason of flooding. She receives £15,000 from her insurance company to meet the restoration costs. Provided the cost of restoration leaves an excess of no more than £750, relief should be available under TCGA 1992 s 23(1)(b). Alternatively, a compensatory receipt of no more than £1,550 may be sheltered under s 23(1)(c), whatever use was made of the monies.

PARTIAL RESTORATION

4.23 The restoration relief under TCGA 1992 s 23(1)(b) is supplemented by a separate relief under TCGA 1992 s 23(3). Compensation which would otherwise be chargeable under s 22(1)(a) or (b) only, which is derived from an asset which is not lost or destroyed, is relieved from an immediate charge so far as concerns that part which is applied in restoring the asset in question. Relief is given in the normal way, by deducting the part so applied in restoration from allowable expenditure upon a subsequent disposal of the asset. Any part of the compensation not so applied is immediately chargeable.

EXAMPLE

Rachel owns some property which was originally acquired for £10,000, but which is now worth £500,000. Her property is damaged and her insurers agree to pay £80,000 compensation.

Of that £80,000, some £76,000 is applied in making good the damage. As the surplus of £4,000 is 'small' compared with the £80,000 compensation (ie it is not greater than 5%) relief is available under TCGA 1992 s 23(1)(b). Rachel's tax position would, very broadly, be as follows:

	£
Disposal proceeds	80,000
Less:	
Allowable expenditure	(10,000)
Chargeable gain	£70,000

Alternatively, Rachel could ensure that the amount not used for restoration is more than 'small'; for example £5,000 could be retained. In this case the £75,000 applied in restoration may be sheltered under TCGA s 23(3), only £5,000 being chargeable to tax on a part-disposal basis. This result occurs because the allowable expenditure

4.23 *Capital gains tax reliefs*

includes that spent on restoration, whereas a claim under TCGA 1992 s 23(1)(b) is limited by reference to the allowable expenditure immediately before the receipt of compensation.

3 THE REPLACEMENT OF ASSETS LOST OR DESTROYED

4.24 If an asset is completely lost or destroyed, then compensation for that loss or destruction may be relieved from an immediate charge to tax if it is applied in acquiring a replacement asset.

The relief is afforded by TCGA 1992 s 23(4). This section provides for a no gain/no loss disposal in respect of the asset lost or destroyed, and for an adjustment to be made upon a subsequent disposal of the replacement asset. That adjustment reduces the acquisition cost of the replacement asset by the excess of the aggregate of the compensation and any residual or scrap value over the no gain/no loss consideration applicable to the original asset.

The compensation should be applied in acquiring the replacement asset within one year of its receipt, although the inspector has a discretion to extend that period.

EXAMPLE

Maria purchased an antique table for £6,000 in March 1983, which was destroyed by fire in June 1992. The insurance company agreed to pay £32,000, representing its agreed value. Maria purchased another table for £37,000 in April 1993, having received the insurance monies in January of that year.

Maria claims relief under s 23(4). The allowable expenditure in respect of the original table is first ascertained:

	£
Acquisition cost	6,000
Add: Indexation allowance (March 1983–January 1993) 0.659 × £6,000	3,954
Deemed disposal consideration	9,954

The total allowable expenditure of £9,954 is deemed to be the consideration for the disposal of the original table, so that neither a gain nor a loss arises.

So far as concerns the acquisition of the new table, the expenditure in relation to it is reduced as follows:

	£
Acquisition cost	37,000
Less: Consideration for original table less deemed consideration (32,000 − 9,954)	(22,046)
Deemed acquisition expenditure	14,954

Upon a subsequent disposal of the new table, the gain is calculated by reference to the reduced acquisition expenditure of £14,954.

4.25 Indexation allowance upon a subsequent disposal is governed by TCGA 1992 s 57, which provides for the indexed rise to be calculated as if the acquisition expenditure upon the new asset were not reduced. From the resulting amount a deduction is made equal to the indexed rise upon the reduction, as if it were an item of expenditure incurred on the day of the compensation receipt.

EXAMPLE

To continue the example above, upon a subsequent sale of the table by Maria in August 1993 for £40,000, a chargeable gain of £25,046 would be realised. This is calculated by reference to the disposal proceeds of £40,000 less the deemed acquisition expenditure of £14,954. No indexation allowable is available because indexation on the original acquisition cost of £32,000 from April 1993 to August 1993 (0.005 × £32,000 = £160) is less than the indexation adjustment, equal to the allowance on the reduction in base cost of the replacement asset of £22,046 from January 1993 to August 1993 (0.025 × £22,046 = £551).

4.26 There is no provision which defines what is meant by 'replacement'. The normal meaning of the term does not require the new asset to be the same in all material respects, but it should correspond so far as concerns its function and category. For example, a picture should be replaced with a picture, a table with a table and so on.

PARTIAL REPLACEMENT

4.27 Relief under TCGA 1992 s 23(4) is only available if the compensation received is wholly applied in replacing the lost asset. If only part is applied in acquiring a replacement asset then relief is available under TCGA 1992 s 23(5), provided the part not applied is less than the amount of the gain accruing on the disposal of the old asset.

The reference to the gain on disposal would appear to be a reference to the gain computed on the basis that the full amount of the compensation represents the disposal proceeds. Relief is given by reduction of the gain to the amount not applied in acquiring a replacement asset.

EXAMPLE

A picture originally costing £20,000 in March 1983 is completely destroyed in a fire in September 1989. The insurance company underwriting the risk agrees to pay the owner £100,000 representing the picture's market value prior to its destruction, and this is paid in April 1990. The owner purchases a new picture by way of replacement, which costs £70,000, in October 1990.

Relief under s 23(5) is only available if the part not applied in acquiring a replacement asset is less than the gain accruing on the disposal of the original asset. This gain is equal to:

4.27 *Capital gains tax reliefs*

	£	£
Disposal proceeds		100,000
Deduct: Acquisition cost	20,000	
Indexation allowance (March 1983–April 1990) $0.505 \times £20{,}000$	10,100	
		(30,100)
Chargeable gain		69,900

The part not applied in acquiring a replacement asset at £30,000 is less than the gain of £69,900, and therefore relief is available.

The gain of £69,900 which would otherwise be realised is reduced to £30,000, being equal to the amount not applied in acquiring a replacement asset.

The acquisition cost of the new picture is reduced by £30,000, being that part of the gain sheltered by s 23(5), as follows:

	£
Acquisition cost	70,000
Less: Reduction of gain on disposal of old picture	(30,000)
Deemed acquisition expenditure	£40,000

4 COMPULSORY ACQUISITION

4.28 Where land is acquired under compulsory powers, compensation payable in respect of that land is chargeable to tax in accordance with normal principles. The fact that the land disposal is involuntary does not prevent it from being a disposal within TCGA 1992 s 21(2).

However, the taxation treatment is subject to two specific provisions:

(a) TCGA s 245, which provides for the compensation to be apportioned as between the part relating to the land and the part relating to compensation for disturbance; and
(b) TCGA s 247, which provides roll-over relief if the compensation is applied in acquiring new land.

If the compensation includes an amount in respect of injurious affliction of land retained by the taxpayer, that amount is deemed to be in consideration of a part disposal of the retained land.[1] However, this element may be included in a claim for roll-over relief[2] under TCGA 1992 s 247.

So far as concerns the time of disposal, the position is such that when land is acquired by an authority with compulsory powers otherwise than under a contract, the disposal is regarded as taking place when the compensation is agreed or otherwise determined, for example by arbitration. For these purposes, any variation in the compensation effected upon appeal is taken into account in computing the chargeable gain. If the authority enters on to the land in pursuance of their powers before the compensation is agreed or otherwise determined then that earlier time is treated as the time of disposal.[3]

1 TCGA 1992 s 245(2).
2 By virtue of ibid s 247(6).
3 Ibid s 246.

APPORTIONMENT

4.29 Section 245 of TCGA 1992 provides for the apportionment of compensation paid on the acquisition of land by an authority with compulsory power, where that land either has or could have been acquired under those powers. The section provides for part of the compensation to be treated as 'compensation for loss of goodwill or for disturbance or otherwise'.[1]

The effect may be to disapply a capital treatment in relation to the part apportioned otherwise than in relation to the land itself. In the case of *Stoke on Trent City Council v Wood Mitchell & Co Ltd*[2] the council agreed to purchase land and premises from the claimants, on terms which provided for compensation to be paid for disturbance. The Court of Appeal decided that that part of the compensation so paid was chargeable as a trading receipt. Roskill LJ concluded:

> '... that this legislation is directed, first, to imposing a liability for capital gains tax on compensation for compulsory acquisition on the footing that such compensation is a capital sum received on the disposal of an asset; secondly, ... to enable what may be called the capital element and the income element to be separated by apportionment in such manner as the inspector or on appeal the commissioners may think just and reasonable; thirdly, to exclude from the computation of the capital gain accruing from such disposal any money charged to income tax ...'[3]

The reference to the apportionment being carried out by the inspector or the commissioners on appeal is a reference to the mechanism contained in TCGA 1992 s 52(4).

1 TCGA 1992 s 245(1).
2 [1979] STC 197.
3 Ibid at 203.

4.30 The decision in *City of Stoke on Trent* obliged the Inland Revenue to change their previous practice, whereby any element of compensation in relation to loss of profits was nonetheless included as part of the disposal consideration for capital gains tax purposes. The change in practice was announced in SP8/79, the main part of which provides as follows:

> '... any element of compensation received for temporary loss of profits [which is present in the compensation or price payable by an authority possessing compulsory powers for the acquisition of property used for the purposes of a trade or profession] ... falls to be included as a receipt taxable under Schedule D Case I or II. Compensation for losses on trading stock and to reimburse revenue expenditure, such as removal expenses and interest, will be treated in the same way for tax purposes.'

4.30 *Capital gains tax reliefs*

The change in practice applies to all cases where liability had not been finally determined as at 28 July 1978.

ROLL-OVER RELIEF

4.31 Section 247 of TCGA 1992 provides for roll-over relief upon the acquisition of land by an authority with compulsory powers. The relief applies to land disposed of after 5 April 1982. Where the consideration for the land so acquired is applied in acquiring other land, then any gain realised on the disposal may be rolled over and deducted from the allowable expenditure of the replacement land.

It is not necessary for the authority to exercise its powers, but it is a precondition that:

> '... the landowner did not take any steps, by advertising or otherwise, to dispose of the old land or to make his willingness to dispose of it known to the authority or others.'[1]

Relief is available where the whole of the consideration for the disposal is applied in acquiring replacement land.[2]

---

1 TCGA 1992 s 247(1)(b).
2 Ibid s 247(2).

EXAMPLE

A Ltd has a cloth manufacturing business which is operated from a factory acquired in September 1985 for £165,000. The local authority agrees in October 1989 to purchase the factory for £305,000, as an alternative to exercising its compulsory powers of acquisition. Legal fees of £3,250 are incurred.

If relief is claimed under TCGA 1992 s 247(2), the gain arising upon the disposal of the factory is first ascertained:

	£	£
Disposal consideration		305,000
Less: Acquisition cost	165,000	
Incidental costs of disposal	3,250	
Indexation allowance (September 1985–October 1989) 0.231 × £165,000	38,115	
		(206,365)
Chargeable gain		98,635

Upon a subsequent acquisition by A Ltd of another factory for £325,000, the chargeable gain arising upon the old factory may be rolled over. The allowable expenditure is reduced by the amount of the rolled-over gain:

	£
Acquisition cost	325,000
Less: Rolled over gain	(98,635)
Deemed acquisition cost	226,365

4.32 To qualify for relief the replacement land must be acquired in the four year period beginning 12 months before the disposal of the original land to the acquiring authority. This period may be extended at the discretion of the Inland Revenue.[1]

No relief is available in respect of replacement land to which the private residence exemption may apply on a subsequent disposal within 6 years of its acquisition by the taxpayer.[2]

1 TCGA 1992, s 247(5)(b).
2 Ibid s 248(1). And see *Simon's Taxes* C2.13.

4.33 If a disposal is made before 6 April 1988 and the land was owned on 31 March 1992, a special relief applies in lieu of rebasing, pursuant to TCGA 1992 Sch 4 paras 1 to 4.[1]

1 *Simon's Taxes* C2.116.

Depreciating assets
4.34 If the replacement asset is a depreciating asset, no roll-over relief is given. Instead the gain is held over but becomes chargeable on the earlier of the disposal of the replacement asset or the end of the ten-year period from its acquisition. No adjustment is made to the taxpayer's acquisition cost of the replacement asset.[1] Freehold land cannot be regarded as a depreciating asset, but a leasehold interest with a term of less than 60 years unexpired is.[2]

A claim to roll over the gain may be made upon the subsequent acquisition of land by the taxpayer which is not a depreciating asset before the held over gain becomes chargeable.[3]

1 TCGA 1992 s 248(3).
2 Ibid ss 44(1) and 154(7).
3 Ibid ss 154 and 248.

Compulsory acquisition of freehold by a tenant
4.35 The availability of roll-over relief under TCGA 1992 s 247 is extended by a Statement of Practice,[1] which provides for the relief to be claimed by a landlord in circumstances where leasehold tenants exercise statutory rights to purchase the freehold interest, or require the grant of a new lease. The statutory rights in question are those conferred by the Leasehold Reform, Housing and Urban Development Act 1993.

Section 247 does not require a compulsory purchase to be effected, it is sufficient that the 'buyer' has those powers. Whilst not expressly dealt with in the Statement, it would appear to be the case that relief remains available even if the tenant in question did not acquire the freehold or a new lease under the 'compulsory' procedure, provided that the tenant had the statutory right to acquire. Unfortunately, given some of the complex conditions which may be in question, it may not always be possible for the landlord to be certain as to the tenant's rights.

1 SP 13/93. Before that see SP 7/90.

5 PERSONAL COMPENSATION

4.36 Compensation for personal or professional injury is exempt from capital gains tax by TCGA 1992 s 51(2). The exemption, which applies to individuals, only refers to:

> 'sums obtained by way of compensation or damages for any wrong or injury suffered by an individual in his person or in his profession or vocation . . .'

The exemption covers physical injury, as well as distress, embarassment and loss of reputation or dignity. Damages for defamation or discrimination are obvious examples. Extra-statutory Concession D33, which is appended to this chapter considers the ambit of the exclusion at para 12.

Damages for defamation received by a company may not be sheltered by reason of s 51(2) above. It might therefore be said that such damages are subject to corporation tax on capital gains by reason of the decision in *Zim Properties*; ie on the basis that the taxpayer company disposes of its right to bring an action to sue for defamation, which right is a separate asset within the charge to tax. Relief would appear to be available pursuant to Extra-statutory Concession D33 on the basis that there is no 'underlying asset' to which the damages relate, although it may be possible for the Inland Revenue to argue that the damages make good some loss or disadvantage suffered in connection with the taxpayer's goodwill.

APPENDIX
EXTRA-STATUTORY CONCESSION D33

Capital gains tax on compensation and damages

INTRODUCTION

1 A person who receives a capital sum derived from an asset is treated for the purposes of capital gains tax as disposing of that asset. The case of *Zim Properties Ltd v Procter* [1985] STC 90, (1984) has established that the right to take court action for compensation or damages is an asset for capital gains tax purposes. It follows that a person who receives compensation or damages, whether by court order or arbitration or by negotiated settlement as a result of a cause of action may be regarded as disposing of the right of action. A capital gain may accrue as a result.

THE STRICT POSITION

2 Cost of acquisition
A capital gain will accrue if the capital sum received as compensation exceeds the amount which may be deducted as the cost of acquiring the right of action. A right of action will almost invariably be acquired otherwise than by way of bargain made at arm's length. Special rules for determining the cost of acquisition apply in these circumstances. Where the right of action was acquired on or before 9 March 1981, it is deemed to have been acquired for a sum equal to its market value on the date of acquisition. Where it was acquired on or after 10 March 1981 and there was no disposal of the right of action corresponding to the claimant's acquisition of it, then where—as is usually the case—the taxpayer gave no consideration to acquire it, it is treated as having been acquired without cost.

If the cause of action was held on 31 March 1982 and disposed of on or after 6 April 1988, it will, in accordance with the rules in Finance Act 1988, be deemed to have been disposed of and immediately reacquired at its open market value on 31 March 1982.

If a right of action passes on the death of the claimant, it is treated as acquired at its open market value on the date of death.

In computing the gain or loss, a deduction may be made for any legal and professional fees incurred in pursuing the claim. If the action in respect of a claim of substance fails, or if the expenses exceed the compensation, a capital loss may accrue.

3 Date of acquisition
A right of action accrues and so is acquired by a person for capital gains tax purposes when, for example as a result of a breach of contract or the negligent actions of another person (tort), he or she suffers actual loss or damage.

4 Market value on acquisition
In practice, where relevant, the Board of Inland Revenue will be prepared to accept a valuation which gives rise to neither chargeable gain nor allowable loss.

Capital gains tax reliefs

5 Date of disposal
The right of action is treated as disposed of when a capital sum derived from it is received, and if a series of capital sums is received, each receipt is the occasion of a separate disposal.

6 Rebasing to 31 March 1982
If an asset which was held on 31 March 1982 is disposed of on or after 6 April 1988, the gain or loss is normally computed as if it had been disposed of and immediately reacquired at its open market value on 31 March 1982. If an underlying asset were held on 31 March 1982, but a right of action related to that asset were acquired after 31 March 1982, the rebasing provisions would apply on the disposal of the underlying asset but not on the disposal of the right of action.

7 Reliefs and exemptions
Some forms of compensation are specifically exempted from liability to capital gains tax (see paragraph 12 below) and these remain exempt despite the decision in *Zim Properties*. But other statutory reliefs and exemptions are not available where the receipt of the compensation is regarded as giving rise to a disposal of the right of action, not of any underlying asset to which the relief or exemption might apply. These include deferment relief for compensation applied in restoring or replacing an asset, roll-over relief for the replacement of business assets, retirement relief and private residence relief.

RELIEF BY CONCESSION

8 Where a gain arises on the disposal of a right of action, the case may alternatively, by concession, be treated in accordance with the following paragraphs of this statement.

9 Underlying assets
Where the right of action arises by reason of the total or partial loss or destruction of or damage to a form of property which is an asset for capital gains tax purposes, or because the claimant suffered some loss or disadvantage in connection with such a form of property, any gain or loss on the disposal of the right of action may by concession be computed as if the compensation derived from that asset, and not from the right of action. As a result, a proportion of the cost of the asset, determined in accordance with normal part-disposal rules, and indexation allowance, may be deducted in computing the gain. For example, if compensation is paid by an estate agent because his negligence led to the sale of a building falling through, an appropriate part of the cost of the building may be deducted in computing any gain on the disposal of the right of action.

The gain may be computed by reference to the original cost of the underlying asset, with time-apportionment if appropriate if the asset was acquired before 6 April 1965, or by reference to its market value on 6 April 1965. For disposals on or after 6 April 1988, the gain may be computed in appropriate cases by reference to the value of the asset on 31 March 1982.

10 Other reliefs and exemptions
If the relief was or would have been available on the disposal of the relevant underlying asset, it will be available on the disposal of the right of action. For

example, if compensation is derived from a cause of action in respect of damage to a building suffered by reason of professional negligence, and the compensation is applied in restoring the building, deferment relief under [TCGA 1992 s 23] will be available as if the compensation derives from the building itself and not from the right of action.

Other reliefs which may become available in this way include private residence relief, retirement relief and roll-over relief. The Board of Inland Revenue will be prepared to consider extending time limits in cases where because of a delay in obtaining a capital sum in compensation, the normal time limit allowed for a relief has elapsed. If the right of action relates to an asset which is specifically exempt from capital gains tax, such as a motor car, any gain on the disposal of the right of action may be treated as exempt.

11 No underlying asset
A right of action may be acquired by a claimant in connection with some matter which does not involve a form of property which is an asset for capital gains tax purposes. This may be the case where professional advisers are said to have given misleading advice in a tax or other financial matter, or to have failed to claim a tax relief within the proper time. Actions may be brought in relation to private or domestic matters. Where the action does not concern loss of or damage to, or loss in connection with, a form of property which is an asset for capital gains tax purposes, the approach in paragraph 9 above of treating the compensation as deriving from the asset itself is not appropriate. In these circumstances any gain accruing on the disposal of the right of action will be exempt from capital gains tax.

OTHER POINTS

12 Personal compensation or damages
[TCGA 1992 s 51(2)] provides that 'sums obtained by way of compensation or damages for any wrong or injury suffered by an individual in his person or his profession or vocation' are not chargeable to capital gains tax. The words 'wrong or injury' include breaches of contractual duties and torts (in Scotland, delicts). If the exemption would have applied to damages received for any wrong or injury, it also applies to any compensation for professional negligence in relation to an action in respect of that wrong or injury.

The words 'in his person' are to be read in distinction to 'in his finances' but they embrace more than physical injury so that distress, embarrassment, loss of reputation or dignity may all be suffered 'in the person'. Compensation or damages for unfair or unlawful discrimination suffered 'in the person' and for libel or slander (in Scotland, defamation) would thus be included. Similarly the words 'in his profession or vocation' refer to compensation or damages suffered by an individual in his professional capacity such as unfair discrimination, libel or slander (in Scotland, defamation) as distinct from 'in his finances'. If the compensation is received by the members of a partnership, each member, in Scotland as elsewhere, is treated as receiving a share of the compensation. The exemption is extended by concession to such compensation received by an individual in his trade or employment.

Capital gains tax reliefs

The exemption also extends to compensation received by a person other than the individual who suffered the wrong or injury, such as relatives or personal representatives of a deceased person. It also extends to compensation for emotional distress caused by the death of another person, and compensation for loss of financial support.

It does not apply to compensation for any other wrong or injury suffered by any person other than an individual.

13 Indemnity payments

The principle in *Zim Properties* is not regarded as applicable to payments made under a warranty or indemnity included as one of the terms of a contract of purchase and sale. If after the completion of the sale a payment is made under a warranty or indemnity by the vendor to the purchaser, the purchaser's cost of acquisition in the event of a further disposal is reduced by the sum received, and the sale proceeds of the vendor are adjusted under [TCGA 1992 s 49]. Where such a payment is not made in accordance with the terms of the contract, the principle in *Zim Properties* may apply and the sums received by the vendor or purchaser as appropriate may be identified as capital sums derived from the asset, or from the right of action, depending on the facts of the case.

14 Date of commencement

The concessions and practices set out this Statement will apply to all open cases on the date of issue.

Chapter 5

DIRECT TAXES AND THE DEFENDANT

5.01 Where a payment of compensation is made, the position of the defendant, as the payer, must be considered quite separately from that of the plaintiff. Specifically, it must be considered whether the payment will attract any form of relief in respect of tax. The primary source of relief is as a deduction in computing the profits of the defendant's trade, profession or vocation for the purposes of Case I or Case II of Schedule D.

It may also be considered whether relief is available:

(a) in the case of an investment company as an expense of management;
(b) as a deduction from rental income;
(c) in respect of interest; or
(d) as allowable expenditure for the purposes of computing capital gains.

1 THE GENERAL SCHEME OF THE TAXES ACT

5.02 The charge to income tax under Schedule D is in respect of the annual profits or gains arising or accruing in respect of any trade (Case I) or any profession or vocation (Case II). Section 60 of the TA 1988 refers to the 'full amount of the profits or gains of the year'. When placed in the context of commercial life it is clear that this reference is to the excess of receipts over the expenditure necessary to earn those receipts.

If an item of expenditure may properly be taken into account in computing profits in accordance with generally accepted commercial accounting principles, then that item should be deductible for the purpose of computing profits subject to tax. However, statute expressly prohibits the deduction of certain expenditure, and expressly permits deductions which may not otherwise have been made. In the words of Lord Clyde:

> '... in considering what is the true balance of profits and gains in the Income Tax Acts . . . you deal in the main with ordinary principles of commercial accounting. [The Acts] expressly exclude a number of deductions and allowances, some of which according to the ordinary principles of commercial accounting might be

5.02 *Direct taxes and the defendant*

allowable. But where these ordinary principles are not invaded by Statute they must be allowed to prevail.'[1]

1 *Lothian Chemical Co Ltd v IRC* (1926) 11 TC 508 at 520–521.

5.03 Unless subject to an express statutory provision, the general scheme of the Taxes Act is to allow an item of expenditure if:

(a) it is deductible in accordance with generally accepted commercial accounting principles;
(b) it was 'wholly and exclusively' incurred for the purposes of the trade or profession in question;
(c) it is revenue in nature as distinct from capital; and
(d) it has actually been expended.

If no trade is in existence then no deduction may as a general rule be made. This rule is relaxed in respect of expenditure incurred before the commencement of a trade by giving relief for expenditure incurred up to seven years before its commencement.[1] In addition, there are specific reliefs applicable to expenditure incurred after cessation.

1 TA 1988 s 401. *Simon's Taxes* B3.1204.

PROHIBITED EXPENDITURE

5.04 The primary provision prohibiting the deduction of expenditure is contained in TA 1988 s 74 which applies to the computation of profits under Case I or Case II of Schedule D.

This section provides that in computing the amount of the profits or gains to be charged under Case I or Case II of Schedule D, no sum shall be deducted in respect of the items listed in paras (*a*) to (*q*).

Where a deduction for expenditure is sought, the general words in para (*a*) are normally considered first. This paragraph, which is considered in detail at **5.06** below, applies in respect of:

'(a) any disbursements or expenses, not being money wholly and exclusively laid out or expended for the purposes of the trade, profession or vocation;'

In addition to the general prohibition, a number of specific exclusions also exist, which apply in respect of:

'(b) any disbursements or expenses of maintenance of the parties, their families or establishments, or any sums expended for any other domestic or private purposes distinct from the purposes of the trade, profession or vocation;
(c) the rent of the whole or any part of any dwelling-house or domestic offices, except any such part as is used for the purposes of the trade, profession or vocation, and where any such part is so used, the sum so deducted shall not, unless in any particular case it appears that having regard to all the circumstances some greater sum ought to be deducted, exceed two-thirds of the rent bona fide paid for that dwelling-house or those offices;
(d) any sum expended for repairs of premises occupied, or for the supply, repairs or alterations of any implements, utensils or articles employed, for

the purposes of the trade, profession or vocation, beyond the sum actually expended for those purposes;
(e) *any loss not connected with or arising out of the trade, profession or vocation;*
(f) *any capital withdrawn from, or any sum employed or intended to be employed as capital in, the trade, profession or vocation, but so that this paragraph shall not be treated as disallowing the deduction of any interest;*
(g) *any capital employed in improvements of premises occupied for the purposes of the trade, profession or vocation;*
(h) *any interest which might have been made if any such sums as aforesaid had been laid out at interest;*
(j) *any debts except:*
   (i) *a bad debt proved to be such;*
   (ii) *a debt or part of a debt released by the creditor wholly and exclusively for the purposes of his trade profession or vocation as part of a relevant arrangement or compromise; and*
   (iii) *a doubtful debt to the extent estimated to be bad, meaning, in the case of the bankruptcy or insolvency of the debtor, the debt except to the extent that any amount may reasonably be expected to be received on the debt;*
(k) *any average loss beyond the actual amount of loss after adjustment;*
(l) *any sum recoverable under an insurance or contract of indemnity.'*

Paras (*m*) to (*q*) relate, broadly speaking, to annuity payments, interest and royalties.

In addition to the general terms of s 74, there are further specific provisions[1] which apply to a variety of classes of expenditure, but none are directly in question in relation to compensation payments.

---

1 For which see *Simon's Taxes* B3.1202.

ALLOWABLE EXPENDITURE

5.05 A large number of provisions have been enacted which provide for certain items of expenditure to be allowable in computing profits under Case I or Case II of Schedule D. Of particular relevance are those relating to employees. Four categories of payment may attract relief.

First, expenditure in respect of restrictive undertakings given by employees to which TA 1988 s 313 applies[1] may be deducted by reason of FA 1988 s 73(2).

Second, expenditure on qualifying courses of training for employees with a view to their retraining for future employment otherwise than with their current employer is expressly allowable by virtue of TA 1988 s 589.[2]

Third, a 'redundancy payment' or 'other employer's' payment made in respect of employment wholly in a trade, profession or vocation carried on by the employer is allowable as a deduction pursuant to TA 1988 s 579(2). Any rebate which may be recovered by the employer reduces the deduction available.[3] If the payment is made after the trade (etc) has been discontinued, relief is available by reason of the payment being treated as made on the last day on which the trade (etc) was carried on.[4] The relief is extended to investment companies so as to allow a deduction as an expense of management,[5] as well as circumstances where payment is made in respect of employment wholly in maintaining or managing property where expenses are eligible for relief under TA 1988 s 25(1) or s 28.[6]

5.05 *Direct taxes and the defendant*

Fourth, payments by way of addition to a redundancy payment or to the corresponding amount of any other employer's payment which would have been allowable but for the permanent discontinuance of the trade, profession, vocation or business of the employer are treated as made on the last day on which the trade (etc) was carried on by virtue of TA 1988 s 90. Relief is limited to additional payments to the extent that they do not exceed three times the amount of the redundancy payment or of the corresponding amount of the other employer's payment.[7]

1 TA 1988 s 313 is considered at **6.75** below.
2 *Simon's Taxes* B3.1431.
3 TA 1988 s 579(2)(a).
4 Ibid s 579(2)(b).
5 Ibid s 579(3).
6 Ibid s 579(4).
7 Ibid s 90(2).

2 EXPENDITURE FOR THE PURPOSES OF THE TRADE

5.06 The right to deduct expenditure is limited by the general words in TA 1988 s 74(1)(a) to the effect that expenditure be 'wholly and exclusively laid out or expended for the purposes of the trade'.

The word 'wholly' is concerned with the amount of the expenditure in question, whilst the word 'exclusively' is concerned with the intention or object of the payer. Expenditure which has an element of non-trade purpose may not be deducted, even if the trade purpose was the primary reason for incurring the expenditure.

5.07 In *Mallalieu v Drummond*,[1] a claim by a barrister to deduct expenditure on clothing for use in court was dismissed on the basis that the clothing had a dual purpose. The fact that the clothes in question were purchased solely for use in court was insufficient, as the taxpayer's expenditure served two purposes, namely the purposes of her business as well as her requirement to be clothed. The House of Lords held that expenses of the kind in question were in part for the advantage and benefit of the taxpayer as a human being. The inextricable mix of private and business purposes allowed for no apportionment to be made, and accordingly, the taxpayer's claim for relief was rejected.

Whilst the taxpayer did not have a conscious motive other than that of the etiquette of her profession, the expenditure was also incurred for other objects albeit they did not represent a conscious motive. Lord Brightman said:

> '*I reject the notion that the object of a taxpayer is inevitably limited to the particular conscious motive in mind at the moment of expenditure. Of course the motive of which the taxpayer is conscious is of a vital significance, but it is not inevitably the only object which the commissioners are entitled to find to exist.*'[2]

Similar considerations arose in the case of *MacKinlay v Arthur Young McClelland Moores & Co*[3] in which expenditure incurred by a large firm of accountants in respect of the relocation expenses of a partner was held not to be deductible. The expenditure was tainted by the subsidiary purpose of assisting a partner to move his private residence.

1 [1983] 2 All ER 1095, [1983] STC 665, HL.
2 Ibid at 673.
3 [1989] STC 898.

The decision in Strong

5.08 In *Strong & Co of Romsey Ltd v Woodifield*[1] the taxpayer was a brewing company which also owned licensed houses. A customer sleeping in one of the taxpayer's inns was injured by the falling of a chimney upon him, and as a result the taxpayer company had to pay damages and costs of some £1,490. In the House of Lords, the Lord Chancellor, Lord Loreburn, described the general scheme of the then Taxes Act (Income Tax Act 1842) in the following terms:

> '*That which has to be assessed is the balance of the profits or gains of a trade; that is to say, the sum left after subtracting the proper deductions from the profits and gains. A deduction may be allowed on account of loss, and this is a loss. The Act does not affirmatively state what losses may be deducted. It furnishes merely negative information. A deduction cannot be allowed on account of loss not connected with or arising out of such trade. That is one indication. And no sum can be deducted unless it be money wholly and exclusively laid out or expended for the purposes of such trade. That is another indication. Beyond that the Act is silent.*'[2]

Having reviewed the general scheme of deductions allowed under the Act, his Lordship continued so as to identify the general rule:

> '*I think only such losses can be deducted as are connected with it in the sense that they are really incidental to the trade itself. They cannot be deducted if they are mainly incidental to some other vocation, or fall on the trader in some character other than that of trader.*'

Applying that formula to the circumstances of the taxpayer company his Lordship concluded that:

> '. . . *the loss sustained by the [taxpayer company] was not really incidental to their trade as innkeepers, and fell upon them in their character not of traders but of householders.*'

This approach was echoed by Lord Davey who was of the view that it is not enough that a payment is made in the course of, or is connected with, the trade or is made out of the profits of the trade. To be deductible, the payment must be made for the purposes of earning the profits. Accordingly, no deduction for the expenditure incurred by the taxpayer was available.

1 [1906] AC 448, 5 TC 215.
2 5 TC 215 at 219.

5.09 *Direct taxes and the defendant*

5.09 The approach taken by the House of Lords involved a very fine distinction, which was illustrated by a number of examples. Lord Loreburn noted that a loss sustained by a railway company in compensating passengers for injuries suffered by reason of an accident whilst travelling might be deducted. On the other hand, if a person with a grocers shop became liable for damages because a window shutter from his house above it fell and injured a man walking in the street, the loss would not be deductible.

The point being made would appear to be that a distinction is to be drawn between losses sustained by virtue of a person's ownership and occupation of premises, which are not deductible, and those sustained from plant used for the purposes of the taxpayer's trade, which are. Lord Clyde made a passing reference to the rule in the case of *Renfrew Town Council v IRC*:

> 'Take, for instance, the case of a transport company which unavoidably incurs liability for damages to persons injured by accident. The damages are revenue charges because they are expenses inseparably connected with the conduct of the business from year to year.'[1]

1 (1934) 19 TC 13 at 18–19.

5.10 In practice, the decision in *Strong* would not appear to be rigorously applied by the Inland Revenue, so that damages for wrongful or unfair dismissal of employees and directors, for example, should in general be regarded as deductible. Where such sums can be said to be paid in order to preserve the goodwill of the workforce generally, to avoid adverse publicity and to save management time, there are grounds for saying that the dicta in *Strong* has no application in any event.

Specifically, reference may be made to the following statement of Viscount Cave LC:

> '. . . a sum of money expended, not of necessity and with a view to a direct and immediate benefit to the trade, but voluntarily and on the grounds of commercial expediency, and in order indirectly to facilitate the carrying on of the business, may yet be expended wholly and exclusively for the purposes of the trade.'[1]

1 *British Insulated and Helsby Cables Ltd v Atherton* [1926] AC 205 at 211.

PENALTIES FOR ILLEGAL ACTS

5.11 In *IRC v Von Glehn & Co Ltd*[1] the Court of Appeal refused a deduction in respect of a penalty imposed upon the taxpayer company for a breach of wartime regulations. The penalty in question was a sum:

> '. . . which the persons conducting the trade have had to pay because in conducting it they have so acted as to render themselves liable to this penalty. It is not a commercial loss, and I think when the Act speaks of a loss connected with or arising out of such trade it means a commercial loss connected with or arising out of the trade.'[2]

The dismissal of the taxpayer's argument may be regarded as an example of a wider principle that an expense incurred in consequence of an infraction of the law or as a penalty for doing an illegal act should not be regarded as a deductible expense; businesses can perfectly well be carried on without such infractions. For example, a person dealing in goods who adulterates those goods and is fined in consequence cannot seek to deduct the fine.[3]

In *Von Glehn* the court declined to decide whether damages paid in civil proceedings in respect of carrying on business in a negligent manner could be deducted; it would appear that a deduction may be allowed in some circumstances. Damages for libel may be cited as an example, if the libel is published in the course of a newspaper business. Such a loss may be in the contemplation of the taxpayer and in the nature of a commercial loss.[4]

1 [1920] 2 KB 553.
2 Per Warrington LJ, ibid at 569.
3 Per Lord Sterndale MR, ibid at 564 and 565.
4 *IRC v Warnes & Co* [1919] 2 KB 444, per Rowlatt J at 452.

INTENTION

5.12 In seeking to establish that expenditure was incurred for trade purposes, the taxpayer's intention in incurring the expense must be determined. This is a question of fact for the Commissioners, and should be determined subjectively. If the taxpayer can demonstrate that expenditure was incurred for the purposes of his trade, then no further test need be satisfied to the effect that the expenditure in question resulted in profit.

The relevant test was referred to in *Robinson v Scott Bader Co Ltd*,[1] which was concerned with the secondment of an employee to the taxpayer company's subsidiary. In that case a deduction in respect of the employee's salary was obtained, as the success of the taxpayer company's business depended upon that of its subsidiary:

> '*In my judgment "purpose" contains an ingredient of "intention". It is very difficult, but perhaps not impossible, to determine this without some element of subjectivity. Indeed, in many cases the test will be wholly subjective. When deciding whether or not a solicitor is entertaining a client to lunch, the test must be wholly subjective. The solicitor is entertaining; it may be because it is an old client; it may be because it is the only opportunity to discuss the business. The court has to decide the real purpose . . .*'[2]

The example given is now subject to the statutory prohibition on deducting business entertaining expenses in TA 1988 s 577 but the general principle remains the same. The decision in *Robinson* may be contrasted with that in *Watney Combe Reid & Co Ltd v Pike*[3] where ex gratia payments to tenants of tied houses were made upon their being given notice to quit. A deduction was disallowed on the basis that the taxpayer company's trade did not benefit from the payment, the benefit accrued to another member company within the group.

1 [1981] STC 436.
2 Per Waller LJ, ibid at 439.
3 [1982] STC 733.

5.13 *Direct taxes and the defendant*

5.13 In *Morley v Lawford & Co*[1] a deduction was allowed for payments made pursuant to a guarantee given by the taxpayer in relation to an exhibition from which the taxpayer expected to obtain orders for work. The taxpayer company showed that it had been informed by a representative of the authorities organising the exhibition that guarantors would be given preference on the allotment of contracts for work, and that the guarantee was given with the sole object of obtaining a contract for work. No opportunity to tender for work was in fact given to the taxpayer who accordingly did no work at the exhibition, but this did not prejudice the availability of a deduction.

1 (1928) 14 TC 229.

EXPENDITURE AND OBLIGATION

5.14 To obtain a deduction for expenditure it is not necessary for it to have been payable by reason of some obligation, whether contractual or otherwise, placed upon the payer. There is no rule against the deduction of expenditure with an ex gratia element.

In *Smith v Incorporated Council of Law Reporting for England and Wales*[1] the taxpayer company sought a deduction in respect of a gratuity paid to a reporter upon retirement after long service. The taxpayer was successful before both the Commissioners and on appeal to the High Court, where it was noted that the expectation of receiving a gratuity upon retirement meant that the reporters were willing to accept a lower salary. Similarly, the voluntary discharge of debts by the purchaser of a business, which were the responsibility of the vendor, was allowed in *Cooke v Quick Shoe Repair Service*[2] on the basis that such payments preserved the goodwill of the business so acquired. Conversely, a payment to enhance goodwill should not attract relief as it would be regarded as a capital payment.

1 [1914] 3 KB 674, 6 TC 477.
2 (1949) 30 TC 460.

APPORTIONMENT

5.15 Where expenditure has been incurred in respect of a number of items, some of which are for business purposes and some not, an apportionment should be made and the relevant parts allowed or disallowed as appropriate.

Expenditure in respect of a single item may also be apportioned, where part can be said to have been incurred for the purposes of the payer's trade. Excessive remuneration paid to a director, for example, may be allowed up to the sum which might reasonably have been paid; the excess is disallowed.[1] On the other hand, a non-trading purpose may taint the entirety of the expenditure in question, as in *Ransom v Higgs*[2] in the context of a tax avoidance scheme.

Of particular importance is the rule that no deduction is available for expenditure incurred for mixed purposes, as in *Mallalieu v Drummond* (**5.07** above). In the case of *Bowden v Russell and Russell*[3] a solicitor sought a deduction for expenditure incurred in attending meetings of legal associations in the USA and Canada. Such visits were partly for business reasons and partly for social purposes (his wife accompanied him). The Inland Revenue were successful in their contention that no deduction was available. At no point in time was it possible to say that the solicitor had ceased travelling for business and had started to travel for personal reasons.

1 *Copeman v Flood (William) & Sons Ltd* [1941] 1 KB 202, 24 TC 53.
2 [1974] 3 All ER 949, 50 TC 1.
3 [1965] 2 All ER 258.

Losses suffered by depositors

5.16 The treatment of losses suffered by depositors, as a result of the failure of the Bank of Credit and Commerce International, was the subject of Inland Revenue guidance in the November 1993 issue of the *Tax Bulletin*.

The guidance given was to the effect that such losses may be deductible for the purposes of computing profits under Case I or II of Schedule D if the account in respect of which the loss arose was used for the purposes of the trade, profession or vocation. Such a loss may be deducted 'up to a maximum of the amount normally kept in the account to meet the ordinary banking requirements of the business'. A provision in respect of such an expected loss may also attract relief.

Furthermore, a deduction was expressed to be available for monies lost in respect of accounts 'held solely to facilitate the issue of letters of credit or guarantees to trade creditors' with the proviso that the debts in question be incurred as revenue expenses.

In circumstances where a deduction has been given but monies are received from the Deposit Protection Board for the loss, that receipt is taken into account as a taxable receipt.

3 EXPENDITURE AND PROVISIONS

5.17 The accruals concept of commercial accounting requires revenue to be matched with the expenses incurred in earning it so as to accurately state profits for a given period. This means that expenses should be recognised in the period in which they are incurred, not in a latter period in which they happen to be paid. The convention of 'prudence' plays a part in this matching process by requiring that whenever a judgment is exercised or an estimate made about the future, the pessimistic view should be taken. Profits should not therefore be taken until they are certain, but provision should be made for all losses whether they are realised or not.

In drawing up accounts for a trade, therefore, a provision for future expense may be included, but the general rule for the purposes of computing taxable profits is that no deduction is available unless the expenditure has actually been incurred. In *Mersey Docks & Harbour Board v Lucas*[1] no deduction was available in forming a sinking fund to extinguish debt at a future date.[2]

5.17 *Direct taxes and the defendant*

---

1 (1883) 8 App Cas 891, 2 TC 25.
2 Also see *RTZ Oil and Gas Ltd v Elliss* [1987] STC 512.

5.18 There is however no rule preventing the deduction of amounts which the taxpayer is required to make in the future, provided a sufficiently accurate calculation can be made as to the amounts falling due.[1] In the leading case of *Owen v Southern Railway of Peru Ltd*[2] the taxpayer company claimed a deduction for accrued compensation which it was required to pay under Peruvian law upon employees leaving its service. The compensation payable was determined by reference to the length of service of the employee and his rate of pay.

It was considered that one of two methods could be adopted in relation to the payments. Allowances could be given for the year in which a payment is actually made, alternatively some scheme of current provision could be adopted which was the method for which the appellant contended. After reviewing the factors which would have to be taken into account in calculating the appropriate provision, Lord Radcliffe concluded that the company's calculations could not be accepted as sufficiently accurate to allow the deduction. Furthermore, it was questioned whether a proper method could be found at all and accordingly the taxpayer's appeal was dismissed.

The principles which emerged in *Southern Railway of Peru* were applied in *IRC v Titaghur Jute Factory Ltd*[3] in which a UK company operating in India was successful in obtaining a deduction for a closing provision in its 1971 accounts in respect of its accrued liability to pay leaving gratuities to employees. Such amounts were calculated by reference to salary and length of service, but it was accepted that the provision was a sufficiently accurate computation of the accrued liability at that time:

> '*The true cost to the employer of employing his labour force in a year includes not only the actual sums paid out in salary or wages for that year but also an allowance for the deferred pay of his workforce in respect of the qualifying period of service as that "matures" by the effluxion of time in that year.*'[4]

---

1 *Sun Insurance Office v Clark* [1912] AC 443.
2 [1957] AC 334, [1956] 2 All ER 728.
3 [1978] STC 166, 53 TC 675, 1978 SC 96.
4 Per Lord Cameron [1978] STC 166 at 180.

5.19 The use of provisions was also considered by the High Court in *Johnston v Britannia Airways Ltd*[1] where the taxpayer made a provision each year for the cost of overhauling aircraft engines, which occurred every three to four years. It was held that the provisions made by the taxpayer were adequate for tax purposes:

> '*The court is slow to accept that accounts prepared in accordance with accepted principles of commercial accountancy are not adequate for tax purposes as a true statement of the taxpayer's profits for the relevant period. In particular, it is slow to find that there is a judge-made rule of law which prevents accounts prepared in accordance with the ordinary principles of commercial accountancy from complying with the requirements of the tax legislation.*'[2]

Reference may also be made to the decision in *Gallagher v Jones*.³

1 [1994] STC 763.
2 Per Knox J, ibid at 782.
3 [1993] STC 537.

NOTIONAL EXPENDITURE

5.20 Deductions are limited to real, not notional, expenditure, so that no allowance is available in respect of the value of the taxpayer's own labour,¹ or for the gradual use of a wasting asset,² nor may the deduction exceed the actual expenditure incurred notwithstanding that it might have secured an asset of greater value. Similarly, the taxpayer must prove the actual amount of the expenditure in question; an estimate is insufficient.³

In *IRC v Niddrie and Benhar Coal Co Ltd*⁴ the taxpayer company's appeal against the Inland Revenue's decision not to allow a notional item of expenditure was refused. In that case the company was subject to demurrage claims for the use of wagons for transporting coal. The company never accepted nor paid the demurrage claims, and upon the cancellation of the agreement under which those claims arose and its replacement with a new agreement, the claims were regarded as discharged. The company's argument to the effect that the new contractual arrangements were consideration for the discharge, and that the value of the demurrage claim should be available as a deduction, was dismissed.

If the facts of the case were such that the taxpayer was liable for demurrage, then a provision in respect of that claim could properly have been made in the accounts for, say, year one. If the claim against the taxpayer unexpectedly lapsed for some reason, the provision would be written back in the accounts at that time, say year five. It may be argued that the accounts for year one should not be revised because they accurately showed the profit at that time, having regard to the facts then known.

1 *Oram v Johnson* [1980] STC 222.
2 *Rolfe v Wimpey Waste Management* [1989] STC 454.
3 *St John's School (Mountford & Knibbs) v Ward* [1975] STC 7.
4 (1951) 32 TC 244.

THE RECOVERY OF EXPENSES

5.21 The requirement that an expense should have been incurred is not restricted to the timing implications. A payment which may be recovered from the payee or some other person is not deductible. In *Bolton v Halpern and Woolf*¹ two partners sought to deduct the sum of £14,000 paid by them under a guarantee entered into by a deceased partner, notwithstanding that the sum was subsequently debited to the account of a deceased partner.

> '... I should have thought that prima facie where a payment gives rise directly to a right of recoupment against a third party the latter right must bear the same character as the payment out of which it arises, and if it be right to treat the payment under the guarantee as an expenditure of a revenue nature I cannot, for my part, see how it can be right to ignore ... the inseparable and correlative right to have the expenditure recouped by someone else.'²

5.21 *Direct taxes and the defendant*

Specific provision is also made in TA 1988 s 74(1)(l), at **5.04** above, which prohibits a deduction for a sum recoverable under an insurance or contract of indemnity.

---

1 [1979] STC 761.
2 Per Oliver J, ibid at 770.

---

4 REVENUE AND CAPITAL EXPENDITURE

5.22 As a general rule, expenditure must have a revenue as distinct from a capital nature if it is to be allowed as a deduction in computing the profits of a trade. Expenditure obviously has a capital nature if it is incurred upon the acquisition or disposal of a capital asset, or in the improvement of such an asset.[1] In *'Countess Warwick' SS Co Ltd v Ogg*[2] a payment of £60,000 to be released from a contract for the construction of a ship which would have been a capital asset of the business was held not to be deductible.

---

1 Per Lord Wilberforce in *Tucker v Granada Motorway Services Ltd* [1979] 2 All ER 801 at 804.
2 [1924] 2 KB 292, 8 TC 652.

5.23 The nature of capital expenditure goes wider than indicated above. In *British Insulated and Helsby Cables Ltd v Atherton*,[1] reference was made to the acquisition of assets giving an enduring benefit. That case was concerned with a payment made by the taxpayer company to establish a pension scheme for the benefit of its employees; the payment formed the initial nucleus of the fund and the amount necessary for past years of service to count for pension purposes. The House of Lords held it to be capital in nature. In the words of Viscount Cave LC:

> '... when an expenditure is made, not only once and for all, but with a view to bringing into existence an asset or an advantage for the enduring benefit of a trade, I think that there is very good reason (in the absence of special circumstances leading to an opposite conclusion) for treating such an expenditure as properly attributable not to revenue but to capital.'[2]

In *Tucker v Granada Motorway Services Ltd*[3] the House of Lords were asked to consider the nature of a payment made by the taxpayer company to its landlord in return for the landlord's agreement to vary the terms of a motorway service station lease. Under the lease, the taxpayer company was required to pay rent calculated by reference to gross takings from the site, which included tobacco sales. As tobacco duty increased, the rent became an increasing burden on the taxpayer company, and it sought a variation to exclude the incidence of tobacco duty from the calculation.

The House of Lords[4] held that the payment was capital in nature:

> '... it is a case of once and for all expenditure on a capital asset designed to make it more advantageous. It is true that the lease was non-assignable, so it had no balance sheet value before or after the modification. But it was nonetheless an asset and a

valuable one for the appellants' trade, and, if an asset, was a capital asset. It appears to me to be impossible to divorce the payment from the lease and to regard it as simply a payment intended to increase the appellants' share of the profits. That it may have done, but the parties chose to do it through the medium of a lease . . . Nor in my opinion can the payment be regarded as payment of rent: that would be to confuse the measure, or basis of calculation, of the payment with its nature.'[5]

1 [1926] AC 205, 10 TC 155.
2 [1926] 10 TC 155 at 192.
3 [1979] 2 All ER 801.
4 Lord Salmon dissenting.
5 Per Lord Wilberforce [1979] 2 All ER 801 at 805 and 806.

5.24 Conversely, the decision in *Anglo-Persian Oil Co Ltd v Dale*[1] may be cited as authority for the proposition that a lump sum paid to get rid of an onerous contract is a revenue expense if the payments which would have been made under the contract were revenue in nature. In that case the taxpayer company had appointed agents for an initial term of ten years. The remuneration payable to the agents proved larger and more onerous than had been anticipated, and accordingly the agency was terminated by agreement, subject to the payment by the taxpayer company of £300,000 to the agent. This occurred in 1922, when the agreement had a further two years to run. The Court of Appeal agreed with the taxpayer to the effect that the payment was properly allowable as a deduction. There was no question of the payment being made for goodwill having regard to the relationship between principal and agent. The taxpayer company had merely effected a change in its business methods and internal organisation; its fixed capital remained the same.

Applying the test as stated by Viscount Cave LC in *British Insulated and Helsby Cables v Atherton*,[2] the court decided in favour of the taxpayer in the following terms:

'. . . *in the present case the expenditure brought no [advantage for the enduring benefit of a trade] into existence, as the Company might, at any time, revert to its former method of conducting its business, and place the management of its business . . . in the hands of an agent. The change in the method of carrying on the Company's business . . . has, in fact, resulted in a more economical and efficient working of the Company's trade, and in that sense has proved to be advantageous to the Company's business.'*[3]

1 [1932] 1 KB 124, 16 TC 253.
2 **5.23** above.
3 Per Lawrence LJ [1932] 1 KB 124 at 142 and 143.

5.25 The decision in *Anglo-Persian Oil* would not appear to be applicable in the context of leases, where a tenant has paid to rid himself of the obligation to pay rent. Such payments tend to be treated as capital in nature, on the basis that the tenant is paying to effect a disposal of an asset which is capital in nature. For example in *Cowcher v Richard Mills & Co Ltd*[1] a series of payments was made by the taxpayer tenant under an agreement whereby his landlord accepted the surrender of a lease. It was held that the expenditure was revenue in nature.[2]

5.25 *Direct taxes and the defendant*

---

1 (1927) 13 TC 216.
2 And see *Mallett v Staveley Coal & Iron Co Ltd* (1928) 13 TC 772 and *West African Drug Co Ltd v Lilley* (1947) 28 TC 140.

5.26 Payments which do not secure an asset for the enduring benefit of the taxpayer's trade may nonetheless be treated as capital if the payment is responsible for a permanent change in the structure or organisation of the business. In *Walker v Joint Credit Card Co Ltd*[1] for example, a payment to induce a competitor to cease trading in the same location as the taxpayer company was regarded as capital in nature. The expenditure was regarded as having been made to enhance the taxpayer's goodwill.

In the case of a compensation payment to a director or employee upon the termination of his office or employment, the continuance of which is detrimental to the employer, it is clear that the payment is a revenue expense. Specifically, there is no advantage for the enduring benefit of a trade nor capital asset enhanced. It was stated in *Mitchell v BW Noble Ltd* that:[2]

> 'in the ordinary case a payment to get rid of a servant, when it was not expedient to keep him in the interests of the trade, would be a deductible expense: I leave out of consideration for the moment special cases, as when a servant is dismissed on the ground of a purely personal quarrel, although his staying on would not affect the trade at all. But it seems to me that a payment to get rid of a servant in the interests of the trade is a proper deduction.'[3]

An interesting aspect of the *Mitchell* case was the fact that the payment to the departing director comprised two elements, one relating to his notice period (etc), the other relating to shares which the director held in the company and which were transferred at par to the remaining directors. Whilst the shares were very valuable, it was decided that the payment should not be dissected—the whole amount was paid to induce the director to go, and the calculation of the amount due to him included an element in respect of his shares.

In this respect the constitution of the taxpayer company was such that its share capital was to be held exclusively by those who had the direction and management of the company. When a shareholder ceased to be a director, officer or employee of the company, he was obliged under the Articles of the company to surrender them.

---

1 [1982] STC 427.
2 [1927] 1 KB 719.
3 Per Rowlatt J, ibid at 726.

---

5 COMPENSATION AND THE CESSATION OF TRADING

5.27 Where compensation is paid after the cessation of trading it may not, as a general rule, be deducted even if paid in pursuance of arrangements made prior to the cessation. This general rule is subject to a number of statutory exemptions, considered at **5.05** above. The commentary which follows illustrates the general principles applicable, which apply to amounts falling outside the statutory regime.

In *IRC v Anglo Brewing Co Ltd*[1] payments by way of compensation for loss of office to certain employees were disallowed as they were incurred for the purposes of the winding up:

> '... when we come to the year 1920, the whole thing that [the taxpayer company] wanted ... was to be delivered from their trade, and not to carry it on; and they said: "As an incident of the deliverance of ourselves from our trade, not in order to carry it on, we have got to make some payments, because we cannot turn all these people adrift; it is not a thing that we care to do." So they came to the conclusion that they would make certain payments, because they were not going to carry on the business any longer.'[2]

There was therefore no evidence that the payments were made for the purposes of the trade; ie keeping the trade going and making it pay. Accordingly, no deduction for the compensation payments was available.

---
1 (1925) 12 TC 803.
2 Per Rowlatt J, ibid at 812.

5.28 Redundancy payments to directors and employees upon the taxpayer company being taken over were not deductible in *Peters (George) & Co Ltd v Smith*.[1] In that case the purchaser bound itself by contract to set aside a sum out of the purchase price to compensate directors and employees of the target company and its subsidiary who became redundant. Upon appeal by the Inland Revenue, it has held that the payments were not made pursuant to a decision of the target company for the purposes of its business, but were made by virtue of arrangements agreed as between the purchaser and vendor. There was a mixture of motives in the decision which led to the compensation payments; the positive finding necessary to justify a deduction could not be made out and accordingly the Inland Revenue's appeal was successful.

On the other hand, payments made to employees for the purpose of ensuring that the taxpayer's business is conducted in an orderly way up to the date of cessation were held to be deductible in the case of *O'Keeffe v Southport Printers Ltd*.[2] The central finding of fact by the Commissioners was in the following terms:

> 'The evidence, which we accepted, was that for the company the essential purpose of the agreement was to achieve the closure of its business without impediment, in a manner which would enable it to fulfil its outstanding work commitments and carry out the disposal of its assets without friction and as early as possible.'[3]

This purpose was a trading purpose and accordingly a deduction was allowed. It should be noted that the position is now subject to the provisions of TA 1988 ss 90(1)(a) and 579(2), for which see **5.05** above.

---
1 (1963) 41 TC 264.
2 [1984] STC 443, 58 TC 88.
3 Case stated at para 27 [1984] STC 443 at 454.

6 COMPENSATION AND SHARE OR BUSINESS SALES

5.29 Where compensation is paid to employees or directors in connection with a sale of shares or a business, a deduction may be denied on the basis that the payment represents a distribution of profits, or was paid for the purposes of the sale as distinct from the trade.

In *Overy v Ashford Dunn & Co Ltd*[1] the directors of the taxpayer company were voted compensation of £3,000 each as compensation for loss of office upon the sale of shares in the company. The shareholders effecting the sale were the same as the directors, and the court had little difficulty in deciding that the compensation was in fact a non-deductible distribution of profits. Specifically, there was no finding that the compensation payment for loss of office was necessary to induce the directors in question to retire; this factor distinguished the situation from that in *Mitchell v Noble*.[2] The directors of Ashford Dunn had decided to sell their shares and retire from the business; the compensation payment was merely a device to extract profits accrued to date.

1 (1933) 17 TC 497.
2 **5.26** above.

5.30 In *James Snook & Co Ltd v Blasdale*[1] an agreement for the sale of shares of the taxpayer company provided that the purchaser would procure the company to pay compensation for loss of office to the directors and the auditors, who were to resign. The Commissioners, the High Court and the Court of Appeal all held that the compensation was not an allowable deduction in computing the profits of the company.

The point was made in the High Court that the mere circumstance that compensation is paid on a change of shareholding control does not of itself mean that a deduction will always be denied. However, the evidential burden is higher because it must be proved that the taxpayer company:

> 'considered the question of payment wholly untrammelled by the terms of the bargain its shareholders had struck with those who were to buy their shares and came to a decision to pay solely in the interests of its trade.'[2]

It is clear that the evidential burden is difficult to meet where the persons who take the decision to sell are the same as those who receive the compensation.

1 (1952) 33 TC 244.
2 Per Donovan J, ibid at 251.

5.31 Where provision is made for compensation to be paid as part of the terms of a sale of shares or business, a deduction may be denied on the basis that the expenditure forms part of the consideration for that sale. In *Royal Insurance Co v Watson*[1] an insurance company acquired the business of a rival. The terms of that acquisition stipulated that the services of a certain manager would be retained subject to the taxpayer company having an option to terminate his services upon payment of a lump sum. That option was exercised soon after the business transfer and the House of Lords held that the compensation paid was capital in nature as it related to the business acquisition and was not therefore deductible.

1 [1897] AC 1.

5.32 The requirement that expenditure be incurred wholly and exclusively for the purposes of the trade may deny a deduction for compensation paid upon termination of an employee's or director's contract of service where that termination occurs by reason of the sale of the trade. This was the case in *Godden v A Wilson's Stores (Holdings) Ltd*[1] in which a business was sold on 31 March 1958. Prior to that sale (on 28 March 1958) notice was given to the manager and a payment in lieu of that notice period was made. The termination of the manager's service agreement was regarded as brought about because the company was selling its business and would no longer have need of his services.

In view of this, it was held that the compensation was paid:

> '... not for the purpose of enabling the Company to earn profits but in connection with the sale of the Company's estates and because the Company's business and the Company's ability and capacity to earn profits was coming to an end.'[2]

No deduction was therefore available.

1 (1962) 40 TC 161.
2 Per Plowman J, ibid at 167.

5.33 On the other side of the dividing line, compensation payments to the managing directors of three subsidiary companies after the takeover of the parent company but as part of a group reorganisation were held to be allowable in *IRC v Patrick Thomson Ltd*.[1] In that case, the policy of operation of the subsidiary companies and its new parent (the House of Fraser) were in conflict. The managing director of each subsidiary had, prior to the House of Fraser takeover, virtually complete control of its business whereas the policy of the House of Fraser was one of centralisation; which policy would have involved the eventual liquidation of the subsidiaries. In each case it was considered that the current managing director was not suitable for carrying out the new policy, and accordingly each of the subsidiary directors were terminated and compensation paid as a consequence.

The Court of Session held that deductions should be available to the subsidiary companies for the amounts paid. The subsequent liquidation of the subsidiary companies did not prejudice the availability of a deduction as at the time the service agreements were discharged and the expenditure made, liquidation was only a possibility:

> 'The strongest way that the matter can be put for the Crown is that there was then a present intention to liquidate at some time in the future. But if that is as high as they can put it then they have not in my opinion established that the expenditure was not laid out for the purposes of the trade . . . When the expense was incurred, liquidation might have been delayed beyond the end of the Company's financial year . . .

5.33 *Direct taxes and the defendant*

> *The purpose for which the money was expended is a question of fact upon which the Commissioners are final . . . and they have negatived any connection between this purpose and the subsequent liquidation of the Company. . .'*[2]

---

1 (1956) 37 TC 145.
2 Per Lord Clyde, ibid at 158.

---

7 LEGAL FEES

5.34 Legal fees and other professional expenses may be incurred in a wide variety of circumstances. A deduction for such expenditure may be denied on the basis that it is capital in nature, which may arise where costs are incurred in connection with a capital asset, although this rule is subject to exceptions; for example where the expense is incurred in connection with protecting a capital asset.

In a case concerning a title dispute in respect of land situated outside the UK[1] the decision by the Commissioners to allow a deduction was not disturbed by the High Court:

> '. . . if it could be said that this expenditure had in any way altered the original character of the capital asset which was acquired by the [taxpayer] company I should have taken the view that the payment was in respect of capital, but as the capital asset of the [taxpayer], in my opinion, remained absolutely unaltered, that payment is properly attributable to revenue.'[2]

The scope for obtaining a deduction in relation to capital assets would appear to be limited. As a general rule expenditure incurred with a view to acquiring or bringing a capital asset into existence, or in connection with the realisation of such an asset[3] will not be allowable. Abortive expenditure is subject to the same rule. In *ECC Quarries Ltd v Watkis*[4] no deduction was allowed in respect of costs incurred in making an unsuccessful claim for planning permission to extract gravel.[5] A deduction was also denied in *Pyrah v Annis & Co Ltd*[6] in relation to the costs of making an unsuccessful application for the variation of a road haulier's licence to increase the number of vehicles which the taxpayer could operate.

---

1 Different rules apply for land in the UK chargeable under TA 1988 Sch A.
2 Per Lawrence J in *Southern v Borax Consolidated Ltd* [1941] 1 KB 111 at 118.
3 *Mallett v Staveley Coal and Iron Co Ltd* [1928] 2 KB 405, 13 TC 772.
4 [1975] STC 578, 51 TC 153.
5 The position is now expressly covered by SP 4/78, which states that relief will be accepted in such circumstances.
6 [1957] 1 All ER 196, 37 TC 163.

5.35 In the important case of *IRC v Carron Co*[1] the taxpayer company was successful in a claim to deduct legal fees incurred in obtaining a supplementary charter[2] and of settling an action by a dissenting shareholder. It was held that the expenditure was incurred to remove obstacles to profitable trading, and accordingly could be deducted.

The new charter was not an end in itself, it was merely a stepping stone to the practical purpose of improving the taxpayer's trading potential in that its structure was modernised and additional borrowing powers were secured as a means of engaging managerial staff of the required calibre. So far as concerns the test in *British Insulated and Helsby Cables* in relation to 'an asset or an advantage for the enduring benefit of the trade' a distinction was drawn between the removal of a disability on the one hand, payment for which is revenue, and the bringing into existence of an advantage, payment for which may be capital. So far as concerns the costs associated with the dissenting shareholders, the payments allowed the taxpayer to carry on its business unfettered by the presence of persons who might have caused difficulty.

1 (1968) 45 TC 18, HL.
2 The taxpayer company was incorporated by charter in 1773.

5.36 In *Knight v Parry*[1] no deduction was allowed in respect of costs incurred by a solicitor in successfully defending an action alleging professional misconduct and breach of contract. The action arose in the context of the taxpayer leaving his employment as an assistant solicitor in order to establish his own practice, and allegedly soliciting instructions from a client of his principal.

The taxpayer had two purposes in defending the action. First, to defend himself against the allegation of professional misconduct. Second, to defend himself against a claim for damages. It was held that no deduction was available as the purpose of protecting himself professionally was to ensure that he was not precluded from practicing as a solicitor as distinct from carrying on that practice. In any event, the defence against the claim for damages was clearly not referable to his practice.

The decision is in accordance with that in *Spofforth and Prince v Golder*[2] in which costs incurred by a chartered accountant in defending a charge of fraud were held not to be deductible.

1 [1973] STC 56.
2 [1945] 1 All ER 363, 26 TC 310.

8 INVESTMENT COMPANIES

5.37 For tax purposes an investment company is one whose business consists wholly or mainly of making investments, from which it derives the principal part of its income.[1] As an investment company is not carrying on a trade, its profits are calculated by taking its total income from all sources; for example, rent taxable under Schedule A, interest under Case III of Schedule D and so on. Management expenses and charges on income may then be set off.

There is little in the way of guidance as to what is covered by the term 'management expenses'. TA 1988, s 75 states that it includes commissions

5.37 *Direct taxes and the defendant*

and excludes any expenses otherwise deductible in computing profits; for example, under Schedule A in relation to surveyors fees[2] or advertising for tenants.[3] The restrictive meaning given to the term management expenses is likely to preclude a deduction being obtained by the payer of damages.

1 TA 1988 s 130.
2 *London and Northern Estates Co Ltd v Harris* (1937) 21 TC 197.
3 *Southern v Aldwych Property Trust Ltd* (1940) 23 TC 707.

5.38 As an exception to the general rule, relief for payments made in connection with the termination of an employee's or director's contract should be available, provided sums paid under that contract have attracted relief as management expenses. Specific deductions for employee's redundancy payments,[1] additional redundancy payments,[2] in respect of restrictive undertakings given by employees,[3] and for certain expenditure on qualifying courses[4] (as discussed in at **5.05** above) are in each case available to investment companies as expenses of management.

1 TA 1988 s 579(3).
2 Ibid, s 90(1)(b).
3 FA 1988 s 73(3).
4 TA 1988 s 588(4).

9 INDIVIDUALS AND INTEREST RELIEF

5.39 An award of damages may also involve an award of interest, and the question is therefore raised: can the defendant obtain relief for such expenditure?

Interest may qualify as a trading expense if it is wholly and exclusively incurred for the purposes of the trade, profession or vocation, and was incurred on revenue as distinct from capital. Such interest may be yearly or non-yearly, but if the former and paid to a non-UK resident, relief is only available if the payer deducts tax at the basic rate and accounts to the Inland Revenue for the same.[1] It would therefore appear to be arguable that if a deduction is available in respect of damages, then interest paid in respect of such damages may also be the subject of relief. However, the payment of interest arises by reason of the defendant failing to compensate the plaintiff, as distinct from a payment in respect of a loan where the monies are used for the purposes of furthering the defendant's trade, profession or vocation. It might therefore be argued that the interest is not incurred for any business purpose.

The tax system also affords relief in relation to certain specified qualifying activities detailed in Pt IX of the Taxes Act 1988. Amongst others, interest on loans to buy land,[2] plant or machinery[3] and shares in a close company[4] qualify. The requirement that there be a 'loan' would appear to preclude any relief being available for interest on damages.

1 TA 1988 ss 82 and 349(2).
2 Ibid, s 354.
3 Ibid, s 359.
4 Ibid, s 360.

10 COMPANIES AND INTEREST RELIEF

5.40 A company may deduct 'short' interest as a trading expense. Yearly interest is also deductible provided it is payable in the UK on an advance from a bank carrying on a bona fide banking business in the UK.[1] Whether yearly or short, the interest must satisfy the general requirements of deductibility as for individuals above.

In addition, relief for interest may be afforded by virtue of it being a charge on income pursuant to TA 1988 s 338 where a deduction is available against the 'total profits' of the company. Interest which is not deductible as a trading expense, or incurred by an investment company, may therefore still attract relief. Amongst the various conditions imposed before relief is given, TA 1988 s 338(5)(b) provides that no payment shall be treated as a charge on income if it 'is not made under a liability incurred for a valuable and sufficient consideration'. Because damages are for a breach of contract or tortious act it is difficult to see how this condition could be fulfilled. Accordingly, relief for interest on damages as a charge on income would not appear to be available.

1 TA 1988 337(2).

11 DEDUCTIONS FROM RENTAL INCOME

5.41 The general rules regarding deductions from rent charged to income tax under Schedule A are contained in TA 1988 s 25. Permitted deductions are specified by TA 1988 s 25(2) to mean any payment, excluding interest, in respect of any of the following:

'(a) maintenance, repairs, insurance or management;
(b) any services provided by him [ie the landlord] otherwise than by way of maintenance or repairs, being services which he was obliged to provide but in respect of which he received no separate consideration;
(c) rates or other charges on the occupier which the person chargeable was obliged to defray;
(d) any rent, rentcharge, ground annual, feuduty or other periodical payment reserved in respect of, or charged on or issuing out of land.'[1]

The above is subject to TA 1988 s 25(3) to (9) which, inter alia, prohibit the deduction of expenditure incurred otherwise than in respect of the premises comprised in the lease;[2] and in the case of a payment for maintenance or

5.41 *Direct taxes and the defendant*

repairs, was incurred by reason of dilapidation attributable to a period falling within or in respect of the currency of the rent-producing lease.[3]

1 TA 1988 s 25(2).
2 Ibid, s 25(3)(a).
3 Ibid, s 25(3)(b).

5.42 No deduction may therefore be afforded under s 25 in respect of payments made by the landlord to adjoining landowners in respect of damage suffered to their property. Indeed the restrictive nature of the deductions permitted pursuant to s 25 is likely to prevent deductions being available in most instances involving damages.

EXAMPLE

Paul owns a building let for both residential and office use. In carrying out some alterations to the building he finds himself the subject of an action from his neighbour seeking redress for a loss of light caused by the alterations. After negotiations the claim is compromised by Paul paying the sum of £3,500 in damages. No deduction from rental income is available.

5.43 In *IRC v Wilson's Executors*,[1] a case relating to 'maintenance claims' under the Schedule A system which prevailed prior to the Finance Act 1963 but which remains relevant for the purposes of TA 1988 s 25(2)(a) a deduction was refused for certain legal expenses and compensation paid by a landlord of agricultural property. The amounts were paid following a dispute with a lessee as to the terms upon which his lease should be renewed.

The court noted that a landlord was inevitably going to incur expenses in disputes with tenants, and if the term 'management' could be said to bear a wide meaning such expenses would be deductible. However, the court was of the view that the term should bear a more restricted meaning, so as to include the fees paid to a manager of an estate so far as concerns keeping accounts, collecting rents and in making the necessary disbursements for these purposes. Having regard to this more restricted meaning it was decided that no deduction was available.

The court also noted that from the landlord's standpoint, payment of compensation for improvements which the tenant leaves behind is payment made as the price for those improvements—so that no deduction is available. Compensation for disturbance is payment made as the price of having a free hand to deal in the property—no deduction is available because it relates to the interest of the landlord in the property.

So far as concerns minor items of expenditure incurred in the context of small arbitrations and adjustments, the court was reluctant to disturb the perceived practice of allowing such expenses as a cost of management:

'. . . I should be disposed to include all charges fairly described as business charges incident to the prudent management of the estate, to whomsoever these charges were incurred, not being charges incident to the business in connection with capital matters of a substantial character.'[2]

So far as concerns expenses incurred by the landlord in bringing a claim, the court was of the view that no deduction would be allowable for expenses incurred in a claim for dilapidations.

1 (1934) 18 TC 465.
2 Per Lord Sands, ibid at 476.

12 RELIEF FOR CAPITAL EXPENDITURE

5.44 In circumstances where payments are made for breach of warranty or under an indemnity in connection with a sale of a capital asset, relief for the payment should be available by way of an adjustment to the purchase price received by the vendor. The relevant principles have already been explored in Chapter 3 and are therefore not repeated here.

It should also be noted that relief is available if the expenditure falls within TCGA 1992 s 38(1)(a) which applies to:

> 'the amount or value of the consideration, in money or money's worth, given by him or on his behalf wholly and exclusively for the acquisition of the asset, together with the incidental costs to him of the acquisition . . .'

It follows that if a dispute is settled on terms providing for the payment by one party to another in return for the transfer of the property in dispute, the amount paid will be taken into account upon a subsequent disposal of that property.

5.45 It is more difficult to identify circumstances in which a payment of compensation may otherwise attract relief, although TCGA 1992 s 38(1)(b) (allowable expenditure, at **3.68** above) might be in question in some circumstances. For example, a payment in return for the surrender of some right, such as a right of way, which adversely affects the taxpayer's asset might be taken into account pursuant to this provision.

Chapter 6

THE POSITION OF EMPLOYEES

6.01 The general taxation treatment of compensation is largely irrelevant when analysing its receipt by the holder of an office (such as a director or company secretary) or employment subject to income tax under Schedule E TA 1988. Instead, special considerations apply which are initially considered by reference to:

(a) the general principles of Schedule E;
(b) the application of those general principles to compensatory receipts;
(c) the special statutory scheme, which extends the ambit of the Schedule E charge to compensatory receipts which might otherwise be free of tax under general principles. The primary provisions in this respect are TA 1988 ss 148 and 154;
(d) the relieving provisions of TA 1988 s 188.

The general commentary is then considered by reference to the following specific circumstances:

(a) wrongful and unfair dismissal, as well as dismissal for cause;
(b) retirement;
(c) death or disability;
(d) redundancy.

The chapter concludes with sections on the charge to tax in respect of restrictive covenants, the national insurance implications, PAYE considerations and some miscellaneous planning points not otherwise dealt with. The term 'employee' should be regarded as including office holders unless otherwise stated.

1 GENERAL PRINCIPLES OF SCHEDULE E

6.02 Schedule E imposes a charge to income tax on emoluments from an office or employment. That charge may arise under one of three Cases, depending on the residence status of the employee and source of funds.

6.02 *The position of employees*

Broadly speaking, Case I applies where the employee is resident and ordinarily resident in the UK. Case II applies where the employee is either not resident in the UK or is resident but not ordinarily resident. Case III applies in certain circumstances where the employee performs his employment duties abroad, tax being levied on a remittance basis (see *Simon's Taxes* E4.1).

In addition, para 5 to Schedule E applies to amounts specifically directed as being taxable under it. A charge to tax upon the removal of share restrictions under FA 1988 s 78 is an example.

Neither the term 'office' nor 'employment' is defined by statute. Their characteristics are briefly discussed in this chapter. For a more complete treatment reference should be made to *Simon's Taxes* E4.201 and E4.202.

Office
6.03   The reference to an office is to:

> '. . . a subsisting, permanent, substantive position, which had an existence independent of the person who filled it, and which went on and was filled in succession by successive holders . . .'[1]

Commonly encountered examples include company directors and secretaries. Other examples include trustees, executors and company registrars.

---

1 Per Rowlatt J in *Great Western Rly Co v Bater* [1920] 3 KB 266 at 274.

Employment
6.04   Modern case law equates the term 'employment' with a contract of service, as distinct from a contract for services where the services are supplied by a person in business on his own account. The views of the Inland Revenue in leaflet IR56/NI39 ('Employed or self-employed? A guide for tax and National Insurance') illustrate the general principles which the Revenue apply:

> 'If you can answer "yes" to the following questions, it will usually mean that you are self-employed:
>
> 1 Do you have the final say in how the business is run?
> 2 Do you risk your own money in the business?
> 3 Are you responsible for meeting the losses as well as taking profits?
> 4 Do you provide the major items of equipment you need to do your job, not just the small tools which many employees provide for themselves?
> 5 Do you have to correct unsatisfactory work in your own time and at your own expense?
>
> If you can answer "yes" to the following questions, you are probably an employee:
>
> 1 Do you yourself have to work rather than hire someone else to do it for you?
> 2 Can someone tell you at any time what to do or when and how to do it?
> 3 Are you paid by the hour, week, or month? Can you get overtime pay? Though even if you are paid by commission or on a piecework basis you may still be an employee.

4 Do you work set hours, or a given number of hours a week or month?
5 Do you work at the premises of the person you are working for, or at a place or places they decide?'

Taxable emoluments

6.05 Schedule E imposes a charge to tax '. . . in respect of any office or employment on emoluments therefrom . . .'. The term 'emoluments' is defined by TA 1988 s 131 as including '. . . all salaries, fees, wages, perquisites and profits whatsoever'.

Given that the charge is one to income tax, it has been argued that payments of a capital nature ought to be excluded. Such arguments would appear to have little merit given the incidence of tax on lump sum payments (although the House of Lords in *Tilley v Wales*[1] refused to go so far as to abolish the distinction[2]).

The wide ambit of the term emoluments, which is not considered to be exhaustive, is such that any payment of money is a taxable emolument subject only to it being referable to the employment. It is therefore the causal connection which determines the scope of charge. A payment made partly in respect of an employee's services and partly for some other purpose should be apportioned on a fair and reasonable basis, and tax charged accordingly. For such an apportionment reference may be made to *Mairs v Haughey*.[3]

1 [1943] 1 All ER 280.
2 Per Lord Thankerton, ibid at 284.
3 [1992] STC 495 at 516–518.

THE CAUSAL CONNECTION

6.06 The nature of the causal requirement was expressed by Upjohn J (in *Hochstrasser v Mayes*) as follows:

'. . . *payment must be made in reference to the services the employee renders by virtue of his office and it must be something in the nature of a reward for services past, present or future.*'[1]

The decision of the House of Lords in *Shilton v Wilmhurst* (**6.18** below) may now be regarded as providing the more complete test. In that case Lord Templeman, having first noted that emoluments may be provided by persons other than the employer, was of the view that:

'Section [19(1)] is not limited to emoluments provided in the course of employment; the section must therefore apply first to an emolument which is paid as a reward for past services and as an inducement to continue to perform services and, second, to an emolument which is paid as an inducement to enter into a contract of employment and to perform services in the future. The result is that an emolument "from employment" means an emolument "from being or becoming an employee".'[2]

His Lordship continued:

6.06 *The position of employees*

> 'The authorities are consistent with this analysis and are concerned to distinguish in each case between an emolument which is derived "from being or becoming an employee" on the one hand, and an emolument which is attributable to something else on the other hand, for example, to a desire on the part of the provider of the emolument to relieve distress or to provide assistance to a home buyer. If an emolument is not paid as a reward for past services or as an inducement to enter into employment and provide future services but is paid for some other reason, then the emolument is not received "from the employment".'

1 [1959] Ch 22 at 33.
2 [1991] 3 All ER 148 at 151.

6.07 The provision of assistance to a home buyer would appear to be a reference to *Hochstrasser v Mayes* in which the taxpayer was successful in arguing that a payment by his employer to assist the taxpayer to move was not a taxable emolument. A more obvious example of a payment outside the scope of Schedule E would include compensation in respect of damage inflicted on an employee's property. However, it is more difficult to draw the distinction if the compensation is paid in respect of the loss of a right enjoyed by the employee under his employment contract.

In determining the causal connection the court is not tied to the terms of any contractual agreement. In the case of *Pritchard v Arundale* (**6.29** below) an expression of consideration for a share transfer was not regarded as conclusive.

The identity of the payer
6.08 The identity of the payer should not be important in deciding whether a particular receipt is an emolument, only the motive for the payment is relevant. However, an employee will have a harder task in seeking to demonstrate that a payment from his employer is not a taxable emolument as opposed to a payment from a third party.

The decision in *Calvert v Wainwright*[1] may be used to illustrate the point. That case was concerned with tips received by an employed taxi-driver which were held to be taxable emoluments on the basis that they were given in the ordinary course as a reward for services. The distinction between tips which are taxable, and those which are given on personal grounds and so exempt, was commented upon:

> 'Some people have the same taxicab every morning to take them to their work. The cab calls in the morning as a matter of course and takes the passenger home at night. The ordinary tip given, in those circumstances, would be something which would be assessable, but supposing at Christmas, or when the driver is going for a holiday, the hirer says: "You have been very attentive to me, here is a £10 note," he would be making a present, and I should say it would not be assessable since it has been given to the man because of his qualities, his faithfulness, and the way he has studied the passenger's interests and has always been available.'[2]

1 [1947] 1 All ER 282.
2 Per Atkinson J, ibid at 283.

6.09 Notwithstanding the supposed irrelevance of the payer's identity, it is difficult to think of a £10 gift at Christmas given by an employer to his employee being viewed in the same manner given the more onerous burden of proof:

> 'If the provider of the emolument is the employer who has an interest in the performance of the contract, the court may find difficulty in accepting that the emolument was not "from the employment" but from something else. The difficulty is not so great where a person who is not the employer provides an emolument because such a person may well be activated by motives other than desire to see that the employee enters into or continues in the employment of another.'[1]

1 Per Lord Templeman in *Shilton v Wilmhurst* [1991] 3 All ER 148 at 152.

Gratuities
6.10 Gratuities are not chargeable to income tax in the hands of an employee if made primarily for personal reasons. The restricted nature of the exemption was considered in *Moore v Griffiths*[1] in which payments were made by the Football Association to Bobby Moore following his captaincy of England in their World Cup victory of 1966. Those payments were held to be free of income tax:

> 'In my judgment . . . I think it would be wrong to regard the payment to Mr Moore as being something in the nature of a reward or remuneration for services. The true purpose of the payment was to mark his participation in an exceptional event; namely, the winning of the World Cup Championships—exceptional because the cup is open for competition only every four years and has never before been won by this country. In other words, the payment had the quality of a testimonial or accolade rather than the quality of remuneration for services rendered.'[2]

For a more complete discussion reference may be made to *Simon's Taxes* E4.451.

1 [1972] 1 WLR 1024.
2 Per Brightman J, ibid at 1034.

2 THE APPLICATION OF GENERAL PRINCIPLES

6.11 Specific legislative provisions apply to the receipt of compensation by employees, but their application is subject to the operation of general Schedule E principles. These are best considered by reference to the various circumstances in which compensation may be paid; essentially, upon commutation of pension rights, termination or amendment of the employment contract, as an inducement upon termination and for the loss of personal rights.

6.12 *The position of employees*

Commutation of pension rights

6.12 The decision in *Tilley v Wales*[1] is authority for the proposition that a payment in exchange for the surrender of pension rights does not constitute a taxable emolument within TA 1988 s 19(1). In the House of Lords, Viscount Simons followed the unanimous view of the members of the Court of Appeal to the effect that:

> '... a pension is in itself a taxable subject-matter distinct from the profit of an office, and, if an individual agrees to exchange his right to a pension for a lump sum, that sum is not taxable under Schedule E.'[2]

The commutation of pension rights subject to the special statutory code is set out at **6.34** below. For the loss of lump sums otherwise payable upon retirement, reference should be made to the case of *Hunter v Dewhurst* at **6.25** below.

---

1 [1943] 1 All ER 280.
2 Ibid at 282.

Payments upon termination

6.13 As a general rule compensation paid upon the termination of the contract of employment does not fall within the ambit of TA 1988 s 19(1). In *Henley v Murray*[1] the managing director of a company resigned following a request to that effect by the board of directors. Under the employment contract his appointment should have continued for a further nine months or so and the company therefore paid him the amount he would have received had he continued to be so employed. The Court of Appeal held that the compensation received was not assessable to income tax.

The court's view as to the nature of the compensation was unanimous. In the words of Jenkins LJ:

> 'The only possible conclusion ... seems to me to be that the payment in question was not a payment of remuneration, but was one made in consideration of the taxpayer, at the request of the company, giving up his right to continue to be employed by the company down to [the end of the contractual term] and to earn and receive his contractual remuneration down to that date.'[2]

In reaching that conclusion, payment was analysed in the following manner:

> 'It is not suggested that the payment was a mere gratuity, nor is it suggested that the payment was in the nature of additional remuneration for the services which the taxpayer had already performed in the past for the stipulated reward, nor is it suggested that there was an arrangement of the nature sometimes met with under which, in effect, the holder of the office is given the equivalent of leave of absence on full pay for the residue of the contractual term. There is no evidence of any such arrangement.'

The conclusion was inevitable:

'It was a simple case of resignation under which the office was to be immediately vacated, and no further services were to be performed. Accordingly, by a process of elimination, I arrive at the conclusion that this sum can only be regarded on the facts of this case as paid to the taxpayer in consideration of his surrendering his right to serve, and receive remuneration, to the end of his contractual agreement.'

1 [1950] 1 All ER 908, 31 TC 351.
2 [1950] 1 All ER 908 at 911.

6.14 The principle in *Henley v Murray* does not extend to all compensation payments paid upon termination. Two situations may be distinguished, namely where payment is conditional upon the continued performance of services, or where it is reserved in the contract of employment.

CONDITIONAL PAYMENTS

6.15 A payment which is conditional upon the employee's continued service is a taxable emolument, as the contract of employment still exists and the employee performs services thereunder.

Notwithstanding the general rule, the Inland Revenue would appear to be willing to accept that a payment conditional on continued service for a short period consistent with the reasonable needs of the employer's business is not a taxable emolument. This view was expressed in the context of redundancy situations only in Statement of Practice SP 1/81 (now withdrawn, see **6.73** below).

RESERVED PAYMENTS

6.16 Payments reserved in the contract of employment are taxable in full. In *Dale v De Soissons*[1] the employee's service contract provided for a payment to be made as 'compensation for loss of office' if terminated by the employer before the agreed three-year term. The contract was so terminated and the compensation paid. The Court of Appeal held that the sum was assessable to income tax under Schedule E. In the words of Sir Raymond Evershed MR the sum:

'was something to which [the employee] became entitled as part of the terms on which he promised to serve . . .'[2]

It is clear that a contractual obligation to pay the sum was regarded as a prerequisite to it being charged to income tax. This may occur where the obligation is included at the outset by way of a written term in the contract. It may also occur where the obligation is subsequently incorporated in the contract by an oral or written agreement.

It is easy to agree to make a payment upon termination, especially immediately before the termination in question. However, the decision in *De Soissons* should not be regarded as meaning that an agreement between employer and employee as to the terms upon which termination is to take place will prejudice the taxation treatment of the compensation then paid.

6.16 *The position of employees*

Compensation so paid is not derived from an entitlement under the employment contract. In *Clayton v Lavender*[3] the managing director of the employing company in question wrote to the taxpayer in the following terms:

> '... I am sorry to learn ... that you do not wish to remain with us after the term of your Agreement. Because of [our] continuous development ... it will be necessary for me to find another Consultant. In these circumstances, I suggest that we terminate your agreement upon the following lines: We will pay you £4,000 per year for one year ... and £2,000 for the next ...'[4]

Such an offer is often avoided on the basis that the compensation may be regarded as a reserved payment and so fully taxable. That perceived risk would not appear to be well founded, as the compensation paid was held to be free of tax. Stamp J considered the effect of the agreement in the following light:

> '... if payment is agreed to be made to an employee in consideration of his agreeing that he shall not in future perform any obligations to his employer and that the employer shall not be entitled to require his services, the payment is a payment in consideration of the surrender by the recipient of his rights in respect of the office.'[5]

---

1 [1950] 2 All ER 460, 32 TC 118.
2 [1950] 2 All ER 460 at 462.
3 (1965) 42 TC 607.
4 Ibid at 610.
5 Ibid at 612.

6.17 Three points may be made as to the nature of the obligation required in order for the principle in *De Soissons* to apply. First, the terms of the contract may only permit variation in a certain manner, most commonly by requiring that any amendment be in writing. An oral agreement to make a payment in such circumstances may not therefore be taxable by reason of *De Soissons*.

Second, where the employee has no contractual right to receive compensation but does have an expectation of receiving it based on the past custom of his employer, it is sometimes suggested that the compensation is taxable under the principle. In the absence of any authority to this effect, the better view would appear to be that such compensation is not so chargeable.

Third, the terms of the contract may give the employer a right to pay the employee in lieu of notice, but without placing him under an obligation to pay that amount. It is considered that the principle would not apply to a payment so made following the exercise of that right by the employer.

Inducements upon termination

6.18 A payment to induce an employee to leave his current employment and take up new employment elsewhere and to perform services in the future is a taxable emolument, by virtue of the decision of the House of Lords in *Shilton v Wilmhurst*[1] notwithstanding that the payer does not directly benefit from those services.

The case concerned the transfer of Peter Shilton from Nottingham Forest FC to Southampton FC, as a result of which two payments were made to him.

First, the payment of £80,000 by Southampton as an inducement to enter into a contract of employment with them and perform services. It was agreed that this payment was a taxable emolument.

Second, the manager of Nottingham Forest indicated to Mr Shilton that if he agreed to the transfer, the club might be willing to make a payment to him for so consenting. He agreed to the terms and Nottingham Forest paid him £75,000. In the House of Lords it was unanimously held that the payment was a taxable emolument. This decision overturned that of both the High Court and Court of Appeal, who did not consider the payment to be an emolument on the grounds that Nottingham Forest had no direct or indirect interest in the performance of the contract.

---

1 [1991] 3 All ER 148, [1991] STC 88.

6.19 Lord Templeman delivered the only judgment in the House of Lords. His Lordship rejected any test based on an interest in the performance of the new employment:

> 'There is nothing in [s 19(1)] or the authorities to justify the inference that an "emolument from employment" only applies to an emolument provided by a person who has an interest in the performance by the employee of the services which he becomes bound to perform when he enters into the contract of employment.'[1]

That rejection was made with a certain degree of relief given the perceived problems in defining the relevant interest required. So far as inducements upon termination are concerned, his Lordship was of the view that TA 1988 s 19(1) applies to:

> '... an emolument which is paid as an inducement to enter into a contract of employment and to perform services in the future.'[2]

In this respect, his Lordship regarded the payments from Southampton FC and Nottingham Forest FC as indistinguishable, notwithstanding the powerful motive in the form of the transfer fee for Nottingham Forest FC to offer the inducement. His Lordship concluded that the £75,000 was paid:

> '... as an emolument in return for the taxpayer agreeing to act as or become an employee of Southampton and for no other reason. The taxpayer accepted the emolument of £75,000 in return for agreeing to act as or become an employee of Southampton just as he accepted £80,000 from Southampton for the same reason. The taxation consequences to the taxpayer should be and are the same. The taxpayer sought and obtained the aggregate sum of £155,000 for his agreement to enter the employment of Southampton. It did not matter to the taxpayer whether the £155,000 was paid wholly or partly by Southampton or Nottingham Forest or some other third party.'[3]

---

1 [1991] 3 All ER 148 at 155.
2 Ibid at 151.
3 Ibid at 153.

6.20 *The position of employees*

6.20 The position post *Shilton* must now be that payments made to induce a person to take up new employment are fully taxable under Schedule E notwithstanding that the payment is made by that person's past employer. This may be encountered in two further situations. First, upon the transfer of a business where the existing employer is seeking to induce employees to accept new employment. Second, where the employer can no longer afford to employ the person at his or her current salary and is seeking to induce the person to obtain employment elsewhere.

Distinguishing Shilton

6.21 It is of course open for the courts to distinguish the decision in *Shilton v Wilmhurst* on the facts, and this occurred in *Mairs v Haughey*.[1]

The case was concerned with the privatisation of the Belfast shipbuilders, Harland and Wolff, pursuant to which the taxpayer was offered new employment by a company established by the management as an alternative to redundancy. The offer terms provided for a payment to be made to the taxpayer calculated as the aggregate of:

(i) 30% of the sum which he would otherwise have received under Harland and Wolff's redundancy scheme;
(ii) £100 for every complete year of service to date subject to a minimum payment of £700.

Both elements were paid in one lump sum to the taxpayer by Harland and Wolff, which therefore stood in the same relative position as Nottingham Forest FC did to Peter Shilton.

The Court of Appeal (Northern Ireland) held that the first element represented compensation for the loss of contingent rights under the original redundancy scheme, and did not therefore constitute a taxable emolument. The second element was taxable as an inducement to enter into the new employment.

In giving judgment in favour of the taxpayer, Hutton LCJ referred to *Shilton v Wilmhurst*, and following the guidance therein was of the opinion that the first element of payment:

'. . . was not, in law, taxable under Schedule E as an emolument "from" employment. A person would not have received the payment unless he had been an employee of Harland and Wolff but . . . that is not sufficient to render the payment assessable. I consider . . . that the payment would not have been made to him "in return for acting as or being an employee"; on the contrary, I think that the payment would have been made to him because he was ceasing to be an employee and to cushion him against the hardship of losing his employment.'[2]

In reaching that conclusion, reference was made to the statement of agreed facts which provided as follows:

'The purpose of the scheme and its predecessor statutory scheme was to help deal with the human problems arising from the contraction of the shipbuilding industry, by the provision of enhanced benefits to redundant employees.'

---

1 [1992] STC 495.
2 Ibid at 519.

Amendments to the contract of employment

6.22 On the basis that an employee is giving up rights under his contract of employment, as distinct from the provision of services, a payment for an agreement to vary that contract should not in principle be regarded as an emolument from employment. However, the courts have been reluctant to accept that such a payment falls outside the income tax net when the contract continues.

The general principles which emerge from a review of the relevant case law are that a payment is taxable when it represents:

(a) advance remuneration;
(b) compensation for the loss of part of the remuneration package or other rights directly connected with the taxpayer's employment;
(c) an inducement to return to employment following a dispute.

ADVANCE REMUNERATION

6.23 A payment of advance remuneration is a taxable emolument. For example, the variation of an employment contract providing for the payment of a lump sum subject to a reduced salary thereafter. As a very limited exception to the general rule, a payment in respect of rights which could not be enjoyed whilst the employment was current may fall outside TA 1988 s 19. The decision in *Hunter v Dewhurst* (see **6.25**) may be regarded in this light.

THE LOSS OF RIGHTS

6.24 Compensation paid in recognition of the loss of part of the employee's remuneration package, or other rights directly connected with the taxpayer's employment represent taxable emoluments. The taxable nature of such payments represents the dividing line with the loss of personal rights, which do not give rise to tax.

The decision of the Court of Appeal in *Hamblett v Godfrey*[1] illustrates the nature of the rights on the taxable side of the line. That case was concerned with civil servants employed by the Crown at GCHQ, the intelligence service headquarters. In 1983, the right to belong to a trade union and certain other rights under the employment protection legislation were withdrawn, on grounds of national security. The employees were offered the option of being transferred to another branch of the civil service or remaining and suffering the withdrawal of those rights. The taxpayer in question remained and received a payment of £1,000 expressed to be in recognition of the loss of rights previously enjoyed.

The taxpayer was assessed to income tax on the £1,000 on the grounds that it constituted an emolument from her employment and the Court of Appeal agreed with the Inland Revenue's contentions. The basis for that decision was explained by Purchas LJ:

> '[The] approach that the court should take . . . is to consider the status of the payment and the context in which it was made. The payment was made to recognise the loss of rights.'[2]

6.24 *The position of employees*

The rights which had been lost were then examined:

'*The rights, the loss of which was being recognised, were rights under the employment protection legislation, and the right to join a union or other trade protection association. Both those rights, in my judgment, are directly connected with the fact of the taxpayer's employment. If the employment did not exist, there would be no need for the rights in the particular context in which the taxpayer found herself.*'

Once the source of the payment was ascertained, it was clear that it constituted a taxable emolument.

---

1 [1987] STC 60.
2 Ibid at 69.

6.25 The decision in the GCHQ case should be contrasted with that of the House of Lords in *Hunter v Dewhurst*.[1] The taxpayer in that case was the chairman and a director of a company. His contract provided for 'compensation' equal to five years' salary to be paid upon his retirement. The taxpayer wished to retire but he was persuaded to remain as a director on a part-time basis, at a greatly reduced rate of remuneration. The agreement to continue had the consequence of reducing the compensation payment of £12,900 which would otherwise be due upon the taxpayer's retirement. It was therefore agreed that the taxpayer would waive his right to compensation upon retirement in return for a lump sum payment of £10,000.

The House of Lords held that the lump sum payment was not chargeable to income tax. The basis for the decision was that the payment was in recompense for contingent rights enjoyed by the taxpayer. Conversely, if the contingency element is missing, so that the payment relates to a right which could be enjoyed during the term of the contract, compensation for its surrender will be taxable. Cases which fall into this category include *McGregor v Randall*[2] where a one-off payment for agreeing to forgo future commission was made.

---

1 (1932) 16 TC 605.
2 [1984] 1 All ER 1092.

INDUCEMENTS AND DISPUTES

6.26 The payment of an inducement to return to work following a dispute is fully taxable. In *Holland v Geoghegan*[1] salvage rights enjoyed by refuse collectors were withdrawn by the employing borough council. That withdrawal resulted in strike action being taken by the refuse collectors, which was settled by the payment of compensation for their loss.

The High Court held that the compensation payments were taxable. In deciding that the payments constituted emoluments from employment, the court regarded the overriding purpose in making the payments to be:

'. . . *to secure that the borough's employees should cease to strike and return to work while a new agreement was negotiated to include an incentive bonus scheme, during which time the taxpayer would be entitled only to his salary, and would have no further cash receipts from the proceeds of sale of salvage.*'[2]

It was therefore concluded that:

'... the main purpose of the borough was to get the taxpayer back to work, and the money when received by him was a form of substituted remuneration for his former rights to share in the proceeds of sale of the salvage.'

1 [1972] 3 All ER 333.
2 Per Foster J, ibid at 342.

Loss of personal liberty

6.27 The judgment of Lord Templeman in *Shilton v Wilmhurst* recognised that compensation for the loss of personal rights, not directly connected with the recipient's employment, does not constitute a taxable emolument. Accordingly, the decisions in *Jarrold v Boustead*[1] and *Pritchard v Arundale*[2] remain good authority.

1 [1964] 3 All ER 76.
2 [1971] 3 All ER 1011.

6.28 In *Jarrold v Boustead* a payment was made to the taxpayer upon signing as a professional rugby player for Hull Football Club Ltd. By signing he lost his amateur status; a disqualification for life. The taxpayer was successful in persuading the Court of Appeal that the payment was non-taxable compensation for the loss of the various rights which he would otherwise enjoy as an amateur player, those rights being personal and so outside the scope of Schedule E. In deciding in favour of the taxpayer, Lord Denning MR agreed with the decision of the commissioners at first instance, to the effect that:

'... the payment ... was quite separate from the engagement of [the taxpayer's] services and was not the payment of remuneration in advance. It was, we think, merely an inducement to [him] which he accepted, to put himself in a position in which he could be employed by the Hull Football Club and to relinquish his amateur status.'[1]

In agreeing with the commissioners, it was noted that there was no element of disguised remuneration, Mr Boustead was otherwise employed at full rates of pay.

1 [1964] 3 All ER 76 at 80.

6.29 In *Pritchard v Arundale* (a case which was distinguished in *Glantree Engineering v Goodhand*[1]) consideration was given to the taxpayer in the form of shares upon him agreeing to leave private practice as a senior chartered accountant and join a company as joint managing director. The fact that consideration was given in the form of shares is not relevant, the same principles would apply if it were paid in money.

6.29 *The position of employees*

The case was decided in favour of the taxpayer by Megarry J, sitting in the High Court. Two extracts from his statement are of particular relevance. First, the circumstances of the share transfer:

> '... it is of some importance to observe that in the present case the shares are being transferred on an out-and-out basis in consideration of the taxpayer entering into a contract whereunder his employment was to commence not forthwith but within a little over six months ... The taxpayer might have died before he had rendered any services whatever to the company, and yet there is no provision for him to return any of the consideration; and many other instances may be imagined of the taxpayer never in fact rendering services to the company.'[2]

Second, the evidence as to the taxpayer's loss:

> 'If a professional man in his middle years gives up his career and embarks on some quite different activity, he is most unlikely to be able to pick up his former profession as soon as his other activities end, for to a greater or less degree he will have grown rusty in his skills and knowledge and will have ceased to be in close daily contact with his professional brethren.'[3]

---

1 [1983] STC 1.
2 [1971] 3 All ER 1011 at 1022.
3 Ibid at 1023.

6.30 In both *Jarrold v Boustead* and *Pritchard v Arundale* the non-returnable nature of the benefits in question was a decisive factor. The decisions may be contrasted with that in *Riley v Coglan*,[1] another case dealing with the loss of amateur status. The £500 payment there in question was returnable if the taxpayer ceased to provide his services, with the result that the payment was regarded as made in return for services and was therefore taxable. In deciding against the taxpayer, Ungoed-Thomas J construed the agreement as follows:

> '... the £500 was paid to him subject to the liability to repay a proportionate part if during the course of his career he did not make himself available to play. Therefore, the £500 was to be a running payment for his making himself available to serve the club when required to do so.'[2]

Notwithstanding the reference to repayment by way of liquidated damages, his Lordship was clear that the £500 was paid to the taxpayer in consideration of his agreement to serve the club.

---

1 [1968] 1 All ER 314.
2 Ibid at 319.

---

3 THE SPECIAL STATUTORY SCHEME

6.31 The general Schedule E principles are subject to a special scheme by virtue of TA 1988 s 148, subject to the relieving provisions of TA 1988 s 188 and TA 1988 s 154. Each section is considered in turn below. The impact of

The special statutory scheme **6.33**

TA 1988 ss 590–612 in respect of retirement, and of TA 1988 s 313 in respect of restrictive covenants are considered at **6.59** and **6.74** below respectively.

The ambit of section 148

6.32 The general principles of the Schedule E charge remain important, because TA 1988 s 148 only applies to payments not otherwise chargeable to tax. Sub-section (2) applies to:

> 'any payment (not otherwise chargeable to tax) which is made, whether in pursuance of any legal obligation or not, either directly or indirectly in consideration or in consequence of, or otherwise in connection with, the termination of the holding of the office or employment or any change in its functions or emoluments, including any payment in commutation of annual or periodical payments (whether chargeable to tax or not) which would otherwise have been so made.'

The importance of the general position is best illustrated by way of example. If compensation is paid to settle a claim for wrongful dismissal, as in *Henley v Murray*, then s 148 is applicable. If the compensation were paid pursuant to an express contractual agreement to this effect, as in *Dale v De Soissons*, the payment would be taxable as an emolument in accordance with general principles and the section would not be in question. Whether or not a charge arises under s 148 or some other provision is important. The relieving provisions contained in TA 1988 s 188 only apply to payments chargeable under s 148.

6.33 It is useful to consider the effect of s 148 by reference to its constituent parts. In considering the ambit of the charge it should be noted that the causation net is cast very wide. A legal obligation is not a necessary precondition to the charge, so that payments of an ex gratia nature may fall within it. It should also be noted that there are no time restrictions on the application of the section, so that a payment made, say, one year after termination of the relevant contract, will still fall within it.

The ambit of the charge may be restated as applying to payments made either directly or indirectly in consideration or in consequence of, or otherwise in connection with:

(a) the termination of the employment;
(b) any change in the functions of the employment;
(c) any change in the emoluments of the employment,

as well as the commutation of annual or periodical payments (whether chargeable to tax or not) which would otherwise have been made but for that commutation.

The section therefore applies to payments following termination by agreement, wrongful or unfair dismissal, as a result of injury or by reason of redundancy. The section also applies where there is any change in the nature of the employee's job or level of remuneration. In each of these instances, the required causal connection is relaxed. It is sufficient for payment to be made in connection with the event. The reference to payment, both direct

6.33 *The position of employees*

and indirect makes it clear that liability cannot be avoided by routing payment via a third party.

6.34 The case of *Hunter v Dewhurst*, the facts of which are considered at **6.25** above, may be used to illustrate the breadth of s 148. In that case a payment was made to the taxpayer so as to compensate him for the partial loss of a lump sum upon retirement, such loss arising as a result of his agreement to work on a part-time basis at a reduced salary.

If the case were decided today, it is considered that the compensation would fall within s 148(2). This is because it was made 'in . . . consequence of, or otherwise in connection with . . . [a] change in [the employment's] emoluments'. This result occurs because it was the salary reduction which had the effect of reducing the taxpayer's lump sum on retirement, and was therefore the reason for making the compensation payment.

Because the section also applies to compensation paid for the commutation of annual or periodical payments which would otherwise have been due, the payment made in commutation of pension rights in *Tilley v Wales* (at **6.12** above) would now fall to be taxed under s 148(2). If the commutation relates to the employee's entire pension and arises by reason of a rule contained in the relevant pension scheme, it may fall to be charged under TA 1988 s 599, for which see *Simon's Taxes* E7.218.

THE IDENTITY OF THE PAYEE

6.35 The identity of the payee is irrelevant for the purposes of s 148. Receipt by the employee's spouse or any relative[1] or dependant (ie a person maintained by the employee) or by any other person on behalf of or to the order of the employee, is assessable in the same manner as direct receipt by the employee.

---

1 As defined by TA 1988 s 839(8).

BASIS OF ASSESSMENT AND REPORTING REQUIREMENTS

6.36 Payments chargeable under s 148 are not 'emoluments', and so the receipts basis of assessment provided for by TA 1988 ss 202A and 202B does not apply. Instead, s 148(4) provides that the payment is regarded as received upon the date of commutation, termination or change as appropriate.

The provider of any benefit chargeable under s 148 is obliged to report the particulars of that benefit to the Inland Revenue within 30 days of the end of the tax year in which it was provided. For example, a payment made following the termination of an employment contract in August 1993 must be reported no later than 5 May 1994.

BENEFITS IN KIND UPON TERMINATION

6.37 The termination of an employee's contract often results in the provision of benefits in kind to the employee in addition to cash payments. In common with the position regarding cash payments, it must first be asked whether the benefit is already chargeable to tax. If so, the provisions of s 148 are inapplicable. Whether this results in more tax becoming due may depend upon the nature of the benefit, and in this respect the position can be very different from that applicable to cash payments because of the different valuation basis that may apply.

Benefits are charged by reason of s 148(3), which provides that valuable consideration other than money is treated as a payment of money equal to its value at the time it is given. Any exemption from charge as to the first £30,000 (pursuant to TA 1988 s 188) must therefore take into account that value together with the amount of any cash payments.

The requirement to value the benefit is presumably a direction to take into account the benefit's market value to the recipient (whether the recipient can turn the benefit to account or not would appear to be irrelevant). In many cases, the market value will be readily ascertainable, but the provision of benefits such as free or subsidised air or rail travel would require valuation by reference to the period over which the benefit was to be made available and the likely extent of use. This method of valuation can result in a very different tax liability to that where the benefit is chargeable on the normal basis.

6.38 Save where benefits are charged by reference to a specific formula, as is the case with cars, the normal basis provides for benefits to be charged by reference to the marginal cost to the employer of providing the benefit, for which see *Pepper v Hart*.[1] That marginal cost may often be different from the value of the benefit. The different basis of valuation is particularly important in the context of so-called in-house benefits. Subject to the impact of the £30,000 or other exemption, it may be advantageous to provide benefits which are taxable on the normal basis, and thereby outside the scope of s 148. This is best illustrated by way of example.

EXAMPLE

In *Pepper v Hart*, the in-house benefits in question were the provision of school places for school masters' sons at a concessionary rate of one-fifth of the fees normally charged. Such benefits are used for the purposes of this example.

Harry's employment with a private school is terminated during the Summer recess. The school provides him with:

(i) a cash payment of £20,000 and
(ii) agrees to allow his son to complete his education at the school under the concessionary fee arrangement available to schoolmasters. Harry's son has a further three years to go and the concessionary fee for each year is £3,000. The full amount of the fees would otherwise be £15,000 for each year.

If Harry were to be charged under s 148, his total assessable benefits would be in the sum of

(i) £20,000 plus
(ii) £45,000 minus £9,000 made good, less
(iii) the £30,000 golden handshake exemption. Tax would therefore be due on £26,000.

However, the agreement to provide the school place could be included as part of Harry's contract of employment. The £20,000 payment would then be sheltered by

6.38 *The position of employees*

the £30,000 exemption, and the benefit of the school place would not have a marginal cost above the £3,000 annual contribution. No tax would therefore be due.

---

1 [1992] STC 898.

OBLIGATIONS INCURRED BEFORE 6 APRIL 1960

6.39 Of minor significance now, payments otherwise chargeable under s 148 are exempted by sub-s (6) if made in pursuance of an obligation incurred before 6 April 1960. The obligation in question must be a legal not merely a moral one.[1]

---

1 *Mercer v Pearson* (1975) 51 TC 213.

The ambit of section 154

6.40 So called 'higher-paid' employees earning £8,500 or more and directors are subject to a special charging regime in respect of benefits in kind, by virtue of TA 1988 Ch II, Pt V. A general head of charge is established by TA 1988 s 154 which provides as follows:

> '(1) . . . where in any year a person is employed in employment to which this Chapter applies and—
>
> (a) by reason of his employment there is provided for him, or for others being members of his family or household, any benefit to which this section applies; and
> (b) the cost of providing the benefit is not (apart from this section) chargeable to tax as his income,
>
> there is to be treated as emoluments of the employment, and accordingly chargeable to income tax under Schedule E, an amount equal to whatever is the cash equivalent of the benefit.'

The charge is aimed at the provision of benefits in kind which would otherwise escape taxation under TA 1988 s 19(1). However, the receipt of cash can constitute a 'benefit' for the purposes of s 154 (see *Wicks v Firth*[1] and *Mairs v Haughey*[2]). It is therefore necessary to consider whether compensation, which is not taxable under TA 1988 s 19(1), but which would otherwise be taxable under TA 1988 s 148 (and so fully or partially relieved) falls to be taxed under s 154(1). This was the secondary argument raised by the Inland Revenue in *Mairs v Haughey*.

---

1 [1981] STC 28.
2 [1992] STC 495.

CAUSATION

6.41 For a benefit to be charged under s 154, it must have been derived 'by reason of' the employment in question. The causation test is easier to satisfy than under TA 1988 s 19(1) as the word 'therefrom' there used constitutes a stricter test. The test was considered by Lord Denning:

> '*It seems to me that the words "by reason of" are far wider than the word "therefrom" in [s 19(1)]. They are deliberately designed to close the gap in taxability which was left by the House of Lords in* Hochstrasser v Mayes. *The words cover cases where the fact of employment is the causa sine qua non of the fringe benefits, that is, where the employee would not have received fringe benefits unless he had been an employee. The fact of employment must be one of the causes of the benefit being provided, but it need not be the sole cause, or even the dominant cause. It is sufficient if the employment was an operative cause—in the sense that it was a condition of the benefit being granted.*'[1]

Lord Chief Justice Hutton in *Mairs v Haughey*, considered Lord Denning's test to be too wide and expressed a preference for the views of Oliver LJ in the same case:

> '*Speaking only for myself I do not, in the case of this legislation, find the philosophical distinction between a "causa causans" and a "causa sine qua non" helpful. I see no reason why a benefit "derived" from the employment (to use the words of the chapter title) necessarily has to be invested with an intention on the part of the employer to remunerate the employee for the performance of his duties. One is directed to see whether the benefit is provided by reason of the employment and in the context of these provisions that, in my judgment, involves no more than asking the question "what is it that enables the person concerned to enjoy the benefit?" without the necessity for too sophisticated an analysis of the operative reasons why that person may have been prompted to apply for the benefit or to avail himself of it.*'[2]

By way of explanation:

> '"*Causa causans" is supposed to mean a cause which causes, while "causa sine qua non" means, I suppose, a cause which does not, in the sense material to the particular case, cause, but is merely an incident which precedes in the history or narrative of events, but as a cause is not in at the death, and hence is irrelevant.*'[3]

The distinction has not been otherwise referred to in this chapter for reasons which Lord Wright also expressed:

> '*I cannot help deprecating the use of Latin or so-called Latin phrases in this way. They only distract the mind from the true problem which is to apply the principles of English law to the realities of the case.*'[4]

As the relevant test applicable under s 154 may be said to rest somewhere at or between the views of Lord Denning and Lord Oliver the use of Latin could not be avoided here.

---

1 In *Wicks v Firth* [1982] STC 76 at 79.
2 [1992] STC 495 at 525.
3 Per Lord Wright in *Smith, Hogg & Co Ltd v Black Sea & Baltic General Insurance Co Ltd* [1940] AC 997 at 1003.
4 Ibid.

6.42 So far as concerned the application of the test in *Mairs v Haughey*, it

6.42 *The position of employees*

was decided that the compensation in that case was paid by reason of the surrender by the taxpayer of his contingent right to receive payments under the redundancy scheme, as distinct from his employment. It remains to be seen whether the Inland Revenue might establish the charge under s 154 as a 'catch all' provision for compensation payments which would otherwise be chargeable under TA 1988 s 148 and therefore relieved under TA 1988 s 188.

The distinction drawn between remuneration for services and compensation for the surrender of an employee's right to provide services appear to make it unlikely that s 154 could apply to termination payment generally. Taxpayers may also seek to rely on the exemption from charge which is available to those who 'make good' the benefit.

MAKING GOOD

6.43 It was decided in *Mairs v Haughey* that even if the compensation fell within s 154, it was 'made good' by the employee and so not charged by reason of TA 1988 s 156(1), which provides as follows:

> '*The cash equivalent of any benefit chargeable to tax under section 154 is an amount equal to the cost of the benefit, less so much (if any) of it as is made good by the employee to those providing the benefit.*'

The employee in *Mairs v Haughey* had made good the benefit by reason of his giving up a contingent right (ie to the redundancy benefits). It is not necessary for the benefit to be made good with money—a non-pecuniary compensation suffices provided it does not consist of the provision of services.

The ability to make good the benefit by giving up rights may therefore ensure that no charge can arise under s 154. However, it was clear in *Mairs v Haughey* that the compensation actually paid did not overvalue the rights being given up; only 30% of the amount payable on redundancy was paid by way of compensation.

A further requirement is that the benefit be 'made good by the employee to those providing the benefit'; a loss of rights is not enough, the employer must receive value. This was obviously the case in *Mairs v Haughey* where the employer was released from his obligation to make redundancy payments. A loss of rights which does not directly benefit the employer financially would not have the same result.

4 EXEMPTION AND SECTION 188

6.44 A charge under TA 1988 s 148 may be relieved, in whole or in part depending on the circumstances of payment and its amount, by reason of TA 1988 s 188. Exemptions from charge in the context of:

(a) termination by reason of death or disability;
(b) restrictive covenants; and
(c) retirement

are considered in detail below. Exemptions are also provided (at TA 1988 s 188(1)) in respect of:

> '(e) any terminal grant, gratuity or other lump sum paid under any Royal Warrant, Queen's Order, or Order in Council relating to members of Her Majesty's forces, and any payment made in commutation of annual or other periodical payments authorised by any such Warrant or Order;
> (f) a payment of benefit under any superannuation scheme administered by the government of an overseas territory within the Commonwealth, or of compensation for loss of career, interruption of service or disturbance made in connection with any change in the constitution of any such overseas territory to persons who, before the change, were employed in the public services of that territory;'

6.45 Where the employment in question involved foreign service, two reliefs are in question. First, complete exemption from charge under TA 1988 s 188(3). Second, partial exemption under TA 1988, Sch 11, para 3. In either case it is first necessary to define the term 'foreign service'.

The meaning of foreign service
6.46 Foreign service is defined by TA 1988, Sch 11, para 10 as meaning:

(i) for service before 1974–75 not chargeable under Case I of Schedule E for the year 1956–57 onwards (before that not chargeable under any such Case); or
(ii) for service after 1973–74 not chargeable under Case I of Schedule E or eligible for the 100% deduction provided for by TA 1988 s 193(1) (or relieved under para 1 of Sch 2, Finance Act 1974 or para 1 of Sch 7, Finance Act 1977).

ABSOLUTE EXEMPTION

6.47 Complete exemption is available pursuant to TA 1988 s 188(3) if the employment in question included foreign service by the employee, and that service comprised either:

> '(a) in any case, three-quarters of the whole period of service down to the relevant date; or
> (b) where the period of service down to the relevant date exceeded ten years, the whole of the last ten years; or
> (c) where the period of service down to the relevant date exceeded 20 years, one-half of that period, including any ten of the last 20 years.'

EXAMPLE

John is employed by A Ltd, for whom he undertakes mining surveys outside the UK for long periods of time. His employment is wrongfully terminated on 1 January 1994, and A Ltd agrees to pay him compensation of £50,000 in consequence.

If John had been with A Ltd for eight years, of which six years had comprised foreign service, the payment would be exempt from tax by reason of condition (a) above. A period of less than six years would be insufficient for the purposes of this condition.

If John's employment were for a period of 17 years, of which the last 11 years had comprised foreign service, condition (a) would not be satisfied, but exemption would be afforded by condition (b).

6.47 *The position of employees*

If John's employment were for a period of 22 years, the first five and last eight years of which comprised foreign service, neither condition (a) nor (b) would be satisfied, but exemption would be afforded by condition (c).

PARTIAL EXEMPTION

6.48 Partial exemption in respect of foreign service may be made available under TA 1988 Sch 11 para 3 if no absolute exemption is available. Relief is given on a proportional basis, as follows:

> '*In computing the charge to tax in respect of a payment chargeable to tax under section 148, being a payment made in respect of an office or employment in which the service of the holder includes foreign service, there shall be deducted from the payment a sum which bears to the amount which would be chargeable to tax apart from this paragraph the same proportion as the length of the foreign service bears to the length of the service before the relevant date.*'

The partial relief is in addition to any available under TA 1988 s 188(4) as to the first £30,000 of any payment.

EXAMPLE

To continue the example at **6.47**, if John's employment was for a period of eight years of which only three constituted foreign service, no absolute exemption would be available. However, three-eighths of the payment would be relieved, equal to £18,750. The remaining £31,250 would be relieved as to £30,000 by reason of TA 1988 s 188(4), leaving the sum of £1,250 only subject to tax.

6.49 For the purposes of the partial exemption the relevant date in calculating the exempt part is the date of termination of or change in the contract or, in a case involving the commutation of annual or other payments the date from which the termination or change takes effect (TA 1988 Sch 11 para 9).

5 TERMINATION GENERALLY, WRONGFUL AND UNFAIR DISMISSAL

6.50 Compensation for termination, not reserved in the contract, will be subject to tax under TA 1988 s 148 subject to any applicable reliefs under TA 1988 s 188. This treatment is applicable to termination generally, which includes wrongful and unfair dismissal. However, special considerations apply in respect of termination by reason of:

(a) retirement;
(b) death or disability; and
(c) redundancy,

which are considered below.

As mentioned above, a payment which escapes tax under s 148 by virtue of s 188 should not be taxable under TA 1988 s 154. This is because the employee is being compensated for a loss arising as a result of termination; the benefit is not being provided because he is an employee performing duties for his employer. It might also be said that the employee gives value for the benefit, namely his rights under the Employment Protection (Consolidation) Act 1978.

Lump sum payments upon termination, commonly known as 'golden handshakes', chargeable under s 148 escape tax as to the first £30,000 by reason of s 188. The exemption is a general one; its availability does not depend upon factors such as disability or foreign service. If the compensation exceeds the financial limit then the excess is fully chargeable to income tax at the recipient's marginal rate of tax. The forerunner of the current exemption was first introduced by the Finance Act 1960 for payments not exceeding £5,000. The current limit was introduced by the Finance Act 1988, and its operation simplified by the removal of the previous system of 'top slicing' relief. For the relief of payments prior to 6 April 1988 see *Simon's Taxes* E4.809 and E4.810.

The exemption is available in relation to each particular employment. Therefore a person's contract could be terminated and the exemption fully used as against the resulting compensation, but if that person subsequently obtained another job which was also terminated, the full amount of the relief would still be available, irrespective that such payments occurred in the same tax year.

Associated employments

6.51 To prevent the benefit of the exemption being obtained more than once in relation to the same employment or from the same employer s 188(5) contains certain restrictions. Their effect is to aggregate multiple payments in respect of the same employment, as well as in respect of different employments with the same employer or associated employers.[1] It is further provided that the exemption is to be applied against income of an earlier period before a later one, but subject to that rateable deduction on account of the exemption should be made. This may be illustrated by example.

---

1 Determined by reference to the definition of 'control' in TA 1988 s 840. See TA 1988 s 188(7).

EXAMPLE

Philip is employed full time by B Ltd and he is also a director of a subsidiary company called C Ltd. Philip's employment and office are both terminated at the same time.

B Ltd agrees to pay Philip compensation in the sum of £40,000. C Ltd agrees to pay compensation in the sum of £6,000. Of the total £46,000 only £30,000 is exempted pursuant to s 188. The benefit of the exemption is divided rateably as between the two payments. The result is that £26,087 and £3,913 remains tax free of the £40,000 and £6,000 payments respectively.

If the facts were changed so that termination was not contemporaneous, but involved termination by C Ltd on 1 April 1993, and by B Ltd on 7 April 1993 the resulting payments would be assessable in different tax years, namely 1992/93 and 1993/94 respectively.

In this case the £6,000 paid by C Ltd would be free of tax because it relates to the

6.51 *The position of employees*

earlier period (ie 1992/93). The £40,000 paid by B Ltd would be tax free as to the first £24,000 representing the remaining exemption available.

Costs
6.52 Costs incurred by an employee in securing compensation for termination or other amount taxable under TA 1988 s 148, are not, strictly speaking, deductible for the purposes of the £30,000 limit.[1]

This somewhat harsh rule is relaxed by Extra-statutory Concession A81, which provides that no charge will be imposed on payments made by the former employer:

> '— direct to the former employee's solicitor; and
> — in full or partial discharge of the solicitor's bill of costs incurred by the employee only in connection with the termination of his or her employment; and
> — under a specific term in the settlement agreement providing for that payment.'

---

1 *Warnett v Jones* [1980] STC 131; which was concerned with the then limit of £5,000.

6.53 If the dispute goes to court then the concession applies to payments made by the employer in accordance with a court order. The concession only applies to legal costs, not accountancy or other professional fees. The concession does not confer a general right to deduct costs; the circumstances are limited to those instances where an apportionment is agreed (or imposed by the court) between the employee and employee. In negotiating settlements, therefore, provision should be made for legal costs as part of any compensation package.

Preserving the exemption and claims for relief

6.54 The availability of the exemptions under TA 1988 s 188 can be vulnerable in practice. This is because it is tempting to promise to pay compensation to an employee prior to the termination of his employment. If agreement is so reached between the employee and employer as to the payment of compensation, either of a precise amount or as to its method of calculation, that may operate as a variation of the employment contract. There is a risk that the compensation could then become fully chargeable to tax under TA 1988 s 19(1) by virtue of the decision in *Dale v De Soissons*.

Avoiding agreement

6.55 To safeguard available exemptions, it is recommended that the following guidelines be adhered to:

(a) no agreement should be reached prior to the termination of the employment as to any payment of compensation;
(b) there is, however, no objection to the employer indicating that consideration will be given to the payment of compensation—provided that the indication falls short of a promise to pay;
(c) nor is there any objection to reaching agreement upon termination, as in *Clayton v Lavender* at **6.16** above;

(d) any payment of compensation should not be conditional upon continued service by the employee.

6.56 If an employee is expected to work out his notice, or otherwise continue to work for a short period, the continuing co-operation of the employee will be required. That co-operation may be safeguarded without prejudicing the taxation treatment by promising to consider making compensation payments after the contract has terminated—provided that promise falls short of an enforceable contractual obligation.

Procedure
6.57 It is also good practice to adhere to a number of procedural guidelines:

(a) the date and circumstances of termination should be evidenced in writing;
(b) a record should be kept of any discussion of compensation payments, especially where the employee continues to work. Board minutes or attendance notes are satisfactory;
(c) board or other approval for compensation payments should be recorded;
(d) if the employee in question is a director or the company secretary, he should not be a party to any board meetings at which any payment of compensation is to be considered.

CLAIMS FOR RELIEF

6.58 Relief under TA 1988 s 188 for payments taxable under TA 1988 s 148 is not automatic; the employee must make a claim (see TA 1988 s 188(6)) but there is no particular form for this. Additionally, no time limit is expressed for the making of the claim, so that the normal period will apply which is the period of six years from the end of the fiscal year in which the payment is chargeable to income tax.

6 RETIREMENT

6.59 Payments made upon the termination of an employee's contract by reason of retirement are now rarely regarded by the Inland Revenue as falling within the TA 1988 s 148 charge. Instead such payments are likely to be regarded as taxable in full, without the benefit of the £30,000 exemption, on the basis that they constitute 'relevant benefits' within TA 1988 s 612 and are therefore taxable under TA 1988 s 595. The charge to tax applies without the benefit of exemption unless the payments derive from, essentially, an approved scheme.[1]

The views of the Inland Revenue are set out in SP 13/91, and apply to payments made after 31 October 1991. Their previous practice was to regard payments made upon retirement as potentially within TA 1988 s 148.

---

1 *Simon's Taxes* E7.211.

6.60 *The position of employees*

THE MEANING OF RETIREMENT

6.60 The term 'retirement' is not defined for the purposes of the taxes legislation. The dictionary meaning refers to the act of withdrawal from an occupation or business activity. Whilst the term is associated with the sense of complete withdrawal from an occupation or business activity, it is recognised that a person may retire yet still have some commercial interests which occupy a small part of his time.

A number of hypothetical circumstances were explored in an exchange of correspondence between the Institute of Chartered Accountants of England and Wales and the Inland Revenue.[1] The Institute queried whether a retirement situation occurred in the following circumstances, which are detailed together with extracts from the Revenue response:

'(a) *A person who has worked for the company for 20 years leaves at age 45 to take a senior position in another company.*

Response: *A senior executive changing jobs at age 45, obviously as part of his or her normal working career, is not retirement.*

(b) *A long-service employee leaves to take a senior position in another company at the age of 60.*

Response: *This is a borderline case which would depend very much on the precise circumstances. But, given the age, this might well be regarded as retirement, despite the new appointment.*

(c) *A division of the company is sold and the 55 year old manager responsible for running it leaves to take a job with the purchaser.*

Response: *The action of the employee does not look to be consistent with retirement but with maximising his opportunities to continue working until normal retirement age.*

(d) *A person in his 50s has a heart attack and is advised by his doctor to leave and seek a less stressful position.*

Response: *The circumstances set out may well be treated as retirement.*

(e) . . .

(f) *An employee aged 50 leaves to take a job nearer home to be able to nurse her aged parents.*

Response: *This again is a borderline case. The example described probably would not be regarded as retirement bearing in mind the age of the employee, and the fact that she obtained further work. But, the decision might go the other way if the employee left to nurse a relative without seeking a further job, especially if she was nearer the normal retirement age for her job.*'

---

1 *Simon's Tax Intelligence* 1992, at 1003 to 1006.

6.61 It can be seen from the responses that the age of the taxpayer is considered to be an important factor. The conclusions reached in situations (a), (c) and (f) appear to be correct. However, it is difficult to regard situation (b) as retirement unless the new position merely requires a nominal amount of time to be expended by the employee. The age factor would appear to have been given excessive prominence. In addition, situation (d) would not appear to be an example of retirement, since the employee intends to continue his work, merely in a less stressful position.

The nature of a retirement benefits scheme

6.62 Central to the revised view of the Inland Revenue published in SP 13/91 is the definition of a 'retirement benefits scheme' as provided by s 611, namely '. . . a scheme for the provision of benefits consisting of or including relevant benefits . . .'

For these purposes 'relevant benefits' is defined by TA 1988 s 612(1) as meaning:

> '. . . any pension, lump sum, gratuity or other like benefit given or to be given on retirement or on death, or in anticipation of retirement, or in connection with past service, after retirement or death, or to be given on or in anticipation of or in connection with any change in the nature of the service of the employee in question, except that it does not include any benefit which is to be afforded solely by reason of the disablement by accident of a person occurring during his service or of his death by accident so occurring and for no other reason.'

There are, therefore, two distinct elements to consider. First, the nature of relevant benefits. Second, that of a scheme.

RELEVANT BENEFITS

6.63 The wide ranging nature of the definition is apt to cover all payments connected with retirement. The facts in *Hunter v Dewhurst* (**6.25** above) may be used to illustrate the scope of the definition. In that case a payment was made in order to compensate the taxpayer for the reduction in the lump sum retirement payment which would otherwise have been made to him but for his continuing to serve as a director on a part-time basis at a reduced rate of remuneration. The change to a part-time basis of employment may be said to bring the compensation payment within the ambit of TA 1988 s 612 as it is a lump sum benefit given 'in connection with [a] change in the nature of the service of the employee in question'.

In *Hunter v Dewhurst*, that change occurred against the background of an existing scheme for payments to be made upon retirement.

SCHEMES

6.64 For the purposes of TA 1988 s 612(1) the term 'scheme' is given a particularly wide meaning. It includes not only those established by deed, agreement, or series of agreements but also those established by 'other arrangements'. The meaning is extended so as to include those which relate only to:

(a) 'a small number of employees, or to a single employee'; or
(b) 'the payment of a pension starting immediately on the making of the arrangements'.

A scheme may exist notwithstanding that only one employee is the object of it. Additionally, circumstances involving simultaneous decision and payment are expressly brought within the definition—but only in relation to pensions.

6.65 The reference to pensions only in the context of payment starting immediately on the making of arrangements does place some limits on the

6.65 *The position of employees*

extended definition. It is clear that a promise to pay a pension to an employee falls within the meaning of a scheme; there is either a pre-existing arrangement to pay or one comes into existence when the first payment is made. This is not the case however with a lump sum, or other once and for all benefit. To be subject to income tax under TA 1988 s 595 there must be a pre-existing arrangement.

The making of an ex gratia financial provision upon retirement should not be sufficient to bring the payments in question within charge under TA 1988 s 595. There must be some additional factor to bring the payment within charge. The Inland Revenue are understandably reluctant to concede that lump sums and benefits may be taxable under the more favourable regime of TA 1988 s 148. The examples given in the Statement of Practice SP 13/91 reflect this in that they are overly restrictive. The following illustrations are regarded by the Inland Revenue as fully taxable:

> '(1) *a decision at a meeting to make an ex gratia payment on an employee's retirement; or*
> (2) *where, say, a personal manager makes an ex gratia payment under a delegated authority or on the basis of some outline structure or policy; or*
> (3) *where it is common practice for an employer to make an ex gratia payment to a particular class of employee.*'

That the illustrations are too restrictive may be demonstrated by recourse to the meaning of the term 'arrangement'.

Schemes and the meaning of arrangements
6.66 It is clear that the term 'arrangement' is a word of the widest possible import. It was considered by the Court of Appeal (in the context of the Restrictive Trade Practices Act 1956 s 6(3)) in the leading case of *Re British Basic Slag Ltd's Agreements*.[1] Willmer LJ had this to say of the term:

> '*Though it may not be easy to put it into words, everybody knows what is meant by an arrangement between two or more parties. If the arrangement is intended to be enforceable by legal proceedings, as in the case where it is made for good considera- tion, it may no doubt properly be described as an agreement. But the statute clearly contemplates that there may be arrangements which are not enforceable by legal proceedings, but which create only moral obligations or obligations binding in honour. . . [When] each of two or more parties intentionally arouses in the other an expectation that he will act in a certain way, it seems to me that he incurs at least a moral obligation to do so. An arrangement as so defined is therefore something "whereby the parties to it accept mutual rights and obligations".*'[2]

The term was also considered by Diplock LJ, who noted that arrange- ments may be made in many ways, but that it was sufficient to constitute one between two parties (referred to as A and B) if:

> '(i) *A makes a representation as to his future conduct with the expectation and intention that such conduct on his part will operate as an inducement to B to act in a particular way; (ii) such representation is communicated to B, who has knowledge that A so expected and intended, and (iii) such representation or A's conduct in fulfilment of it operates as an inducement, whether among other inducements or not, to B to act in that particular way.*'[3]

1 [1963] 2 All ER 807.
2 Ibid at 814.
3 Ibid at 819.

6.67 These comments bring home the requirement of mutuality. The following points may therefore be made in respect of the Inland Revenue's illustrations:

(a) So far as concerns a decision at a meeting, it is clear that no arrangement will exist if the meeting occurs after the employee's retirement.
   A decision to make a payment, taken before retirement, may constitute an agreement on the basis that it becomes part of the employee's contract. Otherwise, it may only be an arrangement if the element of mutuality is satisfied and this will not be the case merely because a decision has been taken, it must be communicated to the employee and raise an expectation of receiving the sum in question.
(b) The existence of delegated authority would not appear by itself to result in the existence of arrangements. An outline policy might, provided the employee in question is aware of it, otherwise there would be no expectation of payment on his part.
(c) The existence of a common practice may be sufficient to result in arrangements existing, but only if that practice is universally applied or the employee has the requisite expectation.

7 DEATH OR DISABILITY

6.68 Payments made because of an employee's death or disablement fall within the charge to income tax under TA 1988 s 148. However, TA 1988 s 188 provides an absolute exemption. Such compensation is also excluded from tax in the context of the retirement provisions. Further, there can be no question that such compensation falls within the ambit of TA 1988 s 154, because it is not referable to the employment contract.

The exemption is provided for by TA 1988 s 188(1)(a), which applies in respect of two types of payments, namely those:

'... [1] made in connection with the termination of the holding of an office or employment by the death of the holder, or [2] made on account of injury to or disability of the holder of an office or employment.'

PAYMENTS FOLLOWING DEATH

6.69 Payments made following the termination of employment by reason of death are the subject of a wide exclusion. They merely need to be made 'in connection' with that termination to so qualify, which should cover all possible circumstances. The only question which arises goes to the status of death in service benefits provided to employees as part of their remuneration package. Are such payments subject to tax in full as being reserved payments or are they free of tax?

6.69 *The position of employees*

It is clear that payments made by an insurer following the payment of premiums by the deceased person's employer are outside the scope of income tax. The position regarding uninsured benefits (ie where the employer meets the cost himself) might be thought to be less clear. On one view payments so made are sums reserved under the contract of employment, and so taxable in full by reason of the decision in *Dale v De Soissons* (**6.16** above). The better view however is to regard such payments as outside the scope of income tax, on the basis that such a payment does not represent a reward in respect of services (the employee cannot enjoy his reward) but is made to relieve distress. It is understood that the Inland Revenue do not regard sums so paid as within the charge to income tax.

PAYMENTS FOLLOWING INJURY OR DISABILITY

6.70 The second element of exemption under TA 1988 s 188 would appear to be more narrowly drawn as it applies only to payments made 'on account of' the injury or disability in question. However, it is considered that the different wording does not import a more restrictive regime than that in relation to death. The different wording merely reflects the fact that death can have no result other than termination. Injury or disablement may result in termination or a change in the functions or emoluments of the injured person's employment; in either case as referred to in TA 1988 s 148(2).

At one stage the Inland Revenue were of the view that a gradual decline in physical or mental ability leading to incapacity was not a disability within TA 1988 s 188. In the light of a decision of the Special Commissioners, that view was changed with effect from 6 January 1981. It is now accepted that disability covers:

> '... not only a condition resulting from a sudden affliction but also continuing incapacity to perform the duties of an office or employment arising out of the culmination of a process of deterioration of physical or mental health caused by chronic illness.'[1]

Whilst the revised view is welcome it would appear to remain too restrictive. Specifically, why refer to 'chronic illness'? Either a disability exists or it does not; the section draws no distinction between disabilities caused by 'chronic' or other illnesses.

---

1 SP 10/81.

---

8 REDUNDANCY

6.71 Payments made upon the termination of an employee's contract through redundancy usually fall to be taxed by reference to TA 1988 s 148. Accordingly the first £30,000 will be exempt from charge by reason of TA 1988, s 188.

Redundancy does not, in itself, impute a different tax treatment than is the case with wrongful dismissal. A separate heading is appropriate however, as it allows consideration of two factors peculiar to redundancy situations. Those factors are first the status of statutory redundancy payments, and second, the status of payments made under voluntary schemes adopted by employers as well as made generally, in the light of the Inland Revenue's views contained in Statement of Practice SP 1/81.

The term 'redundancy' is defined by s 81(2) of the Employment Protection (Consolidation) Act 1978. Dismissal is regarded as being by reason of redundancy if it is wholly or mainly attributable to:

> '(a) the fact that his employer has ceased, or intends to cease, to carry on the business for the purposes of which the employee was employed by him, or has ceased, or intends to cease, to carry on that business in the place where the employee was so employed, or
> (b) the fact that the requirements of that business for employees to carry out work of a particular kind, or for the employees to carry out work of a particular kind in the place where he was so employed, have ceased or diminished or are expected to cease or diminish.'

A detailed consideration of the circumstances which constitute redundancy is beyond the scope of this book. Reference may be made to Part III, Volume 1 of *Harvey on Industrial Relations and Employment Law* (Butterworths), in which the definition is explored in the following introductory manner:

> 'It will be seen that the definition incorporates three main ideas: the employer is closing down his business altogether ("the business disappears"), or else he is closing down his business in the place where the employee is employed ("the workplace disappears"), or else he finds that his business no longer needs the employee's skills ("the job disappears"). But this last element—the disappearing job—may come about in two ways, though they overlap: either the business needs less of that sort of work or else the business can get by with fewer employees to do it. A classic example of the former arises from changing raw material—plastic replaces wood or metal, and the carpenter or welder is replaced by an injection moulder. A classic example of the latter is replacing men with machines: one computer can do the work of dozens of accounts clerks, although there is no diminution in the amount of accounting work required.'[1]

---

1 *Harvey*, at para 302.

STATUTORY REDUNDANCY PAYMENTS

6.72 Statutory redundancy payments are exempted from the general charge to income tax, but may be taken into account under TA 1988 s 148 (see ss 579(1) and 580(3)). They are therefore taxable subject to the £30,000 golden handshake exemption or absolute exemption (ie sums paid under Royal Warrant, by Commonwealth government or in respect of foreign service) as the case may be.

This treatment applies only to a 'redundancy payment' or 'employer's payment', and in respect of the latter only in so far as it is not in excess of the former. The reference to a redundancy payment is to that amount payable which is computed in accordance with Sch 4 of the Employment Protection

6.72 *The position of employees*

(Consolidation) Act 1978, by reference to the employee's length of service, weekly pay and a factor which increases with the employee's age.

The reference to an employer's payment is a reference to a redundancy payment for which the employer is liable to pay (which if the employer is insolvent may be satisfied out of government funds following application to the Secretary of State), or a payment under an agreement between the employer and one or more trade unions recognised by the Secretary of State under s 96 of the 1978 Act. The taxation status of an employer's payment in excess of the corresponding redundancy is subject to the principles considered in the following paragraph.

Voluntary redundancy payments

6.73 The Inland Revenue adopt a more relaxed approach to non-statutory termination payments upon redundancy than to payments upon wrongful dismissal or termination generally. That approach was originally detailed in Statement of Practice SP 1/81, in which the Inland Revenue accepted:

> '. . . that in the case of a genuine redundancy the only tax liability on lump sum payments made under redundancy schemes is under [s 148], even though the payment may be calculated by reference to the length of service or the amount of remuneration, or is conditional on continued service for a short period consistent with the reasonable needs of the employer's business.'

A 'genuine redundancy' was regarded as existing if four conditions were met, namely:

(a) a redundancy situation existed within the meaning of the Employment Protection (Consolidation) Act 1978;
(b) the employee receiving payment had been continuously in the service of the employer for at least two years;
(c) payments were not made to selected employees only; and
(d) such payments were 'not excessively large in relation to earnings and length of service'.

To a large extent, the four conditions are self-explanatory but two points may be made. First, the fact that only some employees will receive payment should not result in condition (c) being breached; the condition is to prevent the making of discretionary payments under the guise of redundancy. Selection by reference to some objective factor, for example minimum service, will not be in breach of the condition unless the objective factor is designed to exclude all but certain beneficiaries. Second, the requirement that payments be less than excessive would not appear to be a direction to consider the amount payable under the voluntary arrangement as compared to the statutory entitlement, if any. The amounts payable should be considered by reference to the employee's remuneration.

The Inland Revenue's practice was revised following the decision of the House of Lords in *Mairs v Haughey*, and Statement of Practice SP 1/94 was introduced to replace SP 1/81. The revised practice is less restrictive in that no mention is now made of the four conditions previously detailed. The revised practice is contained in the appendix following this chapter.

9 RESTRICTIVE COVENANTS

6.74 Payments made in consideration of a restrictive covenant, given in the employment context, are subject to the specific statutory regime of TA 1988 s 313 which charges such payments to income tax under Schedule E. The section was introduced by the Finance Act 1950 in order to reverse the decision in *Beak v Robson*[1] in which it was decided that amounts paid to a director under a non-competition covenant were not taxable.

1 [1943] 1 All ER 46.

6.75 The charge to tax is widely drawn, applying to sums paid in respect of employees past, present or future who give:

'... *an undertaking (whether absolute or qualified, and whether legally valid or not) the tenor or effect of which is to restrict him as to his conduct or activities* ...'

Where such an undertaking is given, the section charges to tax sums paid '... in respect of the giving of the undertaking or its total or partial fulfilment ...'. The identity of the recipient of that payment is irrelevant. Where consideration is provided in a form other than money, market value is substituted and the section applies as if a sum equal to that value has been paid (TA 1988 s 313(4)). The position of non-monetary benefits is therefore subject to the same valuation considerations as those chargeable under TA 1988 s 148.

In *Vaughan-Neil v IRC*[1] it was held that a payment to a barrister to induce him to take on employment and thereby cease private practice was not taxable under s 313. The section does not extend to payments for undertaking to perform the very duties which are inseparable from the employment itself.

The charge to income tax by reference to restrictive covenants only applies if the consideration given would not otherwise be subject to tax. This is a reference to the position under general Schedule E principles.

The charge to tax does not apply to those employees chargeable to tax under Schedule E, Case III; ie the remittance basis for foreign emoluments.

1 [1979] 1 WLR 1283, 54 TC 223.

Undertakings given before and after 9 June 1988

6.76 Payments for undertakings given before 9 June 1988 are subject to an unusual tax treatment. The payment is deemed to be paid net of basic rate tax, the recipient receiving a notional credit for the same so that he is liable to pay further amounts of tax only if he is subject to charge at the higher rate.

This advantageous treatment was removed by the Finance Act 1988, which provided for the whole amount received to be subject to tax by reference to the recipient's marginal rate of tax in the normal way. The changes introduced by the Act apply to undertakings given after 8 June 1988.

6.76 *The position of employees*

However, the 1988 changes also provided that payments for undertakings given after the relevant date would be deductible for the purposes of computing profits assessable to income tax so far as the employer is concerned. For payments made under the pre-1988 regime, deductibility must be considered by reference to normal principles. This may result in a restriction if the payments are considered to be capital in nature; for example, on the basis that the employer's goodwill is enhanced as was the case in *Associated Portland Cement Manufacturers Ltd v Kerr*.[1]

---

1 [1946] All ER 68.

RESTRICTIONS UPON TERMINATION

6.77 Payments taxable under s 313 are excluded from the ambit of TA 1988 s 148. They are therefore taxable in full if paid in connection with the termination of the employee's contract; none of the exemptions from charge associated with termination in TA 1988 s 188 may apply. In many instances, an employer will seek to ensure that he has the benefit of restrictive covenants upon termination, for example as to non-competition. If the employee gives an undertaking not to compete, in respect of which he receives payment, that sum will be fully taxable.

That position must be contrasted with an instance where the employee's restrictive covenants extend beyond termination so that no new covenants are obtained upon termination. No element of compensation so paid upon termination will be taxable under s 313; it is not paid either in respect of the undertaking being given or its fulfilment.

Between the two situations, grey areas exist. For example, where the covenants are subject to dispute or the employer wishes to withhold payment for a period so as to be sure that the employee does not compete in circumstances where the employer is reluctant to rely on his legal remedies. The true tax position will depend on the circumstances. In the case of dispute it is suggested that if compensation is paid on terms that the employee recognises the validity of the existing restriction, it will be taxable under TA 1988 s 148. In the case of delayed payment, common law rights of set-off may be relied upon in the event of the employee being in breach. Provision for liquidated damages is likely to be regarded as payment for total or partial fulfilment, and therefore taxable in full under s 313.

Any apportionment between amounts paid by way of general compensation upon termination and those paid in respect of restrictive covenants must be on a fair and reasonable basis.

10 NATIONAL INSURANCE

6.78 National insurance contributions are due from both employee and employer by reference to the employment income paid to the employee. The former is obliged to pay primary Class 1 contributions at a variable rate of up to 10% (with effect from 5 April 1994) on earnings, subject to an upper earnings limit beyond which further contributions are not due. For 1994/95 the upper limit is £430 per week, which equates to an annual limit of £22,360. Employers are obliged to pay secondary Class 1 contributions at a variable rate of up to 10.2% without limit. In view of the cap upon the employee's liability, the national insurance cost is primarily a matter of concern to employers.

The liability to pay national insurance contributions on payments made in the circumstances discussed in this chapter depends upon their status for income tax purposes, and in particular whether they are taxable in accordance with general Schedule E principles, under TA 1988 s 148 or s 313.

EARNINGS

6.79 National insurance is only due in respect of payments which count as 'earnings' for the purposes of s 3 of the Social Security Contributions and Benefits Act 1992. That section provides that '. . ."earnings" includes any remuneration or profit derived from an employment'. This short definition may for all practical purposes be regarded as identical with the concept of taxable emoluments within TA 1988 s 131, so far as regards cash payments. In addition, cash payments chargeable under TA 1988 s 313 are specifically regarded as earnings (by reason of s 4(4) of the 1992 Act) but non-cash benefits chargeable under TA 1988 s 313 are not so regarded.

It therefore follows that national insurance contributions are not due in relation to:

(a) Cash payments or benefits chargeable under TA 1988 s 148, whether in excess of £30,000 or otherwise;
(b) Non-cash benefits chargeable to tax under TA 1988 s 313.

EARNINGS AND BENEFITS IN KIND

6.80 National insurance was essentially conceived of as a tax (to use the term widely) on cash payments, not benefits in kind. Partly to prevent avoidance and partly to harmonise the basis of charging national insurance and income tax, provision has been made for charging certain benefits in kind.

Benefits may be subject to charge by reason of a specific provision. This is the case in relation to cars and petrol; the charge for which follows the income tax liability, which liability is dependent on continued employment. The provision of a car and/or petrol taxable under TA 1988 s 148, on the other hand, is not liable to national insurance.

Benefits may also be subject to charge if they fall within the list of assets specified in Sch 1A of the Social Security (Contributions) Regulations SI 1979/591. The assets in question include shares, loan stock, warrants and options amongst others. The list is aimed at preventing the avoidance of national insurance by providing benefits in a cash convertible form.

11 THE PAYE SYSTEM

6.81 The PAYE system has been in operation for some 50 years; it was first introduced with effect from the tax year 1944–45. The essence of the system

6.81 *The position of employees*

is to require the deduction of tax by employers from payments of emoluments to employees. The deductions are calculated on a system of cumulative withholding over the year, a proportion of the employee's tax allowances being made available for each payment by reference to the length of the payment period.

Statutory authority for the system is derived from TA 1988 s 203 under which detailed regulations have been made: the Income Tax (Employments) Regulations SI 1993/744.

THE OBLIGATION TO DEDUCT

6.82 The general obligation to make deductions on account of tax is contained in SI 1993/744 reg 14 which applies to '. . . the occasion of any payment of emoluments to the employee . . .'. The term 'emoluments' is widely defined by reference to the full amount of any income to be taken into account in assessing liability under Schedule E.

Accordingly, the obligation to deduct applies to payments which are:

(i) fully chargeable to income tax, whether by reason of general Schedule E principles, under TA 1988 s 313 or TA 1988 s 154; and
(ii) chargeable under TA 1988 s 148 but only to the extent that it is not relieved under TA 1988 s 188.

Deductions on account of tax are calculated by reference to the employee's marginal rate of tax. A termination payment may therefore be paid subject to deduction on account of tax at 40%. However, a more limited obligation to deduct applies if the payment is made after the issue to the employee of Form P45. In this case the employer should only deduct on account of tax at the basic rate (SI 1993/744 reg 24).

Payments made after the death of the employee are subject to normal deduction rules (SI 1993/744 reg 27).

THE NATURE OF THE OBLIGATION

6.83 The PAYE system imposes an obligation upon the employer to deduct and account for the income tax due on any payment of taxable emoluments. If the employer does not deduct a sufficient amount on account of tax, the Inland Revenue will first look to the employer for the underpayment to be made good.

Although any deductions are made on account of the employee's income tax liability, the employee is under no general obligation to reimburse the employer in respect of any sums claimed by the Inland Revenue. The employer may recover under-deductions by deducting further amounts from future payments to the employee, but this remedy is not available if the employee has ceased to be employed.

6.84 If circumstances are such that the status of any compensation payment upon termination is open to doubt, the employer should obtain a suitable form of indemnity from the employee.

Employee liability

6.85 Notwithstanding the general rule, the Inland Revenue may look to the employee to make good any under-deduction under the PAYE system in two limited circumstances. Those circumstances are provided for by SI 1993/744 reg 42 which applies to any underpayment in respect of which:

> '(2) . . . the collector, on being satisfied by the employer that he took reasonable care to comply with these Regulations and that the under-deduction was due to an error made in good faith, may direct that the amount of the excess shall be recovered from the employee, and, where the collector so directs, the employer shall not be liable to pay the amount of that excess to the collector.'

Alternatively:

> '(3) . . . the Board, if they are of the opinion that an employee has received his emoluments knowing that the employer has wilfully failed to deduct the amount of tax which he was liable to deduct . . . may direct that the amount of the excess shall be recovered from the employee, and, where the Board so direct, the employer shall not be liable to pay the amount of that excess to the collector.'

In both cases it will be seen that any relief is discretionary. In circumstances where the employer has obtained professional advice as to the taxation status of any payment and an inadequate deduction on account of tax has been made in reliance of that advice, it is thought that relief should be available.

Under-deductions and 'gross ups'

6.86 If an insufficient deduction on account of tax is made by the employer, which the employer makes good to the Inland Revenue, there is a risk that the payment made in respect of tax may be regarded as a further payment of emoluments, and so on. The reason for this potential 'gross up' liability is contained in SI 1993/744 reg 22, which provides:

> 'Where the employer makes a payment to or for the benefit of the employee in respect of his income tax, the amount of the emoluments which the employer pays to the employee shall be deemed . . . to be such a sum as will include the amount assessable on the employee in respect of the payment made by the employer in respect of the employee's income tax.'

EXAMPLE

Stephen's employment with A Ltd is terminated with immediate effect. In consequence of that termination, A Ltd pay Stephen £30,000. No tax is deducted from the payment which is made before the issue of Form P45.

It is subsequently ascertained that the payment was reserved in Stephen's employment contract, and was therefore fully taxable. Assuming a marginal rate of 40% to be applicable, a further £20,000 will be due from A Ltd; ie on the basis that the £30,000 received was net of tax at 40%.

6.87 *The position of employees*

12 PLANNING

6.87 The planning opportunities which exist in relation to compensation payments to employees have, to a large extent, been incorporated in the general text of this chapter. The main opportunities revolve around the exemptions associated with the charge to tax under TA 1988 s 148 and the different methods for valuing benefits in kind. Some other miscellaneous planning points are considered below.

Pension scheme contributions and annuity purchases

6.88 Neither a special contribution to an approved retirement benefit scheme, nor the purchase of an annuity from a Life Office which is approved under TA 1988 Ch I Pt XIV, are regarded as giving rise to a charge to tax under TA 1988 s 148 if made to an employee upon his employment being terminated.

The authority for this is contained in Statement of Practice SP 2/81, which provides as follows:

> '1 Where, as part of an arrangement relating to the termination of an employment, an agreement is reached between the parties for the employer to make a special contribution to an approved retirement benefit scheme in order to provide benefits for the employee, the Revenue will not seek to charge such a payment under [TA 1988 s 148] provided that the retirement benefits are within the limits and in the form prescribed by the rules of the scheme.
> 2 Similarly, they will not seek to charge the payment under [TA 1988 s 148] where the employer purchases an annuity for his former employee from a Life Office, so long as the transaction is approved under [TA 1988 Pt XIV Ch I].'

6.89 The contribution can only be paid if the augmentation is within Inland Revenue limits. The limits depend on factors such as the level of benefits already provided and the member's age, salary and service and the Inland Revenue regime under which the member's benefits are provided. The facility is particularly valuable where a member is 'uncapped' in the scheme but will be 'capped' under his new employer's scheme. For these purposes 'capped' is a reference to the restriction of pensionable salary to the earnings cap of £76,800 (1994/95) and generally applies to new entrants to a scheme from 1 January 1989.

Contract formation

6.90 In drafting employment contracts, it should be noted that the inclusion of provision for the mandatory payment of compensation upon termination is generally undesirable. Payments so made will be liable to income tax in the hands of the employee in question, without the availability of the £30,000 'golden handshake' or other TA 1988 s 188 exemption.

There would appear to be no objection to the inclusion of a payment in lieu of notice clause, provided that it does not give the employee the right to call for payment—any election must be at the discretion of the employer.

Distributions

6.91 In view of the availability of tax exemptions for compensation upon termination, it might be tempting in some circumstances to artificially inflate such payments. This is most likely to occur in the context of companies controlled by a small number of individual shareholders, where the termination in question relates to one of those individuals' employment contracts.

Any overpayment may, to that extent, be recharacterised as a distribution by the employing company under TA 1988 s 209(4) with the attendant obligation to account for Advance Corporation Tax on the same. If the payment was made by an unincorporated business such as a partnership, the recharacterisation could take the form of drawings.

6.91 *The position of employees*

APPENDIX
STATEMENT OF PRACTICE SP 1/94

1 TA 1988 ss 579(1), 580(3) provide that statutory redundancy payments shall be exempt from income tax under Schedule E, with the exception of any liability under s 148.

2 Lump sum payments made under a non-statutory scheme, in addition to, or instead of statutory redundancy pay, will also be liable to income tax only under TA 1988 s 148 provided they are genuinely made solely on account of redundancy as defined in the Employment Protection (Consolidation) Act 1978 s 81. This will be so whether the scheme is a standing one which forms part of the terms on which the employees give their services or whether it is an ad hoc scheme devised to meet a specific situation such as the imminent closure of a particular factory.

3 However, payments made under a non-statutory scheme which are not genuinely made to compensate for loss of employment through redundancy may be liable to tax in full. In particular, payments which are, in reality, a form of terminal bonus will be chargeable to income tax under Schedule E as emoluments from the employment under TA 1988 s 19(1). Payments made for meeting production targets or doing extra work in the period leading up to redundancy are examples of such terminal bonuses. Payments conditional on continued service in the employment for a time will also represent terminal bonuses if calculated by reference to any additional period served following issue of the redundancy notice.

4 The Revenue is concerned to distinguish between payments under non-statutory schemes which are genuinely made to compensate for loss of employment through redundancy and payments which are made as a reward for services in the employment or more generally for having acted as or having been an employee. As arrangements for redundancy can often be complex and provide for a variety of payments, it follows that each scheme must be considered on its own facts. The Revenue's practice, in these circumstances, is to allow employers to submit proposed schemes to their inspectors of taxes for advance clearance.

5 An employer or any other person operating a redundancy scheme, who wishes to be satisfied that lump sum payments under a scheme will be accepted as liable to tax only under TA 1988 s 148 should submit the full facts to the inspector for consideration. Applications for clearance should be made in writing and should be accompanied by the scheme document together with the text of any intended letter to employees which explains its terms.

Chapter 7

STRUCTURED SETTLEMENTS

7.01 Compensation for personal injury is free of tax in view of the specific exemption from capital gains tax provided by TCGA 1992 s 51(2) and the exemption from income tax upon interest thereon (TA 1988 s 329(1)). In many personal injury cases it will not be necessary to consider the taxation treatment of the award further. However, if the personal injuries involved are particularly serious, different considerations may apply.

In serious personal injury cases, the plaintiff's compensation usually includes an amount earmarked for investment with a view to providing the plaintiff with sufficient income to meet his ongoing care costs, living expenses and so on. Whilst the compensation is itself free of tax, that freedom does not extend to the income or capital gains subsequently realised from it to meet the plaintiff's expenses. Structured settlements seek to eliminate the tax charge upon the investment return.

The use of structured settlements was originally pioneered in the United States and Canada. In both jurisdictions they are arranged so as to avoid tax on the periodic payments made, and have become a common device. Their use in the UK is a more recent development.

1 INTRODUCTION

7.02 The essence of a structured settlement is very simple. The defendant insurer meeting the claim pays it by way of instalments, which are deemed to be instalments of the capital debt of the award in the hands of the plaintiff, and therefore received free of tax.

The mechanics of the instalment payments are provided by the defendant insurer purchasing an annuity on the plaintiff's life. The insurer then receives the monthly annuity net of income tax at the basic rate (currently 25%) and pays the gross amount to the plaintiff to satisfy that part of the total award which has been structured. The income element of the annuity does not give rise to a charge to tax so far as the insurer is concerned because of the corresponding obligation upon the insurer to pay the plaintiff. The instalments are in the nature of revenue expenditure fully deductible for

7.02 *Structured settlements*

the purposes of computing the insurer's taxable profits. This allows the cost to the insurer of meeting the claim to be reduced, because the income arising in respect of the annuity is effectively passed on to the plaintiff without incurring a charge to tax. In the words of Potter J:

> '... the plaintiffs seek to take advantage of provisions of revenue law, or at least the interpretation of those provisions which is currently acceptable to the Inland Revenue, which appear to render a structured settlement beneficial in actions involving large awards for future financial losses, in particular in relation to long-term care.'[1]

The beneficial treatment was simply stated:

> '... under the terms of such a settlement, a defendant's insurers pay out somewhat less money than would be necessary to meet a single lump sum award, assessed on conventional lines and paid over to the plaintiff, while the plaintiff obtains the benefit of annual payments greater than the income which would have arisen from investment by the plaintiff of the lump sum award.'

EXAMPLE

John suffers injuries in a car accident, caused by the negligence of Philip. Compensation for John's injuries is agreed in principle in the sum of £500,000 of which £350,000 is suitable for structuring. At anticipated rates of return of 10%, John will receive a gross £35,000 per annum. Assuming tax thereon at 25%, John's net annual return is £26,250 which is the annual return required in order to meet the cost of providing care for John.

Compensation payable by way of instalments under a structured settlement remains free of tax. If one were adopted, Philip's insurers could offer to pay, say, £29,000 per annum. The funding cost to the insurer, again assuming a 10% return, will be £290,000. In this simplified example, John receives an enhanced annual return and the defendant insurers obtain a saving of £60,000.

---

1 In *Kelly v Dawes* (1990) *Times*, 27 September, QBD July 14 1989. Extract from transcript prepared by Beveley F. Nunnery & Co.

---

2 THE DECISION IN *KELLY V DAWES*

7.03 The decision in *Kelly v Dawes* was the first example of a case in which a structured settlement was approved in the UK. It therefore sets the scene for future applications. The proceedings arose from a road accident in which the plaintiff suffered serious injury, and her husband was killed. The facts of the accident were not considered by the court, there being no dispute as to liability. The application was therefore concerned only with the amount and form of the compensation to be paid.

7.04 The calculation of the compensation was made in the context of the serious injuries which the plaintiff suffered, leaving her in a permanent vegetative condition so that the cost of long-term health care was a prime concern in computing an award. On the conventional basis of calculation the appropriate figure was agreed in principle in the sum of £427,500.

Under the terms of the proposed structured settlement, the sum payable was reduced to £410,000. Of this, £300,000 was to be appropriated by the insurers to the purchase of an annuity. The structured settlement therefore resulted in a discount to the defendants of £17,500 to the lump sum which would otherwise be paid.

The principal features of the settlement were as follows:

(a) a lump sum of £110,000 was to be paid immediately, so as to make available a substantial contingency fund;
(b) the remaining £300,000 was to be appropriated by the insurers to secure an annuity to pay the plaintiff the sum of £25,582 per annum;
(c) the annual payments were index-linked and guaranteed for a period of ten years.

Shared benefit

7.05 It was demonstrated to the court that the rate of return available to the plaintiff under the proposed arrangement would exceed that from the traditional mix of gilt and equity investment which would otherwise follow from a conventional award. It was also shown that if compensation was awarded on the conventional basis, the fund available to the plaintiff was likely to be exhausted in 12–15 years and thereafter the plaintiff would be wholly reliant upon the state. The plaintiff's life expectancy was 20 years.

The proposed arrangement therefore offered significant advantages to the plaintiff. In addition, the insurer would benefit from the £17,500 discount to the amount which would otherwise be paid on a conventional basis. Potter J commented:

> *'The "discount" . . . has been agreed on the basis that, since the benefits to the . . . plaintiff under the structure contemplated (as opposed to a single lump sum settlement) will considerably exceed £17,500, the defendants should be permitted also to participate in the benefits resulting from the reduced levels of taxation which will be payable.'*

7.06 It was considered that the shared benefit should not be prejudicial to the plaintiff, because of the fiscal advantages available:

> *'. . . I have to be satisfied that the interests of the . . . plaintiff are fully protected. Normally, no doubt, that involves ensuring that a plaintiff receives the highest possible payment on offer from the defendants; however, if it be that the . . . plaintiff's interests are better protected by receipt and/or expenditure of a reduced sum which will ultimately yield a greater benefit, I see no objection in principle to the differential proposed . . .'*

Judicial acceptance of the sharing of the fiscal benefits is fundamental to the use of structured settlements; if this element were absent, no incentive would exist for the insurer to negotiate.

3 STRUCTURED SETTLEMENTS IN PRACTICE

7.07 The decision in *Kelly v Dawes* paved the way for structured settlements to be used in personal injury cases, and it is understood that a significant number have since been approved to date. From a practical point of view, the most pressing considerations are likely to relate to:

(a) their suitability in particular circumstances and relative merits compared with the adoption of a conventional award; and
(b) the application of the Inland Revenue's view on their tax effect.

Suitability

7.08 An immediate factor in determining whether a structured settlement is suitable is the size of the likely award in question—the smaller it is, the less suitable a structured settlement is likely to be. Some commentators have expressed the view that the threshold could fall to as low as £50,000 if structured settlements become the preferred and accepted method of provision in personal injury cases.

In addition to the size of the award, a number of general factors should be taken into account before a structured settlement is adopted in any particular case. Some of those factors militate against their use, but in general the advantages are likely to outweigh the disadvantages by a considerable margin.

7.09 So far as the plaintiff is concerned, two principal disadvantages exist. First, a structured settlement is an inflexible arrangement; once it is in place the terms cannot be varied. The circumstances of the plaintiff may subsequently change with the consequence that the arrangement becomes inappropriate. For example, the plaintiff may need to meet some unexpected capital expenditure, although structured settlements include a contingency fund which is intended to be used in such circumstances. Second, the plaintiff loses the opportunity to use the lump sum payment which would otherwise have been made.

If the plaintiff dies earlier than expected, his estate will not benefit from the structured element of his award unless it includes some form of death benefit or guaranteed minimum payment period. In practice, guaranteed minimum payment periods are popular and are relatively cheap to purchase. The existence or otherwise of some form of death benefit or guaranteed payments is not regarded as a concern of the court. In *Kelly v Dawes*, Potter J was of the view that '. . . it is the protection of, and benefits to, the plaintiff in her lifetime which concern me and not the interests of future beneficiaries from her estate'.

7.10 Against the disadvantages to the plaintiff, three principal advantages may be weighed. First, the plaintiff is not at risk of the money running out whether by reason of inadequate investment returns eating into the underlying capital or otherwise. Second, the agreed payments may be made for a guaranteed minimum period and/or include an index-linked element. Third, the plaintiff does not have to concern himself with the investment of the capital sum and the risks this may entail, nor incur the costs associated with the same. The plaintiff has the security of receiving a known inflow of funds and may budget for expenditure accordingly.

7.11 Whilst disadvantages may also be identified so far as the defendant insurer is concerned, these are likely to be of less importance than those applicable to the plaintiff. A structured settlement does involve some extra administrative work for the insurer which is compensated through the discount available to the defendant.

The mechanics of financing the payments by way of annuity may give some cause for concern. This is because the insurer is obliged to pay the agreed instalments to the plaintiff in full. Against that, the insurer will receive payments under the annuity taken out to match the obligation, but it is understood that the Inland Revenue regard the life office as under an obligation to pay the annuity subject to deduction on account of income tax which it claims back later. Whilst the arrangement remains fiscally neutral, the insurer is put at a cash flow disadvantage.

The Revenue view

7.12 The taxation status of structured settlements remains untested in the courts. In *Kelly v Dawes* its use was approved on the basis of Inland Revenue agreement as to its taxation status, no ruling was made by the court. In giving that approval, Potter J commented:

> '*I have not heard argument on, let alone decided, the question of whether the present interpretation in fact represents a true application of the taxation provisions concerned. Nonetheless I feel justified in assuming that the interpretation will continue to apply for the time being. Even if it does not, it seems to me practically inconceivable that any future change in the law or in revenue practice which reverses its effect would be applied retroactively to settlements already entered into on the faith of the interpretation, let alone to payments already made.*'

The Inland Revenue interpretation referred to has not been embodied in any Statement of Practice or Extra-statutory Concession. Instead, reference should be made to the guidance note and model agreement issued by the Association of British Insurers.

MODEL AGREEMENT

7.13 The use of structured settlements was the subject of extensive discussions between the Inland Revenue and the Association of British Insurers. Those discussions resulted, on 9 July 1987, in a guidance note and model agreement being issued. The guidance note explains that the Inland Revenue had accepted that periodic payments to a plaintiff, funded by an annuity purchased by the insurer from a separate life office, may be treated as instalments of capital rather than income, and therefore exempt from tax.

The model agreement provides a standard form for use in structured settlement cases. The schedules attached to it provide for the four different kinds of payments anticipated to be the most commonly used, namely:

7.13 *Structured settlements*

(a) basic terms providing for a series of ascertained amounts over an agreed period;
(b) as per (a) above, but indexed so as to take inflation into account;
(c) basic terms for periodic payments but determinable upon the death of the plaintiff, subject to an option to receive a minimum amount;
(d) as per (c) above, but indexed so as to take inflation into account.

The model agreement is reproduced in the second appendix to this chapter.

Clearance

7.14 The Inland Revenue approval of the ABI's model agreement relates to its use in principle only. Its adoption in any particular case results in a provisional form of approval only.

In circumstances where judicial or Court of Protection approval is required for the adoption of a structured settlement, the specific agreement of the Inland Revenue should be obtained. Otherwise it is not compulsory to obtain clearance. Whether this should be sought will depend upon the form of the structure and the past experience of the professional advisers involved. Applications for specific agreement may be made direct to the Financial Institutions Division of the Inland Revenue (at Somerset House, London WC2R 1LB).

Procedural guidelines

7.15 In *Kelly v Dawes* some guidelines were suggested as to the information which should be placed before the court in respect of future applications. Those guidelines have now been superseded by a Practice Note which provides for the following to be lodged:

> '1 *copies of originating process or pleadings, if any;*
> 2 *an opinion of counsel assessing the value of the claim on a conventional basis (unless approval has already been given) and, if practicable, the opinion of counsel on the structured settlement proposed;*
> 3 *a report of forensic accountants setting out the advantages and disadvantages, if any, of structuring, bearing in mind the plaintiff's life expectancy and the anticipated costs of future care;*
> 4 *a draft of the proposed agreement as approved by the Inland Revenue (and by the Treasury where the defendant or other paying party is a health authority);*
> 5 *sufficient material to satisfy the court that enough capital is available free of the structure to meet anticipated future capital needs: particular reference to accommodation and transport needs will usually be helpful in this context;*
> 6 *sufficient material to satisfy the court that the structure is secure and backed by responsible insurers;*
> 7 *evidence of other assets available to the plaintiff beyond the award which is the subject of the application;*
> 8 *in cases where the plaintiff is under mental disability the consent of the Court of Protection.*'[1]

---

1 Structured settlements: court's approval, [1992] 1 WLR 328.

4 TAXATION TREATMENT

7.16 The Inland Revenue view of the taxation treatment of structured settlements has been expressed and is open for use by defendants and their insurers. It is noted however that the Inland Revenue's view is concessionary, and the ABI's guidance note expressly refers to the existence of other factors causing the Inland Revenue to take a different view. What then is the correct interpretation of the law?

Capital by instalments

7.17 Central to the concept of structured settlements is the payment of compensation by way of instalments, which nonetheless retain their capital nature so far as the plaintiff is concerned. No case has yet been decided which considers this from the point of view of a claim for damages for personal injury. Judicial authority on the subject tends to be concerned with commercial arrangements. Authority for the proposition that instalments may retain a capital nature may be considered by reference to two decisions of the Court of Appeal, namely *IRC v Ramsay*,[1] and *Dott v Brown*.[2]

1 (1935) 20 TC 79.
2 [1936] 1 All ER 543.

7.18 In *Ramsay*, the respondent agreed to purchase a dental practice for a primary price of £15,000. That figure was subject to subsequent increase or decrease depending on the level of net profits subsequently realised in respect of the practice. A payment of £5,000 was made on completion, and the balance was to be satisfied by yearly payments for the next ten years of 25% of the profits of the practice. If the amounts so paid were more or less than the £15,000 purchase price then it was treated as correspondingly increased or decreased as appropriate.

The Court of Appeal came to the conclusion that the annual sums payable were instalments of the capital sum for the acquisition of the dental practice. In coming to that conclusion, it was first necessary to distinguish between capital instalments and annuities. The manner in which payments were made did not determine the issue. In this respect Lord Wright MR considered that payments retained their capital nature if the instalments in question could be said to be '. . . merely the method and the manner and the form in which a lump sum is paid'. The fact that the amount of the instalments could fluctuate was not regarded as necessarily inconsistent with those instalments being capital.

A review of the agreement revealed that the initial price of £15,000 was never lost sight of; the instalments were payable in discharge of that debt which was subject to increase or decrease as a result of the level of profits from the practice. The spreading of the instalments over the ten-year period allowed the purchaser to pay for the business out of its profits, rather than having to borrow in order to satisfy the same by way of a lump sum payment. Finally, the agreement made no reference to the amounts being paid by way of income. So far as contingencies were concerned, it was possible for the vendor to die before the full price was paid, in which case no further

7.18 *Structured settlements*

instalments were due. Conversely, should the purchaser die, his estate would remain liable.

On these facts, Lord Wright MR felt justified in deciding that the instalments were capital in nature. There were sufficient reasons making it desirable for the parties to adopt the arrangement; at no point was there any reference to income and the fact that the amount payable was subject to change did not affect the matter one way or another.

Both Lords Romer and Greene agreed with this view. Of particular interest are the views of Lord Romer as to the choice faced by the parties to such an arrangement.

Choice
7.19 In distinguishing between instalments of capital and annuities, Lord Romer drew attention to the choice that a person has in the form of return upon the sale of an asset. That choice was illustrated by example:

> *'If a man has some property which he wishes to sell on terms which will result in his receiving for the next 20 years an annual sum of £500, he can do it in either of two methods. He can either sell his property in consideration of a payment by the purchaser to him of an annuity of £500 for the next 20 years, or he can sell his property to the purchaser for £10,000 . . . to be paid by equal instalments of £500 over the next 20 years.'*[1]

So far as concerned the sale of the dental practice, Lord Romer was clear as to the method of disposal adopted:

> *'. . . I am satisfied that the vendor here has adopted the second of the two methods to which I have referred; in other words, that the vendor has in fact sold the property for a capital sum part of which, in certain events, is payable by annual instalments.'*

---

1 (1935) 20 TC 79 at 98.

THE DECISION IN *DOTT V BROWN*

7.20 The case of *Dott v Brown*[1] was heard by the Court of Appeal just three months after *Ramsay*. *Dott* was concerned with a covenant to pay two sums of £1,000 each on 31 March 1933 and 1934 and further sums of £250 on each succeeding 31 March for so long as the payee should live, in satisfaction of an antecedent debt of some £9,000 to £10,000.

As with *Ramsay*, it was decided that the instalments were capital, not payments of income. Two principles may be identified from the decision. First, there is a presumption that consideration for the liquidation of the debt will share the same capital or income nature of the debt itself. Second, the possibility that the instalments paid would fall short of the full debt by reason of their ceasing upon the death of the payee did not deprive the payments of their capital nature.

As to the first principle, Scott LJ noted that:

> *'You start here with the antecedent debt of £9,000 to £10,000 which by the agreement of compromise was to be liquidated in a certain manner. You have therefore the presumption that the consideration for this liquidation would be a capital payment of the same kind as the debt itself—not an income payment—unless the*

transaction makes it quite clear that an annuity was being bought, so to speak, by the release of the debt.'[2]

As to the second principle, the very real possibility of the creditor receiving less than the amount due was considered to be the essence of the compromise reached between the parties. That compromise did not alter the capital nature of the instalment payments.

---

1 [1936] 1 All ER 543.
2 Ibid at 551.

PRELIMINARY CONCLUSIONS

7.21 The following preliminary conclusions may be drawn from the decisions in *Ramsay* and *Dott*:

(a) if the settlement is conceived and thought of in capital terms, a capital treatment will apply;
(b) if a capital debt is being liquidated, it is presumed that the consideration for the liquidation is also capital unless evidenced clearly to the contrary;
(c) the fact that the amounts being paid are contingent, may fluctuate, or could exceed or be less than the primary obligation does not deprive them from being capital in nature.

In applying the above it is necessary to have regard to substance of the settlement in question, not merely the form in which it takes.

Income-producing assets

7.22 Where an asset is sold in return for instalments intended to replace the income lost by reason of the asset sale, a different treatment will apply to that in *Ramsay*. Such instalments will be regarded as income; this represents the reverse of the principle that a settlement conceived and thought of in capital terms will attract a capital treatment.

The decision of the House of Lords in *IRC v Church Comrs*[1] may be cited as authority for the reverse principle. The essential facts were that the Church Commissioners sold various leasehold reversions in property for £720,000 to the incumbent tenant in return for ten yearly rent charges of £96,000 per annum.

The House of Lords held that the receipts could not be regarded as capital, even in part, but were wholly income receipts. The income treatment was found to apply by reason of the nature of the bargain concluded by the parties:

> 'The essential feature of the negotiations and of the bargain, as shown by the documents, was that Land Securities did not wish, on any account, to pay a lump sum for the properties. This is so found in terms. The Church Commissioners, on their side, wished to maintain their existing income by rentcharges for a longer period.'[2]

7.22 *Structured settlements*

As to the figures used:

'The figure of £720,000 was not an agreed purchase price or even an agreed valuation. It was, as I understand it, simply a checking figure in the calculations, worked out on the basis of 18 years' purchase price . . . of the existing rents of £40,000. The bargain was always thought of in income terms, and was concluded on income terms, and there is nothing in the documents which gives to the transaction, or to any element in it, a capital character.'

This view was endorsed by Lord Morris of Borth-y-Gest who regarded the transaction as nothing more 'than the replacement of one income-producing property, namely the reversion, for another . . . namely, the rent charge'.

---

1 [1976] 2 All ER 1037.
2 Per Lord Wilberforce, ibid at 1044.

7.23 The decision in *Church Commissioners* is important for three reasons. First, it demonstrates the reverse principle to that in *Ramsay* and *Dott*; a settlement thought of in income terms will be subject to an income treatment. This is the case if an income-producing asset is being replaced with another such asset.

Second, the Crown raised a general argument to the effect that when the payment of the purchase price of a capital asset is spread over a number of years, each payment should be treated as containing a capital element and an income element. The income element, it was argued, reflects the deferred character of the payment. This general argument was dismissed.

Third, some consideration was given to the Crown's secondary argument that instalment payments may be dissected as between the capital and interest elements.

DISSECTION

7.24 The basis for the 'dissection' argument raised by the Crown in the Church Commissioners case was put by Lord Wilberforce:

'Dissection is, at least as a plain case, permissible if the parties who are buying and selling a capital asset, having agreed on a price, then make provision for payment of that price by instalments, the amount of which is so calculated and shown to be calculated as to include an interest element.'[1]

---

1 [1976] 2 All ER 1037 at 1043.

7.25 The case of *Vestey v IRC*[1] was considered by Lord Wilberforce in the context of the above proposition. That case is particularly important to the taxation of structured settlements. The dicta of Lord Romer as to the parties choice between income and capital was specifically considered in it.

The facts of *Vestey* show a clear intention to use the decisions in *Ramsay* and *Dott* to the taxpayer's advantage upon the sale of shares. The value of the shares was approximately £2 million. On an actuarial basis, the annual sum payable for £2 million over 125 years at an interest rate of 2% was £43,670. The taxpayer agreed to sell his shares for a purchase price of

£5,500,000 to be paid without interest by 125 yearly instalments of £44,000.

On the evidence put forward, it was decided that the purchase price included an interest element. For income tax purposes it could therefore be dissected into capital and interest. That decision was reached notwithstanding the statements of law propounded by Lord Romer in *Ramsay* as to the choice between income and capital, nor those propounded by Lord Greene MR in *IRC v Wesleyan and General Assurance Society*[2] to the same effect.

1 [1961] 3 All ER 978.
2 [1946] 2 All ER 749.

7.26 The decision in *Vestey* would appear to be capable of explanation in the following brief manner. Common sense demands that an apportionment be made. The inflated nature of the purchase price is clearly distinguishable from the facts in both *Ramsay* and *Dott*, so allowing the court a certain freedom from the constraints of precedent. The freedom was exercised by following the words of Sir Wilfrid Greene MR in *Sothern-Smith v Clancy*[1] who appended to his words concerning the payment of capital by instalments the following:

'*If to the instalments there is added an element of interest, that element would presumably attract tax as being an annual profit or gain.*'

Clearly no interest element was 'added' in *Vestey*; the sale was concluded upon a purchase price of £5.5 million without reference to the shares' value of £2 million. In ascertaining the true nature of the transaction however, evidence extrinsic to the share sale agreement was admitted to show the addition made.

Vestey was a borderline case, and represents the high water mark of the dissection principle.[2] Can it be said to apply to structured settlements, with the result that instalment payments so made should also be dissected?

1 [1941] 1 All ER 111.
2 Per Lord Wilberforce in *IRC v Church Comrs* [1976] 2 All ER 1037 at 1045.

Dissection and structured settlements

7.27 In many ways, the use of a structured settlement is analogous to the facts and decision in *Vestey*. The instalments are paid over an agreed period of years, and the return is calculated by reference to a fixed rate of return each year, demonstrated to yield a greater benefit than investment of the lump sum. An argument can therefore be made that the dissection principle applied in *Vestey* could be applied to a structured settlement. The true position is unclear given the complexities in this difficult area; it is noted that a number of arguments may be made against this.

First, the nature of the agreement between the plaintiff and defendant in a structured settlement does not involve the inflation of the compensation otherwise due by reference to an interest factor over the instalment period. The agreement is founded upon comparative investment yields under the structured settlement on the one hand and traditional investment on the other. To apply the dissection principle to a structured settlement would

7.27 *Structured settlements*

appear to require an extension of the dissection principle. It is unlikely that any extension would be admitted having regard to the view that the decision in *Vestey* marks the high water mark of the principle.

Second, the obligation upon the insurer to pay instalments may cease upon the death of the plaintiff. The capital and interest elements are not therefore separately identifiable as such when the agreement is adopted. In *Vestey*, the interest and capital elements were easily dissected, but this is not the case with a structured settlement as the amount ultimately payable will depend upon the life of the plaintiff which is uncertain. However, if the settlement provided for a wholly-guaranteed return, irrespective of death, the same distinction could not be made.

Third, the arrangement does not involve the sale of an asset in the sense of tangible property, as was the case in *Vestey*. It involves the compromise of a claim for compensation for personal injury, although that claim might be regarded as an 'asset' for capital gains tax purposes.

Structured settlements and the *Ramsay* doctrine

7.28 As discussed in Chapter 1 the essence of the *Ramsay*[1] doctrine is to look at any composite transaction as a whole, so as to tax it by reference to the end result achieved, not each individual step in the transaction.

It is not considered that the doctrine is applicable to structured settlements in their current form, on the basis that no 'preordained series of transactions' exists as formulated by Lord Brightman in *Furniss v Dawson*.[2] In particular, the four essential features identified by Lord Oliver in *IRC v Bowater*[3] are not satisfied. If the inserted step or intermediate transaction is equated with the instalment payments, the following feature identified by Lord Oliver is absent:

> '. . . that there was at that time no practical likelihood that the pre-planned events would not take place in the order ordained, so that the intermediate transaction was not even contemplated practically as having an independent life . . .'[4]

The settlement is of course subject to earlier determination upon the death of the plaintiff, whose life span determines the number of instalments due. At the time of entering into the settlement, the number of instalments due cannot necessarily be identified, in the absence of a guaranteed element. In any event, the instalments represent the very essence of the settlement and so have an independent life. Accordingly, structured settlements would not appear to be subject to the *Ramsay* doctrine.

---

1 *W T Ramsay Ltd v IRC* [1981] STC 174, 54 TC 101, HL.
2 [1984] 1 All ER 530, 55 TC 324.
3 [1988] 5 TC 476.
4 Ibid at 507.

Conclusions

7.29 Any agreement reached as between the plaintiff and defendant's insurers regarding the amount required to settle the action is presumed to be capital unless there is evidence clearly to the contrary. While the calculation of the amount to be paid may depend in part upon income considerations, this should not be regarded as constituting the replacement of one income-producing asset with another within the ambit of the decision in *Church Commissioners*. It may also be argued that an agreement does not raise the possibility that the settlement is being thought of in income rather than capital terms on the basis that any reference to income is limited to calculation only; however, it is noted that the plaintiff is likely to view the instalment payments in income terms.

Finally, it falls to be considered whether the indexation of instalments may be said to rebut the presumption that the instalments should be wholly treated as capital. In this respect the cases are perhaps not quite as helpful as they might have been; this is function of time—*Ramsay* was heard in 1935 and *Dott* in 1936, when the incidence of inflation was not such a fundamental concern. However, in neither case was it considered relevant that the instalments could fluctuate or exceed the original obligation to pay; the inclusion of an indexation provision should not therefore affect the capital treatment.

Whether the Inland Revenue's 'concessionary' view can be said to represent a correct interpretation of the law remains uncertain. It is clear however that any Inland Revenue attack against the use of structured settlements could be vigorously resisted.

COMPENSATION AS A CHARGEABLE GAIN

7.30 One further aspect which has been considered by some commentators is whether the availability of the exemption provided by TCGA 1992 s 51 in relation to 'compensation . . . for any wrong or injury' is prejudiced by the use of a structured settlement.

Specifically, there is an argument to the effect that the right to the capital instalments represents a separate asset for capital gains tax purposes on the basis of *Zim Properties Ltd v Procter*[1] (for which see Chapter 4). Instalment payments would be regarded as part disposals in relation to that asset, requiring separate calculations of the gain or loss thereby accruing. Whether a gain or loss accrues would be determined by reference to the value of the right at acquisition and at each part disposal, in consequence of the decision in *Marren v Ingles*.[2]

In the author's view this argument is without merit. The scope of the exemption afforded by s 51 is defined by reference to the wrong or injury suffered by the plaintiff. Sums obtained by way of structured settlement retain their character as compensation in respect of the wrong or injury in question. If the section made reference to, say, 'gains accruing on the disposal of rights to compensation or damages for any wrong or injury' (in common with TCGA 1992 s 51(1) in respect of gaming winnings) then the position might be different.

---

1 [1985] STC 90.
2 [1980] STC 500, for which see Chapter 4.

7.31 *Structured settlements*

5 THE INSURER AND THE LIFE OFFICE

7.31 In paying compensation for personal injury, an insurer carrying on general insurance business is in a unique position. The payments it makes are deductible for the purposes of computing its profits chargeable to corporation tax. Further, the purchase of an annuity in order to secure its obligations to make periodic compensation payments may be treated as a deductible expense, on the basis that it represents a reinsurance premium.

The position is different in the case of a mutual insurance company however, as mutuals do not pay corporation tax given that they 'trade' only with their members. On the other hand mutuals pay tax on investment income, which would include payments under an annuity purchased to secure the settlement obligation.[1] The fiscal advantages of structuring a settlement are not therefore directly available to a mutual insurance company, although it would appear to be possible in some circumstances to allow the mutual to take advantage of the benefits by an indirect structure to which the defendant is a party.[2]

---

1 This tax disincentive for mutuals to adopt structured settlements was considered by the Law Commission (Structured Settlements and Interim and Provisional Damages, Consultation Paper No. 125, November 1992).
2 See *Marshall v Westminster City Council* QBD Transcript (8 March 1991, unreported).

7.32 Insurance company taxation is determined by the class of insurance business carried on. A liability insurer meeting a claim for personal injuries will do so as part of its general insurance business which includes fire, motor, marine and transport amongst others. Such business constitutes a trade and it is therefore taxed under Schedule D, Case I in accordance with general principles (subject to the use of a three-year period of account for marine, aviation and transport business).

The receipt of a fully-taxable annuity by the insurer is offset against the corresponding payment made by the insurer to the plaintiff. So far as the insurer is concerned, the adoption of a structured settlement is therefore fiscally neutral, provided the annuity payments are received in full without deduction on account of income tax.

ANNUITIES AND THE OBLIGATION TO DEDUCT

7.33 The purchase of an annuity forms part of the life office's general annuity business. Normally, the life office will be liable to deduct tax at the basic rate from the income element[1] when making payment by reason of TA 1988 s 656—which imposes a statutory requirement to dissect payments as between their capital and income elements. The extent of the income element will depend on the age of the life-assured and annuity term.

The obligation to deduct turns on the income element being chargeable under Case III of Schedule D in accordance with general principles. In this respect, the scheme of s 656 is to identify the treatment applicable to the capital element only. Central to the application of Case III is the concept of receipt as 'pure income profit', as considered in *Earl Howe v IRC*.[2] In the case of a receipt by a liability insurer the amount will be used to fund the corresponding obligation to pay the plaintiff. Can it then be said to be pure income profit and therefore liable to deduction on account of income tax at source?

1 TA 1988 s 348.
2 [1919] 2 KB 336, 7 TC 289.

ANNUITIES AS PURE INCOME PROFIT

7.34 In *Earl Howe* the taxpayer was obliged to pay premiums on life policies taken out following the mortgage of certain properties. He sought to deduct the premiums for surtax purposes on the basis that they constituted annual payments. The taxpayer's argument was rejected. The premiums did not represent pure income profit so far as the insurance company recipient was concerned. The premiums represented receipts to be taken into account in computing the profits of the insurance company.

That a trading receipt could not be an annual payment within Schedule D Case III was illustrated by Scrutton LJ:

> '*It is not all payments made every year from which income tax can be deducted. For instance, if a man agrees to pay a motor garage £500 a year for the hire and upkeep of his car, no one suggests the person paying can deduct Income Tax from each yearly payment . . . [The] annual instalment would not be subject to tax as a whole in the hands of the payee, but only that part of it which was profits.*'[1]

The subsequent decision of the Court of Appeal in the case of *Re Hanbury*[2] may also be cited in support of the importance of 'pure income profit'. In both cases however, the facts and examples given were concerned with payments in consideration of some service or supply as between the payer and payee. This is not so under a structured settlement; the life office pays the annuity in the same manner as if to a private individual, and no supply is being made in return by the insurer other than the original purchase price.

1 (1919) 7 TC 289 at 303.
2 (1939) 38 TC 588.

7.35 Reference may also be made to the case of *Essex County Council v Ellam*[1] in which a Mr Skidmore decided that his mentally handicapped son would benefit from attending a residential course run by a charity. The charity only accepted persons sponsored by their local authorities, who were responsible for their fees. Mr Skidmore agreed with Essex County Council, which was the appropriate authority, to reimburse his son's fees and executed a deed by which he covenanted to pay the relevant amounts. Amounts paid under the deed were paid subject to deduction of tax at the basic rate on the basis that they were annual payments chargeable under Schedule D Case III.

The Inland Revenue refused to repay the amounts deducted to the Council on the basis that the amounts paid under the deed were made in return for services; the payments were not received by the Council as pure income profit. The Court of Appeal agreed with the Inland Revenue. The reason for that agreement was the obligation on the Council to make corresponding

7.35 *Structured settlements*

payments to the charity in respect of the fees for the son. In the words of Dillon LJ. the covering letter to the deed:

> '... clearly earmarked the net payments under the deed of covenant for meeting either directly or by reimbursement [the fees]. A condition was thereby imposed on the council which, if it took the payments, it could not ignore.'[2]

The effect of the condition attaching to the payment was to deprive the payments under the deed of the character of pure income profit. The payments made under the deed only went to cancel the corresponding obligation to pay the charity. Again in the words of Dillon LJ:

> '... it is impossible ... in all the circumstances and in view in particular of the covering letter, to regard the payments by Mr Skidmore under the deed of covenant as pure income of the council without regard to the obligation, which the council took at Mr Skidmore's request, to pay [the fees]. One goes to cancel the other, and there is nothing left to support the council's claim for repayment or to justify deduction of tax by Mr Skidmore under Case III of Sch D.'[3]

---

1 [1989] 2 All ER 494.
2 Ibid at 499.
3 Ibid at 500.

7.36 In a structured settlement it is clear that the insurer cannot receive the annuity without regard to the corresponding obligation to pay an instalment to the plaintiff. However, that obligation is not one which concerns the life office, whether instalments are paid to the plaintiff or not is of no concern to it. This is an obvious difference to the facts which existed in *Ellam*, in which Mr Skidmore had a direct interest in ensuring that the Council made the corresponding payments to the charity. It is also observed that under a structured settlement the insurer is compromising an existing liability to compensate the plaintiff. In *Ellam*, the essence of the agreement was that the council assumed new obligations in return for the payments to be made to it by Mr Skidmore.

7.37 It is therefore difficult to rely upon the decision in *Ellam* as support for the argument that sums paid under an annuity to the insurer are not pure income profit having regard to the counter-stipulation in the case. Whether the Inland Revenue are correct in their assertion that the life office should deduct on account of basic rate tax remains uncertain.

6 OTHER CONSIDERATIONS

7.38 Where the insurer is to fund instalments by way of a purchased annuity, that annuity is normally obtained from a life company separate from the insurer. If it was obtained from a different branch or department of the insurer then it might be argued that the instalments represent an annuity as between the plaintiff and the defendant insurer in view of the direct contractual relationship.

For administration purposes it may be more convenient to arrange for the annuity payments to be paid direct to the plaintiff. To ensure that this does not prejudice the status of the structured settlement, the insurer must remain liable to pay the instalments. Annuity payments from the life insurer therefore should only be made direct if the life insurer is acting as the insurers' paying agent. This may be evidenced in an appropriate form of written agreement.

FINANCIAL REINSURANCE

7.39 The basis for structured settlements rests on the principle that a capital payment may still retain its capital nature even if paid in instalments. The method of funding those instalments is usually met by way of purchased annuity.

The terms of the annuity are not directly relevant to the plaintiff so far as tax is concerned. The obligation of the insurer to pay the plaintiff derives solely from the structured settlement agreement. Accordingly there would appear to be no reason why structured settlements should not also be available where the liability is to be funded by way of so called 'financial reinsurance'. Such reinsurance is usually given by reinsurers located in tax havens who, as a consequence, may accumulate reserves by income retention or capital growth at a faster rate than their counterparts in high tax areas.

LIMITATIONS ON THE CONCEPT OF CAPITAL INSTALMENTS

7.40 The principles upon which structured settlements are based can also operate in reverse, so as to provide for revenue instalments to be paid in respect of an obligation which would otherwise be capital in nature. By way of example, the reverse principle enables a purchaser of a business to convert an earn-out payment for goodwill, otherwise capital expenditure, into a series of annual payments deductible for the purposes of computing taxable profits.

Unfortunately, the circumstances in which this may occur in practice are severely limited by reason of TA 1988 s 125, which was introduced to prevent the use of so-called 'reverse annuity' schemes.[1] The section is mentioned for completeness only; it has no application to payments made under a structured settlement.

---

1 As in *IRC v Plummer* [1980] AC 896.

Structured settlements

APPENDIX 1

Considering the benefits of settling an award for damages in part by a structured settlement rather than wholly as a conventional lump sum

1 BACKGROUND

1.1 Andrew was involved in a serious road traffic accident on 1 May 1988 in which liability was not an issue. He is now a tetraplegic and is fully dependent upon others for his care and attention.

1.2 At the time of the accident he was aged 21 years old and was employed in farm management. He is presently aged 27 years and will not be able to return to work.

1.3 He is unmarried and lives with his parents in a specially adapted bungalow provided by an interim payment. He is currently cared for by a full-time employed carer supplemented by his father. His mother suffers poor health and his father gave up his employment as an agricultural sales representative following the accident in order to care for Andrew. In the future it is intended that as Andrew's father gets older additional care will be provided by a paid carer.

1.4 Andrew's life expectancy has been reduced to the age of 55 years, ie a further 28 years.

1.5 A conventional award for damages has been agreed at £900,000 as follows:

	£	£
Pain suffering and loss of amenity plus interest		115,000
Past losses		
Loss of earnings	20,000	
Aids and equipment	10,000	
Care and attention	40,000	
Travel	5,000	
Accommodation	60,000	
Extra household expenses	2,000	
Holiday costs	2,000	
Less: State Benefits	(22,000)	
Interest on past losses	13,000	
		130,000
Future losses[1]		
Loss of earnings	168,000	
Equipment	90,000	
Care and attention	335,000	
Physiotherapy	30,000	
Travel	30,000	
Extra household expenses	28,000	
Holiday	28,000	
Less: State Benefits	(54,000)	
		655,000
Conventional award		900,000

Appendix 1

---

1 Calculated by reference to a multiplier and multiplicand.

1.6 Andrew has already received interim payments of £150,000 which have been used to provide suitably adapted accommodation, employment of a carer and provision of necessary equipment. Andrew has identified further capital items he requires and estimates the cost at £35,000 (see Schedule 1), including the provision of an electric wheelchair (£15,000) and the replacement of an adapted vehicle (£14,000).

1.7 Andrew therefore has the following sum available to invest to provide for his annual needs:

	£
Conventional award	900,000
Interim payments	(150,000)
Immediate capital needs	(35,000)
Funds available for investment	715,000

1.8 Based on current costs Andrew's essential annual needs inclusive of care costs and ordinary living expenses have been calculated to be £40,000 (see Schedule 1). In addition he requires the following lump sums to replace various capital equipment items such as wheelchairs, vehicles and medical aids.

Years from Settlement	Current cost £	Cost assuming inflation of 5% pa £
5	16,000	20,421
10	35,000	57,011
15	16,000	33,263
20	36,000	95,519
25	16,000	54,182

1.9 In sections 3 and 4 of this example consideration is given to how Andrew's monetary needs, as described above, would be met if his award was paid:

(a) wholly as a lump sum invested conventionally; or
(b) partially as a lump sum, with the balance of £500,000 being used to buy a structured settlement.

1.10 In comparing the two methods of settling the award it has been assumed Andrew will continue to receive State Benefits of £5,500 per annum.

Structured settlements

2 Conventional lump sum settlement

2.1 Funds available for investment amount to £715,000 as follows:

	£
Conventional award	900,000
Less: Interim payments	(150,000)
Immediate capital needs	(35,000)
	715,000

2.2 It is illustrated in Schedule 2 how a lump sum of £715,000 provides for Andrew's future annual needs of £40,000 and periodic capital requirements as adjusted for estimated future inflation of 5% and assuming:

(a) Funds will be invested in a balanced portfolio of gilts and equities (30%/70%) with a return on gilts of 8% and on equities of 3.5%, together with an annual capital growth of 7% for equities.
(b) Tax allowances, bands, and capital gains exemptions will remain at the level of 1994/95. This presents a conservative approach as it is not known whether these allowances will move in line with inflation.

2.3 The model demonstrates that a lump sum of £715,000 only provides for Andrew's needs to the age of 49 years in 2016, being six years short of his reduced life expectancy (Schedule 2). Thereafter, the fund is exhausted and Andrew would be wholly reliant upon the State.

3 Structured settlement

3.1 Structured settlement quotations have been obtained from life insurance companies adopting the following parameters:

(a) Initial investment of £500,000.
(b) Annual sums increasing at 5% and alternatively in line with RPI.
(c) Guaranteed payments for a minimum of ten years should Andrew die within such time, and alternatively no guarantee.
(d) Monthly receipts paid in arrears.
(e) Nil commission to any financial intermediary.

3.2 The most competitive quotations produce:

	1st year's receipt with fixed escalation of 5% pa £	1st year's receipt with movements in line with RPI £
No guarantee period	25,452	29,626
Ten-year guarantee period	25,411	29,580
Difference	41	46

Appendix 1

3.3 The difference in cost between an annuity with no guarantee and one with a ten-year guarantee period is small. In return for his father giving up his job to provide care following the accident Andrew may wish to consider opting for the ten-year guarantee period annuity to provide an income for his parents should he die within ten years of the award being made. We have assumed in this example an annuity with a ten-year guarantee period would be selected.

3.4 A comparison of the annuity escalating by a fixed 5% per annum to that linked to RPI at Schedule 3 illustrates the following:

(a) If RPI is 2% or more over the next ten years, being the guarantee period, then an annuity moving in line with RPI provides cumulative receipts of £323,893 (assuming inflation of 2%) when compared to the fixed 5% annuity which provides £319,617. On this basis the RPI annuity appears a slightly better choice.
(b) If RPI is 1.5% or less over the next ten years, then the fixed 5% escalation appears marginally the better choice as it provides cumulative receipts of £319,617 compared to the RPI annuity of £316,587.
(c) Over Andrew's reduced life expectancy to the age of 55 years the cumulative receipts from the annuities provide:

	Aged 55 cumulative receipts (Schedule 3)
	£000
Fixed 5% escalation	1,484
Moving in line with RPI assumed to be 2%	1,096
" " 3%	1,270
" " 4%	1,478
" " 5%	1,728

Therefore if RPI over the next 28 years is, on average, more than 4.1% per annum then the RPI linked annuity produces the higher cumulative receipts.

3.5 The decision as to whether to adopt a fixed escalation annuity or one moving in line with RPI is difficult to make, especially with RPI currently running at less than 3%. However, although it is the present government's policy to keep inflation low, it is not possible to predict with any accuracy how future levels during the next 28 years may rise. As average RPI over the past 30 years has been approximately 8%, it is considered prudent to adopt an annuity linked with RPI.

3.6 Assuming £500,000 of the award is structured, and a discount of £35,000 has been negotiated with the defendants, the following amount, after allowing for immediate needs, becomes available as a free fund to meet contingencies:

Structured settlements

	£
Conventional award	900,000
Interim payments	(150,000)
Immediate capital needs	(35,000)
	715,000
Cost of structured settlement	(500,000)
Defendant's discount	(35,000)
Professional costs in considering implementation of a structure	(6,000)
Contingency fund	174,000

3.7 The contingency fund aims to provide Andrew with some income and a degree of flexibility in order to cater for any unplanned needs.

3.8 The model at Schedule 4 shows how Andrew's future needs can be provided from a contingency fund of £174,000 together with receipts of capital under a structured settlement increasing in line with RPI (assumed to be 5%). It illustrates that Andrew's needs can be fully provided for up to his life expectancy at age 55 years.

4 CONCLUSION—COMPARISON OF A CONVENTIONAL SETTLEMENT WITH A STRUCTURED SETTLEMENT

4.1 In this example, a conventional lump sum provides for Andrew's needs to the age of 49 years. Thereafter his funds become exhausted and he would be wholly reliant upon the State for the remaining six years of his life expectancy. However a structured settlement fully provides for his needs for his entire life expectancy.

4.2 It should be noted that if Andrew dies before the age of 49 years the conventional award would leave his estate with the greater balance of funds than the structure and contingency fund. In either case the bungalow would also become part of the estate.

Had Andrew any dependants, the extent of his estate on his death may have been an important consideration in deciding whether or not to structure the award. It therefore follows that other considerations need to be taken into account in deciding whether or not a structure is appropriate. In this example as Andrew has no dependants, the extent of his estate is not an important consideration. However, Andrew may wish to consider leaving the bungalow to his parents so that should he pre-decease them then they have a home for the rest of their lives.

4.3 In this example it appears the structured settlement is the most appropriate choice.

Appendix 1

Schedule 1 Andrew's annual needs (in current terms)

	Annual £	Immediate needs for capital items £	Replacement of capital items				
			5 Yrs £	10 Yrs £	15 Yrs £	20 Yrs £	25 Yrs £
Quidic wheelchair			1,175	1,175	1,175	1,175	1,175
Accessories			260	260	260	260	260
Maintenance	150						
Mobile hoist	90	885		885		885	
Portable ramp		250		250		250	
Gewa page turner		1,804		1,804		1,804	
Environmental control system	100	500				500	
Remote door opener	100	800				800	
Home computer	100			1,000		1,000	
Permobile wheelchair	200	15,000		15,000		15,000	
Nissan prairie		14,000	14,000	14,000	14,000	14,000	14,000
Carers	20,000						
Sundry costs	500						
Handyman	200						
Physiotherapy	1,000						
Annual expenditure							
Food	5,720						
Clothes	300						
Entertainment	2,600						
Sundries	600						
Holidays	3,000						
Electric	500						
Telephone	1,000						
Insurance	400						
Cleaner	200						
Vehicle							
Insurance	1,000						
Repairs and servicing	500						
Tyres etc	200						
Petrol and oil	800						
AA/RAC	70						
	39,330	33,239	15,435	34,374	15,435	35,674	15,435
Say	40,000	35,000	16,000	35,000	16,000	36,000	16,000
Inflation of 5%			20,421	57,011	33,263	95,519	54,182

Schedule 2 Net income based on traditional lump sum

Input

Year of settlement	1994	
Age now	27	
Conventional lump sum £	900,000	
Structured lump sum £	500,000	
Disc. for st. settlement £	35,000	
Interim payments	(150,000)	
Total trad. cost £	750,000	
Interest on gilts %	8.00%	
Return on equities %	3.50%	
Rate of inflation %	5.00%	

State benefits £	5,500	
Gilts % of fund	30.00%	
Equities of fund	70.00%	
Personal allowances £	3,445	
Basic rate band £ first	3,000	
Basic rate band £ up to	23,700	
Capital growth %	7.00%	

Pensions at age 65 £		
Immediate needs £	35,000	
Professional costs %	0.25%	
Dealing costs %	1.50%	
CGT limit £	5,800	
Auto Calc	A	
Manual Calc	M	

Sum to invest		
Conventional lump sum and interest		750,000
Immediate needs		(35,000)
	£	715,000
Other income	£	0

For annual needs Years from

End of year during	s'ment (end of year)	Age	Total lump sum £	Gilts annual interest £	Equities annual divis £	Other income (if any) £	Total income £	Income tax @ 20.00% £	Income tax @ 25.00% £	Income tax @ 40.00% £	Total income tax £	Income net of tax £	Pro-fessional costs £	Net inc. to plaintiff £	Annual sum required £	Capital sum required £	State benefits £	(−) or + to fund £	Dealing costs @ 1.50% £	Capital growth @ 7.00% £	CGT on capital growth £	Balance of fund £
1995	1	28	715,000	17,160	17,518	0	34,678	(600)	(5,175)	(3,013)	(8,788)	25,890	(1,788)	24,102	(40,000)		5,500	(10,398)	(156)	34,525	(11,490)	727,481
1996	2	29	727,481	17,460	17,823	0	35,283	(600)	(5,175)	(3,255)	(9,030)	26,253	(1,819)	24,434	(42,000)		5,775	(11,791)	(177)	35,069	(11,708)	738,875
1997	3	30	738,875	17,733	18,102	0	35,835	(600)	(5,175)	(3,476)	(9,251)	26,584	(1,847)	24,737	(44,100)		6,064	(13,299)	(199)	35,553	(11,901)	749,028
1998	4	31	749,028	17,977	18,351	0	36,328	(600)	(5,175)	(3,673)	(9,448)	26,880	(1,873)	25,007	(46,305)		6,367	(14,931)	(224)	35,971	(12,068)	757,776
1999	5	32	757,776	18,187	18,566	0	36,752	(600)	(5,175)	(3,843)	(9,618)	27,134	(1,894)	25,240	(48,620)	(20,421)	6,685	(37,116)	(557)	35,312	(11,805)	743,611
2000	6	33	743,611	17,847	18,218	0	36,065	(600)	(5,175)	(3,568)	(9,343)	26,722	(1,859)	24,863	(51,051)		7,020	(19,169)	(288)	35,498	(11,879)	747,773
2001	7	34	747,773	17,947	18,320	0	36,267	(600)	(5,175)	(3,649)	(9,424)	26,843	(1,869)	24,974	(53,604)		7,371	(21,260)	(319)	35,599	(11,920)	749,874
2002	8	35	749,874	17,997	18,372	0	36,369	(600)	(5,175)	(3,690)	(9,465)	26,904	(1,875)	25,030	(56,284)		7,739	(23,515)	(353)	35,592	(11,917)	749,681
2003	9	36	749,681	17,992	18,367	0	36,360	(600)	(5,175)	(3,686)	(9,461)	26,899	(1,874)	25,025	(59,098)		8,126	(25,948)	(389)	35,463	(11,865)	746,942
2004	10	37	746,942	17,927	18,300	0	36,227	(600)	(5,175)	(3,633)	(9,408)	26,819	(1,867)	24,952	(62,053)	(57,011)	8,532	(85,580)	(1,284)	32,407	(10,643)	681,842
2005	11	38	681,842	16,364	16,705	0	33,069	(600)	(5,175)	(2,370)	(8,145)	24,925	(1,705)	23,220	(65,156)		8,959	(32,977)	(495)	31,794	(10,398)	669,767
2006	12	39	669,767	16,074	16,409	0	32,484	(600)	(5,175)	(2,135)	(7,910)	24,573	(1,674)	22,899	(68,414)		9,407	(36,108)	(542)	31,049	(10,100)	654,067
2007	13	40	654,067	15,698	16,025	0	31,722	(600)	(5,175)	(1,831)	(7,606)	24,116	(1,635)	22,481	(71,834)		9,877	(39,476)	(592)	30,115	(9,726)	634,388
2008	14	41	634,388	15,225	15,543	0	30,768	(600)	(5,175)	(1,449)	(7,224)	23,544	(1,586)	21,958	(75,426)		10,371	(43,097)	(646)	28,973	(9,269)	610,348
2009	15	42	610,348	14,648	14,954	0	29,602	(600)	(5,175)	(983)	(6,758)	22,844	(1,526)	21,318	(79,197)	(33,263)	10,890	(80,252)	(1,204)	25,975	(8,070)	546,797
2010	16	43	546,797	13,123	13,397	0	26,520	(600)	(5,019)	0	(5,619)	20,901	(1,367)	19,534	(83,157)		11,434	(52,189)	(783)	24,236	(7,281)	510,780
2011	17	44	510,780	12,259	12,514	0	24,773	(600)	(4,582)	0	(5,182)	19,591	(1,277)	18,314	(87,315)		12,006	(56,995)	(855)	22,235	(6,218)	468,947
2012	18	45	468,947	11,255	11,489	0	22,744	(600)	(4,075)	0	(4,675)	18,069	(1,172)	16,897	(91,681)		12,606	(62,178)	(933)	19,932	(4,993)	420,776
2013	19	46	420,776	10,099	10,309	0	20,408	(600)	(3,491)	0	(4,091)	16,317	(1,052)	15,265	(96,265)		13,236	(67,763)	(1,016)	17,298	(3,588)	365,705
2014	20	47	365,705	8,777	8,960	0	17,737	(600)	(2,823)	0	(3,423)	14,314	(914)	13,400	(101,078)	(95,519)	13,898	(169,299)	(2,539)	9,624	(956)	202,535
2015	21	48	202,535	4,861	4,962	0	9,823	(600)	(844)	0	(1,444)	8,378	(506)	7,872	(106,132)		14,593	(83,667)	(1,255)	5,825	(6)	123,432
2016	22	49	123,432	2,962	3,024	0	5,986	(508)	0	0	(508)	5,478	(309)	5,170	(111,439)		15,323	(90,946)	(1,364)	1,592	0	32,713
2017	23	50	32,713	785	801	0	1,587	0	0	0	0	1,587	(82)	1,505	(117,010)		16,089	(99,417)	(1,491)	0	0	0
2018	24	51	0	0	0	0	0	0	0	0	0	0	0	0	(122,861)		16,893	0	0	0	0	0
2019	25	52	0	0	0	0	0	0	0	0	0	0	0	0	(129,004)	(54,182)	17,738	0	0	0	0	0
2020	26	53	0	0	0	0	0	0	0	0	0	0	0	0	(135,454)		18,625	0	0	0	0	0
2021	27	54	0	0	0	0	0	0	0	0	0	0	0	0	(142,227)		19,556	0	0	0	0	0
2022	28	55	0	0	0	0	0	0	0	0	0	0	0	0	(149,338)		20,534	0	0	0	0	0

Appendix 1

Schedule 3 Comparison of structured settlement quotations of £500,000 with 5% escalation versus RPI escalation

End of year	Years from s'ment	Age	Structured receipts at 5% fixed £	Cumulative £	Structured receipts at RPI assuming inflation of 1.5% £	Cumulative £	Structured receipts at RPI assuming inflation at 2% £	Cumulative £	Structured receipts at RPI assuming inflation of 3% £	Cumulative £	Structured receipts at RPI assuming inflation of 4% £	Cumulative £	Structured receipts at RPI assuming inflation of 5% £	Cumulative £
1995	1	28	25,411	25,411	29,580	29,580	29,580	29,580	29,580	29,580	29,580	29,580	29,580	29,580
1996	2	29	26,682	52,093	30,024	59,604	30,172	59,752	30,467	60,047	30,763	60,343	31,059	60,639
1997	3	30	28,016	80,106	30,474	90,078	30,775	90,527	31,381	91,429	31,994	92,337	32,612	93,251
1998	4	31	29,416	109,525	30,931	121,009	31,391	121,917	32,323	123,752	33,273	125,610	34,243	127,493
1999	5	32	30,887	140,412	31,395	152,404	32,018	153,936	33,293	157,044	34,604	160,215	35,955	163,448
2000	6	33	32,432	172,843	31,866	184,270	32,659	186,594	34,291	191,336	35,989	196,203	37,752	201,201
2001	7	34	34,053	206,897	32,344	216,614	33,312	219,906	35,320	226,656	37,428	233,632	39,640	240,841
2002	8	35	35,756	242,652	33,829	249,443	33,978	253,884	36,380	263,035	38,925	272,557	41,622	282,463
2003	9	36	37,544	280,196	33,322	282,765	34,650	288,542	37,471	300,506	40,402	313,039	43,703	326,166
2004	10	37	39,421	319,617	34,821	316,587	35,351	323,893	38,595	339,102	42,102	355,141	45,800	372,054
2005	11	38	41,392	361,009	34,329	350,915	36,058	359,951	39,753	378,855	43,786	398,926	48,183	420,237
2006	12	39	43,461	404,470	34,844	385,759	36,779	396,730	40,946	419,800	45,537	444,463	50,592	470,829
2007	13	40	45,635	450,105	35,366	421,125	37,515	434,244	42,174	461,974	47,359	491,822	53,121	523,950
2008	14	41	47,916	498,021	35,897	457,022	38,265	472,509	43,439	505,413	49,253	541,075	55,778	579,728
2009	15	42	50,312	548,333	36,435	493,458	39,030	511,539	44,742	550,156	51,223	592,298	58,566	638,294
2010	16	43	52,828	601,161	36,982	530,439	39,811	551,350	46,085	596,241	53,272	645,570	61,495	699,789
2011	17	44	55,469	656,630	37,537	567,976	40,607	591,957	47,467	643,708	55,403	700,972	64,569	764,358
2012	18	45	58,242	714,872	38,100	606,076	41,419	633,376	48,891	692,599	57,619	758,591	67,798	832,156
2013	19	46	61,155	776,027	38,671	644,747	42,248	675,624	50,358	742,957	59,924	818,515	71,188	903,344
2014	20	47	64,212	840,239	39,251	683,998	43,092	718,716	51,869	794,826	62,321	880,836	74,747	978,091
2015	21	48	67,423	907,662	39,840	723,838	43,954	762,671	53,425	848,250	64,813	945,649	78,485	1,056,575
2016	22	49	70,794	978,456	40,438	764,276	44,833	807,504	55,028	903,278	67,406	1,013,055	82,409	1,138,984
2017	23	50	74,334	1,052,790	41,044	805,320	45,730	853,234	56,678	959,956	70,102	1,083,157	86,529	1,225,513
2018	24	51	78,050	1,130,840	41,660	846,980	46,645	899,879	58,379	1,018,335	72,906	1,156,083	90,856	1,316,369
2019	25	52	81,953	1,212,793	42,285	889,264	47,578	947,456	60,130	1,078,465	75,823	1,231,886	95,398	1,411,768
2020	26	53	86,051	1,298,844	42,919	932,183	48,529	995,985	61,934	1,140,399	78,855	1,310,741	100,168	1,511,936
2021	27	54	90,353	1,389,197	43,563	975,746	49,500	1,045,485	63,792	1,204,191	82,010	1,392,761	105,177	1,617,113
2022	28	55	94,871	1,484,066	44,216	1,019,962	50,490	1,095,975	65,706	1,269,897	85,290	1,478,041	110,436	1,727,548

Schedule 4 Net income from investment of contingency fund and annuity from structured settlement

Input

Year of settlement	1994	State benefits £	5,500	Pensions at age 65 £	0
Age now	27	Gilts % of fund	30.00%	Immediate needs £	35,000
Conventional lump sum	750,000	Equities of fund	70.00%	Professional costs %	0.50%
Structured lump sum	500,000	Personal allowance £	3,445	Dealing costs %	1.50%
Discount	35,000	Basic rate band £ first	3,000	CGT limit £	5,800
Total remaining	215,000	Basic rate band £ next	23,700	Auto Calc	A
Interest on gilts %	8.00%	Capital growth %	7.00%	Manual Calc	M
Interest on equities %	3.50%			1st structured receipt £	29,580
Rate of inflation %	5.00%			Increasing at 5.00% assumed RPI	

Contingency to invest

	£
(incl on Sch of needs)	
Contingency fund	215,000
Immediate needs	(35,000)
Professional fees re structure	(6,000)
	174,000
Other income	0

End of year during	Years from trial (end of year)	Age	Contingency lump sum £	Gilts annual interest £	Equities annual divis £	Other income (if any) £	Total income £	Income tax @ 20.00% £	Income tax @ 25.00% £	Income tax @ 40.00% £	Total income tax £	Income net of tax £	Professional costs £	Net income to plaintiff £	Receipt from structured settlement £	Annual sum required £	State benefits £	(−) or + to fund £	Dealing costs @ 1.50% £	Capital growth @ 7.00% £	CGT on capital growth £	Balance of fund £
1995	1	28	174,000	4,176	4,263	0	8,439	(600)	(499)	0	(1,099)	7,341	(870)	6,471	29,580	(40,000)	5,500	1,551	0	8,602	(700)	183,452
1996	2	29	183,452	4,403	4,495	0	8,897	(600)	(613)	0	(1,213)	7,684	(917)	6,767	31,059	(42,000)	5,775	1,601	0	9,068	(817)	193,304
1997	3	30	193,304	4,639	4,736	0	9,375	(600)	(733)	0	(1,333)	8,043	(967)	7,076	32,612	(44,100)	6,064	1,652	0	9,553	(938)	203,570
1998	4	31	203,570	4,886	4,987	0	9,873	(600)	(857)	0	(1,457)	8,416	(1,018)	7,398	34,243	(46,305)	6,367	1,703	0	10,058	(1,065)	214,267
1999	5	32	214,267	5,142	5,250	0	10,392	(600)	(987)	0	(1,587)	8,805	(1,071)	7,734	35,955	(48,041)	6,685	18,667	(280)	9,304	(876)	203,748
2000	6	33	203,748	4,890	4,992	0	9,882	(600)	(859)	0	(1,459)	8,423	(1,019)	7,404	37,752	(51,051)	7,020	1,125	0	10,039	(1,060)	213,852
2001	7	34	213,852	5,132	5,239	0	10,372	(600)	(982)	0	(1,582)	8,790	(1,069)	7,721	39,640	(53,604)	7,371	1,128	0	10,534	(1,183)	224,330
2002	8	35	224,330	5,384	5,496	0	10,880	(600)	(1,109)	0	(1,709)	9,171	(1,122)	8,050	41,622	(56,284)	7,739	1,127	0	11,047	(1,312)	235,192
2003	9	36	235,192	5,645	5,762	0	11,407	(600)	(1,240)	0	(1,840)	9,566	(1,178)	8,390	43,703	(59,098)	8,126	1,121	0	11,579	(1,445)	246,448
2004	10	37	246,448	5,915	6,038	0	11,953	(600)	(1,377)	0	(1,977)	9,976	(1,232)	8,744	45,888	(59,098)	8,532	(55,900)	(839)	8,498	(675)	197,533
2005	11	38	197,533	4,741	4,840	0	9,580	(600)	(784)	0	(1,384)	8,197	(988)	7,209	48,183	(65,156)	8,950	(805)	(12)	9,628	(957)	205,386
2006	12	39	205,386	4,929	5,032	0	9,961	(600)	(870)	0	(1,479)	8,482	(1,027)	7,455	50,592	(68,414)	9,407	960	(14)	10,002	(1,051)	213,384
2007	13	40	213,384	5,121	5,227	0	10,348	(600)	(978)	0	(1,576)	8,772	(1,067)	7,706	53,121	(71,834)	9,877	(1,130)	(17)	10,383	(1,146)	221,454
2008	14	41	221,454	5,315	5,426	0	10,741	(600)	(1,074)	0	(1,674)	9,067	(1,107)	7,959	55,778	(75,426)	10,371	(1,318)	(20)	10,767	(1,242)	229,641
2009	15	42	229,641	5,511	5,626	0	11,138	(600)	(1,173)	0	(1,773)	9,364	(1,148)	8,216	58,568	(112,460)	10,890	(34,788)	(522)	9,028	(806)	202,551
2010	16	43	202,551	4,861	4,962	0	9,824	(600)	(845)	0	(1,445)	8,379	(1,013)	7,366	61,495	(83,157)	11,434	(2,862)	(43)	9,742	(985)	208,402
2011	17	44	208,402	5,002	5,106	0	10,108	(600)	(916)	0	(1,516)	8,592	(1,042)	7,550	64,569	(87,315)	12,006	(3,190)	(48)	10,008	(1,052)	214,120
2012	18	45	214,120	5,139	5,248	0	10,385	(600)	(985)	0	(1,585)	8,800	(1,071)	7,729	67,796	(91,681)	12,606	(3,547)	(53)	10,265	(1,116)	219,668
2013	19	46	219,668	5,272	5,382	0	10,654	(600)	(1,052)	0	(1,652)	9,002	(1,098)	7,903	71,188	(96,265)	13,236	(3,937)	(59)	10,512	(1,178)	225,006
2014	20	47	225,006	5,400	5,513	0	10,913	(600)	(1,117)	0	(1,717)	9,196	(1,125)	8,071	74,747	(196,597)	13,898	(99,881)	(1,498)	4,633	0	128,260
2015	21	48	128,260	3,078	3,142	0	6,221	(555)	0	0	(555)	5,665	(641)	5,024	78,485	(106,132)	14,503	(8,030)	(120)	5,771	0	125,880
2016	22	49	125,880	3,021	3,084	0	6,105	(532)	0	0	(532)	5,573	(629)	4,944	82,409	(111,439)	15,323	(8,763)	(131)	5,607	0	122,593
2017	23	50	122,593	2,942	3,004	0	5,946	(500)	0	0	(500)	5,446	(613)	4,833	86,529	(117,010)	16,089	(9,560)	(143)	5,395	0	118,285
2018	24	51	118,285	2,839	2,898	0	5,737	(458)	0	0	(458)	5,278	(591)	4,687	90,856	(122,861)	16,893	(10,425)	(156)	5,129	0	112,833
2019	25	52	112,833	2,706	2,704	0	5,472	(405)	0	0	(405)	5,067	(564)	4,503	95,300	(130,100)	17,730	(65,546)	(903)	1,334	0	47,637
2020	26	53	47,637	1,143	1,167	0	2,310	0	0	0	0	2,310	(238)	2,072	100,166	(135,454)	18,625	(14,589)	(219)	1,401	0	34,230
2021	27	54	34,230	822	839	0	1,660	0	0	0	0	1,660	(171)	1,489	105,177	(142,227)	19,556	(16,005)	(240)	653	0	18,638
2022	28	55	18,638	447	457	0	904	0	0	0	0	904	(93)	811	110,436	(149,338)	20,534	(17,558)	(263)	0	(210)	606

APPENDIX 2
ASSOCIATION OF BRITISH INSURERS: MODEL AGREEMENT

PARTIES: (1) _____ ('the Claimant')

(2) _____ ('the Insurer')

WHEREAS:

(1) The Claimant has made a claim against _____ ('the Insured') arising out of _____ ('the Claim')

(2) It is agreed that the Claim shall be settled for £____

AGREED:

1 The Insurer shall be substituted for the Insured to the intent that any liability of the Insured to the Claimant in respect of the Claim shall attach to and be the sole responsibility of the Insurer and that the Insured shall be discharged from any such liability.

2 By way of settlement of the Claim the Insurer shall pay or procure to be paid to the Claimant the sum of £____ and the Claimant shall accept such sum in full and final settlement of the Claim, which is discharged.

3 Subject to the Claimant complying with clause 4 to the satisfaction of the Insurer, the debt of £____ arising under clause 2 shall be discharged by payments by the Insurer to the Claimant in accordance with the Schedule.

4.1 The Claimant shall forthwith take all necessary steps to discontinue any proceedings which have been begun or threatened against the Insurer or the Insured in connection with the Claim.

4.2 The Claimant shall not institute any proceedings against the Insurer or the Insured in connection with the Claim.

DATED: _____

SIGNED: (1) _____ (the Claimant)

(2) _____ (for the Insurer)

Structured settlements

BASIC TERMS

THE SCHEDULE

Amount *Date for payment*

Appendix 2

INDEXED TERMS

THE SCHEDULE

Amount *Date for payment*

Amounts payable under this Schedule shall be increased annually on or after the date of each anniversary of this agreement in proportion to the increase if any in the figure for the General Index of Retail Prices (all items) for the relevant month over the figure for the same month of the preceding year. For the first anniversary the relevant month shall be that for which the monthly Index was last published by the Department of Employment before that anniversary; for the second and subsequent anniversaries the relevant month in the year of the anniversary in question shall be the same as that used in calculating the increase due on the first anniversary. These increases shall take effect each year on the anniversary of this agreement, or on the date of publication of the Index figure for the relevant month, whichever is later.

In the event that in any year the figure for the General Index of Retail Prices (all items) for the relevant month is lower than the figure for the same month of the preceding year (the 'Base Figure'), then:

(1) In that year, the amounts payable under this Schedule shall be the same amount ('the fixed amount') as were paid in the previous year.
(2) In subsequent years, the amounts payable under this Schedule shall remain at the fixed amounts until in any subsequent year (a 'year of RPI increase') the figure for the General Index of Retail Prices (all items) for the relevant month is higher than the Base Figure.
(3) In such a year of RPI increase, the amounts payable under the Schedule shall be increased on or after the date of the anniversary of this agreement in proportion to the increase in the figure for the General Index of Retail Prices (all items) for the relevant month over the Base Figure. Such an increase shall take effect in accordance with the terms of this Schedule.

Structured settlements

TERMS FOR LIFE

THE SCHEDULE

Amount   *Date for payment*

A minimum of _____ payments shall be made under this Schedule, regardless of the date of death of the Claimant, but subject to this no amounts shall be payable after the date of death of the Claimant.

Appendix 2

INDEXED TERMS FOR LIFE

THE SCHEDULE

Amount   *Date for payment*

Amounts payable under this Schedule shall be increased annually on or after the date of each anniversary of this agreement in proportion to the increase if any in the figure for the General Index of Retail Prices (all items) for the relevant month over the figure for the same month of the preceding year. For the first anniversary the relevant month shall be that for which the monthly Index was last published by the Department of Employment before that anniversary; for the second and subsequent anniversaries the relevant month in the year of the anniversary in question shall be the same as that used in calculating the increase due on the first anniversary. These increases shall take effect each year on the anniversary of this agreement, or on the date of publication of the Index figures for the relevant month, whichever is later.

In the event that in any year the figure for the General Index of Retail Prices (all items) for the relevant month is lower than the figure for the same month of the preceding year (the 'Base Figure'), then:

(1) In that year, the amounts payable under this Schedule shall be the same amount ('the fixed amounts') as were paid in the previous year.
(2) In subsequent years, the amount payable under this Schedule shall remain at the fixed amounts until in any subsequent year (a 'year of RPI increase') the figure for the General Index of Retail Prices (all items) for the relevant month is higher than the Base Figure.
(3) In such a year of RPI increase, the amounts payable under the Schedule shall be increased on or after the date of the anniversary of this agreement in proportion to the increase in the figure for the General Index of Retail Prices (all items) for the relevant month over the Base Figure. Such an increase shall take effect in accordance with the terms of this Schedule.

A minimum of _____ payments shall be made under this Schedule, regardless of the date of death of the Claimant, but subject to this no amounts shall be payable after the date of death of the Claimant.

Chapter 8

TAXATION AND QUANTUM

8.01 It will be seen from the preceding chapters that compensation is not always taxed in the same way as the loss to which it relates. If the compensation is to be treated differently from the loss then the question arises: should tax be taken into account in calculating the amount to be paid?

This question is raised in the context of pecuniary losses only. Compensation in respect of a non-pecuniary loss (as discussed in Chapter 1) is not compensation for earnings, income or some other monetary loss subject to tax. Accordingly, compensation for pain and suffering, injury to reputation[1] and so on are not subject to this enquiry.

1 But see *Lewis v Daily Telegraph* at para **2.65** above in respect of damages for defamation.

1 THE RULE IN *GOURLEY*

8.02 The question arose in an extreme form in the personal injury case of *British Transport Commission v Gourley*.[1] In that case the taxpayer was injured as a result of the negligence of the Commission, and was therefore entitled to damages calculated by reference to, inter alia, his lost future income, which was calculated in the sum of £37,720.

The Commission argued that to pay the sum of £37,720 would overcompensate the taxpayer, who would have paid tax on those earnings. It was calculated that had the taxpayer continued to work, income of £37,720 would have yielded a net benefit of only £6,695, the remaining £31,025 would have been paid as tax. The respondent would therefore, so the argument went, be unjustly enriched if he were to receive the full amount which, as damages for personal injury, would be free of tax in his hands. There was, of course, no question of damages for pain and suffering, loss of amenities and for out of pocket expenses being adjusted.

1 [1956] AC 185.

8.03 *Taxation and quantum*

8.03 The House of Lords[1] accepted the appellant's arguments, and decided that tax should be taken into account. Before the decision, the tax position of a plaintiff was generally considered to be an irrelevance in determining the amount of compensation due.[2]

The general principle on which damages are assessed was stated by Lord Reid in the following terms:

> *'A successful plaintiff is entitled to have awarded to him such a sum as will, so far as possible, make good to him the financial loss which he has suffered and will probably suffer as a result of the wrong done to him for which the defendant is responsible.'*[3]

The question which then arose was whether the plaintiff's liability to pay taxes was something which should be regarded as too remote in determining damages. Earl Jowitt raised the question of what damages the defendant should be liable for, and answered in the following terms:

> '... if we apply the dominant rule, we should answer: "He is liable for such damages as, by reason of his wrongdoing, the plaintiff has sustained."'[4]

The application of the rule of law was the dominant consideration, and his Lordship was not deterred from taking the tax position into account:

> '[To] ignore the tax element at the present day would be to act in a manner which is out of touch with reality. Nor can I regard the tax element as so remote that it should be disregarded in assessing damages. The obligation to pay tax—save for those in possession of exiguous incomes—is almost universal in its application. That obligation is ever present in the minds of those who are called upon to pay taxes, and no sensible person any longer regards the net earnings from his trade or profession as the equivalent of his available income. Indeed, save for the fact that in many cases—though by no means in all cases—the tax only becomes payable after the money has been received, there is, I think, no element of remoteness or uncertainty about its incidence.'

---

1 Before a bench of seven Law Lords, Lord Keith dissenting.
2 *Fairholme v Firth & Brown Ltd* (1933) 149 LT 332.
3 [1956] AC 185 at 212.
4 Ibid at 202.

8.04 The rule formulated in *Gourley* is not limited to damages for personal injuries. Lord Goddard expressed the view that it should apply in relation to a wrongful dismissal claim and this view was followed in *Beach v Reed Corrugated Cases Ltd*.[1]

Subsequent case law has applied the rule in a wide variety of circumstances. In *West Suffolk County Council v W Rought Ltd*[2] a local authority compulsorily acquired leasehold factory premises leased to and occupied by the plaintiff for manufacture. Nine months elapsed between the date of the local authority taking possession and the taxpayer recommencing its manufacturing operations. Its claim for compensation[3] included loss of profit during the nine-month interruption. The House of Lords held that the Lands Tribunal should have reduced the award by the amount of tax which the taxpayer would otherwise have borne. The principle in *Rought* is not now considered to be applicable to statutory compensation for compulsory acquisition having regard to the decision in *Stoke on Trent City Council v Wood, Mitchell & Co* (dealt with at **4.29** above).

1 [1956] 1 WLR 807.
2 [1957] AC 403.
3 Under the Acquisition of Land (Assessment of Compensation) Act 1919.

8.05 In *Thomas McGhie & Sons Ltd v British Transport Commission*[1] compensation was paid in respect of a mine following a prohibition on working it. Compensation was paid for the profits lost as a result of the prohibition, and in assessing the amount to be paid the rule in *Gourley* was applied. The taxpayer company argued that for the rule in *Gourley* to apply the compensation must be received free of tax, which was agreed to be the case, and also that it was paid in respect of the loss of profits, earnings or income. It was argued that the compensation was for the loss or sterilisation of a capital asset, as in *Glenboig*,[2] and accordingly there was no question of a deduction being made on account of tax; it was a simple case of being due compensation by reference to the value of the asset lost.

The taxpayer's argument was rejected by the High Court; the decision in *Glenboig* was distinguished on the basis that the compensation was not being paid for the sterilisation of the company's asset but for its loss of profit from not working it. The rule in *Gourley* applied on the basis that it is a principle of the measure of damages and that fiscal liability alone is not conclusive of its application. Because the specific matter in respect of which the compensation was payable was for the loss of profit caused by the mine being left unworked, and such profit would have been taxable if it had been realised, a deduction on account of tax was appropriate:

> '*The essence of the question in relation to each head of damage or each head in any claim for compensation depends on the nature of the item for which the compensation or damages are to be awarded. You do not merely look to the fact that damages are being awarded for negligence, but to the various types of loss or damage asserted as flowing from that negligence.*'[3]

1 [1963] 1 QB 125.
2 *Glenboig Union Fireclay Co Ltd v IRC*, for which see **2.41**.
3 Per Phillimore J [1963] 1 QB 125 at 143.

8.06 Other examples as to the application of the rule in *Gourley* include compensation for lost commission[1] and for the loss of pension rights.[2] In the case of *Hall & Co v Pearlberg*[3] the principle was applied in respect of an action for mesne profits, but this is probably incorrect in the light of the decision in *Raja's Commercial College v Gian Singh & Co*.[4]

In *Hartley v Sandholme Iron Co Ltd*[5] the plaintiff was injured while at work, as a result of which he was away from work for a period of 19 weeks. Under the PAYE basis of tax deduction at source, allowances are allocated throughout the year on a pro-rata basis. As a result of the plaintiff's absence from work the amount of tax deducted from his earnings was too high and he therefore obtained a rebate. The income tax saving to the plaintiff was

8.06 *Taxation and quantum*

deducted from the damages due to him, on the basis that the saving was not too remote to be taken into account because it was a direct consequence of the accident.

1 *Lyndale Fashion Manufacturers v Rich* [1973] STC 32.
2 *Re Houghton Main Colliery Co Ltd* [1956] 1 WLR 1219.
3 [1956] 1 WLR 244.
4 **2.61** above.
5 [1974] STC 434.

THE CONTINUATION OF THE RULE

8.07 The rule in *Gourley* has been subject to much criticism. Apart from the practical difficulties involved in applying the *Gourley* principle, it is a perverse result of the principle that the benefit of an exemption from tax does not help the plaintiff (who is the victim of a tortious act or breach of contract) but the defendant, by reducing the amount otherwise payable. The application of the rule may mean it is less expensive for the defendant to commit a breach of contract than to abide by its terms. This often arises in the context of compensation for the termination of an employee's contract, having regard to the £30,000 exemption available under TA 1988 s 188.

The issue was referred to the Law Reform Committee who reported in July 1958.[1] The committee was divided in opinion, some members favouring retention of the rule and others advocating change. No recommendations were therefore made, and to date there would not appear to be any reason to expect a change in the application of the rule.

1 Seventh Report (Effect of Tax Liability on Damages), 1958, Cmnd 501.

LIMITATIONS

8.08 The rule in *Gourley* does not apply in respect of an action for account, the nature of which is dealt with in Chapter 1. Claims to this effect were rejected in *Re Bell's Indenture*[1] and in *Bartlett v Barclays Bank Trust Co Ltd*.[2]

In the *Bartlett* case it was concluded that whilst there was an argument for taking tax into account in assessing the computation by reduction of what would otherwise be payable, it ought not to be taken into account for the following reasons:

> '... the obligation of a trustee who is held liable for breach of trust is fundamentally different from the obligation of a contractual or tortious wrongdoer. The trustee's obligation is to restore to the trust estate the assets of which he has deprived it. The tax liability of individual beneficiaries, who have claims qua beneficiaries to the capital and income of the trust estate, do not enter into the picture because they arise not at the point of restitution to the trust estate but at the point of distribution of capital or income out of the trust estate.'[3]

1 [1980] 3 All ER 425.
2 [1980] Ch 515.
3 Per Brightman LJ, ibid at 545.

8.09 In *John v James*[1] the court refused to make any deduction on account of tax. The defendant was obliged to account to the plaintiffs for the appropriate percentage of sums received by its subsidiaries. The fact that the defendants might have paid tax on the difference between the sum actually accounted for and that which should have been accounted for was regarded as irrelevant:

> 'Had the defendants accounted as they should have done, they would have paid to the plaintiffs the appropriate percentage of larger sums—X pounds—rather than of the smaller sums—Y pounds—in respect of which they did account. Prima facie what the plaintiffs have lost is the appropriate percentage of X pounds minus Y pounds and, prima facie, that is what they are now entitled to have made good. That is what the defendants must now restore to them.'[2]

So far as concerned the tax costs incurred by the defendant, the court was of the view that:

> 'The fact that the defendants may have paid tax in the United Kingdom or elsewhere on some of or all of the difference between X pounds and Y pounds is essentially irrelevant. If the amount of that tax is to be deducted now, before arriving at the sums to the appropriate percentage of which the plaintiffs are entitled, the plaintiffs . . . will receive less than they would have received had the defendants accounted properly. To that extent the plaintiffs would be penalised because of the defendant's breach of fiduciary duty. In principle that cannot be right.'[3]

---

1 [1986] STC 352.
2 Per Nicholls LJ, ibid at 360.
3 Ibid.

8.10 The second reason given for this refusal to make a deduction on account of tax was the difficulty in calculating the tax involved—which was dependent not only on the incidence of UK tax but also that of seven foreign jurisdictions. Nicholls LJ reviewed the complex inquiry which would be necessary to ascertain what tax would actually be payable by the plaintiff and concluded in the following terms:

> 'Such an inquiry opens up, it seems to me, a real prospect of having to undertake a wide-ranging investigation into the [defendant] group's financial and tax affairs here and overseas over the last fifteen or so years. No doubt . . . the defendants would be prepared to undertake this exercise. But I do not think that the plaintiffs should be required to do so when . . . essentially what is in issue is the payment to the plaintiffs belatedly of sums the defendants ought to have paid years ago.'[1]

---

1 Per Nicholls LJ [1986] STC 352 at 361.

The decision in O'Sullivan

8.11 The decision in *John v James* may be contrasted with that of the Court of Appeal in the earlier decision of *O'Sullivan v Management Agency and Music Ltd*,[1] which was distinguished in *John v James*. In the *O'Sullivan* case the plaintiff, an unknown composer at the time he entered into an exclusive

8.11 *Taxation and quantum*

management contract, was successful in arguing that the contractual arrangements to which he became a party had been obtained by undue influence. In the circumstances the court decided that it was just to set aside the agreements, and the defendants were ordered to account for their profits subject to giving them credit for their skill and labour in promoting the plaintiff.

The order made was to the effect that in computing the sums payable to Mr O'Sullivan for the years in which tax was actually paid by the defendant but was not recoverable (by reason of the six-year limit contained in TMA 1970 s 33), credit should be given to the defendant. That credit was expressed to be for all sums paid by way of tax or which would have been paid but for the utilisation of tax losses, group relief or surrendered advance corporation tax. No such deduction was to be made for sums payable to Mr O'Sullivan within the six-year period.

1 [1985] QB 428.

2 THE RELEVANT RULE

8.12 The relevant rule established by *Gourley*, regarded to be of general application in view of the above-mentioned cases, was referred to in the following terms by the Law Reform Committee:

> '... in awarding damages for loss of income which, if received, would have been taxable as such in the recipient's hands, the gross amount of the damages must be reduced to take into account the plaintiff's tax liability. If, on the other hand, there would be no liability to tax on the sum for the loss of which damages are awarded, then no deduction will fall to be made from the amount of the gross damages.'[1]

It will be seen from the above that there are two conditions precedent which must be satisfied:

(a) the compensation received must be in respect of lost income which would have been subject to tax if it had not been lost; and
(b) the compensation must be free of tax.

The first condition is to the effect that the compensation represents lost income which would have been subject to tax if it had been received by the plaintiff. Whether or not the income would have been so chargeable depends upon the application of the various heads in TA 1988, and this must be decided in the context of a dispute to which the Inland Revenue is not an interested party. The second condition should be considered by reference to the general commentary in Chapter 2.

1 Seventh Report, 1958, Cmnd 501, at p 4.

8.13 The general objections which may be made to taking the tax element into account are threefold. First, the tax saving to the plaintiff may be too remote to be taken into account. For *Gourley* to apply, the tax saving should stem directly from the consequences of the accident. Second, the tax should not be uncertain so that it is a matter for speculation; it should be accurately quantified. Third, the tax element should be something which helps to quantify accurately the extent of the plaintiff's loss.

THE BURDEN OF PROOF

8.14 The burden of proof was not expressly dealt with in *Gourley*. Should the plaintiff demonstrate to the court that the rule in *Gourley* applies on the basis that he must prove his loss and the taxation consequences should be taken into account in respect of it, or should the onus be on the defendant on the basis that he is seeking to reduce the amount otherwise payable?

8.15 In the case of *Barber v Manchester Regional Hospital Board*[1] a deduction on account of tax was made from the award notwithstanding that the court had no information regarding the tax position of the plaintiff.

The decisions in *Hall v Pearlberg*[2] and *West Suffolk County Council v W Rought Ltd*[3] support the view that the burden falls upon the plaintiff to take tax into account in proving his damage. In *Hall v Pearlberg* it was decided that two heads of damage claimed by the plaintiff should not be subject to any deduction on account of tax, notwithstanding the paucity of evidence adduced as to the correct tax position. In the words of Carter QC, Official Referee:

> '. . . the correct conclusion for me to reach is that the plaintiffs have satisfied me that what lies ahead of them is a battle with the Revenue the result of which is very uncertain, and that . . . the balance of probabilities is that they will not obtain any tax advantage by receiving an award of damages . . .'[4]

In the *West Suffolk County Council* case Lord Morton of Henryton expressed the following view in the House of Lords:

> 'It is for the respondents to prove the loss which they have suffered. Their trading year ends on 31 August. They have proved to the satisfaction of the tribunal that they have lost £11,600 profits which they would have made during the trading year [in question], but it is still incumbent upon them to prove their loss after taking into account the incidence of taxation.'[5]

His Lordship continued so as to outline the procedure which might be adopted, by suggesting that the plaintiff submit to the tribunal:

> '. . . (a) a statement of the tax liability which they actually incurred in respect of their trading during the year in question, and (b) an estimate of the tax liability which they would have incurred . . . if they had made this profit of £11,600. These figures would, of course, be open to criticism by the appellants.'

---

1 [1958] 1 WLR 181.
2 [1956] 1 WLR 244.
3 [1957] AC 403.
4 [1956] 1 WLR 244 at 248.
5 [1957] AC 403 at 413 and 414.

8.16 It is thought that the court will apply *Gourley* to cases which clearly fall within its ambit unless the plaintiff can prove otherwise. In *Phipps v Orthodox Unit Trust Ltd*[1] for example, the income tax liability of the plaintiff was considered to be an essential element in the calculation of the damages due to him.

1 [1958] 1 QB 314.

THE GIVING OF PARTICULARS

8.17 It is the duty of a plaintiff claiming 'special damage' (that is to say loss actually incurred up to the date of the trial) to give full particulars showing the amount of the damage claimed. Those particulars must take into account the application of the rule in *Gourley*. As to the particulars which should be provided, a note of caution was sounded in *Phipps v Orthodox Unit Trusts*:

> 'I trust that the matter will be kept in check by the masters and judges applying the principle that particulars should be limited to what is really reasonably necessary to enable the party seeking them to know what case he has to meet.'[1]

This caution is in keeping with the principle in *Gourley* that any deduction on account of tax would be no more than a rough estimate. In the words of Earl Jowitt in *Gourley*:

> 'It would, I think, be unfortunate if, as the result of our decision, the fixation of damages in a running-down case were to involve an elaborate assessment of tax liability. It will no doubt become necessary for the tribunal assessing damages to form an estimate of what the tax would have been if the money had been earned, but such an estimate will be none the worse if it is formed on broad lines, even though it may be described as rough and ready. It is impossible to assess with mathematical accuracy what reduction should be made by reason of the tax position, just as it is impossible to assess with mathematical accuracy the amount of damages which should be awarded for the injury itself and for the pain and suffering endured.'[2]

1 Per Jenkins LJ [1958] 1 QB 314 at 321.
2 [1956] AC 185 at 203 and 204.

8.18 The present practice would appear to have moved away from the above. In 1984 the court in *Shove v Downs Surgical plc*[1] applied the rule in *Gourley* irrespective of complications in the context of a claim for damages for wrongful dismissal. A detailed assessment of the plaintiff's tax position may therefore be required so as to calculate the precise sum which should be paid.

1 [1984] 1 All ER 7.

CALCULATING THE TAX LIABILITY

8.19 In *Gourley* the plaintiff's earned income was so large that no account was taken of his unearned income from investments. Whether such income should be taken into account depends upon the status of the damages, in particular whether they constitute 'special damage', that is to say loss actually incurred up to the date of trial or general damages, that is to say future loss anticipated after the date of trial.

In the context of special damage Lord Goddard said in *Gourley*:

'... *the rate of tax to be taken must, as it seems to me, be the effective rate of income tax, and, if necessary, surtax which would have been applicable to the sums in question if they had been earned. That rate depends on the combination of a number of factors that may vary with each case—allowances, reduced rates, surtax rates, other income of the claimant or his wife, charges or reliefs. The task of determining it may not always be an easy one, but in complicated cases it is to be hoped that the parties, with the help of accountants, will be able to agree figures. If not, the court must do its best to arrive at a reasonable figure, even though it cannot be said to be an exact one.*'[1]

Loss up to the date of trial is therefore to be computed having regard to the actual circumstances of the plaintiff in the pre-trial period. The position is different, however, for anticipated future losses. Dealing with general damages, his Lordship said:

'*In cases where surtax is payable and the rate has been affected by private income, the nature of that private income will be relevant. If it is a life annuity under a will or settlement it may well be expected to continue. If it is disposable investments which might be sold at any time or transferred to a child, less, perhaps little, regard should be had to it.*'

---

1 [1956] AC 185 at 208.

8.20 In applying the rule in *Gourley* to determine the level of general damages, the court should assess the amount due having regard to the current fiscal position of the plaintiff. The relevant considerations include:

(a) tax rates;
(b) the availability of reliefs and allowances, and the incidence of tax planning;
(c) the decision in *Taylor v O'Connor*.[1]

---

1 [1971] AC 115; see **8.25** below.

Tax rates
8.21 In calculating the deduction to be made on account of tax, the possibility of changes in the rates of tax should be ignored. Calculations should be made on the basis that current rates will continue to apply unless it is possible to take account of future tax rates announced but not yet implemented.[1] In *Gourley*, Lord Goddard expressed the following view in the context of a model direction to a jury:

'*No one can foresee whether tax will go up or down, and I advise you not to speculate on the subject but to deal with it as matters are at present.*'[2]

8.21 *Taxation and quantum*

---

1 As in *Daniels v Jones* [1961] 1 WLR 1103.
2 [1956] AC 185 at 209.

8.22 In making a deduction on account of tax, the amount to be deducted is the difference between the actual tax paid on the plaintiff's earnings and the tax which the plaintiff would have paid on the assumed total income. In the words of Orr LJ in *Lyndale Fashion Manufacturers v Rich*,[1] a case concerned with an employee's claim for damages for wrongful dismissal in the gross amount of £495:

> 'In my judgment, the question which . . . has to be posed, namely, how much larger would the tax bill have been if the £495 had been received as additional commission, admits of only one answer, for if a comparison is to be made between a given income and that income with something added, the addition must be treated as the top part of the income. To treat it otherwise would not produce the true amount of the additional tax, since it is the increase in income which attracts the higher rates of tax . . .'[2]

---

1 [1973] STC 32.
2 Ibid at 36.

EXAMPLE

Damages in the net amount of £75 are to be paid, and therefore if the plaintiff's marginal rate of income tax is 25% the sum of £100 is due. If the damages are calculated by reference to the 'average' tax rate after taking account of allowances, an insufficient amount would be awarded. Assuming the plaintiff has taxable investment income of £100, a personal allowance of £20 and is subject to tax at 25% the point may be illustrated by reference to the following table:

	Without damages £	With damages £	Difference £
Income receipt:	100	200	100
Tax due:	20	45	25

Reliefs, allowances and tax planning
8.23 As a general rule the court will take into account the current personal circumstances of the plaintiff for the purposes of computing reliefs and allowances available to him.

In applying the rule in *Gourley* the courts seek to be realistic as to the plaintiff's actual tax position. Evidence of tax planning may be adduced by the plaintiff with a view to restricting the deduction which would otherwise be made. In *Beach v Reed Corrugated Cases Ltd*[1] the court noted that the plaintiff had a large amount of capital which might at any time be sold or transferred. Having regard to the fact that the plaintiff could use covenants to shelter his investment income (in a manner which would not be effective today), the court was of the view that the plaintiff's investment income should not be taken to have an effect on the calculation of damages. This decision was arrived at after taking account of the plaintiff's evidence of his intention to increase amounts paid under covenant, and to make substantial capital provision for his family.

The onus placed upon the plaintiff in this respect would not appear to have been great:

> 'It is common knowledge that, with the present high incidence of taxation on income, those who are fortunate enough to enjoy a large income which is primarily unearned can legitimately and do, in fact, reduce their taxable income substantially . . .'[2]

---

1 [1956] 1 WLR 807.
2 Per Pilcher J, ibid at 814.

EXAMPLE

Mark is successful in a claim for damages for personal injury, and is to be compensated for lost future income of £20,000 per annum. At his marginal rate of 40%, the net benefit is expected to be £12,000 per annum and damages would normally be calculated on that basis.

However, Mark demonstrates that by the use of pension scheme contributions and investments in tax-favoured investments (for example, the Enterprise Investment Scheme) he can expect to shelter the equivalent of £2,000 per annum from tax. No deduction should therefore be made in respect of this element, so that the excess of £18,000 per annum only should be regarded as subject to a deduction.

8.24 In addition to the tax planning opportunities available to the plaintiff in *Beach v Reed Corrugated Cases Ltd* it was noted that since a large proportion of the plaintiff's income derived from investments which might be disposed of at any time, little regard should be had to that income in arriving at the deduction to be made on account of tax from the gross damages due to him.

The decision in Taylor v O'Connor

8.25 In *Taylor v O'Connor*[1] Lord Reid noted that where a lump sum is calculated by reference to the loss of an income stream over a number of years (the multiplier principle), the basis of the calculation provides for the investment of the lump sum by the plaintiff. The investment return is taken into account in fixing the award, but that return is itself subject to tax. If the income loss relates to a long period, the correction required in order to counter-balance tax on the investment return may negate the application of the rule in *Gourley*.

---

1 [1971] AC 115.

EXAMPLE

The correction may be illustrated by reference to the loss of a perpetual income stream. If this was £1,000 per annum and taxed in the plaintiff's hands at 40% so as to yield a net benefit of £600, damages which may be received free from tax should be paid which would yield that benefit if invested. Assuming a 10% return on funds

8.25 *Taxation and quantum*

invested, damages of £10,000 would be due. Such a sum would yield £1,000 per annum which, after tax, gives a net £600. The position is therefore the same as if tax had been ignored altogether and damages calculated by reference to the interest rate only.

8.26 Where damages are being awarded to compensate the plaintiff for a loss of income over a number of years, it is to be expected that the plaintiff will invest the damages in an annuity. Part of each year's annuity payment will represent a tax-free return of capital, but part will represent income subject to tax. The damages therefore have to be increased by an amount necessary to counteract this shortfall.

EXAMPLE

Damages are to be paid so as to compensate the plaintiff for the loss of £3,000 per annum net of tax for the remainder of the plaintiff's life, estimated to be 15 years. To purchase an annuity providing for this return would cost, say, £30,000; but for each payment of £3,000, £2,000 is regarded as a return of capital and £1,000 income. Assuming a tax rate of 25% the plaintiff would be under-compensated by the sum of £250 per annum. The amount of the damages payable should therefore be increased so as to compensate for that income tax charge.

8.27 The rule in *Gourley* is therefore reversed because the net damages are increased so as to take account of taxation:

> '*In* British Transport Commission v Gourley *the net figure after deduction of tax was used for the purpose of assessing damages. Here the net figure should be grossed up to provide the tax which the respondent would have to pay so that she will be able to receive £3,050 net.*'[1]

The reference to £3,050 is to the annual figure to be received free of tax in the taxpayer's hands.

---

1 *Taylor v O'Connor* [1971] AC 115, per Viscount Dilhorne at 139.

---

3 EXTENSION OF THE *GOURLEY* RULE

8.28 Several cases have taken the incidence of tax into account in circumstances where the rule in *Gourley* did not strictly apply. In *Tate & Lyle Food Distribution Ltd v Greater London Council*[1] the plaintiff sought damages in connection with the siltation of a channel serving the plaintiff's jetty on the Thames. The claim comprised two main elements, first the expense of dredging the channel, and second interest on that expense.

It was agreed that damages for the expense would be taxable in the plaintiff's hands but that the actual expense would give rise to a deduction for the purposes of computing profits. This fiscally neutral result was not subject to any adjustment on account of tax. However, it was reasoned that as the actual expense was tax deductible, the real loss for the purposes of computing the interest element was the sum expended after a deduction was made on account of the tax saving.

This reasoning would not appear incorrect. If the plaintiff receives a benefit in the form of a tax deduction then it should be taken into account in determining his net loss. The actual deduction made in the case may well have been excessive however, as little account was taken of the plaintiff's actual liability to corporation tax. Specifically, the availability of allowances to the plaintiff was such that no corporation tax was likely to be due for some time.

1 [1982] 1 WLR 149.

8.29 In *Re Associated Portland Cement Manufacturers Ltd's Application*[1] the incidence of taxation was taken into account in assessing compensation payable by the taxpayer company upon the grant of the right to win and work minerals awarded pursuant to the Town and Country Planning Act 1962. In such circumstances the court is directed to determine what fair and reasonable terms willing parties negotiating outside the statute would have been likely to agree, and compensation is awarded on that basis. This process called for an inquiry into the nature of comparable transactions in the free market.

It was concluded that a property sale for a lump sum was the most likely structure, having regard to the fiscal consequences, and compensation was calculated on this basis.

1 [1966] Ch 308.

GOURLEY AND CAPITAL GAINS

8.30 The decision is *Gourley* is expressed in terms of income tax only. In a situation where compensation is subject to capital gains tax (or corporation tax on capital gains) should this liability to tax be taken into account in computing the damages due? The answer would appear to be 'yes'.

8.31 In *Pennine Raceway Ltd v Kirklees Metropolitan Council (No 2)*[1] the taxpayer company's licence to conduct drag racing was revoked by the local council. As a result the taxpayer sought compensation (under s 164(1) of the Town and Country Planning Act 1971) for loss of income and other costs incurred as a result of the revocation of the original planning permission. After prolonged litigation an award was made in favour of the taxpayer on the basis of lost profits by the Lands Tribunal. The tribunal took the view that the loss of profits would be free of tax in the hands of the taxpayer and made a deduction to reflect the tax which would have been paid had the profits actually been earned.

The Revenue subsequently took the view that the compensation was chargeable as a capital gain, on the basis that it was derived from the licence which was a capital asset within the scheme of the capital gains tax legislation.

The court did not have to decide whether the compensation was properly taxable as income or capital, but took the view that the Inland Revenue's

8.31 *Taxation and quantum*

arguments were correct. Whatever the final analysis, it was clear that the taxpayer would suffer tax in respect of the compensation and accordingly no deductions on account of *Gourley* could be made as this would undercompensate the taxpayer. The appeal was therefore allowed and the compensation increased so as to cancel the effect of the deduction made by the tribunal on account of tax.

1 [1989] STC 122.

WARRANTY CLAIMS

8.32 In a claim for damages for breach of warranty, where some tax benefit accrues to the purchaser by reason of the matter giving rise to the breach, that tax benefit should be taken into account in calculating the purchaser's loss. Support for this statement may be found in the case of *Levison v Farin*,[1] which was concerned with the sale of shares in a trading company on terms whereby the vendor gave certain warranties as to net assets. Because of an adverse change in trading conditions the net assets were less than expected, but the liability of the vendor was reduced having regard to the tax benefit of the losses which caused the reduction in net asset value. It was calculated that the trading loss in question of £7,000 yielded a tax advantage of £2,940 and this was deductible from the damages otherwise due.

The trading losses were of course, enjoyed by the taxpayer company whose shares were the subject of the sale, but it was considered that the purchasers obtained the benefit of the reduced taxation by virtue of their shareholding. Having regard to the general principle that a successful claimant is entitled to have awarded to him such sums as will make good the financial loss which he has suffered, the tax benefit was rightly taken into account. At the date of the trial the benefit was known or could be fairly assessed, and accordingly could not be disregarded as too remote.

In circumstances where it is difficult or indeed impossible to predict the likely tax benefit, no adjustment would appear to be appropriate.

1 [1978] 2 All ER 1149.

8.33 For reasons discussed in Chapter 3, the purchaser's base cost for the shares in the target company is reduced by reason of a warranty claim. The decision in *Levison* should therefore be considered in the context of the capital gains tax position upon the ultimate disposal of the shares.

EXAMPLE

A Ltd purchases the entire share capital of B Ltd for £1m, on terms whereby the vendor warrants that the net asset value of B Ltd is no less than £600,000. It is subsequently ascertained that the net asset value of B Ltd was £560,000 at completion, by reason of trading losses.

A Ltd may claim damages for breach of warranty in the sum of £40,000. On the assumption however that the trading losses may be set off against profits, that claim should be reduced by an amount equal to the tax saving. At the small companies rate of 25%, the tax saving is £10,000 so that the purchaser's claim is reduced to £30,000.

Upon a subsequent sale by A Ltd of its shares in B Ltd, the capital gain will be calculated by reference to a base cost of £970,000 (ie £1m actually paid, less £30,000 repaid under the warranty claim).

Restating the rule

8.34 The rule in *Gourley* has been applied in circumstances where the two conditions precedent to its application (**8.12** above) have not been satisfied. It may therefore be that the decision in *Gourley* is only an example of a more general principle, in that the normal measure of damages is that a successful plaintiff is entitled to receive the full amount of his loss. In calculating his loss, any benefit to the plaintiff should be taken into account; such benefits may include tax savings provided they can be accurately quantified, stem directly from the consequences of the tortious act or breach of contract in question and the taxation treatment giving rise to the benefit is neither uncertain nor complex.

Tax benefits may arise because the taxation treatment of the damages is more favourable than that of the loss to which it relates. Benefits may also arise because the loss itself gives rise to a tax benefit, such as a trading loss which may be offset against profits. The timing of the loss and that of the damages may also result in a benefit, by reference to the allocation of reliefs and allowances or by reference to rates of tax.

8.35 In *Julien Praet et Cie S/A v H G Poland Ltd*[1] damages had to be assessed in respect of an agency agreement relating to Belgian motor insurance. If the insurance premiums in question had continued to be collected, tax would have been due, so that the first condition specified in *Gourley* was satisfied. However, the second condition was not satisfied because damages for the loss would also be subject to tax, but at a much reduced rate.

The High Court declined to make an adjustment so as to reduce the damages on account of the difference in tax rates:

> '... once it is agreed or provided that the damages awarded will be subject to tax, the court inquires no further and does not consider whether the tax liability on the damages would be heavier or lighter than the tax liability on the lost income.'[2]

This approach was approved by the Court of Appeal in the case of *Parsons v BNM Laboratories Ltd*[3] where it was noted that whilst there was some roughness in this justice, this was preferable to an over-assiduous search for perfection.

---

1 [1962] 1 Lloyd's Rep 566.
2 Per Mocatta J, ibid at 595.
3 [1964] 1 QB 95.

8.36 The approach of the court in the *Julien Praet* case might represent the high water mark for a strict interpretation of the rule in *Gourley* having regard to those cases where a less legalistic approach has been taken to computation. In this respect, the approach adopted in *Shove v Downs*

8.36 *Taxation and quantum*

Surgical[1] is to be preferred as it results in the plaintiff receiving compensation for his true loss. In the *Julien Praet* case the fact that no deduction was made resulted in the plaintiff being over-compensated.

1 [1984] 1 All ER 7; see **8.38** below.

4 THE POSITION OF EMPLOYEES

8.37 Compensation may be paid to an employee upon termination without taking into account the tax effect of that payment where the amount is determined by a statutory or contractual formula. There may also be circumstances where it is considered inappropriate to make adjustments on account of tax. Payments in lieu of notice are often calculated by reference to the period of notice in question only. Strictly speaking, such payments may be reduced in anticipation of mitigation, on account of accelerated receipt as well as under the rule in *Gourley*.

8.38 The leading case on the application of the *Gourley* principle to employees is *Shove v Downs Surgical plc*[1] which was concerned with an award of damages for wrongful dismissal. It was noted that any award would be subject to tax only in respect of amounts in excess of £25,000, the relevant figure at the time for the purposes of (what is now) TA 1988 s 188.

The starting point in assessing the award was to calculate the plaintiff's net loss of earnings during the two and a half year notice period to which the plaintiff was entitled. This was calculated by taking the plaintiff's gross salary and deducting amounts on account of income tax, national insurance and contributions to the employer's pension scheme. To this amount was added sums on account of the loss of benefits which would otherwise have been received by the plaintiff in relation to private health cover, life insurance and the provision of the use of a motor car.

This calculation resulted in a total of £70,300 against which £5,000 was deducted on account of the plaintiff's duty to mitigate and £4,571 to reflect early receipt. The net compensation found to be due to the plaintiff was therefore in the sum of £60,729. Because tax was due on any award in excess of £25,000 it was necessary to increase the award to £83,477 which amount, after the payment of tax by the plaintiff, would yield a net benefit of £60,729.

1 [1984] 1 All ER 7.

Application of the rule

8.39 In most cases involving the termination of an employee's contract, the first condition to the effect that the lost income would have been taxable had it been received in *Gourley* will be satisfied, although exemptions exist in the context of overseas employment.

The condition would appear to be satisfied where the employee is subject to tax on the remittance basis under Schedule E, Case III, even though the employee may anticipate enjoying that income free of any liability to pay tax.

8.40 Whether the compensation to be paid to the employee will be free of tax in his hands and therefore satisfy the second condition will depend upon the status of that payment, as considered in Chapter 6. In this respect, freedom from tax may take one of two forms. It may be absolute, for example in relation to foreign service under TA 1988 s 188(3) or partial, for example where the first £30,000 only is subject to exemption.

An absolute freedom from tax gives rise to no difficulties. A sum should be deducted from the gross amount of the damages, which would otherwise be paid, on account of the tax which the employee would have borne on the lost income in question.

EXAMPLE

Jane is to be compensated for the loss of £100,000 income. If she had received the income she would have paid tax at her marginal rate of 40%, so that her net loss is £60,000. The compensation payment, which will be completely free of tax in her hands by reason of TA 1988 s 188(3) is therefore reduced to £60,000.

PARTIAL FREEDOM FROM TAX

8.41 Complications arise when the payment will be received free of tax in part only, usually where the £30,000 'golden handshake' exemption (under TA 1988 s 188(4)) applies but the amount of compensation exceeds this. The correct approach would appear to require that the rule in *Gourley* be applied only to the net £30,000 which escapes tax, the amount in excess of that not being subject to reduction.

EXAMPLE

Michael is to be compensated for the loss of £100,000 income. Had he received it, it would have been subject to tax at the marginal rate of income tax of 40%, so that his net loss is £60,000. The compensation constitutes damages for wrongful dismissal and is therefore taxable only under TA 1988 s 148 so that the first £30,000 is free of tax.

The rule in *Gourley* applies to part only of Michael's loss. For Michael to receive £60,000 net of tax he must be paid £80,000. Of this sum £30,000 will be free of tax, the remaining £50,000 will be subject to tax at 40% and therefore yields a net benefit of £30,000.

8.42 This approach was applied by the High Court in the case of *Shove v Downs Surgical Ltd*,[1] following the decision of the Outer House in *Stewart v Glentaggart Ltd*.[2]

In the former case the court adopted the view that the correct principle to apply:

> '... is to start by estimating the net amount which would have been received by the plaintiff after the deduction of tax from his gross income. That net amount would

8.42 *Taxation and quantum*

represent as realistically as possible his actual loss. Thereafter, in assessing the damages, the court should take into account the plaintiff's liability to tax on the damages awarded so that the net amount received should, so far as possible, equal the net or actual loss suffered.'[3]

---

1 [1984] 1 All ER 7.
2 [1963] SC 300.
3 Per Sheen J [1984] 1 All ER 7 at 9.

8.43 The solution adopted in *Shove v Downs Surgical plc* results in the plaintiff being exactly compensated for his loss and accordingly the primary object of a damages award is satisfied; the plaintiff's financial loss is made good, no more, no less.

SHOVE V DOWNS CALCULATION

8.44 Marie had her employment contract wrongfully terminated on 1 January 1993. The contract was for a fixed term, with three years to run at the date of termination. The terms of that contract provided as follows:

1 an annual salary of £50,000;
2 contribution of £2,000 per annum towards Marie's personal pension plan;
3 provision for health care, at a cost of £300 per annum;
4 company car, taxable on the income tax scale rates as a benefit equal to £2,770 per annum so far as the car is concerned, and £630 so far as fuel is concerned. The aggregate benefit of that car and petrol to Marie based on AA figures is in the sum of £5,000 per annum.

The first stage in the calculation is to establish the net loss to Marie. This is achieved by ascertaining the yearly tax cost, deducting that from her total yearly remuneration and multiplying the result by the unexpired term of her contract of three years. The result (assuming tax rates and bands for 1992/93 to remain in force) is as follows:

	£
Salary	50,000
Car	2,770
Health care	300
Petrol	630
	53,700
Less:	
Personal allowance	(3,445)
Taxable remuneration	50,255

Tax on £50,255:

£0	to £2,000 @ 20% =	400
£2,000	to £23,700 @ 25% =	5,425
£23,700	to £50,255 @ 40% =	10,622

	£
National Insurance (21,060 − 2,807 @ 9%) =	1,643
Total tax cost	18,090
Net yearly benefit:	
Salary	50,000
Car + petrol (value)	5,000
Pension contribution	2,000
Health care	300
Less: tax	(18,090)
Net benefit	39,210

Net loss over three years : £39,210 × 3 = £117,630

The second stage in the calculation is to take the net loss and reduce this by reference to (i) mitigation and (ii) discount for early receipt. This will of course depend on whether Marie has good prospects for obtaining other employment and the expected salary thereon as to item (i), and prevailing interest rates as to item (ii).

For the purposes of this example, it is assumed that the second stage of the calculation produces a figure of £78,867 after deducting (i) the sum of £30,000 on account of mitigation and (ii) £8,763 on account of accelerated receipt at the rate of 10%. Any reduction on account of early receipt should be made after taking mitigation into account.

The third stage in the calculation is to 'gross up' the net loss of £78,867 in order to arrive at the amount which should be paid to Marie so as to leave her with that amount net of tax. The termination of Marie's employment occurred late in the 1993/94 tax year. Any receipt is subject to tax at the higher rate of 40%, being Marie's marginal rate of tax:

	£
Amount to be grossed up:	78,867
Less—tax free amount	(30,000)
Amount to be grossed up	48,867

Calculation to gross up £48,867 :

$$\frac{48,867}{60} \times 100 = 81,445$$

The gross payment is therefore:

Tax free amount	30,000
Amount subject to tax at 40%	81,445
Total amount due	111,455

8.45 *Taxation and quantum*

THE TIMING OF THE TERMINATION

8.45 The charge to tax pursuant to TA 1988 s 148 arises by reference to the termination of the employment contract in question. The timing of that termination can affect the amount of damages due, depending upon where the termination falls relative to the end of the tax year.

EXAMPLE

Robert has his employment contract wrongfully terminated on 30 April 1994. The contract provided as follows:

(a) a notice period of one year;
(b) a salary of £80,000 per annum.

His net loss is first calculated as follows:

	£
Salary	80,000
Less:	
Personal allowance	(3,445)
	76,555

Tax on £76,555:

£0	to £3,000 @ 20% =	600
£3,000	to £23,700 @ 25% =	5,175
£23,700	to £76,555 @ 40% =	21,142

National Insurance	
(£22,360 − 2,964 @ 10%) =	1,940
Total tax cost	28,857

Net yearly benefit:

Salary	80,000
Less: tax	(28,857)
Net loss over one year:	51,143

Assuming no reduction by reference to mitigation nor discount for early receipt it is necessary to 'gross up' the net loss of £51,143 in order to arrive at the amount which should be paid to Robert so as to leave him with that amount net of tax. For these purposes the £30,000 exemption (TA 1988 s 188) is presumed to be available:

	£
Amount to be grossed up:	51,143
Less—tax free amount	(30,000)
personal allowance	(3,445)
	17,698

The position of employees 8.45

Calculation to gross up £17,698:

Amount	Rate	Tax	Net
0 – 3,000	20%	600	2,400
3,000 – 23,397	25%	5,099	15,298
			17,698

The gross payment is therefore:

Tax free amount	30,000
Tax free personal allowance	3,445
Amount subject to tax @ 20%	3,000
Amount subject to tax @ 25%	20,397
Total amount due	56,842

It should be noted that because the termination occurred early in the 1994/95 tax year, the calculation of damages takes into account the availability of his personal allowance and in grossing up it is necessary to calculate through the income tax bands.

If the termination had occurred on 1 April 1994 the position would have been very different. In this case the first part of the calculation would have remained almost the same; the different rates of tax for the last five days in the 1993/94 tax year would have had a very limited effect and are not therefore computed.

Again assuming no reduction by reference to mitigation nor discount for early receipt it is necessary to gross up the net loss of £51,143. Because termination occurred almost at the end of the 1993/94 tax year any receipt of damages by Robert will be taxable at the higher rate of 40%, having regard to his income in the year, and no element of his personal allowance is available. Accordingly:

	£
Amount to be grossed up:	51,143
Less—tax free amount	(30,000)
	21,143

Calculation to gross up £21,143:

$$\frac{21,143}{60} \times 100 = 35,238$$

The gross payment is therefore:

Tax free amount	30,000
Tax free personal allowance	—
Amount subject to tax @ 20%	—
Amount subject to tax @ 25%	—
Amount subject to tax @ 40%	35,238
Total amount due	65,238

The difference in cost between termination on 30 April 1994 as distinct from 1 April 1994 is therefore in the sum of £8,396.

5 GOURLEY SITUATIONS: A SUMMARY

8.46 The commentary which follows is intended as a selective summary of the application of the *Gourley* rule on a situation by situation basis.

(a) Personal injury—damages for non-pecunary loss such as pain and suffering are not subject to deduction on account of tax. Damages for loss of earnings are so subject (*British Transport Commission v Gourley* [1956] AC 185).
(b) Defamation—general damages awarded to individuals are not compensation for the loss of taxable income, and accordingly no deduction on account of tax is appropriate. Awards in favour of a company however may be subject to a deduction (*Lewis v Daily Telegraph Ltd* [1964] AC 234 and **2.65** above).

Special damages may replace lost income and therefore be subject to income tax in accordance with general principles, with the result that no deduction on account of tax is appropriate (**2.67** above).
(c) Damage to trading stock—damages for the destruction of or damage to trading stock should be subject to income tax (**2.15** above) and accordingly no deduction on account of tax should be made.
(d) Mesne profits—having regard to the decision in *Raja's Commercial College v Gian Singh & Co Ltd* [1976] 2 All ER 801 compensation for unlawful occupation of land should be subject to income tax so that no deduction on account of tax is appropriate (**2.61** above).
(e) Contractual breach—to the extent that damages for contractual breach may be regarded as income subject to tax, no deduction on account of tax is appropriate. This treatment may be disapplied if the receipt is regarded as capital in nature, in which case a deduction might be appropriate on facts analogous to those in *Van Den Berghs Ltd v Clark* at **2.27** above.
(f) Employment contracts—if the compensation may be received free or partially free of tax a deduction should be made. In calculating the deduction the basis of calculation established in *Shove v Downs Surgical plc* [1984] 1 All ER 7 should be followed.

Chapter 9

VALUE ADDED TAX

9.01 Value added tax (VAT) is charged on the supply of goods and services in the United Kingdom.[1] It is also chargeable upon the importation of goods from places outside the community, and acquisition of goods in the United Kingdom from other member states of the European Community. The standard rate of tax is 17.5%, but certain supplies are specifically exempted from the charge[2] whilst others attract relief by a reduction in the rate to 0%.[3]

VAT is essentially a tax on consumption; it is largely excluded as a business expense by allowing tax incurred for business purposes to be recovered by way of a credit mechanism.

So far as compensation is concerned, the incidence of VAT raises two primary questions:

(a) should VAT be charged in respect of compensation?
(b) to what extent may VAT incurred upon legal fees and other professional costs in defending or pursuing a claim for compensation be recovered?

---

1 VATA 1994, s 1.
2 Ibid, Sch 9.
3 Ibid, Sch 8.

9.02 VAT is payable by the person effecting the supply, not the recipient of that supply.[1] For the cost to be passed to the recipient, it is necessary to contractually bind the recipient by including the VAT element in the price for that supply. An agreement to pay compensation should expressly address the incidence of tax, and where appropriate make provision for this to be paid in addition to the compensation agreed.

In circumstances where the parties to an agreement consider the payment to be outside the scope of tax for the reasons explored below, but the payer has agreed to pay the tax in addition if the Commissioners of Customs & Excise take a different view, an appropriate form of wording might read as follows:

> 'It is the intention of the parties that the sum payable hereunder should be regarded as outside the scope of VAT by reason of its compensatory nature, provided always

9.02 *Value added tax*

> that [the plaintiff] shall be entitled to charge and [the defendant] shall be liable to pay VAT in addition to the sum payable hereunder upon the issue of a VAT invoice for the same.'

There are variations on the above. For example, it might be appropriate to include provisions regulating the conduct of an appeal against an assessment to tax.

---

1 VATA 1994 s 1(2).

---

1 THE CHARGE TO TAX

9.03 For VAT to be due, a number of conditions must be satisfied; VATA 1994 s 4(1) provides as follows:

> 'Tax shall be charged on any supply of goods or services made in the United Kingdom, where it is a taxable supply made by a taxable person in the course or furtherance of any business carried on by him.'

For tax to be due there must be a 'supply' in the United Kingdom of goods or services. Furthermore, that supply must be a 'taxable supply' (ie zero- or standard-rated, as distinct from exempt) made by a 'taxable person'. There must also be a link with that person's business in that the supply is made in the course or furtherance of it. A full review of each element is outside the scope of this book, but of particular importance in the context of compensation is the identification of taxable persons and the nature of a supply.

Taxable persons

9.04 A person who makes or intends to make taxable supplies is a taxable person while he is, or is required to be, registered for VAT.[1] A person is required to register if the value of his taxable supplies exceeds the prescribed limit. From 1 December 1993, a person is required to be registered if:

(a) at the end of any month, the value of taxable supplies made in the past year has exceeded £45,000; or
(b) at any time, there are reasonable grounds for believing that the value of taxable supplies to be made in the next 30 days will exceed £45,000.[2]

Once registered a person may apply for cancellation if it can be shown that the value of taxable supplies in the period of one year then beginning will not exceed £43,000.[3] For registration purposes the value of the supply of goods or services which are capital assets of the business (save for land which is not zero-rated) is disregarded.[4]

---

1 VATA 1994 s 3(1).
2 Ibid, Sch 1 para 1(1).

3 Ibid, Sch 1 para 1(3).
4 Ibid, Sch 1 paras 1(7) and 1(8).

9.05 In most cases the status of parties to a dispute will be clear. However, the limit may be in question in certain circumstances, for example in the context of the termination of a contract for services with a self-employed consultant.

EXAMPLE

David is a self-employed consultant who provides services to A Ltd. He receives in the region of £35,000 per annum for his services, and is not registered for VAT. David and A Ltd decide to discontinue the arrangement, and it is agreed that A Ltd will pay £30,000 to David as compensation for the termination of his contract. In addition, A Ltd agrees to pay a further £20,000 for the acquisition of certain intellectual property rights. For reasons which are discussed below, the compensation element is outside the scope of VAT, but not the further payment in consideration of the intellectual property rights.

The £20,000 should therefore be taken into account in determining whether David should be registered. It might be the case that no registration is necessary if the intellectual property rights could be classified as capital assets. Furthermore, no registration is required if David can show that the value of taxable supplies in the year then beginning falls below the current threshold of £43,000 as referred to above.

The meaning of 'supply'

9.06 The term supply is 'of the widest import'.[1] It includes supply by way of contract for sale, hire purchase, licence, lease and so on. In most business dealings there is little doubt that a 'supply' has been made; attention is more likely to focus on whether it is a supply of goods or services, and whether that supply is standard rated, zero rated or exempt.

In the context of damages, however, the precise scope of the term 'supply' assumes considerable importance because of the general principle, explored below, to the effect that a compensatory payment falls outside the scope of VAT. Section 5(2) of the 1994 Act provides as follows:

'(a) "supply" in this Act includes all forms of supply, but not anything done otherwise than for a consideration;
(b) anything which is not a supply of goods but is done for a consideration (including, if so done, the granting, assignment or surrender of any right) is a supply of services.'

1 Per Griffiths J in *Customs and Excise Comrs v Oliver* [1980] STC 73 at 74.

9.07 Whether dealing with limb (a) or (b) above the term 'consideration' is central to the meaning of supply. It should be noted that the term cannot be construed in the light of its technical meaning in English domestic law, as it is used in both the Second and Sixth Directives whose object is to harmonise

9.07 *Value added tax*

the laws of member states to the European Community. It clearly includes money, but it also includes the promise to do something under a contractually binding agreement, or the actual doing of something. For these purposes it is immaterial whether the supplier received or directly benefited from the consideration in question; so that a transfer of goods by A to B in return for B providing services to C constitutes consideration.

In the case of *Trafalgar Tours Ltd v Customs and Excise Comrs*[1] it was noted in the Court of Appeal that:

> '... the expression "consideration" ... means everything which the supplier has received or is to receive from the purchaser, the customer or a third party for the relevant supplies. The one important qualification is this. The concept of receipt for this purpose is not to be confined to mere physical receipt; anything which is received by persons for and on behalf of the supplier must be treated for this purpose as received by the supplier himself.'[2]

1 [1990] STC 127.
2 Per Slade LJ, ibid at 135.

9.08 The mere fact that a person has received money or some other valuable benefit does not mean that a supply has taken place. There must be a direct link between the supply and the consideration, and the existence of such a link is dependent upon the nature of the agreement reached between the parties. Where there are difficulties in ascertaining the nature of a supply, or whether one has been made, reference should be made to the contractual arrangements in question. In looking at the nature of that agreement, regard must be had to its substance and reality; this does not allow a written agreement to be disregarded unless it can be said to be a sham.

THE REQUIRED LINK

9.09 In the case of *Apple and Pear Development Council v Customs and Excise Comrs*[1] a ruling was sought from the European Court of Justice in respect of the status of a mandatory annual charge levied by the Council. The charge was levied pursuant to the statutory powers of the Council and was paid by the growers from whom it was levied. The functions of the Council related essentially to advertising, the promotion and improvement of apples and pears.

The Court decided that the concept of supply effected for a consideration presupposed the existence of a direct link between the supply provided and the consideration received. Applying that principle to the case in question, it was decided that the exercise of the Council's functions did not constitute a supply of services effected for a consideration.

The services supplied by the Council were for the benefit of the industry as a whole, and any benefits derived by individual growers were obtained indirectly by reference to the overall benefit. It was therefore possible that only some growers would benefit from the exercise of specific activities by the Council. No relationship existed between the level of benefits which individual growers obtained and the levy paid, and the charges were imposed by virtue of statutory as distinct from contractual rights.

1 ECJ case 102/86, [1988] STC 221.

9.10 In the context of damages generally, a person does not deliver goods or provide services against payment. Compensation is paid because of the defendant's breach of contract or tortious act. There is no reciprocal performance; damages are not awarded for goods supplied or services provided but because the defendant has caused loss and is therefore bound to eliminate that loss whether under a contract or pursuant to general principles. Consequently, it is argued that the payment of damages cannot constitute consideration for a supply.

So far as VATA 1994 s 5(2)(b) is concerned, it would not appear that the plaintiff is doing something for a consideration. The enforcement of his rights to compensation should not involve a surrender of rights which constitute a supply of services.

As a general rule no award of damages by the court should be regarded as consideration for a supply. However, if the action in question is a means of enforcing the supplier's right to payment for a supply (ie an action for money payable, as discussed at **1.06** above) the position is different. For example, a sale of goods on credit to a person who subsequently refuses to pay remains a supply for the purposes of VAT, and if the supplier enforces his right to payment by way of a court order, the character of the monies paid remains unaltered.

9.11 The analysis is less clear if the parties to a dispute settle without recourse to a trial. In the case of *Neville Russell*[1] the appellant entered into a lease, upon payment of £300,000 by the landlord by way of an inducement to take it. The Tribunal held that the £300,000 was consideration for a supply of services, namely the execution of the lease by the appellant. In the words of Lord Grantchester:

> '. . . the acceptance by a tenant of the lease of the demised premises involves the execution of the counterpart lease and acceptance of the grant. In my opinion, this is something done. Further, in my view, where a sum of money is paid for that to be done as in the present case, it is a supply of services for a consideration for tax purposes.'[2]

Could it therefore be said that where a plaintiff agrees to refrain from pursuing his rights to damages against a person in consideration for a sum by way of settlement that the plaintiff is doing something for a consideration, which constitutes a taxable supply of services?

1 [1987] VATTR 194. Reference may also be made to the earlier decision in *Gleneagles Hotel plc* [1986] VATTR 196.
2 [1987] VATTR 194 at 206.

The approach of Customs & Excise

9.12 Prior to 19 November 1987, the Commissioners of Customs & Excise had taken the view that payments of compensation made pursuant to a court order were outside the scope of VAT, but that payments under out-of-court

9.12 *Value added tax*

settlements were taxable. This policy was reviewed on 19 November 1987 when the treatment of out-of-court settlements was brought into line with awards of the court. The policy review was in response to the decision in *White's Metal Company*[1] in which sums paid to settle an action in tort were held to be outside the scope of tax.

The revised policy, applicable to payments made in respect of settlements of disputes, after proceedings had been commenced by service of originating process or the appointment of an arbitrator, is as follows:

> '... where such payments are in essence compensatory and do not relate directly to supplies of goods or services, they are outside the scope of VAT. This will be so even if the settlement is expressed in terms that the payment is consideration for the plaintiff's agreement to abandon his rights to bring legal proceedings. But payments will remain taxable if, and to the extent, that they are the consideration for specific taxable supplies by the plaintiff, eg where the dispute concerns payment for an earlier supply, or where the plaintiff grants future rights to exploit copyright material under the settlement.'[2]

1 LON/86/686Z.
2 HM Customs & Excise Press Release, 19 November 1987.

9.13 In circumstances where there is no dispute as to the actual supply of goods or services but the dispute relates to price, then a settlement under which a reduced price is payable will result in the same tax consequences as if the supply had originally been made in consideration of that reduced amount.

For example, A Ltd supplies materials to Z Ltd for a price of £1,000, but upon inspection it is established that the materials do not meet the required standard. The payment of a lesser amount, say £600, is in consideration of the supply made and VAT is due by reference to this lesser amount. A credit note should be issued by A Ltd so as to reduce the value upon which value added tax is accounted from £1,000 to £600.

9.14 In the case of *Cooper Chasney Ltd*[1] the sum of £30,000 was received by the taxpayer company in settlement of a dispute concerning the use of the name 'INFOLINK' and a logo. This payment was held to be made in consideration of a supply of services by the company.

The terms of the settlement went beyond the provision of compensation for past breaches in relation to the use of the trade name in dispute. The appellant agreed to change its name from 'Info-link Publishing and Communications Resources Limited' to Cooper Chasney Limited, to refrain from using the 'INFOLINK' trade name or logo and to withdraw applications made for registration of trade and service marks.

A direct link was therefore established between the amount paid to and supplies made by the appellant, and VAT was due accordingly. The supply in question was that of services, pursuant to what is now para 4 of Sch 5 to the 1994 Act, which applies to payments in consideration for the acceptance of an obligation to refrain from pursuing or exercising any business activity, or any copyrights, patents, licences, trade marks or similar rights.

1 LON/89/1409Z.

9.15 The decision in *Cooper Chasney Ltd* attracted attention amongst practitioners as it could be seen to throw doubt on the guidance issued by Customs in 1987. The Law Society therefore approached Customs, and a note of the outcome was published in the *Law Society's Gazette*.[1]

The following points were made:

(a) Customs confirmed that they were satisfied that the general approach in the 1987 Press Notice remained correct;
(b) liquidated damages, whilst not involving litigation, would generally be within the spirit of the 1987 Press Notice unless it could be said that the plaintiff was giving up a separate right;
(c) damages for past infringement must be distinguished from permission to continue acts in the future, which constituted taxable supplies. Where a settlement comprised both elements, Customs would accept a reasonable apportionment;
(d) in circumstances where litigation results in a price reduction being effected in respect of a supply on which VAT has already been accounted for, the supplier may issue a credit note in respect of the supply and repayments made accordingly;
(e) interest on damages is outside the scope of VAT.

1 (1992) 9 September at p 32.

THE USE OF CREDIT NOTES

9.16 In general the value of any supply of goods or services is fixed at the time when it is contracted for. However, it is common to adjust the price in order to take into account subsequent events, and this is reflected by the ability of the supplier to issue credit notes.[1]

In circumstances where compensation is paid outside the scope of VAT there is no question of a credit note being issued so as to adjust the value of a supply in respect of which the compensation arises. On the other hand, where litigation results in the consideration for a supply being reduced, the supplier should issue a credit note so as to recover that part of the tax paid but not ultimately due.

1 Notice 700, paras 60 to 63.

2 THE APPLICATION OF THE GENERAL PRINCIPLE

9.17 In the case of *Leslie Reich*[1] in which the appellant was assessed to tax in respect of the receipt by him of £35,000, that amount was paid in settlement of proceedings brought by the appellant in the High Court against Hogg Robinson (Travel) Ltd.

The nature of the litigation was summarised by Mr Johnson, the tribunal chairman, in the following terms:

9.17 *Value added tax*

> '. . . the Appellant was suing Hogg Robinson for commission allegedly earned by having provided, at its request, accounts and information introducing it to a chain of "travel shops" . . . which were on offer for sale. The Appellant . . . [obtained] a signed written agreement laying down the scale of his fees for a transaction before proceeding to do the work in respect of such fees. After obtaining the agreement of Hogg Robinson to pay his fee, and providing the accounts and information mentioned, the Appellant received a short letter from Hogg Robinson to say that it did not wish to proceed further. A while later, he learned . . . that Hogg Robinson had in fact proceeded to acquire the particular chain of "travel shops" without further contacting him. He accordingly raised an invoice for the amount of his agreed sale fee, and when this was not paid, took Hogg Robinson to court.
>
> Hogg Robinson's defence was that the Appellant had not effected the introduction resulting in the acquisition, and that accordingly the Appellant was not entitled to his fee.'[2]

After negotiations the action was settled, at the door of the court, by Hogg Robinson paying to the appellant the sum of £35,000, which sum represented a substantial proportion of his claim for £45,000 plus costs.

1 MAN/92/454.
2 Ibid at 4 and 5.

9.18 Customs argued that the amount paid in settlement should be regarded as paid in consideration of a supply of services, namely the work carried out by the appellant which was in dispute, and VAT assessed accordingly. It was submitted that the legal proceedings instituted by the appellant to recover the sum in question were merely incidental to the actual supply.

Against this the appellant submitted that the amount paid represented the value of the compromise of the dispute to the parties, as distinct from the value of a supply made by the appellant which was in dispute.

The tribunal found for the appellant. The amount paid was not the full amount of his claim for services rendered, it was an agreed estimate of the value of that claim. The sum paid could not be said to be directly linked to the provision of services by the appellant, the amount paid was inclusive of costs and, of course, a settlement avoided the potential embarrassment and/or financial loss which the appellant might cause Hogg Robinson.

Mr Johnson commented that:

> '. . . it is in my view one situation where a taxpayer sues and recovers judgment for the amount of an invoice on which value added tax is properly chargeable as being in respect of a supply; it is quite another situation where judgment has not been obtained, no admission has been made that a taxable supply was ever made, and to avoid the embarrassment of a trial a sum is paid by way of compromise. The one situation fortifies the view that a taxable supply was made; the other situation leads to the conclusion that it will never be established that a taxable supply has been made.'[1]

1 MAN/92/454 at 7.

9.19 It would appear that the outcome in *Leslie Reich* would have been different if the terms of the settlement were such that Hogg Robinson accepted that it had received the services in dispute. In such a case a direct link would exist between the consideration paid by way of settlement and a supply for the purposes of VAT.

In *Galaxy Equipment (Europe) Ltd*[1] a claim by the appellant to recover as input tax an amount shown as VAT upon an invoice was dismissed, as the invoice related to a claim for compensation outside the scope of the charge to tax. The invoice was raised by a customer of the appellant which had purchased material from the appellant for the manufacture of wet suits. The material proved to be faulty and so the customer raised the invoice in dispute in respect of which the appellant claimed the VAT shown on it.

Customs' argument, which was accepted by the tribunal, was that the quality of the material sold was guaranteed, and under that guarantee the customer had been repaid the full replacement value of the garments. Any such payment was therefore by way of compensation for the loss sustained by the customer and so outside the scope of tax.

---

1 MAN/91/1457.

Liquidated damages

9.20 The nature of liquidated damages was considered in some detail in the case of *Holiday Inns (UK) Ltd*[1] which was concerned with a payment of £2,000,000 to a management company for the loss of future fees following the termination of the management agreement by notice.

The appellant carried on the business of managing hotels, and from March 1984 had managed the Holiday Inn in Croydon which was owned by the Croydon Hotel Leisure Company Ltd. The management of the hotel was governed by a written agreement between the two companies, which was renewable in 2004. Differences arose between the parties about the way the hotel was being managed, and the owner wanted to terminate the agreement but could not do so unless there was a so-called 'Event of Default'. There was no such event in question, so the parties to the agreement agreed to a variation to it whereby the owner was given a right of termination, subject to paying all sums due up to the termination date and paying a lump sum by way of liquidated damages in the sum of £2,000,000. The variation was agreed on 31 August 1990, and notice of termination was given on 18 December 1990. Liquidated damages were paid in consequence of that termination at the end of the relevant notice period.

---

1 MAN/91/1475.

9.21 Customs conceded that in general liquidated damages are outside the scope of VAT, but argued that in this case the payment was for the surrender by the appellant of his right to manage the hotel. The appellant 'did' something for a consideration, by entering into the new agreement. There was therefore a direct link between the consideration paid and the services supplied by the appellant.

The tribunal found in favour of the appellant. The status of the August contract was considered to be a variation of the original management contract; it simply added a new term providing for an additional method of

9.21 *Value added tax*

termination. Having regard to the terms of the management agreement, and in particular the fees reserved therein, it was considered that the £2,000,000 payment was a genuine pre-estimate of damages and therefore conformed to the classic exposition of liquidated damages.[1] The payment was therefore in essence compensatory, and there was no direct link between the payment and any supply of services.

---

1 Lord Dunedin, *Dunlop Pneumatic Tyre Co Ltd v New Garage and Motor Co Ltd* [1915] AC 79.

9.22 Because the August contract merely provided for a new term which might or might not have led to termination, it could not be said that there was a supply by reference to its execution.

Mr Rowland QC, the tribunal chairman, summarised the position in the following terms:

> '... looking at the reality of the situation from the point of the parties the Management Agreement was no longer working satisfactorily in the sense that there were substantial disputes about the way the hotel was being run and [the hotel owners] were anxious to end the contract. But they were unable to do so under the existing termination clause which required default to be proved as the only available cause of action. [The hotel owners] were unable to prove default and so eventually the parties agreed upon a way of ending the contract without proof of default. [The hotel owners] were empowered, if they so wished and within a certain time, to serve a notice of termination. If they did that they would have to pay [the appellant] £2,000,000 agreed compensation for the loss of future management fees.'[1]

VATA 1994 s 5(2)(b) was not in question, because nothing was 'done' for a consideration:

> '[the appellant] was a purely passive party to this procedure; it did not have to do anything once [the hotel owners] had set in motion the termination procedure. [The appellant] had no option but to allow termination to take its course. And that is what happened; [the hotel owners] paid £2,000,000 as compensation for loss of future fees. [The appellant] did nothing ...'

It was therefore concluded that the payment was in essence compensatory and could not be said to relate directly to a supply of goods or services made by the appellant. It was not consideration for a specific taxable supply and was therefore outside the scope of VAT.

---

1 MAN/91/1475 at 27 and 28.

LEASING CONTRACTS

9.23 The decisions in *Holiday Inns* should be contrasted with that in *Leigh*[1] in which a 'fine' paid by a hirer of goods upon their late return amounted to consideration for the use of those goods.

The treatment of lease termination was discussed by the Law Society and Customs, as a result of which the following commentary was published:

> 'Customs have agreed a "joint statement of practice" (JSP) with the principal leasing association in order to avoid contractual arguments and any ambiguity over

The application of the general principle **9.25**

the correct VAT treatment of termination payments and rebates/refunds of rentals arising under equipment leases. The object of the JSP is to establish a common treatment which provides that:

(1) all lease termination payments may be treated as being in respect of taxable supplies, ie of the right to terminate. Here the termination payment is usually calculated by reference to the amount of rental payments outstanding under the primary lease period; and

(2) where on expiry or termination of an equipment lease, the lessee receives from the lessor a rebate or refund of rentals, no adjustment for VAT previously charged need be made. However, credit notes should be endorsed "This is not a credit note for VAT purposes".

Importantly, the JSP does not override any contractual arrangements in force. If the lessors wish to revert to the terms of their original agreements, they may do so. For example, lease termination payments may arise on default by a lessee which are by way of liquidated damages and therefore outside the scope of VAT.

Taxpayers who were not within the major leasing associations could rely on this agreement, but they would not necessarily be aware of it. It was confirmed that local VAT offices had knowledge of it.'[2]

---

1 [1990] VATTR 59.
2 *Law Society Gazette* (1992) 9 September at p 32.

CANCELLATION CHARGES AND DEPOSITS

9.24 As discussed above, liquidated damages remain outside the scope of VAT, but it does not follow that all payments made following a breach of contract will be so treated. Two cases may usefully be referred to, *Customs and Excise Comrs v Moonraker's Guest House Ltd*[1] and *Customs and Excise Comrs v Bass plc*.[2]

---

1 [1992] STC 544.
2 [1993] STC 42.

9.25 In the *Moonraker* case, holiday accommodation was provided in the Scilly Isles, which accommodation was standard rated. When booking, a deposit of 25% of the total was due, the balance being paid upon arrival. If the booking was cancelled, the appellant sought to re-let the accommodation. If successful, the deposit was returned but if not the full amount remained due and the deposit was retained as part-payment.

The appellant was successful before the tribunal but on appeal the High Court found in favour of Customs & Excise. It was decided that when the deposit was paid it was a payment on account of rent and so standard rated. The deposit became the property of the appellant upon payment and a supply therefore occurred at that time. If the deposit was subsequently returned the appellant was able to claim the VAT previously paid in respect of it.

In *Bass* the appellants owned hotels which had a standard cancellation charge for customers who failed to arrive and take up their booking. The cancellation charge was equal to the full price of the hotel room which was made available on a guaranteed basis; the customer could arrive at any time and the room would be available. The court took the view that hotel

9.25 *Value added tax*

accommodation was being made available, and that the cancellation charge represented the fee for such accommodation; it was up to the customer to decide whether or not to use the room. Accordingly, tax was due in full upon the charge made.

9.26 In contrast, deposits taken as security or to show 'good faith' will not create a tax point when they remain the property of the payer. In *Nigel Mansell Sports Co Ltd v Customs and Excise Comrs*[1] the tribunal held that 'deposits' paid by customers in respect of Ferrari sports cars could not be regarded as creating a tax point as at the time the deposit was paid because no contract to supply a car then existed. The money was deposited by a person who wished to be treated as a potential purchaser, and whilst the deposit was utilised if he did purchase a car it was otherwise repayable within 48 hours of a request to this effect.

1 [1991] VATTR 491.

DEPOSITS AND PROPERTY TRANSACTIONS

9.27 The purchaser of property will usually be required to pay a deposit upon exchange of contracts, which will either be held as 'agent for the vendor' or as 'stakeholder'. In the former case, the deposit becomes the property of the vendor and VAT is due if the transaction in question is one to which the standard-rated provisions apply. If the contract is never completed, the deposit may be forfeited by the purchaser. In these circumstances no supply of property has been made, and the forfeited deposit cannot be consideration for such a supply but is damages for breach of contract and is outside the scope of charge. The vendor should issue a credit note to the purchaser in respect of the deposit, whether returned or not.

On the other hand, a deposit held as stakeholder does not create a tax point as the deposit does not become the property of the vendor. If the deposit is forfeited, the same analysis as for deposits paid as agent of the vendor applies, save that no credit note need be issued.

MESNE PROFITS AND ARREARS OF RENT

9.28 Mesne profits is another term for damages for trespass, being damages accruing to a landlord from the continued occupation of land by a tenant after that right of occupation has ceased.[1] They can only be claimed from the date when the tenant became a trespasser, which may be from the time the landlord seeks entry or the service of a writ. They do not arise if the tenant is holding over with the consent of the landlord.

The position of such profits is clear. Customs have accepted that an award of mesne profits is not consideration for a supply whether in respect of the land or by reference to services.[2]

1 *Bramwell v Bramwell* [1942] 1 All ER 137.
2 Law Society press release, 14 October 1992.

9.29 However, care must be taken to distinguish between mesne profits on the one hand and arrears of rent on the other. Any receipt of the latter is consideration for a supply under the lease in question. Accordingly, VAT is due if the landlord has exercised his 'option to tax'.[1]

Provided the landlord is either on cash accounting, or rent demands have been made without involving the issue of a VAT invoice, there is no cash flow disadvantage. In most cases however, a tax point would have been created by the issue of an invoice. If agreement is reached so that a sum less than the rental arrears claimed is paid, it is necessary to issue a credit note for the difference, so that the landlord may recover the same.

In circumstances where both arrears and mesne profits are claimed, and the landlord and tenant agree to settle the claim for less than the total amount, Customs' practice is to regard the rent arrears as settled in priority to the mesne profits.

1 Under VATA 1994 Sch 10 para 2.

THE IMPORTANCE OF CONSENT

9.30 Compensation for the infringement of a person's rights must be distinguished from a payment in return for the agreement of a person to give up those rights.

For example, if the owner of a piece of land had the benefit of a right of way over an adjoining piece of land, which was blocked by the adjoining landowner, he may receive damages for his loss which would be outside the scope of charge. On the other hand, an agreement to forfeit his rights in consideration of a payment from his neighbour may constitute a standard-rated supply. A similar example may be given in the context of rights to light.

COMPULSORY PURCHASE

9.31 Customs take the view that if a person is obliged to dispose of property under a compulsory purchase order, that person is making a supply for VAT purposes.[1] The status of that supply will be determined by reference to the normal rules applicable to property transfers, but broadly speaking most acquisitions will be exempt unless the person has exercised the so-called 'option to tax'.[2]

1 Notice 742B at para 11.
2 VATA 1994 Sch 10 para 2.

9.32 It is clear that Customs' view is correct if a transfer of land is made voluntarily, albeit in the knowledge that the land could be compulsorily purchased. What is less clear is the status of compensation paid by reason of compulsory acquisition where the landowner has done nothing to assist the authority exercising its powers of acquisition, ie if the landowner merely sits back and has his land taken from him, against his will, can it be said that he has made a supply?

Two arguments may be put forward which support the view that no supply is made. First, it may be argued that there is no supply made in the course or furtherance of the landowner's business because compulsory acquisition is not a normal business activity. Second, it may be argued that

9.32 *Value added tax*

the compensation paid to the landowner as a result of the compulsory acquisition does not have the quality of consideration because there is no bargain as between the landowner and the authority. While not directly on the point, it is noted that in *Tolsma v Inspecteur der Omzetbelasting Leeuwarden*[1] the European Court of Justice was of the view that a supply of services is effected for 'consideration' only if:

> '... there is a legal relationship between the provider of the service and the recipient pursuant to which there is reciprocal performance, the remuneration received by the provider of the service constituting the value actually given in return for the service supplied to the recipient.'[2]

Against this it is noted that the compensation is, effectively, the purchase price paid by the authority for the land. Whilst there may have been no element of consent on the part of the landowner, there may be said to be a direct link between the compulsory acquisition and the compensation paid.

1 [1994] STC 509, a case concerning donations made by passers-by voluntarily to Mr Tolsma who played a barrel organ on the public highway.
2 Ibid at 516.

9.33 It is understood that whilst Customs adhere to the view stated at **9.31** above, they are willing to concede that certain compensation payments may fall outside the scope of tax. Such payments may include those for disturbance or injurious affliction of land retained by the landowner.

INDEMNITIES FOR COSTS

9.34 As a general rule, the payment of another party's costs as a term for the granting of some right will be part of the consideration for the grant. For example, a payment by a prospective tenant on account of his landlord's costs in granting a lease will be part of the consideration for that lease.

However, Customs accept that if a tenant is exercising rights already granted under the lease on terms that require the tenant to make good any legal or other ordinary costs, such as a surveyor, incurred by the landlord, then that reimbursement of costs is not regarded as consideration for a supply by the landlord to the tenant.[1] Any VAT charged to the landlord in respect of the costs may be deducted by the landlord, provided he has exercised his 'option to tax' in respect of the building in question (ie on the basis that such costs will then be attributable to the standard rated supplies made by the landlord in respect of the building).

1 Notice 742B, para 15.

EXAMPLE

Emily agrees to assign her lease in respect of an office suite, but under the terms of the lease must obtain her landlord's consent to assign. The lease provides for Emily to indemnify her landlord for the costs of giving consent, and the costs amount to £200 plus VAT. If Emily's landlord can fully recover the VAT element of the costs, Emily need pay only £200, which payment is outside the scope of VAT. If the landlord cannot fully recover the VAT element, Emily should pay £200 plus that part of the VAT which the landlord cannot recover. This VAT cost cannot be recovered by Emily, because the legal services were not supplied to her.

Further examples may be given in relation to the exercise by a tenant of a right to sub-let, or make alterations.

STATUTORY COMPENSATION

9.35 Customs accept that compensation paid by a landlord to a tenant under the terms of the Landlord and Tenant Act 1954 or the Agricultural Holdings Act 1986 is outside the scope of tax.[1] It is necessary for the compensation to be paid in accordance with the statutory procedures in order to be so treated; ie a 'notice to quit' must be served, and complied with by the tenant.

1 Notice 742B, para 13.

INTEREST

9.36 It is clear that interest for late payment awarded by the court is outside the scope of tax.[1] There would appear to be no reason to distinguish between interest awarded by the court, settled as between the parties or provided for in the contract.

1 *BAZ Bausystem AG v Finarnzamnt München für Köpershaften*, ECJ case 222/81 [1992] ECR 2527.

3 THE FORM OF SETTLEMENT

9.37 As discussed above, Customs originally took the view that the method by which a dispute was settled could determine the VAT treatment. Payments under court orders were regarded as outside the scope of VAT but out-of-court settlements were not. This view was reviewed in 1987, but the terms of the revised view issued in November of that year still referred to the institution of legal proceedings. Customs subsequently indicated in a meeting with the Law Society[1] that payments made before proceedings had been commenced may also qualify to be treated as outside the scope of VAT, but no general guidance was given.

1 23 October 1991.

9.38 In *Holiday Inns (UK) Ltd*[1] Mr Rowland QC, the tribunal chairman, doubted that the form in which two parties to a dispute settled their differences should alter the taxability of payments made in connection with that dispute. Specifically, the institution of legal proceedings should not be regarded as a condition precedent in avoiding the payment of VAT. Whilst not expressly dealt with in *FMS Management Services*[2] the apparent absence of legal proceedings did not prevent the £30,000 payment there in question from being regarded as outside the scope of VAT.

9.38 *Value added tax*

The position would therefore appear to be that the form adopted to settle a dispute between parties at arm's length will not affect the VAT position. In this respect the examples given by Mr Rowland QC in the *Holiday Inns* case as methods of settlement between two parties may usefully be set out:

> '(i) They may settle for payment of damages or compensation after a writ or originating process has been issued.
> (ii) They may obtain a court order on consent, the draft of which has been agreed.
> (iii) They may have the action struck out by consent with no court order.
> (iv) They may settle on terms endorsed on counsel's brief which is simply a form of contract.
> (v) They may draw up and sign terms of settlement in the form of an agreement without a court order.
> (vi) They may enter into an agreement settling their differences before *action brought*—an agreement which may be in the same terms as after a *writ has been issued.*
> (vii) If the parties to a dispute have agreed to a court order any alleged breach of terms of settlement is dealt with by the court.
> (viii) If such parties elect not to have a court order any alleged breach can only be dealt with by suing on the contract (that is, the terms of settlement agreed).'[3]

---

1 MAN/91/1475.
2 LON/92/722.
3 MAN/91/1475 at 23.

---

4 THE PAYMENT OF THIRD PARTY COSTS

9.39 Where a defendant is obliged or agrees to pay damages, provision is usually made for the legal costs incurred by the plaintiff in pursuing his claim. Such legal costs will themselves invariably be subject to VAT, which may be recovered in whole or in part by the plaintiff if the plaintiff is a taxable person.

The liability upon the defendant to pay the plaintiff's costs is essentially one of indemnity, so the actual amount paid should be equal to the legal costs exclusive of VAT together with any element of VAT which is not recoverable by the plaintiff. It is not possible for the defendant to recover the VAT element on the plaintiff's costs, as no supply was actually made to the defendant in respect of the legal services in question.

The general principles to apply were published by the Law Society in the following terms:

> '(a) the solicitor whose costs are to be paid should deliver a tax invoice to his or her own client. If his or her client is not a registered taxable person, it is permissible to deliver a VAT inclusive bill without distinguishing the VAT element, although this would not be a common practice;
> (b) if the solicitor's client is a registered fully taxable person, and the supply of legal services is obtained for the purposes of the client's business, the client will be entitled to an input tax credit in which case the indemnifying party need only pay the costs exclusive of VAT;

(c) if the solicitor's client is not a registered fully-taxable person and cannot obtain input tax credit, the indemnifying party is liable to pay the costs and VAT as well. However, the indemnifying party cannot recover the VAT;
(d) where the solicitor's client is a partly-exempt registered taxable person, paragraph (b) above applies only to the extent that the client can obtain credit for input tax. Paragraph (c) applies to the balance;
(e) in no circumstances may a tax invoice be issued by the client's solicitor to the paying party who is not in law entitled to receive an input tax credit as the services have not been rendered to him. The paying party should therefore receive a note of the other party's costs in such terms that the note cannot be mistaken for a tax invoice issued to the paying party.'[1]

---

1 *Law Society's Gazette* (1992) 28 October at 43.

EXAMPLE

A Ltd contracts with Z Ltd to supply goods. The goods delivered do not meet the specification detailed in the contract; they are returned and Z Ltd sues for damages for the breach. After negotiations it is agreed that A Ltd will pay £65,000 in settlement of Z Ltd's claim. This amount is outside the scope of VAT. In addition, A Ltd agrees to pay B Ltd's legal costs which come to £10,000 plus VAT of £1,750. Z Ltd is partially exempt, and is only able to recover 65% of its VAT. Accordingly, A Ltd pays £10,612.50 (ie £10,000 plus £612.50 being 35% of £1,750).

9.40 The use of the indemnity principle for paying costs is not appropriate where the compensation in question is consideration for a supply, in which case amounts paid on account of costs will follow the status of the supply in question.

EXAMPLE

Andrew and Robert are in dispute as to the ownership of certain intellectual property rights. The dispute is settled in circumstances where £5,000 is paid by Robert for past infringements and a further sum of £20,000 is paid for the acquisition of those rights. Robert agrees to pay Andrew's legal costs of £3,000 (exclusive of VAT). It is agreed that £1,000 of the legal fees relate to the action for past infringement and £2,000 relates to the negotiations for the sale of the rights.

Assuming Andrew is partially exempt, and may recover only 35%, Robert is liable to pay the following:

(a) £5,000 compensation for past infringement which amount is outside the scope of VAT;
(b) £1,113.75 on account of costs relating to (a) above, representing £1,000 plus £113.75, being 65% of the VAT element of £175;
(c) £22,000 plus £3,850 VAT on account of the acquisition of the intellectual property rights (ie £20,000 plus £2,000 legal costs which element forms part of the consideration of the sale).

Robert may recover the VAT incurred in item (c) above, subject to the normal rules concerning recovery.

5 VAT AND EMPLOYEES

9.41 A cash payment to an employee upon the termination of his employment or other event giving rise to compensation has no VAT effect. Whilst an employee might be seen to be making a supply there is no business in respect of which it is made.

However, if the employer (who is a taxable person) transfers property to the employee then there are VAT implications. VATA 1994 Sch 4 para 5(1) provides for a supply of goods to be regarded as made:

> '... where goods forming part of the assets of a business are transferred or disposed of so as no longer to form part of those assets, whether or not for a consideration ...'

Invariably, goods will be transferred for no consideration in the case of an ex gratia benefit or for a consideration not wholly in money; ie the employee agreeing not to pursue an action against his employer. Unless a value is attributed to the goods transferred as part of any settlement and such value is fair, the valuation rules in VATA 1994 Sch 6 para 6(2) will apply, which provide for an open market basis of valuation as follows:

> 'The value of the supply shall be taken to be—
>
> (a) such consideration in money as would be payable by the person making the supply if he were, at the time of the supply, to purchase goods identical in every respect (including age and condition) to the goods concerned; or
> (b) where the value cannot be ascertained in accordance with paragraph (a) above, such consideration in money as would be payable by that person if he were, at that time, to purchase goods similar to, and of the same age and condition as, the goods concerned; or
> (c) where the value can be ascertained in accordance with neither paragraph (a) nor (b) above, the cost of producing the goods concerned if they were produced at that time.'

9.42 Any asset regarded as supplied pursuant to para 5(1) may of course be subject to exemption or zero-rating if it falls within one of the relevant categories (residential property for example).

Where a motor car is disposed for no consideration (ie as an ex gratia benefit) then it is regarded as outside the scope of VAT provided no credit for input tax was given upon its acquisition by the employer.[1] Tax will be due if a car is being provided as part of a compensation package upon termination of an employee's contract. However, the operation of the so-called 'margin scheme' usually results in the tax cost being reduced to nil.[2]

---

1 Value Added Tax (Cars) Order 1992 SI 1992/3122, art 4(1)(c).
2 Ibid at art 8.

---

6 THE RECOVERY OF TAX

9.43 To be entitled to credit for input tax (ie VAT charged on goods and services supplied to the taxpayer, or upon importation or acquisition) it is

The recovery of tax **9.45**

necessary to satisfy the conditions of VATA 1994 s 26 to the effect that the supply was made to the person claiming credit and the tax was paid in respect of 'goods or services used or to be used for the purpose of any business carried on or to be carried on by him'.

Input tax may only be deducted by a taxable person in respect of a supply made to him. In the case of *Turner*[1] the taxpayer was denied a deduction in respect of VAT on legal costs for which he was liable following an unsuccessful action. The legal costs in question were those supplied to the defendant to the action; no deduction was available because the legal services were not supplied to the taxpayer.

1 *Turner (t/a Turner Agricultural) v Customs & Excise Comrs* [1992] STC 621.

9.44 Certain input tax is specifically identified as non-deductible under a variety of statutory provisions. Legal and other professional costs incurred within the context of an action for compensation are subject to the general principles of recovery, specified in VATA 1994 s 26. This section provides for the recovery of input tax by a taxable person which is attributable to the following supplies made or to be made in the course or furtherance of that person's business:

(a) taxable supplies;
(b) supplies outside the United Kingdom which would be taxable supplies if made in the United Kingdom;
(c) supplies specified by Treasury order.

9.45 For most taxable persons the attribution and recovery of input tax is straightforward, but the position becomes complex for persons who make partly exempt and partly-taxable supplies, or those engaged in non-business as well as business activities. Such issues are outside the scope of this book, but in broad terms input tax which is attributable to the making of taxable supplies may be recovered in full. Input tax used in making exempt supplies may not be recovered. Input tax which falls into neither category, which may include general overhead expenses, is recovered on a proportional basis by reference to the proportional value of taxable and exempt supplies made by the taxpayer.[1]

1 Value Added Tax (General) Regulations SI 1985/886, Pt V.

EXAMPLE

A Ltd engages in two types of business. First, the provision of consultancy services which is standard rated. Second, the provision of insurance which is wholly exempt. A Ltd incurs the following VAT expenses:

(a) £400 in connection with materials for a client presentation for consultancy services;
(b) £650 on computer equipment used for A Ltd's insurance business;
(c) £1,000 on rent for office space used for both the consultancy and the insurance business.

9.45 *Value added tax*

In this simplified example the £400 may be recovered in full, but no recovery may be made in respect of the £650. If the insurance business comprises 35% of turnover and the consultancy business 65%, the £1,000 may be recovered as to £650.

BUSINESS PURPOSE TEST

9.46 Input tax must be incurred on goods or services which are used or to be used for the purposes of the business of the recipient. The tribunals have frequently had to decide whether goods or services were obtained for business purposes, and in deciding whether this is the case a subjective test is applied.

The relevant test to apply was set out in *Ian Flockton Developments Ltd*:[1]

> *'The test is were the goods or services which were supplied to the taxpayer used or to be used for the purposes of any business carried on by him? The test is a subjective one: that is to say, the fact finding tribunal must look into the taxpayer's mind as it was at the relevant time to discover his object. Where the taxpayer is a company, the relevant mind or minds are those of the person or persons who control the company who are entitled to and do act for the company.'*[2]

1 [1987] STC 394.
2 Per Stuart-Smith J, ibid at 400.

BUSINESS BENEFIT

9.47 It is not enough that a particular expense benefits the business in question. To be recoverable, the expense must be for the purpose of the business. A company which meets the legal fees of an employee against whom an action is brought may demonstrate a business benefit in that the company is seeking to ensure that the employee continues to be available for work, but the expenses in question may not be for the purposes of the business.

Expenses incurred in connection with the defence of criminal charges against a director or employee of a company[1] or the taxable person himself as a sole proprietor[2] have been held to be non-deductible because the expenses could not be said to be for business purposes.

1 *Britwood Toys Ltd* LON/86/280.
2 *Wallman Foods Ltd* MAN/83/41.

9.48 In *Customs and Excise Comrs v Rosner*[1] the taxpayer, who owned and managed a private educational establishment, was charged with conspiracy to defraud in relation to the provision of false information under the Immigration Act 1971 and assisting persons in making false representations about being genuine students. He pleaded guilty.

A credit for input tax was claimed by the taxpayer in respect of the costs of his defence, and was successful before the tribunal. On appeal however, the High Court found in favour of Customs. It was noted that business benefit was not the test for deductibility, otherwise any expenditure incurred for the purposes of defending a proprietor of a one man business would be deductible. To be deductible there must be a connection, a nexus, between the expenditure and the business so that offences which relate directly to trading activities provide the necessary connection. The court was of the view that Mr Rosner failed to satisfy this test:

> 'In the present case the facts seem to me to make it abundantly clear that the only conclusion must be that the criminal offences in respect of which the legal expenses claimed were incurred were offences which, whilst they had a connection with the business in the sense that it would appear as though the immigration offences related to people who might become students of the business, were not offences which related to the carrying on of the business. They were sufficiently removed from the purpose of the business to mean that the expenditure was not expenditure incurred for the purpose of the business.'[2]

1 [1994] STC 228.
2 Per Latham J, ibid at 231.

9.49 In *P&O European Ferries (Dover) Ltd*[1] the taxpayer company spent around £3.5m on the defence of seven individual members of its staff charged with manslaughter as a result of the *Herald of Free Enterprise* disaster at Zeebrugge on 6 March 1987.

The company received advice that it was at risk from being charged with 'corporate manslaughter' and that the defence of the company depended on the success of the prosecution in relation to the charges against the individual employees. The legal director of the P&O Group ensured that each of the possible defendants had professional representation of a standard approved by him, and the individual solicitors worked with the company in planning the defence.

The tribunal accepted that in addition to the criminal law reason for ensuring an adequate defence, the company had had regard to the following consequences which were likely to result from a conviction:

(a) the P&O Group as a whole would be affected by reason of adverse publicity;
(b) the quoted price of P&O shares on the Stock Exchange could fall;
(c) negotiations with the National Seamen's Union in a dispute concerning manning and works levels would be affected;
(d) loss of staff morale; that the company was seen to be supporting to the full the defence of its staff was a bid to bolster morale;
(e) loss of certain insurance advantages.

1 LON/91/214, 2532.

9.50 The case for Customs was that no deduction was available because the legal services in question were to the individuals, not the company. This argument was rejected by the tribunal; the company was the client of each solicitor having regard to the fact that the company paid the fees, approved the choice of solicitor and gave instructions. It did not matter that the individual employees also received the benefit of those services.

A further argument raised by Customs was that the expenditure was for the benefit of the company but not for the purposes of its business. Again,

9.50 *Value added tax*

the tribunal rejected this argument; the costs were incurred to protect the company's business irrespective of the substantial benefit conferred upon the seven individuals in question. Accordingly, the company's appeal was allowed in full.

INSURANCE CLAIMS

9.51 Prior to 1 January 1985 Customs regarded the supply of legal services to a person defending an action against him covered by insurance as being supplied to his insurer, if the claim was subrogated. Because insurance is mostly an exempt activity, this VAT could not be recovered by the insurer, nor by the policy-holder because the services were not supplied to him.

This practice was changed from 1 January 1985[1] so as to allow the policy-holder to treat the services as supplied to him and therefore eligible for recovery.

---

1 Press Notice 960, 31 December 1984.

INDEX

Index entries are to paragraph numbers, those in italic referring to the appendices by chapter number and, where appropriate, appendix number.

ABI (Association of British Insurers), 7.13
Actions. *See* LEGAL ACTIONS
Agency agreements, 2.22–2.24
Agreements, compensation for variation, 2.29–2.30
Annuities
   capital instalments, distinguishing between, 7.19
   obligation to deduct tax, 7.33
   pure income profit, as, 7.34–7.37
   structured settlements, 7.02, 7.11
Apportionment, 4.29–4.30, 5.15
Arising basis
   profits from land, 2.62–2.63
Assets
   compulsory acquisition, 4.28–4.35
   damaged, restoration
     reliefs 4.15–4.23
   depreciating, 4.34
   destruction, 3.53
     reliefs for replacement, 4.24–4.27
   disposals, 3.43
     part, 3.44–3.46
       statutory relief, 3.47–3.48
       TCGA s 22 provisions, 3.49–3.51
         physical damage compensation, 3.52–3.53
   dissipation, 3.53
   forfeiture or surrender, 3.55
   income producing, 7.22–7.27
   insurance, 3.54
   loss, 3.52
     reliefs for replacement, 4.24–4.27

Assets – *cont*
   nature, 3.16–3.17
     benefit of an action for damages, 3.36–3.37
     acquisition of right to sue, 3.42
     causal link, 3.40–3.41
     nature of the right, 3.38–3.39
     claims to statutory compensation, 3.26–3.27
     Davenport v Chilver decision, 3.31–3.35
     freedom from charge, 3.28–3.30
     Kirby v Thorn EMI, 3.24–3.25
     Marren v Ingles, 3.21–3.23
     O'Brien v Benson's Hosiery decision, 3.18–3.19
     Zim Properties Ltd v Procter, 3.36–3.42
   non-chargeable, 3.07
   property, 3.16, 3.20
   rights of action as. *See* RIGHTS OF ACTION
   use or exploitation, 3.56
   wasting, 4.21
   See also CAPITAL ASSETS
Associated employments, 6.51
Association of British Insurers, 7.13

Basic pecuniary losses
   breach of contract, 1.19–1.21
   income tax, subject to, 2.06
   tort, 1.31
Benefits in kind
   national insurance, 6.80
   termination, upon, 6.37–6.38

Index

Bereavement, 1.39
Breach of contract
  compensation relating to trading stock, 2.18
  damages, 1.04, 1.15–1.17, 1.18
  loss of profits, 2.19
  losses, 1.18–1.29
Business sales, compensation and, 5.29–5.33
Business structure
  compensation for acts having great effect on, 2.26–2.28

Cancellation charges
  VAT, 9.24–9.26
Capital assets
  concept of use and, 2.37
  identification, 2.08–2.10
  realisation, 2.41–2.44
  See also CAPITAL RECEIPTS
Capital expenditure
  relief for, 5.44–5.45
  revenue expenditure and, 5.22–5.26
Capital gains tax, 3.01–3.02
  assets
    disposals, 3.43
      allowable expenditure and deductions, 3.68–3.69
      amount or value of consideration, 3.70
      enhancement expenditure and preservation of title, 3.71–3.72
      chargeable gains, 3.57
        contingent liabilities, 3.59–3.61
        disposal consideration, 3.58
        indemnities, 3.65–3.67
        warranties or representations, 3.62–3.64
      dissipation, 3.53
      forfeiture or surrender, 3.55
      indexation, 3.73
        calculation, 3.74
      insurance, 3.54
      loss, 3.52
      part, 3.44–3.46
        statutory relief, 3.47–3.48, 4.14
      TCGA s 22 provisions, 3.49–3.51
        physical damage compensation, 3.52–3.53
    nature of. *See* ASSETS: NATURE
  charging requirements of 1992 Act, 3.15

Capital gains tax – *cont*
  consideration chargeable to income tax, 3.09–3.11
  exemptions and reliefs, 3.06–3.07
  income, and, 3.08
  income expenditure exclusion, 3.13–3.14
  insurance receipts, 3.54
  losses, 3.05
  non-chargeable assets, 3.07
  personal compensation, 4.36
  profits or gains, 3.12
  rates and payment, 3.04
  reliefs, 4.01–4.02
    compulsory acquisition of land, 4.28
    apportionment, 4.29–4.30
    depreciating assets, 4.34
    freehold by tenants, 4.35
    roll-over relief, 4.31–4.35
    damaged assets, restoration, 4.15–4.16
    limitations, 4.20
    partial restoration, 4.23
    small receipts, 4.22
    TCGA s 23, relieving provisions, 4.17–4.19
    wasting assets, 4.21
  defendants, 5.44–5.45
  Extra-statutory Concession D33. *See* EXTRA-STATUTORY CONCESSION D33
  lost or destroyed assets, replacement, 4.24–4.26
  partial replacement, 4.27
  Zim Properties decision, 4.02–4.14
  residence status, 3.03
  rule in *Gourley*, 8.30–8.36
  termination payments, 3.12
Capital payments
  annuities, distinguishing between, 7.19
  limitations, 7.40
  structured settlements, 7.17–7.19
Capital receipts
  classification of compensation as. *See* INCOME TAX: COMPENSATION CHARGEABLE UNDER SCHEDULE D, CASES I OR II
  revenue receipts and, the dividing line, 2.31–2.34
  See also CAPITAL ASSETS
Case law, limitations, 2.07
Cessation of trading, compensation and, 5.27–5.28
CGT. *See* CAPITAL GAINS TAX

Index

Chargeable gains. *See* CAPITAL GAINS TAX
Commutation of pension rights, 6.12
Compensation
  business sales, and, 5.29–5.33
  capital gains tax. *See* CAPITAL GAINS TAX
  cessation of trading, and, 5.27–5.28
  employees, 6.11
    See also SCHEDULE E
  Gourley rule. *See* GOURLEY RULE
  income tax. *See* INCOME TAX
  payable under settlements, 1.04
  personal or professional injury, 4.36, 7.01
  physical damage, 3.52–3.53
  revenue or capital, 2.02–2.03
  statutory. *See* STATUTORY COMPENSATION
  structured settlements. *See* STRUCTURED SETTLEMENTS
  tax on, 1.01–1.03
  tax planning. *See* TAX PLANNING AND COMPENSATION
  tax relief for defendants, 5.01
  trading stock and, 2.15–2.18
  use of term, 1.02
  VAT. *See* VALUE ADDED TAX
Compulsory purchase
  VAT on payments, 9.31–9.33
Conditional payments, 6.15
Connected persons
  asset disposals between, 3.58
Consequential pecuniary losses
  breach of contract, 1.22–1.25
  income tax, subject to, 2.06
  tort, 1.31–1.34
Consideration
  link with supply, 9.09–9.11
  VAT meaning, 9.06–9.07
Contingent liabilities
  capital gains tax, 3.59–3.61
Contracts
  amount due under, 1.06
  breach. *See* BREACH OF CONTRACT
  damages. *See* BREACH OF CONTRACT: DAMAGES
  legal effect destroyed, 1.07
  quasi–contracts, 1.07–1.10
  See also EMPLOYMENT CONTRACTS
Contracts to supply, 2.25
Corporation Tax
  chargeable gains. *See* CAPITAL GAINS TAX
  compensation chargeable. *See* INCOME TAX

Costs incurred by employees in seeking compensation, 6.52–6.53

Damages
  actions for, as assets, 3.36–3.42
  amounts contracts. *See* BREACH OF CONTRACT: DAMAGES
  exemplary, 1.16
  liquidated, 1.17
  nominal 1.15
  normal measure, 1.15
  torts. *See* TORT: DAMAGES
  compensation payable under settlements, 1.04
  general, 2.64–2.66
  Gourley rule, 8.19–8.20
  legal action falling outside the scope of the term, 1.05
  meaning and definition in English law, 1.04–1.05
  nature, 1.04–1.14
  personal injury, interest, 2.59
  special, 2.64, 2.67
  Gourley rule, 8.19
  trespass, 2.60
Death, 6.68
  payments following, 6.69
Defamation, 2.64–2.67
Defective performance, 1.20
Defendants
  direct taxes and, 5.01–5.45
  shared benefit, 7.05–7.06
  use of term, 1.02
Delayed performance, 1.20
Depositors
  losses suffered by, 5.16
Deposits
  VAT, 9.24–9.26, 9.27
Directors. *See* EMPLOYEES
Disabilities, payments following, 6.70
Disturbance, compensation, 2.45

Earnings cap, 6.89
Emoluments
  definition, 6.05
Employees
  associated employments, 6.51
  benefits in kind
    national insurance, 6.80
    termination, upon, 6.37–6.38
  conditional payments, 6.15
  costs incurred in seeking compensation, 6.52–6.53

251

Index

Employees – *cont*
   death, 6.68
      payments following, 6.69
   disabilities, payments following, 6.70
   employment contracts, amendments, 6.22
      advance remuneration, 6.23
      inducements and disputes, 6.26
      loss of rights, 6.24–6.25
   foreign service, 6.46–6.49
   golden handshakes, 6.50
   injury, payments following, 6.70
   liability to PAYE, 6.85
   loss of personal liberty, 6.27–6.30
   lump sum payments upon termination, 6.50
   making good, 6.43
   payments to, 6.01
      defendants' deductible expenditure, 5.05
      distributions, 6.91
      Gourley rule, 8.37–8.38
         application of the rule, 8.39–8.40
         partial freedom from tax, 8.41–8.43
         calculation, 8.44
         timing of termination, 8.45
      pension scheme contributions and annuity purchases, 6.88–6.89
      planning, 6.87–6.91
      Schedule E operation. *See* SCHEDULE E
      VAT, 9.41–9.42
   redundancy, 6.71
      employers' payments, 6.72
      statutory payments, 6.72
      voluntary payments, 6.73
   relevant benefits, 6.62–6.63
   reserved payments, 6.16–6.17
   restrictive covenants, 6.74–6.75
      restrictions upon termination, 6.77
      undertakings given before and after 9 June 1988, 6.76
   retirement, 6.59
      meaning, 6.60–6.61
   retirement benefits schemes, 6.62–6.67
   termination
      benefits in kind upon, 6.37–6.38
      inducements, 6.18–6.21
      payments, 6.13–6.14
         conditional, 6.15
         reserved, 6.16–6.17
      Shilton v Wilmhurst, 6.18–6.21
      wrongful and unfair dismissal, 6.50
Employment, 6.04

Employment contracts, 6.90
   amendments, 6.22
      advance remuneration, 6.23
      inducements and disputes, 6.26
      loss of rights, 6.24–6.25
Equity, actions in, 1.11
Ex gratia payments, 2.68–2.71
Expenditure
   obligation, and, 5.14
   provisions, and, 5.17–5.19
   relief for, 2.52–2.54, 5.01–5.45
Expenses
   recovery of, 5.21
Expenses caused
   breach of contract, 1.24
   tort, 1.33
Expenses rendered futile
   breach of contract, 1.21, 1.25
   tort, 1.34
Extra-statutory Concession D33, 4.03
   strict position, 4.04
      application, 4.05
      date of acquisition, 4.06–4.07
      rights and values, 4.08
      terms, 4.09
         no underlying assets, 4.12–4.13
         other reliefs and exemptions, 4.14
         underlying assets, 4.10–4.11
   text, *4*

Fiduciary duty, breaches, 1.13
Financial reinsurance, 7.39
Foreign service, 6.46–6.49

Gains prevented
   breach of contract, 1.23
   tort, 1.32
Golden handshakes, 6.50
Gourley **rule,** 8.02–8.06
   burden of proof, 8.14–8.16
   criticism, 8.07
   employees, compensation paid to, 8.37–8.38
      application of the rule, 8.39–8.40
      partial freedom from tax, 8.41–8.43
      calculation, 8.44
      timing of termination, 8.45
   extension of the rule, 8.28–8.29
      capital gains, 8.30–8.31
      restating the rule, 8.34–8.36
      warranty claims, 8.32–8.33
   general damage, 8.19–8.20
   limitations, 8.08–8.10
   O'Sullivan decision, 8.11

Gourley rule – *cont*
  relevant rule, 8.12–8.13
    particulars, 8.17–8.18
    reliefs, allowances and tax
      planning, 8.23–8.24
    tax liability calculation, 8.19–8.20
    tax rates, 8.21–8.22
    Taylor v O'Connor decision, 8.25–
      8.27
  special damage, 8.19
  summary, 8.47
Gratuities, 6.10

Illegal acts
  penalties for, 5.11
Income tax
  capital gains tax and, 3.08–3.11
  compensation chargeable under
    Schedule D, Cases I or II, 2.01
    agency agreements, 2.22–2.24
    agreements, variation, 2.29–2.30
    business structure, 2.26–2.28
    capital assets
      concept of use, 2.37
      identification, 2.08–2.10
      realisation, 2.41–2.44
    case law, limitations, 2.07
    compulsion immaterial, 2.04
    contracts to supply, 2.25
    defamation, 2.64–2.67
    disturbance, 2.45
    enduring benefits, 2.10
    ex gratia payments, 2.68–2.71
    expenditure, relief for, 2.52–2.54
    general principles and trading
      receipts, 2.02–2.03
    intention, 2.13
    Lloyd's losses, 2.35–2.36
    loss of profits, 2.19–2.21
    price reductions, 2.39–2.40
    principles, 2.05–2.06
    pursuing claims, 2.72–2.73
    recurrence, 2.09
    revenue and capital receipts,
      dividing line, 2.31–2.34
    specific status, 2.14
    total and partial loss, 2.38
    trading receipts and assessment,
      2.46
      relating back, 2.47–2.51
    trading stock, 2.11–2.12, 2.15–
      2.16
      insurance recoveries, 2.17
      breach of contract
        compensation, 2.18

Income tax – *cont*
  defendants' deductible expenditure
    allowable expenditure, 5.05
    apportionment, 5.15
    business sales, compensation and,
      5.29–5.33
    cessation of trading, compensation
      and, 5.27–5.28
    employees, payments to, 5.05
    expenditure and obligation,
      5.14
    expenditure and provisions, 5.17–
      5.19
    intention, 5.12–5.13
    investment companies,
      management expenses, 5.37–
      5.38
    legal fees, 5.34–5.36
    losses suffered by depositors,
      5.16
    notional expenditure, 5.20
    penalties for illegal acts, 5.11
    prohibited expenditure, 5.04
    recovery of expenses, 5.21
    revenue and capital expenditure,
      5.22–5.26
    share sales, compensation and,
      5.29–5.33
    Strong decision, 5.08–5.10
    Taxes Act general scheme, 5.02–
      5.03
    trade, for purposes of, 5.06–5.08
  interest chargeable under Schedule
    D, Case III, 2.55–2.57
    assessment, 2.58
    damages for personal injury, 2.59
    land, profits from, charged under
      Schedule A, 2.60–2.61
      assessment, 2.62–2.63
    rule in *Gourley*, 8.01–8.29, 8.37–
      8.46
Indemnities
  capital gains tax, 3.65–3.67
Indemnities for costs
  VAT, 9.34
Indexation
  capital gains tax, 3.73
Inheritance tax
  ex gratia payments, 2.68
Injury, payments following, 6.70
Injury to reputation, 1.38
**Inland Revenue Statement of Practice
  SP 1/94,** 6
Insurance
  late delivery, 2.40
  loss of profits, 2.19
  stock destruction recoveries, 2.17

Index

Insurers in structured settlements
  annuities
    offset against payments, 7.32
    purchase, 7.31
    taxation, 7.32
Interest
  compensation regarded as, 2.55–2.59
  relief
    companies and, 5.40
    individuals and, 5.39
  VAT, 9.36
Investment companies
  management expenses, 5.37–5.38

Land
  compulsory acquisition, 4.28–4.35
  profits from, 2.60–2.63
Leasing contracts
  VAT, 9.23
Legal actions
  account, for, 1.12
  account of profits, 1.13
  equity, 1.11
  falling outside the scope of the term 'damages', 1.05
  money payable, 1.06
  quasi–contract, 1.07
  statutes, claiming money under, 1.14
Legal fees, 5.34–5.36
Libel, 2.64–2.67
Life offices in structured settlements
  annuities, obligation to deduct basic rate tax, 7.33
Liquidated damages, 1.17
  VAT, 9.20–9.22
Lloyd's losses
  compensation, 2.35–2.36
Loss of personal liberty, 6.27–6.30
Losses
  assets, 3.52–3.53
  basic pecuniary, 1.19–1.21
  capital gains tax, 3.05
  consequential pecuniary, 1.22–1.25
  non-pecuniary, 1.26–1.29
  profits. *See* PROFITS: LOSS OF
  suffered by depositors, 5.16
  total and partial, 2.38
Lump sum payments upon termination, 6.50

Making good, 6.43
Management expenses
  investment companies, 5.37–5.38

Mental distress, 1.29
  Race Relations Act 1976, discrimination, 1.38
Mesne profits, 2.61
  VAT, 9.28–9.29
Mistakes of fact, 1.07
Model agreement, structured settlements, 7.13, *7.2*
Money payable, actions for, 1.06

National insurance, 6.78
  earnings, 6.79
  benefits in kind, 6.80
Non-pecuniary losses
  breach of contract, 1.26–1.29
  income tax, not subject to, 2.06
  tort, 1.35–1.39
Non-performance, 1.20
Notional expenditure, 5.20

Office, 6.03
Office holders. *See* EMPLOYEES

Pain and suffering, 1.36
PAYE system, 6.81
  employee liability, 6.85
  obligation to deduct, 6.82–6.84
  under–deductions and 'gross ups', 6.86
Pecuniary losses. *See* BASIC PECUNIARY LOSSES; CONSEQUENTIAL PECUNIARY LOSSES
Penalties
  illegal acts, 5.11
  liquidated damages, 1.17
Pension rights, commutation, 6.12
Personal injury
  interest on damages, 2.59
  structured settlements. *See* STRUCTURED SETTLEMENTS
Physical inconvenience and discomfort, 1.27, 1.37
Plaintiffs
  shared benefit, 7.05–7.06
  use of term, 1.02
Price reductions, 2.39–2.40
Profits
  chargeable to capital gains tax, 3.12
  loss of, compensation for, 2.19–2.21
  pure income profit, annuities as, 7.34–7.37
Prohibited expenditure, 5.04
Property
  nature of assets, 3.16, 3.20

Index

Property transactions
  VAT on deposits, 9.27
Provisions, 5.17–5.19
Pure income profit, annuities as, 7.34–7.37

Quantum, taxation and, 8.01–8.46
Quantum meruit, 1.09–1.10
Quasi–contract, actions in, 1.07
  partial recoveries, 1.08
  quantum meruit, 1.09–1.10

Race Relations Act 1976
  discriminatory acts, 1.14
  mental distress, damages for, 1.38
Rebasing
  capital gains tax, 3.73
Recovery of expenses, 5.21
Redundancy, 6.71
  definition, 6.71
  employers' payments, 6.72
  payments to employees, 5.05
  statutory payments, 6.72
  voluntary payments, 6.73
Relation back
  interest, 2.58
  trading receipts, 2.47–2.51
Relevant benefits, 6.62–6.63
Rent arrears
  VAT, 9.28–9.29
Rental income
  deductions, 5.41–5.43
Representations. *See* WARRANTIES OR REPRESENTATIONS
Reputation, injury to, 1.38
Reserved payments, 6.16–6.17
Residence
  capital gains tax, 3.03
Restrictive covenants, 6.74–6.75
  restrictions upon termination, 6.77
  undertakings given before and after 9 June 1988, 6.76
Restrictive undertakings
  payments to employees, 5.05
Retirement, 6.59
  meaning, 6.60–6.61
Retirement benefits schemes, 6.62–6.67
Revenue expenditure
  capital expenditure, and, 5.22–5.26
Revenue receipts
  capital receipts and, the dividing line, 2.31–2.34
  classification of compensation as. *See* INCOME TAX: COMPENSATION CHARGEABLE UNDER SCHEDULE D, CASES I OR II

Reverse annuities, 7.40
Rights of action, 3.36–3.42, 4.02
  date of acquisition, 4.06–4.07
  Extra–statutory Concession D33. *See* EXTRA-STATUTORY CONCESSION D33
  rights and values, 4.08
  strict position application, 4.05
  structured settlements, 7.30

Schedule A
  profits from land, 2.60–2.61
  assessment, 2.62–2.63
Schedule D
  Cases I or II, compensation chargeable under, 2.01
  Case III
    annuity payments, 7.33
    compensation regarded as interest, 2.55–2.59
Schedule E
  exemption and Taxes Act s 188, 6.44–6.45
    absolute exemption, 6.47
    foreign service, 6.46–6.49
    partial exemption, 6.48–6.49
  general principles, 6.02
    application, 6.11
    advance remuneration, 6.23
    commutation of pension rights, 6.12
    conditional payments, 6.15
    contract of employment amendments, 6.22
    inducements and disputes, 6.26
    loss of personal liberty, 6.27–6.30
    loss of rights, 6.24–6.25
    reserved payments, 6.16–6.17
    termination inducements, 6.18–6.21
    payments, 6.13–6.14
    Shilton v Wilmhurst, 6.18–6.21
  causal connection, 6.06–6.07
  emoluments, 6.05
  employment, 6.04
  gratuities, 6.10
  office, 6.03
  payer's identity, 6.08–6.09
  retirement, 6.59
    meaning, 6.60–6.61
    retirement benefits schemes, 6.62
    relevant benefits, 6.63
    schemes, 6.64–6.65
      arrangements, and, 6.66–6.67

255

Index

Schedule E – *cont*
  Taxes Act special statutory scheme, 6.31
    s 148, 6.32–6.34
      basis of assessment and reporting requirements, 6.36
      benefits in kind upon termination, 6.37–6.38
      death, 6.68
        payments following, 6.69
      disabilities, payments following, 6.70
      obligations incurred before 6 April 1960, 6.39
      payee's identity, 6.35
      redundancy, 6.71
        employers' payments, 6.72
        statutory payments, 6.72
        voluntary payments, 6.73
      termination, wrongful and unfair dismissal, 6.50
        associated employments, 6.51
        avoiding agreement, 6.55–6.56
        claims for relief, 6.58
        costs, 6.52–6.53
        preserving the exemption, 6.54
        procedure, 6.57
    s 154, 6.40
      causation, 6.41–6.42
      making good, 6.43
    s 313
      restrictive covenants, 6.74–6.75
      restrictions upon termination, 6.77
      undertakings given before and after 9 June 1988, 6.76
Settlements
  compensation payable under, 1.04
  See also STRUCTURED SETTLEMENTS
Share sales
  compensation and, 5.29–5.33
Slander, 2.64–2.67
Social discredit, 1.38
Statutory compensation
  claims to, 3.26–3.27
  VAT, 9.35
Stock. *See* TRADING STOCK
Structured settlements, 7.01
  advantages to plaintiffs, 7.10
  annuities, 7.02, 7.11
    obligation to deduct tax, 7.33
    payment direct to plaintiffs, 7.38
    pure income profit, as, 7.34–7.37

Structured settlements – *cont*
  benefits against conventional lump sums, *7.1*
  description, 7.02
  disadvantages to plaintiffs, 7.09
  financial reinsurance, 7.39
  Kelly v Dawes decision, 7.03–7.06
  insurers
    annuities
      offset against payments, 7.32
      purchase, 7.31
    independence from life office, 7.38
    taxation, 7.32
  life offices
    annuities
      obligation to deduct basic rate tax, 7.33
    independence from insurer, 7.38
  practice, 7.07
    guidance note, 7.13
    model agreement, 7.13, *7.2*
    Inland Revenue view, 7.12
    clearance, 7.14
    procedural guidelines, 7.15
    suitability, 7.08–7.11
  shared benefit, 7.05–7.06
  taxation treatment, 7.16
    capital by instalments, 7.17–7.19
      Dott v Brown decision, 7.20
      presumed capital unless contrary evidence, 7.29
      substance rather than form, 7.21
    chargeable gains, 7.30
    income–producing assets, 7.22–7.23
    dissection, 7.24–7.27
    Ramsay doctrine, 7.28
Supply
  link with consideration, 9.09–9.11
  VAT meaning, 9.06–9.08

Tax
  avoidance, 1.40
    Ramsay doctrine, 1.45–1.47
  compensation, on, 1.01–1.03
  planning and compensation. *See* TAX PLANNING AND COMPENSATION
  quantum, and, 8.01–8.46
  structured settlements. *See* STRUCTURED SETTLEMENTS: TAXATION TREATMENT
  See also CAPITAL GAINS TAX; INCOME TAX; INHERITANCE TAX; VALUE ADDED TAX

Index

Tax planning and compensation
    genuineness of transactions, 1.41–1.44
    Ramsay doctrine, 1.45–1.47
    tax avoidance, 1.40

Taxes Act 1988
    general scheme, 5.02–5.05

Termination
    benefits in kind upon, 6.37–6.38
    Gourley rule, 8.37–8.45
    inducements, 6.18–6.21
    payments, 3.12, 6.13–6.14
        conditional, 6.15
        reserved, 6.16–6.17
    Shilton v Wilmhurst, 6.18–6.21
    wrongful and unfair dismissal, 6.50

Third parties
    costs, payment of, VAT, 9.39–9.40
    payments to, recoverable from defendants, 1.07

Tort
    damages, 1.04, 1.15, 1.30
    loss of profits, 2.19
    losses, 1.31–1.39

Trading receipts and assessment, 2.46–2.51

Trading stock
    compensation, 2.15–2.18
    statutory definition, 2.11–2.12

Training courses
    payments to employees, 5.05

Trespass, 2.61, 9.28–9.29

Value added tax (VAT), 9.01–9.02
    charge to tax, 9.03
    consideration
        link with supply, 9.09–9.11
        meaning, 9.06–9.07

Value added tax (VAT) – *cont*
    credit notes, 9.16
    Customs and Excise approach, 9.12–9.15
    employees, compensation to, 9.41–9.42
    general principle application, 9.17–9.19
        cancellation charges and deposits, 9.24–9.26
        consent, importance of, 9.30
        compulsory purchase, 9.31–9.33
        deposits and property transactions, 9.27
        indemnities for costs, 9.34
        interest, 9.36
        leasing contracts, 9.23
        liquidated damages, 9.20–9.22
        mesne profits and arrears of rent, 9.28–9.29
        statutory compensation, 9.35
    recovery of input tax, 9.43–9.45
        business benefit, 9.47–9.50
        business purpose test, 9.46
        insurance claims, 9.51
    settlements, form of, 9.37–9.38
    supply
        link with consideration, 9.09–9.11
        meaning, 9.06–9.08
    taxable persons, 9.04–9.05
    third party costs, payment of, 9.39–9.40

Warranties or representations
    capital gains tax, 3.62–3.64

Warranty claims
    Gourley rule, 8.32–8.33